Educating in Ethics Across the Professions: A Compendium of Research, Theory, Practice, and an Agenda for the Future

A Volume in:
Ethics in Practice

Series Editors:
Robert A. Giacalone
Carole L. Jurkiewicz

Ethics in Practice

Series Editors:
Robert A. Giacalone
John Carroll University

Carole L. Jurkiewicz
University of Colorado, Colorado Springs

Books in this Series

Educating in Ethics Across the Professions: A Compendium of Research, Theory, Practice, and an Agenda for the Future

Richard M. Jacobs

INFORMATION AGE PUBLISHING, INC.
Charlotte, NC • www.infoagepub.com

Library of Congress Cataloging-In-Publication Data

The CIP data for this book can be found on the Library of Congress website (loc.gov).

Paperback: 978-1-64802-983-7
Hardcover: 978-1-64802-984-4
E-Book: 978-1-64802-985-1

CONTENTS

SECTION 1
EDUCATING IN ETHICS: PROFESSIONS WITH A FOCUS UPON THE PERSON SERVED

SECTION 4

EDUCATING IN ETHICS: RECONCEIVING PROFESSIONAL ETHICS EDUCATION

9. **Teaching Applied Ethics Across the Professions: Educating the Spirit *in* Ethics**... 185
    Richard M. Jacobs

10. **The Core Values of the Service Professions and an Effective Curriculum to Help Students Internalize Them** 213
    Neil Hamilton

    Epilogue: Educating in Ethics: Today's Desired Reality and Agenda for the Future 231
    Richard M. Jacobs

    Biographies 253

DEDICATION

To Don Menzel—ethics educator, lifetime learner, and respected servant leader—who formed generations of students *in* ethics.

—RMJ

ACKNOWLEDGEMENTS

This edited volume represents a collaborative effort on the part of its editor and the distinguished scholars contributing to it.

Oftentimes overlooked in a volume like this is the critical role of reviewers who selflessly devote hours to evaluate the original manuscripts and provide commentary to strengthen what already represents a contribution to each author's profession.

Of the 47 recognized scholars nominated to serve as reviewers for this volume, 25 were selected. Representing an array of professions, each has taught applied ethics for years if not decades and graciously offered to review one chapter in his/her area of expertise.

This volume's reviewers include:

Jennifer L. Bartlett
Associate Professor
Georgia Baptist College of Nursing

Sheri K. Bias
Associate Professor, Human Resources Lead
Faculty, Saint Leo University

Robert Beauregard
Professor Emeritus
Columbia University Graduate School of
Architecture, Planning, and Preservation

Johannes Brinkmann
Professor Emeritus—Department of Strategy
and Entrepreneurship
Norwegian Business School

Educating in Ethics Across the Professions: A Compendium of Research, Theory,
Practice, and an Agenda for the Future, pages xi–xiii.
Copyright © 2023 by Information Age Publishing
www.infoagepub.com

R. Michael Cassidy
Professor and Dean's Distinguished Scholar
Boston College Law School

Jeffrey K. H. Chan
Assistant Professor in the Humanities, Arts,
and Social Sciences Cluster
Singapore University of Technology and Design

Daniel R. Coquillette
J. Donald Monan, SJ, University Professor
Boston College
Visiting Professor, Harvard Law School

Lorraine Corfield
Lead—Healthcare Ethics and Law
Keele University (UK)

Shannon E. French
Professor of Philosophy and Law and Inamori
Professor in Ethics
Case Western Reserve University

Stuart C. Gilman
Senior Partner, Global Integrity Group

Carole L. Jurkiewicz
University of Colorado Springs

Pauline M. Shanks Kaurin
Professor of Professional Military Ethics
Admiral James B. Stockdale
Chair in Professional Military Ethics
US Naval War College

Jesse Kirkpatrick
Research Assistant Professor
Acting Director of the Institute for
Philosophy and Public Policy
George Mason University

Thomas Lennerfors
Professor of Industrial Engineering and
Management
Uppsala University (Sweden)

Kris Lines
Senior Lecturer and ABS Academic Offences
Officer
Ashton University School of Law (UK)

Robert Maranto
21st Century Chair in Leadership—Department
of Education Reform
University of Arkansas

Joé T. Martineau,
Assistant Professor of Business Ethics and
Management
HEC Montréal

William J. Mea
Visiting Research Fellow Institute for National
Strategic Studies
National Defense University

Cristóbal Miralles
Industrial Engineering Department
Polytechnic University of Valencia (Spain)

Andrew N. Papanikitas
Honorable Tutor in General Practice—Nuffield
Department of Primary Care Health Sciences
University of Oxford (UK)

Stefan Perun
Associate Teaching Professor
Department of Public Administration
Villanova University

Catherine Robichaux
Assistant Professor
The University of Texas Health Science Center

James Svara
Visiting Professor
University of North Carolina-Chapel Hill School
of Government
Fellow of the National Academy of Public
Administration

Huw Thomas
Emeritus Reader—School of Geography and
Planning, Cardiff University (UK)
Honorary Professor—School of Natural and
Built Environment, Queen's University (Belfast)

Tuna Taşan-Kok
Professor of Urban Governance and Planning
University of Amsterdam

Connie M. Ulrich
Lillian S. Brunner Chair
Professor of Nursing and Professor of Medical
Ethics and Health Policy
University of Pennsylvania School of Nursing

Eli Wald
Charles W. Delaney Jr. Professor of Law
University of Denver Sturm College of Law

Stephanie Witt
Professor, Director of Training
School of Public Service
Boise State University

Each reviewer's contribution has assisted in sharpening the discourse about teaching applied ethics both in their professions and, more importantly given this volume's purpose, across the professions. This substantive contribution, implicit in the significance of this volume's contents for those who currently teach or will be teaching applied ethics across the professions, represents an important professional service that I want not only to acknowledge individually but also to express my gratitude to each personally and publicly.

—*Richard M. Jacobs*
Editor

FOREWORD

Stuart C. Gilman
Global Integrity Group

There is much to be done. It must begin within professional education programs in universities and technical schools....The following essays provide
a path through which this can be done. For that reason, I commend these
essays, with the hope that they will encourage both research and practice in
the critical, cross-disciplinary ethics questions that will inform the future of
ethics in the professions.

—Stuart C. Gilman

The focus of this collection of essays is the role of ethics in professional education. Further, it explores the common normative and compliance threads woven
across disciplines and practices. However, without a context, the articles analytical importance might not seem as significant as they are. My hope is that my
professional experience over the past 50 years will help frame these essays and
highlight their value in initiating a critical dialogue around inculcating ethics as
the gold standard in any profession.[1]

---

[1] Like many other professionals, I have had multiple careers: a decade as a university professor;
professor at the Federal Executive Institute, Executive Director of a Center for Risk Management

---

*Educating in Ethics Across the Professions: A Compendium of Research, Theory,
Practice, and an Agenda for the Future,* pages xv–xxi.
Copyright © 2023 by Information Age Publishing
www.infoagepub.com

THE PROBLEM

Over the past decade, there has been an assault on ethics and integrity programs both in the United States and internationally. In the U.S. federal, state and local ethics programs have been disbanded, defunded, or ignored. The once-vaunted federal inspectors general were often neutered by an executive who fired or intimidated any who would dare criticize members of the administration for ethics violations or corruption. The Office of Government Ethics and the Office of Special Counsel (protecting whistleblowers and preventing political abuse) were ignored or undermined by putting compliant political appointees in place. This dissipation of ethics bodies also occurred in almost every state in the U.S.

Outside of government, oversight bodies such as bar associations for lawyers and state medical boards appear to be unable to discipline even the most egregious violations of their ethics principles. Lawyers filing frivolous lawsuits in political issues are rewarded by millions of dollars in donations, far more than they have made in their normal practice. Doctors who peddle the most implausible preventions and cures for disease have their medical licenses renewed without any consequences. This is even more egregious because they then use online vehicles to sell worthless, and sometimes dangerous, "natural" remedies.

The mass availability of the Internet has magnified the problem but not only for the "professionals" who sell their services online. The Internet has fostered social media and mega-sales networks (e.g., Amazon, eBay) that might claim ethical responsibility in their public pronouncements but ignore ethical norms in their practice. Arguably, society have been victimized by media organizations created only to maximize profits, sell worthless products, or distort news to favor ideological causes.

Internationally, ethics offices and oversight bodies responsible for ethics in professions have been dissolved and undermined. In some instances, heads of those organizations have been imprisoned, forced to flee their country and were subject to violence.

THE SOLUTION

Professional education is the best way to recapture the fundamental ethical foundations and why they are essential to disciplines and practices.

All professions have both empirical and normative elements that inform both what they do and make their work valuable. These elements adapt to evidentiary changes in "facts," technology, and culture. Although ethical principles remain constant, they often have to be re-articulated because of changes in a profession or society. In an important way, professional cultures are invented (Wagner, 1981).

in Engineering Systems, executive at the Office of Government Ethics and the Treasury Department Inspectors General office, president of an ethics non-profit, Head, of the UN Global Program against Corruption, and now more than a decade as an ethics and anti-corruption expert for U.S. Executive Departments, international bodies, businesses and governments in over 30 countries.

Part of that invention includes the adoption of norms of behavior based upon ethical values that are sometimes clearly stated, sometimes assumed.

Unfortunately, most instruction in disciplines and practices focuses upon the empirical and technical while often ignoring the ethical questions fostered by new changes in approach or technology. Most disciplines overlook the fact that the vast majority of practitioners will work within a bureaucracy. Schön points out that "the lives of professionals in our society are bound up with the lives of formal bureaucratic organizations through which most work will be done. For engineers, physicians, lawyers, architects, teachers and social workers, bureaucracies are the institutional settings of professional practice" (Schön, 1983, p. 326).

Within an institutional setting ethical frames of reference are crucial. Ethics provides the guard rails that are essential to creating a discipline or practice. Without proper guard rails, professionals can destroy or undermine their profession which then is a danger to society. Professions become corrupt once their foundational values become aspirational tokens or irrelevant.

WEAK PROFESSIONAL ETHICS LEADS TO BAD OUTCOMES

Many times, ethical obligations are informal, sometimes informed by one or more generic statements of value (e.g., the Hippocratic oath). Often, these value systems are made concrete through policies, regulations, and/or laws (Gilman, 2005). But when ethical norms are vague, open to broad interpretation, or are not enforced, violations can become a cultural norm. In my experience, even the most corrupt individuals have a rational (in their own minds) narrative to explain why what they did wasn't bad or served a greater good.

As an advisor to the United Nations, I helped adjudicate a case of one of their doctors who had stolen several hundred thousand doses of penicillin, selling them on the black market. When confronted, he defiantly confessed stating that he used the money to pay tuition for his daughter to go to Harvard Medical School. When she returned to her own country (according to the doctor), she would save more lives than the penicillin would have. The head of the UN medical program told him the penicillin would have saved over 30,000 lives and prevented crippling diseases affecting tens of thousands a year.

Organizations can often be blind to their vulnerability because of vague notions of ethical vulnerability. In a meeting in 2000, involving an auditing by inspectors general, several of us had a conversation with a senior executive at Arthur Anderson. At the time, Anderson was one of the "big five" auditing firms. The senior executive argued that IGs were not independent. I pointed out that at any time a client of an auditing firm could fire the auditing firm and go to another which could force the auditor to comply with the clients wishes to narrow or change the audit. He responded that Arthur Anderson was so large that they didn't need to bend to a client. Within a year, the Enron scandal destroyed Arthur Anderson because their Texas office was desperate to keep Enron as a client. Senior leadership had no idea about the flimsy ethical structure on which the entire company was built.

In addition, good financial decisions can lead to very bad unintended consequences. In an international banking institution, an individual accused of a violation within the bank had the right to a judicial review if they chose to do so. The rules required a panel of eight judges from eight different countries to sit in a panel at the body's headquarters. Travel, accommodations, and accompanying staff (sometimes for months) could cost up to US$800,000. The director of personnel had a "better" idea: He offered one staff member accused of stealing a computer an alternative if he did not take advantage of the judicial panel. If he retired immediately, the bank would pay him US$100,000 along with full retirement benefits. Others heard about this resolution and within 18 months, 11 more staff were accused of minor theft and paid to retire. Efficient institutional solutions to problems can encourage unethical behavior. My job was to protect the rights of staff while at the same time to redesign the appeals system to make it less burdensome.

Without strong professional norms, personal loyalty or ideology can trump ethics. In the early 1990s as a senior official at the Office of Government Ethics, I was asked to give the ethics lecture to the Plebes (1st year students) at the U.S. Naval Academy. I was somewhat surprised at being loudly booed when I mentioned the ethical failings of Colonel Oliver North. I did my best to point out that it was not specifically the Iran-Contra Affair that I was speaking about, but rather the personal misuse of some of those funds received from Iran. Syphoning off moneys from the agreement, North had built a swimming pool and other luxury upgrades to his home under the guise of upgrading security. North's failings began at the Naval Academy as documented in a book about four naval academy graduates, two national heroes and two who were criminally indicted as Timberg's (1996) *The Nightingale's Song* chronicles.

Engineering and architecture are also vulnerable to being blind to the ethical implications of their practice. Perhaps the most famous example is safety testing of the Chrystal Palace, the show piece of the first international world's fair in London in 1851. William Paxton and William Barlow won the award to build the largest glass building until that time. After the building was finished, there was great fear the building would collapse with all of the visitors passing through it. It was decided to test it by marching 100 young army engineers on to the floor and, to test its tensile strength, they were required to jump up and down on the floor (Addis, 2006). Although not resulting in disaster, there were certainly more ethical ways to test the strength of the building.

WHY ETHICS IS CRITICAL IN PROFESSIONAL EDUCATION

If integrity is essential to professions, and being a "professional" means abiding by a professions norms and standards, then what is to be done?

It begins with professional education.

Perhaps a first step is to identify how ethical values apply to professionals generally, and to the discipline and practice specifically (Lewis & Gilman, 2012, pp. 115–140). Courses usually present these as values through examples. While this is important, it is vital to recognize that individual students can see these issues through different lenses. For some, their only concern in an ethical violation is whether they will be punished.

Recently, in a discussion with an Assistant Secretary at a large, U.S. Executive Branch department, he confessed to lying about conflicting financial interests that his wife held (and he was obligated to have sold). After all, he asked, "What is the likelihood of being caught and, even if I am caught will anyone in this administration do anything about it?" Sadly, his behavior was modeled by other political appointees in the department.

Some students respond to broad ethical principles, asking "Will I be punished and others believe it is important to obey authority?"[2] Any ethics education must be able to speak to all of these perspectives (Kohlberg, 1981).

A second step is to provide professionals with analytical tools necessary to examine an ethical problem. Ethical issues arise in professions because of problems that cannot be resolved otherwise or when conflicts arise about whether a technical issue raises ethical questions. Natural law, Kantian (deontological approach) as well as act and rule utilitarianism are often useful to have students work through dilemmas. Applying them in the class setting can get them tuned to recognize their value in a professional environment (Gilman, 1994).

There are positive examples of professionals recognizing ethical dilemmas because of their professional education. Norm Augustine, former CEO of Lockheed-Martin corporation, told of arriving at his office and on his desk was a large, thick envelope. When he opened it, he found a copy of a competitor's bid on a hundred-million-dollar defense contract. He did not look at it, but instead called the Inspector General at the Department of Defense. The IG took the document and Augustine told him that Lockheed was withdrawing their bid. The IG was puzzled and asked, "But you said that you didn't look at it." "I didn't," he responded, "but some people will not believe it if we win the contract. What I was taught in engineering school was that the only thing we have to sell is trust."[3]

A third step is to distinguish between normative ethical values and compliance ethics, explaining how they can complement each other. Too often instructors see normative ethics in conflict with compliance ethics. Almost all compliance, laws, regulations, and policies in organizations stem from basic ethical principles. If there is a difference, normative ethics leads down the straight path of ethical values while compliance ethics is the outer edge of ethical behavior, an "electric" third rail. This third rail should be the guide in granting licenses to practice, laws,

---

[2] In the hundreds of classes I have taught, I found that students fell into Lawrence Kohlberg's categories of moral analytical categories: obedience, self-interest, conformity, authority, social contract, and universal ethical principles. Although Kohlberg is focusing upon moral development of children, my experience suggests that in every ethics course students view their ethical obligations through these lenses (Kohlberg, 1981).

[3] The example was used in a presentation at a meeting at the Ethics Resource Center in 2003. Validated by the Defense Department IG present.

and regulations in public service and ethical compliance in business as exemplified in the U.S. Corporate Sentencing Guidelines (2018).

ABOUT THIS VOLUME

This volume and its collection of essays takes this discussion and puts the elements into a multi-disciplinary focus. It should not be surprising that there are common ethical dilemmas among professions. This is especially true as professions continue to develop sub-disciplines and practices. It is now common for individuals to hold degrees and practices in multiple disciplines (e.g., medical doctors with law degrees, engineers with legal or medical specialties, or business professionals having degrees and licenses in several other disciplines).

Professional degree-granting institutions should have required ethics courses. Additionally, technical courses should pay attention to the ethical choices that professionals have to make. As important, accrediting bodies have an important role in ensuring that ethics is reflected in their accrediting and licensing of individuals to practice. They also act in clear cases of ethical violations. State medical boards and bar associations are increasingly reticent to police bad actors. One of the few very strong ethics programs is overseen by the International City-County Mangers Association. ICMA not only enforces ethics of their members but also cities who hire those managers. (ICMA, 2021) However, in my own discipline, Public Administration, both major associations have only aspirational ethics codes with no requirements for ethics or even basic enforcement.

There is much to be done. It must begin within professional education programs in universities and technical schools. A student's understanding how to reason through ethical dilemmas is essential to effectively practicing their craft. The following essays provide a path through which this can be done.

For that reason, I commend these essays, with the hope they will encourage both research and practice in the critical, cross-disciplinary ethics questions that will catalyze the future of ethics in the professions.

REFERENCES

Addis, B. (2006). The Crystal Palace and its place in structural history. *International Journal of Space Structures, 21*(1), 3–19.

Gilman, S. (1994). Many hands, dirty hands and no hands: Bringing applied ethics in public management. In N. Preston (Ed.), *Ethics in the public sector: Education and training* (pp. 219–231). Federal Press.

Gilman, S. (2005). *Ethics codes and codes of conduct as tools for promoting an ethical and professional public service* [monograph]. PREM, World Bank Publications.

International City-County Managers Association. (2021). *Ethics Guidance*. https://icma.org/search?keyword=ethics&date=All&page=0

Kohlberg, L. (1981). *Essays on moral development, Vol. I: The philosophy of moral development*. Harper & Row.

Lewis, C., & Gilman, S. (2012). *The ethics challenge in public service: A problem-solving guide* (3rd ed.). Jossey-Bass Publishers.

Schön, D. (1983). *The reflective practitioner: How professionals think in action.* Basic Books.

Timberg, R. (1996). *The nightingale's song.* The Free Press.

United States Sentencing Commission. (2018). *Amendments* [webpage]. https://www.ussc.gov/guidelines/201guidelines-manual/2018-chapter-8.2.1.

Wagner, R. (1981). *The invention of culture.* University of Chicago Press.

PROLOGUE

THE PRESENT REALITY v. THE DESIRED REALITY

Richard M. Jacobs

Villanova University

> Liberating applied ethics educators from within the silos of their indepen-
> dent disciplines and professions to think about their important and valuable
> craft across the professions—the formation of ethical professionals—pro-
> vides ethics educators a roadmap to traverse the pathway leading to the
> desired reality.
>
> —*Richard M. Jacobs*

Over the course of the past three decades, I've learned good deal about the gulf
demarcating theoretical ethics from applied ethics.

Interacting with both theorists and practitioners during two terms as Chair of
the American Society for Public Administration's (ASPA) Section on Ethics and
Integrity in Governance, four years of service as Acquisitions Editor for the public
administration ethics journal *Public Integrity*, delivering numerous presentations
at professional conferences and in-service trainings, and mentoring faculty who
were new to the teaching of applied ethics, I've learned that when confronting
ethical dilemmas, forming the "mind" to apply ethical principles to guide one's

Educating in Ethics Across the Professions: A Compendium of Research, Theory,
Practice, and an Agenda for the Future, pages xxiii–xxxi.
Copyright © 2023 by Information Age Publishing
www.infoagepub.com

deliberations—helpful as this is for professional practice—proves insufficient to the complex intricacies of actual practice, as many professionals assert. Likewise, forming the "hand" to work with the tools of administration to solve the problems of practice skillfully—helpful as this is for successful professional practice—also proves insufficient for deliberating conscientiously when confronting ethical dilemmas, as many theoretical ethicists assert.

This gulf is nothing new, of course, one Aristotle (1958) described in his *Nicomachean Ethics* more than two millennia ago. Calling the practice of ethics "applied philosophy," Aristotle envisioned the integration of theory and skill through judicious reflection upon practice and making what today might be called "aesthetic" judgments that promote the "good," like good healthcare and engineering practice, for example. Two millennia later, Sennett (2008) described this process by invoking the metaphor of "craftsman" to demonstrate how a professional integrates the mind, hand, and heart in a personal, idiosyncratic way exhibiting human excellence in a variety of endeavors requiring aesthetic judgments.

Then too, having taught applied ethics for the past three decades to graduate students enrolled in programs representing four professions (education, criminal justice, nursing, and public administration), I've learned about a second gulf, this one demarcating professors who teach theoretical ethics from those who teach applied ethics. The former are suspicious of the latter—and, for the most part the suspicion is deserved, I'd observe—because many who teach applied ethics don't possess a sufficient intellectual formation in theoretical ethics. The latter view the former with suspicion—and, for the most part, this suspicion is also deserved, I'd observe once again—because they don't possess a sufficient breadth of real-world, hands-on experience to address the vagaries involved in professional practice systematically.

Complicating matters, I've also learned about a third gulf, this one demarcating those who teach skills-related professional training courses in professional colleges, schools, and departments from their colleagues who teach applied ethics. For a variety of reasons, the former are wary of the latter's presence, arguably the most prominent reason being that ethics courses filch valuable instructional time. These professors believe the time expended upon an ethics course is wasteful and that professional licensing agencies are better positioned to teach the content, once again the operative assumption being that an ethics course adds little if any value to the curriculum. Across the professions, accrediting associations—like the Network of Schools of Public Policy, Affairs, and Administration (2019) (NASPAA) for public administration—implicitly promote this belief as their standards don't require including an ethics course in the curriculum, either as a required or elective course. While the contents are said to represent an important aspect of professional training, they're not so important that they deserve a standalone course, whether required or not. Instead, they should be divvied up across the curriculum, interspersing them, as appropriate, into the syllabi of the curriculum's more important, required and elective courses.

Further complicating matters, while students may be interested in learning ethics and studying ethical theory as well as thinking critically and deliberatively about ethical principles, this interest oftentimes is disjointed from what constitutes their primary interest—learning how to do the kinds of things experts do and making the kind of good decisions experts in those professions make. In addition, students believe devoting the time required to immerse themselves in the study of ethics would be better devoted to what they perceive are the more essential courses, namely, those imparting the skills necessary for successful professional practice. In all of this reasoning, the operative assumption is that even if being an ethical professional is important, its contents are secondary—an "add on"—to professional practice.

Taking my cue from Aristotle, I've spent a good deal of time over the past three decades attempting to bridge these three gulfs and surmount the complications they've spawned.

Relying upon my academic training in philosophy, ethics, and pedagogy as well as my study and practice of educational leadership as a school principal, I've written 5 books and more than 30 articles, each focusing explicitly or implicitly upon applied ethics. Assuming that ethics is the bedrock foundation upon which professional practice is constructed and not just some lauded but nonessential "add on" to professional training, my objective has been to offer more substantive discussions concerning applied ethics to two audiences: those who teach and those who practice applied ethics (Jacobs, 2021). Taking my cue from Aristotle and Sennett, I wrote each publication with the intention of assisting readers to form themselves as ethical professionals by integrating ethical theory (the "mind"—knowing what's right) and professional skill with the "hand"—doing things *right*—and the "heart"—doing right *things*, as Bennis and Nanus (1985, p. 21) would say.

Those three decades evidenced a sea change, however, and I found myself working against a rising tide which was moving ethics from the center to the periphery of MPA curriculua nationally. For example:

- Even though the number of NASPAA accredited MPA programs with standalone ethics courses (required or elective) increased from 23% in 1981 to 64% in 2002 (with an indeterminate number of programs incorporating ethics into other professional training courses) (Jurkiewicz, 2002), 15 years later the percentage declined to 11% (Jurkiewicz, 2017).
- Svara and Baizhanov attribute this decrease to NASPAA's 2001 accreditation standards which had the effect of reducing the number of ethics courses by decreasing the focus of those standards upon ethics while increasing its focus upon values. Then, in its 2006 revised standards, NASPAA only reinforced its declining emphasis upon ethics (2019, p. 86).

Despite this sea change, I did accomplish what some may consider an "astonishing" achievement: Not only did I convince my departmental colleagues to introduce a standalone ethics course into the MPA curriculum but also to make it a requirement for all degree-seeking students.

Wondering whether my experience was idiosyncratic, I undertook a retrospective study of the literature of public administration ethics education several years ago during *Public Integrity's* first 20 years (*Public Integrity* is the scholarly journal for public administration ethics). As it ends up, my experience wasn't idiosyncratic but was shared by others who have taught applied ethics across the public service professions.

This finding piqued my interest, expanding my thoughts beyond the now familiar terrain of public administration ethics. I asked, "Does this portrait depict the experience of those who teach applied ethics *across the professions*?" (Jacobs, 2021). Motivated to research the published literature associated with the teaching of applied ethics across the professions, I limited this investigation to include only accredited professional training programs. The project's landscape was wide, spanning the healthcare professions to the military profession and just about every profession in between.

I discovered the three gaps and complications I had experienced also evidencing themselves in the public service professions across the professions, albeit in diverse contexts, situations, and circumstances. Common to all, however, was the struggle for legitimacy, evidencing itself in similar challenges. More interestingly, those teaching applied ethics across the professions were also attempting to improve their craft by applying ethical theory to the vagaries of their profession's idiosyncratic practice. Lastly, they shared a singular goal: For students to form their minds, hands, and hearts sufficiently *in the classroom* so they would demonstrate basic what Cooper and Menzel (2013) have called "ethical competence." This achievement offered those who teach applied ethics evidence of and a ground for hope that their students one day in an indeterminate future would demonstrate increased ethical competence beyond the classroom *in professional practice*.

The seed of that finding, published in a symposium issue of *Public Integrity* (Jacobs, 2019), germinated over the next year into this volume's purpose: To provide those who currently teach or will be teaching applied across the professions today a candid *terminus ad quo* and an agenda leading toward the desired *terminus ad quem*.

Assuming that ethics can be taught (Bok, 1976), that purpose implied this volume's three goals:

1. To provide an historical overview identifying how research, theory, and practice concerning teaching applied ethics have evolved in the professions included in this volume to this day;

2. To identify today's topics, contested ideas, and challenges concerning the teaching of applied ethics discussed in each profession's literature; and,

3. To suggest what today's applied ethics educators should consider if they are to improve the teaching of applied ethics across the professions.

All along, my assumption has been that achieving these three goals would re-conceive applied ethics education in a way that would make it possible for those who teach applied ethics today to collaborate *across* their professions and make demonstrable progress toward the desired *terminus ad quem* they share individually and perhaps collectively *within* their professions.

Liberating applied ethics educators from within the silos of their independent disciplines and professions to think about their important and valuable craft across the professions—the formation of ethical professionals—provides a road-map for traversing the pathway leading to the *terminus ad quem*, what Oettingen (2012) calls the "desired reality." With this volume's contents providing a candid *terminus ad quo*, the hope is that today's applied ethics educators will be better positioned to assess progress toward the *terminus ad quem* and, thus, to evidence how collaboration across the professions can function to dissolve the sources of suspicion that historically have produced those three gulfs as well as the complications they have spawned which, it should be observed, have been of little benefit to the professions and their practitioners as well as those who aspire to be professionals and those who teach them.

This volume represents an important if not necessary first step forward, that is, if those who have contributed to this volume and their successors are to bring this volume's purpose to fulfillment by achieving its three goals. To the degree each contributor has assisted in constructing that candid *terminus ad quo*—what Oettingen (2012) would call the "present reality"—that can promote collaboration across the professions moving forward, even if that means taking baby steps at first, their honesty and humility in narrating their history may make it possible for others to narrate a very different "present reality" one day in the not-too-distant future—today's "desired reality." This reality will evidence itself not only in the classroom but also, and more importantly beyond it, in demonstrated ethical competence on the part of the professionals they have educated in ethics *across* the professions.

A NOTE TO READERS ABOUT THE CONTENTS OF THIS VOLUME

Examining and reflecting upon the contents of each of this volume's chapters dedicated to teaching applied ethics in eight very different professions, what I discovered in my 2019 study became glaringly apparent yet once again, namely, variance is present among two variables though not uniformly so:

- The degree to which each profession has identified its core values and guiding principles; and,

- A curriculum that engages pre-professionals in experimenting with those core values and guiding principles.

Four of those professions boast professional associations and licensing requirements and are more explicit about their core values and guiding principles, though vague about what they denote. Variance is also exhibited in terms of curricula, for example, the healthcare professions and professions whose general focus is the betterment of society by promoting the common good. While the other four professions also have professional associations, they don't have licensing requirements. Even so, variance is evident in their core values and principles as well as a required curriculum for acculturating pre-professionals into the profession, for example, the professions whose general focus is upon the community, stakeholders, and clients.

Considering this variance, I formulated a matrix to rank those eight professions:

- The degree each chapter demonstrates core values and guiding principles (ranked from implicit to explicit); and,
- A curriculum that experiments with those core values and guiding principles (from a focus upon functional conduct to deliberating about those core values and guiding principles) (see Figure 1).

This ranking made it possible to arrange the chapters into what constitutes this volume's first three sections:

- *Section 1*: Educating *in* applied ethics in professions with a focus upon the person served.
  - ○ Legal Ethics
  - ○ Medical Ethics
  - ○ Nursing Ethics
- *Section 2*: Educating *in* applied ethics in professions with a focus upon the community/entity served.
  - ○ Engineering Ethics
  - ○ Urban Planning Ethics
  - ○ Business Ethics
- *Section 3*: Educating *in* applied ethics in professions with a focus upon preserving/sustaining the society served.
  - ○ Public Administration Ethics
  - ○ Military Ethics

A third type of variance was also evident, namely, whether the curriculum has a required course (ranging from no course to an elective course and, finally, to a required course). As significant a factor this is, I found it overly complicating matters for the purpose of ordering the chapters. Thus, I have excluded this fac-

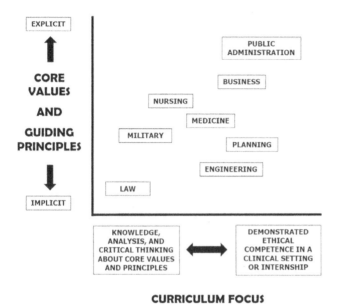

FIGURE 1.   Situating the Variability of the Eight Professions Studied

tor from these considerations but include it in the considerations detailed in the Epilogue.

Prior to reading and considering the contents of this volume, readers might find it helpful to plot where they currently view their profession positioned along those two axes. Then, while reading the contents, to revise their profession's current position (if necessary) to reflect better where they believe it might currently be positioned, reflecting upon what this repositioning connotes for teaching applied ethics in that profession. Lastly, having read this volume's contents, to make a final determination regarding where readers now believe their profession is currently best positioned—establishing a *terminus ad quo*—and where they believe it ought to be positioned—establishing a *terminus ad quem.*

I don't make this suggestion idly because the variance between the *terminus ad quo*—today's "present reality"—and the *terminus ad quem*—today's "desired reality"—provides a pathway forward for readers to improve the teaching of applied ethics in their profession. It will also enable readers to envision a continuous, progressive, and developmental approach to applied ethics education that focuses upon preparing pre-service professionals in the classroom to demonstrate basic ethical competence in the practice of their self-chosen profession. Then, once they immerse themselves in the practice of their profession as in-service professionals, to build upon and extend that foundation with the objective of becoming ethically competent, ethical professionals.

While that's helpful for applied ethics educators teaching *within the professions*, developing a shared vision concerning the teaching of ethics represents the substantive purpose of this volume: To break down those artificially constructed disciplinary silos that insulate those who teach applied ethics *across the professions*. By collaborating as a "learning community" whose members form a "community of practice" (DiBella & Nevis, 1998), those who teach applied ethics across the professions will be better positioned to resolve the nettlesome issues confronting them, especially defining "applied ethics" as an important field of inquiry and assessing the development of ethical competence at both the pre-service and in-service levels.

Identifying the unique, substantive, and invaluable contribution those who teach applied ethics across the professions make to the formation of ethical professionals will go a long way to mute, if not silence those who have maintained that applied ethics, in general, and a standalone ethics course, in particular, don't "add value" to the professional training curriculum.

> —*Richard M. Jacobs*
> *Villanova University*

REFERENCES

Aristotle. (1958). Nicomachean ethics. In *The pocket Aristotle* (pp. 158–274, W. D. Ross, Trans.). Washington Square Press.

Bennis, W., & Nanus, B. (1985). *Leaders: The strategies for taking charge* (p. 21). Harper & Row.

Bok, D. (1976). Can ethics be taught? *Change, 8*(9), 26–30.

Cooper, T. L., & Menzel, D. C. (2013). *Achieving ethical competence for public service leadership*. Routledge.

DiBella, A. J., & Nevis, E. C. (1998). *How organizations learn: An integrated strategy for building learning capability.* Jossey-Bass.

Jacobs, R. M. (2019, March). Teaching public administration ethics: A 20-year *Public Integrity* Retrospective. *Public Integrity, 21*(Sup 1). https://think.taylorandfrancis.com/teaching-public-administration-ethics/

Jacobs R. M. (2021). Ethics education in the professions: Those who have taught and what they have taught. In D. C. Poff & A. C. Michalos (Eds.), *Encyclopedia of business and professional ethics* (pp. 1–6). Springer. https://doi.org/10.1007/978-3-319-23514-1_1187-1

Jurkiewicz, C. L. (2002). The influence of pedagogical style on students' level of ethical reasoning. *Journal of Public Affairs Education, 8*(4), 263–274.

Jurkiewicz, C. L. (2017). *Teaching ethics: Demonstrated approaches and outcomes*. A paper delivered at the NASPAA Annual Conference, Washington, DC.

Network of Schools Public Policy, Affairs, and Administration. (2019). *NASPAA accreditation standards.* https://www.naspaa.org/sites/default/files/docs/2019-11/

NASPAA%20Accreditation%20Standards%20-%202019%20FINAL%20with%20 rationale.pdf

Oettingen, G. (2012). Future thought and behaviour change. *European Review of Social Psychology, 23*(1), 1–63. https://doi.org/10.1080/10463283.2011.643698

Sennett, R. (2008). *The craftsman.* Yale University Press.

Svara, J. H., & Baizhanov, S. (2019). Public service values in NASPAA programs: Identification, integration, and activation. *Journal of Public Affairs Education, 25*(1), 73–92. https://doi.org/10.1080/15236803.2018.1454761

INTRODUCTION

Carole L. Jurkiewicz
University of Colorado

To progressively reflect upon oneself and the ethical foundations one uses to define his or her character comprises a system that is internally consistent, and to attain that habituation requires instruction by someone without a stake in the outcome beyond ensuring the individual is challenged to think logically, critically, and of the ethical consequences to themselves, others, and their profession into the long-term....Essentially, ethics educators are drill sergeants, breaking down superficial belief systems and helping the individual reconfigure themselves.

—Carole L. Jurkiewicz

The enduring criticality of ethics as a topic of study for society in general, and the most effective methods of teaching it, have developed over the centuries to hold a scientific structure of its own. Variations to the scope of professions to which the general studies needed specific applications continues across time, as new fields, sub-fields, and evidence of impact become more salient. What remains pre-eminent is an interest in defining ethical conduct compared to its opposite, which remains a point of debate in itself, as well as the ability to establish either/or conclusions or a continuum of right vs. wrong with considerations interjected as

Educating in Ethics Across the Professions: A Compendium of Research, Theory, Practice, and an Agenda for the Future, pages xxxiii–xxxvi.
Copyright © 2023 by Information Age Publishing
www.infoagepub.com
xxxiii

sidebars. In such a timeless and fluid environment, this volume regarding teaching ethics across professions bravely takes on this topic broadly applied by authors with decades of experience in trying to be most impactful, yet remaining dynamic addressing the societal and moral challenges in their fields as they shifted in congruence with their diversifying student populations and the growing body of research from which both draw their examples and to which they contribute.

The core challenge in teaching ethics across any profession is first overcoming the ingrained belief that people intuitively know the difference between right and wrong. Individuals glean notions of what's ethical from their parents perhaps, their teachers, friends, media, authority figures, books, games, etc., and they internalize ideas of what is right without thinking through whether the pieces of their moral proclamations fit together, or even if ethics is a system which needs to logical, consistent, and represents who they believe themselves to be or merely a collection of assertions. Most people think they're more ethical in comparison to others and can rationalize all sorts of behaviors by believing that they meant well, that their intentions were unassailable. When these ethical positions are challenged by life events, individuals tend to look outside themselves for who might be responsible for the alternative admonitions: video games, parents, society, rules, laws, a boss....but when these excuses fail it's the person him/herself and their system of beliefs as a professional who are held to account.

It's this internal development of a system of moral contentions, or an ethical framework, which effective ethics instructors emphasize and upon which this volume focuses. Learning to be ethical is challenging, but teaching it is even more difficult. It's easy to point to a set of rules, laws, or codes to follow, as if it confers on the individual an innate sense of propriety that requires none of the moral questioning and deliberation that results in the development of consistent principles and personal accountability. A checklist can be printed, laminated, condensed onto a wallet card, placed on posters, and can then be dismissed as been there, done that. To progressively reflect upon oneself and the ethical foundations one uses to define his or her character comprises a system that is internally consistent, and to attain that habituation requires instruction by someone without a stake in the outcome beyond ensuring the individual is challenged to think logically, critically, and of the ethical consequences to themselves, others, and their profession into the long-term.

What this requires of ethics educators is that they have developed an ethical system that defines them, that they've gone through the struggle to do so as well as having employed it to resolve dilemmas in their lives. And after doing that they must set aside their personal beliefs and tolerate students' ambiguities, unwillingness to be pinned down, the startling moments when they realize what they have professed is at best illogical and hasn't been used to guide their behavior but excuse it. Essentially, ethics educators are drill sergeants, breaking down superficial belief systems and helping the individual reconfigure themselves. The chapters here are clustered by professions in overlapping fields of practice and theory and, thus, similar foundations for ethics instruction.

THE TECHNICAL PROFESSIONS

Drs. Lozano and Hui, in their respective chapters on engineering and urban planning, champion the centrality of developing technical expertise in their students as these skill sets have moved human life forward in quality, safety, science, and learning, yet with that capability to advance humanity it has an equal and possibly more impactful ability to destroy it, as they ably detail. With the power to change the trajectory of human life comes great responsibility for protecting humankind. The need for both professional knowledge and moral discernment is amplified in the chapters of McMorrow and Sims, who detail how teaching technical "know-how" must be integrated with ethical "why-for" as the fields of law and business have a distinct and profound social responsibility that exceeds their shareholder accountability. All four provide actionable pedagogical tools and justifications for ethical development in that progresses in sync with technical knowledge.

THE HEALTHCARE PROFESSIONS

Drs. Moorlock and Grace discuss in their chapters that which most individuals ultimately conclude: Those licensed to hold our very life in their hands as physicians and nurses should have effective ethics education. Yet what is alarming are their cogent and timely arguments that the ethical training in these fields is not sufficient. Extreme time pressures, the sheer volume of information one needs to absorb, and the autonomy with which these trained professionals fulfill their responsibilities exacerbate the need for timely, internalized ethical understanding that has been proven effective. When a sense of moral accountability has not been ingrained during one's formation as a professional, even the enormity of the potential consequences—threats of litigation or the loss of a license—prove insufficient to the challenge to conduct oneself as an ethical professional.

THE PUBLIC SERVICE PROFESSIONS

Dr. West chronicles the changing nature of what is commonly viewed as public sector ethics and illustrates that it differs little from the proprietary and nonprofit fields. While the sectors have specific demands that are profession-specific, the development of a broad-based moral understanding remains pre-eminent. Drs. Whetham and Corbett emphasize that moral understanding is a factor in character development, something the military in particular inculcates by introducing values training to stress how values are at the core of effective responses to a range of dilemmas. What is intriguing is the concern Whetham and Corbett pose for machines making ethical decisions based upon presumed values and algorithms. It's a topic that will become increasingly significant as technology progresses more rapidly than its implications can be understood, accentuating the importance of ethics education in the technical professions.

RECONCEIVING PROFESSIONAL ETHICS EDUCATION

Drs. Jacobs and Hamilton speak to the importance of internalizing an education in ethics in order to address the challenges in a world defined by change and globalization, that which humans have in common more so than what separates us. Perhaps circling back to the development of character as configured by Aristotle or Socrates and then applying it to professionals required to make ethical judgements that affect a range of citizens is warranted amidst sometimes conflicting codes and priorities. As Hamilton has echoed the idea, teaching ethics ideally results in the ability to mature morally throughout one's life rather than memorizing a static rubric of understanding. To instill a lifelong pursuit of developing one's character and applying it within a professional framework requires, as they argue, values development. Whereas Jacobs advocates an individualistic approach and Hamilton a macro one, each arrives at the same conclusion: Effective ethics education across the professions requires the instructor to be both intentional and accountable.

Given the focus on values-based character development, ethics educators can actually be harmful. If they advocate for their personal system or a religious dogma rather than teach others how to develop their own, they've failed. If they haven't completed the process for themselves, they're not capable of the selflessness and empathy required to teach applied ethics. If they're not capable of critical thought, they can't effectively teach. If they have a legalistic, rule-bound orientation they can even measurably reduce the ability of their students to think and behave ethically. Ethics education makes a difference, and that difference can be positive or negative.

The lament over the state of ethicality in the professions continues to grow while trust in organizations of all types is at an all-time low. The public asks why organizations appear so self-serving, harmful to citizens, and those leading organizations only care about the bottom line or how their positions benefit themselves. Organizations and the people in them, left to their own devices, will not stumble upon ethicality. Creating codes of conduct won't change it. And rarely do internal ethics training programs enable employees to understand and demonstrate ethicality over the long term, more so they become conversant with compliance programs, laws, or rules around which they can devise avoidance mechanisms. It is folly to presume these are a replacement for applied ethics education, as this books both details and demonstrates.

SECTION 1

EDUCATING IN ETHICS: PROFESSIONS WITH A FOCUS UPON THE PERSON SERVED

Chapter 1: Legal Ethics

If students are not forewarned and prepared for this possible disconnect for the individual lawyer, wearing a mask by day and then taking it off at night, they can quickly become demoralized. Whether called cognitive dissonance, or lawyering through the third person point of view, there is a human toll.

—*Judith A. McMorrow*

Chapter 2: Medical Ethics

Because ethics is taught to medical students in a relatively understandable and superficial way, there is a risk that doctors end up thinking that what they are taught about ethics is all there is to know, without appreciating the complexity or nuance that lies behind claims that they often take to be uncontroversial.

—*Greg Moorlock*

Chapter 3: Nursing Ethics

Without preparation as critical inquirers, who are willing to question how what is being proposed is likely to meet practice aims, the ability to resist deprofessionalization movements will be weakened....But it is not clear the discipline's scholars, leaders, and educators are paying attention to these threats.

—*Pamela Grace*

CHAPTER 1

TEACHING LEGAL ETHICS IN A CLIENT-CENTERED PROFESSION

Judith A. McMorrow

Boston College Law School

This chapter surveys the history, current challenges, and future of teaching legal ethics. It proceeds through foundation information about the growth of the legal profession, the move to legal education and away from apprenticeships as the initial training site for lawyers, and the evolution of codes and rules of professional conduct for lawyers. With law schools situated as the starting point for the training in legal ethics and professional responsibility, the chapter then explores in more detail the central challenges to teaching legal ethics: the obligation of partisan zeal in a profession that also requires personal commitment to embracing this role, the orientation to representing both sides, the ethical blindness that role-differentiated behavior can promote, and the challenge of discussing personal and professional values and wellbeing in the logical enterprise of law. The chapter concludes by asserting the greatest challenge to teaching legal ethics is insufficient space, time, and skill to teach and learn to talk values in a client-centered, rules-oriented profession.

Keywords: Legal Ethics, Professional Responsibility; Ethical Blindness

The calling of legal educators is a high one—to prepare future professionals with enough understanding, skill and judgment to support the vast and complicated system of the law needed to sustain the United States as a free society worthy of its citizens' loyalty. (Sullivan et al., 2007a, p. 11)

Educating in Ethics Across the Professions: A Compendium of Research, Theory, Practice, and an Agenda for the Future, pages 3–21.

INTRODUCTION

Lawyers in the United States are embedded in our rule-of-law political system and culture. They appear on every side of most contested social, cultural, and political issues. Over time, ethical norms have developed to support this role, leading eventually to the development of a "law of lawyering" that affirmatively supports the lawyer's ability to advocate for all sides. Once a lawyer accepts a representation, the lawyer engages in role-differentiated behavior in which the lawyer becomes an advocate for the point of view of their client, not necessarily of their own. Although lawyers may choose which clients to represent, and withdraw if there is a serious disruption in the relationship, once the lawyer accepts the representation the lawyer is required to represent the client competently, and many argue zealously, within the bounds of the law. This framing of the lawyer's professional ethical responsibility to clients minimizes concern for the third party or public interest consequences of the client's legal goals, setting up an inherent tension in ethical decision making between legal ethics and larger social and individual norms.

The process of both doing and teaching legal ethics evolves from these core features of lawyering. Exercising judgment in this context requires more than mere knowledge of rules, but also character and habits of thoughtful deliberation, concepts difficult to teach when a student is in law school and at the beginning of their professional journey. An additional concern is that lawyers are deeply embedded within our rule-of-law system and obtain significant advantages from their semi-monopoly. This in turn creates obligations on lawyers to bear some responsibility for systemic flaws, including vastly unequal access to legal services and substantive law doctrines and implementation issues that may create or perpetuate unfairness. These are the challenges of teaching legal ethics.

This chapter proceeds through foundation information on the growth of the legal profession, the move to legal education and away from apprenticeships as the initial training site for lawyers, and the evolution of codes and rules of professional conduct for lawyers. With law schools situated as the starting point for the training in legal ethics and professional responsibility, the chapter then explores in more detail the central challenges to teaching legal ethics: the obligation of partisan zeal in a profession that also requires personal commitment to embracing this role, the orientation to representing both sides, the ethical blindness that role-differentiated behavior can promote, and the challenge of discussing personal and professional values and wellbeing in the logical enterprise of law.

EVOLUTION OF THE LEGAL
PROFESSIONAL AND LEGAL ETHICS

The Growth of a Legal Profession

Lawyers emerged as a regulated profession, with all the complex baggage that term implies, in the 20th century. In the early history of the American bar, lawyers were relatively unencumbered by regulation or a need to define the essence of their craft, in large measure because ours was an amorphous enterprise. In the seventeenth century, "the practice of law was far from being recognized as a profession, or even a reputable calling" (Chafee & Morison, 1933, p. xxiii). By the mid-eighteenth century, lawyers functioned typically as individual practitioners, who spent long hours in court on issues such as debt collection, land disputes, and criminal matters (McKirdy, 1976). The task of drafting legal documents was shared with nonlawyers. Some lawyers supplemented their income through non-legal activities: land speculation, farming, retail, transportation, and, lending. They often were involved in local political affairs, either by holding office or as a spokesman for both the powerful and the disenfranchised. Twenty five of the 56 signers of the Declaration of Independence were lawyers (Warren, 1911).

As the profession moved into the 19th century, American lawyers operated in a relatively open market and competed with both lawyers and laypersons for work outside the courtroom. There continued to be little functional need to demarcate the difference between law practice and other activities. The bulk of lawyers in the 19th century practiced as generalists. Apprenticeship was the primary method of training new lawyers, and even this requirement weakened when several states and territories abolished or greatly abbreviated apprenticeships in the early 1800s (Abel, 1989, p. 40). Lawyers also continued to play a significant role in national politics. De Tocqueville's compelling commentary noted the predominance of lawyers in American political life. This reflects one dimension of lawyering— the vision of the lawyer-statesman practicing a public profession (Gordon, 1990; Neal, 1967).

In the second half of the 19th century lawyers began organizing bar associations, generally gathering the elite lawyers into their midst (Abel, 1989, pp. 44–45). University-based legal education began to supplant apprenticeships as the primary method of training, with Harvard Law School's Socratic method leading the way by envisioning law as a science (Coquillette & Kimball, 2015). The move to legal education as the entry point to practice married the craft aspects of lawyering with the academic habits and attributes of a university. By the late 1920s, this marriage was largely completed and law schools were producing a growing number of lawyers.

The American Bar Association (ABA), a voluntary professional organization founded in 1878, became an increasingly powerful voice and convinced states to tighten entry by imposing requirements to practice law, such as graduating from an accredited law school and passing the bar exam. As the business world became more complex, lawyers also faced increasing competition from other occupations (Christensen, 1980). Professional associations "sought to ward off incursions by title insurance companies, credit and collection agencies, banks and trust companies, accountants, automobile clubs, mortgage and insurance companies, and lay representatives seeking to appear before administrative agencies" (Abel, 1989, p. 112).

The profession was increasingly successful in obtaining monopoly status over certain activities, often by emphasizing the importance of "professional" aspects of lawyering, including specialized knowledge and habits of conduct. State statutes prohibiting the unauthorized practice of law spread throughout the states and courts began to issue pronouncements defining the practice of law to include in legal practice activities beyond appearance in court (Christensen, 1980, pp. 181–182). A new era of legal practice had taken root and over the early and mid-20th century lawyers would work collectively to expand the definition of the legal practice through unauthorized practice statutes. In general, the statutes do not define the "practice of law" but asked whether a particular activity constitutes the "unauthorized" practice of law. What constituted "unauthorized practice" was and continues to be determined on a case-by-case basis. The phrase "practice of law" generally focuses on giving legal advice or drafting legal documents, but these terms provide only modest insights. Legal Zoom helps individuals draft legal documents; consulting groups advise corporations on a wide range of issues with legal dimensions, including compliance with regulatory requirements, tax advising, creating, and maintaining pensions and a host of other activities that are commonly shared by both lawyers and other professionals, all without running afoul of the unauthorized practice of law statutes. But there continues to be large sectors of work that are customarily understood to be the practice of law, such as law firms offering business and advisory services. In return for the benefit of a statutorily imposed, albeit fuzzy, monopoly, a patchy and weak system of self-regulation began to take hold.

It is important to acknowledge that the formation of a legal profession in the early-20th century, identified by those who received the benefits of a statutory monopoly, provided a mechanism to exclude or restrict opportunities for applicants who were black, Jewish, immigrants, female, or otherwise different. Limited access to legal education served as one important barrier. When applying to join the bar, the development of "character and fitness" requirements served as another barrier for those seeking to become a lawyer. As renowned professor Deborah Rhode (2018) has powerfully noted, defining and assessing character and fitness is notoriously difficult and incorporates the inequalities extant within society. While the professionalism project has a sad and exclusionary theme in its emergence, there is another important theme of professionalism that reflects concern for ethical conduct, good judgment, a commitment to justice, pro bono services and habits of practice that support the rule of law (Stuckey & Others, 2007, pp. 59–67).

While many lawyers work on relatively non-controversial commercial and litigation activity, lawyers are also deeply embedded in our constitutional and political system, which has a significant influence on legal ethics and professional responsibility. For example, the lawyer's role in the criminal justice system is embedded in the U.S. Constitution in the 6th Amendment right to counsel. The right to counsel means, in theory, that the presence of a lawyer will be a check on government overreach when asserting its power to bring criminal actions. Consequently, criminal defense lawyers may choose not inquire about the client's actual guilt because the lawyer is engaging in the constitutionally guaranteed role of requiring the government to overcome the presumption of innocence and prove its case beyond a reasonable doubt.

The standard conception of the lawyer's role is grounded in litigation and the adversary system, in which each side presents its best case before a neutral decision-maker (judge or jury) (Luban, 2007). This activity represents one area of legal services. Due to our strong rule of law society where contested issues routinely become legal issues, lawyers may become change agents for social justice by representing those seeking new rights and liberties. They also represent the status quo resisting those claims. Lawyers have taken the lead on movements to both limit and support abortion, protect or limit access to guns, and almost all major social issues, such as civil rights, environmental protection, education, and law reform. Implicit in this use of law to shape social movements is the concept that each side should present the value of its case in the light most favorable to its point of view, within the bounds of the law. While somewhat oversimplified, the idea that each side has legal counsel to help craft the best point of view in theory should assure better quality outcomes. Of course, there is a vast gap between the theory and practice, given that many individuals do not have access to counsel in civil matters. In addition, over half of lawyering happens outside the adversary system and without a neutral fact-finder, which undermines the adversary system justification in these areas of practice. Nonetheless, the *habits* of adversarial presentation are embedded in the training and conduct of U.S. lawyers. Note that adversarial does not mean unpleasant or uncivil. Rather, in this context it means that the lawyer will present the best case for their client's goal.

The Legalization of Legal Ethics and Professional Responsibility

Legal practice through the middle of the 20th century proceeded with a widely understood but unwritten concept of the lawyer's role and of legal ethics. Economic and social advancements in the 20th century led to a rapid expansion of the U.S. legal profession. The number of lawyers began to grow and the areas in which they practiced diversified. Memorializing or codifying the lawyer's ethical and professional obligations was a natural next step, particularly as the legal profession was seeking to expand and maintain its monopoly status.

The first effort to articulate a systematic description of legal ethics was through the 1908 Canons of Ethics. The precatory Canons were a cluster of statements that focused heavily on proper behavior, with aspects of traditional ethics: duties to courts, representing your clients' interests, and maintaining confidentiality. The mid-20th-century saw a rapid rise in the number of lawyers needed to support the expanding economy and population. This led to a concomitant need to provide a more robust statement of legal ethics. In 1969, the ABA produced the Model Code of Professional Responsibility. Organized around nine core principles, with ethical considerations, the Model Code was intended to serve as a basis for both professional discipline and a guide for lawyers. The Model Code became a body of law as states adopted it as the codified rules of professional responsibility that would be applied in their jurisdiction. The flaws in the Model Code were quickly evident: the canons were too general and the rules to be applied too imprecise. Rules for self-protection rather than client protection, such as broad prohibitions on lawyer advertising, weakened the weight of the Model Code. Watergate, emerging soon after the adoption of the Model Code, would shake the legal profession because so many of the senior leadership were lawyers who were actively involved in the cover-up. The ABA went back to the drawing board and in 1983 produced the Model Rules of Professional Conduct which were crafted to look like any regulatory scheme, with black letter rules and commentary to assist in the interpretation of the rules. The Rules of Professional Conduct have been embraced by almost every state, with some local variations (American Bar Association, 2020b).

Note the evolution over a 70-year span from *Canons*, to *Code*, to the modern *Rules*, and the change from *Ethics*, to *Professional Responsibility*, to *Conduct*. This represents the legalization of legal ethics. The more precise Rules of Professional Conduct serve the institutional goal of trying to implement an effective system of professional discipline but made the language of ethics less prominent in the discussion. Ethical discernment and decision-making became less dominant as the focus on rules and the floor of proper behavior increased. As noted below, there are areas in the Rules of Professional Conduct that state a lawyer "may" take an act, which functionally leaves the decision of how to proceed to the lawyer's professional judgment. But the overall tone of the Model Rules is a focus on the floor of right behavior.

Of course, it is not surprising that the legal profession moved to the legalization of legal ethics. As Wendel (2011) has noted, legalization of legal ethics asks lawyers to use very familiar skills of precise analysis and application of facts to doctrine that are inherent in the craft of lawyering. Policy plays an important role in understanding and interpreting the rules, but when focusing on the rules larger ethical principles have weight only if they are incorporated into the black letter rule. And if the underlying goal of the rules is to support professional discipline, then institutional values such as notice of wrongdoing are essential. But a wide range of ethical values and concerns are left to the lawyer's discretion or are simply not captured by the rules. For example, a lawyer "may reveal information relating to the representation of a client to the extent the lawyer reasonably believes necessary…to prevent reasonably certain death or substantial bodily harm" (Model Rule 1.6(b)(1)) (American Bar Association, 2020b). How to exercise that discretion can be a heart-wrenching process and the Rules give little guidance about how to exercise it. As developed below, complexity in decision-making, institutional pressures, and cognitive biases can also skew how a lawyer sees and interprets the rules in particular fact settings. This poses significant challenges to ethics education because the presence of rules understandingly can dominate and overwhelm nuanced discussion of morals and values, both personal and professional. As Green has observed, beyond the rules are "the profession's guiding beliefs, standards and ideals, including a commitment of legal reform, improving the administration of the law, and governing society through the rule of law—an ambitious agenda for several dozen hours of classroom instruction" (Green, 2018, p. 4).

Further complicating the picture, in addition to the legalization of legal ethics through rules pronounced by the state bar, the regulation of lawyers throughout different practice settings was expanding. Courts have developed a rich jurisprudence in conflict of interests, contact with represented persons, and duties of candor to the court. Tax practitioners will be particularly attentive to the regulation of lawyer conduct by the Department of Treasury, business lawyers practicing before the Securities and Exchange Commission will be sharply attentive to the SEC pronouncements regarding lawyer conduct, and intellectual property practitioners will need to know the Patent and Trademark Office (PTO) Rules of Professional Conduct (Coquillette & McMorrow, 2011). An additional source of doctrine and insights on lawyer conduct comes from malpractice and breach of fiduciary duty lawsuits. When teaching legal ethics and professional responsibility, professors have a surprisingly large body of law to cover.

ETHICS EDUCATION AND CHALLENGES

Regulatory Requirements in Ethics Education

The Supreme Courts of the various states control the requirements for admission to the bar. Most states require applicants to graduate from an ABA accredited law school. Accredited law schools are governed under the ABA Standards and Rules of Procedure for Approval of Law Schools (American Bar Association, 2020a). Under Standard 302 on Learning Outcomes:

Standard 302. LEARNING OUTCOMES
A law school shall establish learning outcomes that shall, at a minimum, include competency in the following:
a. Knowledge and understanding of substantive and procedural law;
b. Legal analysis and reasoning, legal research, problem-solving, and written and oral communication in the legal context;
c. Exercise of proper professional and ethical responsibilities to clients and the legal system; and
d. Other professional skills needed for competent and ethical participation as a member of the legal profession.

Two of the four core learning outcomes refer to the law school's requirement to include competency in "ethical" responsibilities to both clients and as a member of the legal profession. The standards offer little guidance in implementing these goals beyond Standard 303, which states that law schools must offer "one course of at least two credit hours in professional responsibility that includes substantial instruction in rules of professional conduct, and the values and responsibilities of the legal profession and its members." Given the large body of law of lawyering described above, a 2–3 credit course leaves very little room to do more, such as grounding professional responsibility in larger ethical theory and digging into the messy implementation of rules to complex facts.

The law school regulations are themselves just the bottom line, or minimum requirements. Rhode actively promoted the teaching of legal ethics through the "pervasive method," where a wide range of courses address ethical issues in particular settings (Daly et al., 1995; Rhode, 1995). Many schools have upper-level courses in tax ethics, prosecutorial ethics, business ethics, and the like. Clinics are often the centerpiece for thoughtful teaching of legal ethics in context, so that student prosecutors, defense counsel, representatives of children, immigrants, and a host of other legal settings can dig more deeply into their role within a system, the tensions that arise, and the habits of practice they need to develop to navigate the thicket of concerns. But the foundation course continues to be "Professional Responsibility" or similarly named course.

Although this chapter focuses primarily upon how law schools teach legal ethics and professional responsibility, law schools are not the only locus of professional responsibility education. Almost every state also requires applicants to the bar to pass a Multistate Professional Responsibility Exam, a two-hour test on the content of the Model Rules. Students study and take the MPRE during law school and may have passed it before taking their law school legal ethics course. This reflects the understanding that a law school legal ethics course may linger over some topics and include ideas not contained in the Model Rules. Many courts and bar associations have developed creeds of civility and professionalism (Preston & Lawrence, 2015). Many states are now also requiring a professionalism or similar course on norms and values that new entrants to the bar must take. In addition, 47 states require lawyers to engage in continuing legal education, which typically includes 2–3 hours of professional responsibility or ethics. The content of the Continuing Legal Education (CLE) courses mirrors the content of law school courses, but often focuses on current issues in practice.

Critiques of Legal Education and Preparation for Ethical Practice

Over the last 30 years, several efforts have been made to critique and offer suggestions to improve legal education, including education on professionalism (Wald, 2021). The 2007 Carnegie Report on Educating Lawyers; Preparation for the Profession of Law ("Report") offered a fairly sharp critique of the legal profession, stating: "The profession of law is fundamental to the flourishing of American democracy. Today, however, critics of the legal profession, both from within and without, have pointed to a great profession suffering from varying degrees of confusion and demoralization." Addressing this concern, they note, requires "enthusiastic participation of the nation's law schools" (Sullivan, summary, p. 3). The Report found that the challenge of legal education is "linking the interests of legal educators with the needs of legal practitioners and with the public the profession is pledged to serve—in other words, fostering what can be called civic professionalism" (Sullivan et al., 2007a, p. 4). The Report also found law schools provide rapid socialization into legal thinking—seeing both sides, sifting through facts and precedents, using precise language, understanding the application of and conflicts in rules—predominantly through the Socratic method. Students are often put into a role to think about what each side would say, a client-centered teaching method that hones the ability to craft client-centered legal arguments. This also reinforces a client-centered ethical norm noted above. The unintended consequence in this strong emphasis on developing analytical skills is there is significantly less time and attention given to the social or ethical dimensions of the lawyer's conclusions and her subsequent actions. The haphazard method of addressing moral concerns students may have leads to cynicism. In addition, the overemphasis on developing analytical skills leaves less room for addressing the complexity of the use of law in actual practice.

A second major concern asserted by the Report is law school's failure to provide focus on developing a stronger professional identity. The Report stated: "Despite progress in making legal ethics a part of the curriculum, law schools rarely pay consistent attention to the social and cultural contexts of legal institutions and the varied forms of legal practice" (p. 6). Change in legal education usually occurs incrementally. A major initiative that would focus on ethics and professionalism faces the same headwinds of all professional education, "[T]here is always too much to accomplish in too little time" (p. 8). The Report recommended that law schools offer a more integrated curriculum that brings together doctrine and analysis, introduction of facets of practice, and exploration of the identity, value, and dispositions of the fundamental purpose of the legal profession. This proposal reflects both a conceptual and pedagogical change in how law schools approach student learning by moving away from too much reliance on "Professional Responsibility" as a standalone course. An integrated model, they assert, would better meet student needs for "a dynamic curriculum that moves them back and forth between understanding and enactment, experience and analysis" (Sullivan, summary, p. 8).

The 2007 Clinical Legal Education Association (CLEA) also published a critique of legal education. Focusing upon Best Practices and the development of professionalism, CLEA urged law schools to include: a commitment to justice; respect for the rule of law; honor, integrity, fair play, truthfulness and candor; sensitivity and effectiveness in working with diverse clients and colleagues; and, nurturing quality of life when engaged in legal practice (Stuckey & Others, 2007, pp. 59–67).

Clinics are a very good place to provide this type of professional development. The Carnegie Report and Best Practices built upon the 1992 ABA Task Force on

Legal Education and the Profession (known as the MacCrate Report, named after the chair) which focused on creating a continuum of professional development that integrates skills and values into legal education and continues as the lawyer proceeds into the profession (American Bar Association, 1992). The MacCrate Report was influential in expanding skills-based instruction, clinics, and externships in law schools.

Embedded in all of these critiques of legal education is an understanding that the task of improving the formation of professional identity rests not solely upon professors who teach professional responsibility but also every professor within the law school. But, it can be acknowledged, the professional responsibility of professors should be at the forefront of this conversation.

These major critiques of legal education have built momentum for an increasing focus on professionalism as a social movement in legal education. As Wald observes, there is some tension between the professional identity rhetoric of the organized bar and the "the actual and desired professional identity of United States lawyers" in daily practice. As he notes, "generalized responsibilities and values of the profession such as competence, loyalty, justice, equality, fairness, integrity, and ongoing professional learning cannot serve as a suitable professional foundation because the practice of law is increasingly diverse and contextualized" (Wald, 2021, p. 686). This leads back to the central challenge of addressing the contextual nature of professional ethics.

These three critiques of legal education offer the same theme of pushing law schools to bridge the gap between theory and practice and focus more on ethics and professional development. The devil, however, is always in the details. With this background, we can now explore the underlying tensions in the role assigned to lawyers that makes legal ethics education so difficult.

The Duty of Zealous Representation, Role-Differentiated Behavior, and Ethics

One of the major challenges to legal ethics education is grappling with the inherent tension of the duty of zealous representation, role-differentiated behavior, and integration of the personal moral judgment of lawyers. To become a member of the bar, lawyers must take an oath of office. Although the words might differ slightly, the oath is similar to the presidential oath in the U.S. Constitution. For example, the oath of office for lawyers in New York is set out in Sec. 1, Article XIII of the New York state constitution.

> I do solemnly swear (or affirm) that I will support the constitution of the United States, and the constitution of the State of New York, and that I will faithfully discharge the duties of the office of [attorney and counselor-at-law], according to the best of my ability.

An oath is a deeply personal commitment. As Horwitz (2019) has noted, an oath of office emphasizes individual duty that connects the individual to the office assumed. An oath demands a commitment to serve with virtue and honor, both of which require an internal point of view.

Once the lawyer takes that personal oath of office, the lawyer accepts the responsibility to faithfully discharge the "duties of the office." Functionally, the lawyer has a professional obligation to engage in role-differentiated behavior and represent clients competently, and many would argue zealously, within the bounds of the law. This is sometimes described as the external point of view. For example, the lawyer must advocate, within the bounds of the law, for positions that are favorable to the client even if the lawyer finds them distasteful or repugnant. This tension represents one major challenges in teaching legal ethics and professional responsibility. Most lawyers have taken a position on behalf of the client that the lawyer does not believe is good law or good policy, even though the position is within the bounds of the law. As Luban (2020) notes, legal ethics faces a moral problem with partisan zeal. Some scholars urge that lawyers should not experience moral discomfort for playing an established role within our rule of law system (Wendel, 2011). But lawyers do sometimes express sharp discomfort with this role (Markovits, 2003; Schiltz, 1999).

The Rules of Professional Conduct offer help on the margins in reconciling this inherent tension. Lawyers are subject to professional discipline if they commit a criminal act that reflects on their honesty, trustworthiness, or fitness as a lawyer (Rule 8.4(b)) or if they assist a client in committing a criminal act. Whether the line has been crossed is determined by a separate institutional actor, a criminal court. But there are other prohibitions which sound like clear lines between proper and improper partisan zeal, but which turn out to be less helpful than they appear. Lawyers are also subject to professional discipline if they "engage in conduct involving dishonesty, fraud, deceit or misrepresentation," (Rule 8.4(c)), or "engage in conduct that is prejudicial to the administration of justice" (Rule 8.4(d)) (American Bar Association, 2020b). Each of these must be interpreted in light of the role-differentiated behavior required by lawyers. It is not dishonest to fail to volunteer information that is otherwise not required to be disclosed, even if this potentially misleads the listener. It is not misconduct to engage in puffery or exaggeration in negotiation. And on and on.

In daily practice, lawyers have a wide range of discretion in how to behave, with underlying pressure to make choices that advocate the interests of clients within the bounds of the law. The habits of client-centered interpretation of law flows into the lawyer's interpretation of the Rules of Professional Conduct. This can turn the Rules of Professional Conduct into just one more regulatory hurdle for the lawyer to parse and get around if possible (Wilkins, 1990). Even in areas that provide the lawyer discretion, it can be extremely difficult to develop a thoughtful and nuanced discussion of the exercise of discretion in practice. This is how lawyers build practical wisdom.

Implicit in this client-centered use of the Rules of Professional Conduct is the tension in balancing the autonomy interests of lawyer and client. In most circumstances, lawyers may refuse to represent a client or withdraw if a moral disagreement arises (Rule 1.16). But when the representation begins, the clients are themselves moral agents and a lawyer's assistance in providing the client a voice within a legal system is a valid goal. The client's goals and the means to achieve them are usually determined in dialogue with the lawyer. At least in areas left to the lawyer's discretion, there is strong reason that lawyers should act in a way that is likely to promote justice (Simon, 1998). In areas where decisions are made in consultation with the client, where legal counseling will take place, the lawyer's relationship with their clients is inward looking. Under Rule 1.2(d), "A lawyer shall not counsel a client to engage, or assist a client, in conduct that the lawyer knows is criminal or fraudulent, but a lawyer may discuss the legal consequences of any proposed course of conduct with a client and may counsel or assist a client to make a good faith effort to determine the validity, scope, meaning or application of the law." In addition, "[i]n representing a client, a lawyer shall exercise independent professional judgment and render candid advice. In rendering advice, a lawyer may refer not only to law but to other considerations such as moral, economic, social and political factors that may be relevant to the client's situation" (American Bar Association, 2020b).

Note that the language makes advising on non-legal factors optional. Some argue this is quite right (Wendel, 2011). After all, few lawyers are trained ethicists and there is a concern of the lawyer putting overbearing pressure on the client to adhere to the lawyer's own moral judgment rather than the client's judgment. There is something vaguely arrogant about lawyers identifying themselves as moral counselors.

There is also a powerful justification for lawyers to engage in a moral dialogue with their clients (Vischer, 2006). To treat the client as a presumptively amoral actor denigrates the client's moral autonomy. Why should lawyers assume that clients only care about money or winning at all costs? A thoughtful dialogue with the client about the non-legal consequences of pursuing the client's goals is in theory a laudable goal. As Tremblay (2003) has noted, however, this idea of moral counseling has not turned out to be a significant movement within law. One major challenge is the surprising difficulty in having a firm factual foundation for making a moral judgment. Legal disputes often have changing facts and lawyers often defer to the clients if there is a good faith basis for a different interpretation of the facts. A good faith basis is key. Courts have disciplined lawyers for engaging in deliberate ignorance and ignoring strong facts that call into question the lawyer's factual claims (In re Giuliani, 2021). But facts are often contested in the midst of representation.

Training students to open up a moral dialogue with their clients also encounters significant headwinds. Law schools train students to be very precise in language and define their terms. As soon as one introduces the idea of "moral dialogue," many students and lawyers become uncomfortable. They understandably ask for a definition of what constitutes morality or a moral judgment and few legal ethics educators have the expertise or time for an in-depth discussion. The conversation is quite easy when good ethics (being cooperative, disclosing in the close case, etc.) also constitutes good strategy and the conduct will promote the client's goals. But what about circumstances where the legally allowed conduct is good for the client but causes harm to third persons or other public interest concerns? The client-centered obligation pushes the lawyer to engage in the conduct that causes third party harm. Another complication is the wide range of settings in which new lawyers practice. In a large firm, new lawyers may have little client contact and no involvement in assessing the client goals, as new lawyers operate within the confines of the firm's culture and ethical infrastructure. Many new lawyers do not have an opportunity to engage in the habits of meaningful discussion with their clients.

When lawyers are engaged in a client dialogue, one method lawyers can use (and students can be taught) is to focus upon the likely public reaction should information become known. For example, in the modern practice of law, it is increasingly difficult to keep a client's conduct confidential, especially corporate actors with many individuals who have relevant knowledge. In addition, reporting requirements to government agencies, client data breaches, and electronic copies that are easily shared create many opportunities for client conduct to be known even when the lawyer successfully maintains strict confidentiality. If a client pursues conduct that, while legal, also causes harm to third persons or the body politic and it becomes known and reported in the news, how would the public react? Would it be a public relations fiasco? This is one avenue to tap into common morality. But there are those occasional cases where the matter includes binary choices that beg for a discussion about that fundamental question, "Is this the right thing to do?" rather than "Am I legally allowed to do this?" Most legal ethics or professional responsibility courses have time to discuss one or two examples of this moment. And the course can analytically frame the tension and choice presented to the lawyer. But most Professional Responsibility courses do not have time or context to help the student internalize the deeply personal and professional decision they may face.

A corollary of the role differentiated behavior is the concept of "non-accountability." Model Rule 1.2(b) states that "[a] lawyer's representation of a client, including representation by appointment, does not constitute an endorsement of the client's political, economic, social or moral views or activities" (American Bar Association, 2020b). That language attempts to separate the lawyer from the consequences of the lawyer's actions via a positive rule. Non-lawyers might reasonably ask "Why not?" The answer to why non-accountability might be appropriate in some or even many situations goes back to role-differentiated behavior. If we believe in the rule of law and believe that legal processes will advance the general good, then at least in litigation there is social value to having diverse points of view represented. This argument holds up relatively well in a litigation context, in which we have at least the formal attributes of the adversary system—lawyers for each side and a neutral judge. Criminal defense lawyers have the strongest justification for their role. They are charged to require the state to prove guilt beyond a reasonable doubt. That level of proof is embedded in the legal system as a check upon the power of the state, so serving that role is serving a constitutional function. In civil litigation matters, lawyers point to the adversary system and note there is an opposing party who is serving as a check. But relying on the system to justify non-accountability requires an analysis of the moral value of the adversary system (Luban, 2007). Most law schools, however, take the adversary system as a given, not a concept that needs justification.

The concept of non-accountability grows weaker as lawyers move outside of litigation settings (McMorrow & Scheuer, 2011). In transactional work or lobbying, the internal tension between one's own beliefs and the legal position of the client can cause huge dissonance. An external statement from the Rules of Professional Conduct that the lawyer is not accountable will only hold up to protect the lawyer from being sanctioned under the rules. It cannot address the question of moral accountability, reintroducing the oath of office. The lawyer is committing on a personal level to promote the interests of the client and the rule of law. To reconcile this tension, lawyers tend to gravitate to clients and causes they believe in, or at least can live with.

This reality—that lawyers are committed to competently (and many believe zealously) represent their clients and may, but are not required to, refer to larger moral concerns, poses a significant challenge in teaching legal ethics. A deeper exploration of the value of allegiance to the legal system and the value of the adversary system, along with an honest recognition of the tensions that can arise, requires time and nuanced attention. A detailed case study in which the students can work through the tensions, discuss them and challenge each other, and begin to develop a vocabulary that more sharply identifies the tensions, increases their skills in having a dialogue with clients, and pushes them to decide where their line is—that place they will not go, even if it is legal—takes time.

If students are not forewarned and prepared for this possible disconnect between their professional role and personal values, wearing a mask by day and then taking it off at night, they can quickly become demoralized. Whether called cognitive dissonance or lawyering through the third person point of view, there is a human toll (Markovits, 2003; Schiltz, 1999). Most states have developed programs to address depression and substance abuse by lawyers. Although a Professional Responsibility class is a very good place to start such discussion, the weight of the large body of law governing lawyers makes it very difficult to dig deeply into this issue.

Institutional Pressures, Psychological Distortions, and Ethical Blindness

Legal ethics is also framed as an individual obligation, treating the lawyer as an autonomous decision-maker. The Rules of Professional Conduct also regulate individual lawyers, not the law firm or other institutions in which they practice. (This is in contrast to emerging regulatory models in the U.K. and Australia, which regulates the firm as well as the individual lawyer) (McMorrow, 2016). The focus upon the individual ignores institutional structural flaws that can put tremendous pressure on the lawyer to disregard the obligations of the RPC as well as the larger moral or ethical dimensions of their conduct. Both these pressures and client-focused lawyering can lead to ethical blindness, where the lawyer literally cannot "see" the ethical dimensions of their conduct (Eldred, 2012; Hall, 2009).

Institutional pressures can influence individual decision making in multiple ways. When the pressure comes from client-centered lawyering, the lawyer may essentially be saying "The system made me do it!" by taking advantage of a scrivener error of opposing counsel or putting compliance with the duty of confidentiality over the interests of a third person incarcerated for a crime this person did not commit. That is reflected in the role-differentiated behavior above.

A second form of institutional pressure comes from policies from the practice setting (e.g., law firm, in-house counsel, government lawyer, public interest representation) that push against compliance with professional obligations. A law firm may have high billable hour requirements, which pressures individual lawyers to "pad" their bills (i.e., to lie to the firm and the client about the amount of work they performed). Lawyers working in house for a corporation may experience significant pressure to find ways to allow profitable business to proceed and minimize the legal risks. A prosecutor's office may have a strong push for a high conviction rate, which puts pressure on the assistant prosecutors to interpret disclosure obligations narrowly, resulting in failure to disclose exculpatory information. A non-profit may feel pressure to pursue a policy that may not be in the interests of the current client but will yield better outcomes for the larger cause they are pursuing. A public defender's office may be underfunded and impose high caseloads on their lawyers, which ultimately requires the lawyer to engage in triage and may undermine the competence of the lawyer and/or her communications with the client.

Cognitive processing also pushes toward ethical blindness. Legal services usually involve evaluating facts in light of the applicable law. But as noted above facts are often not stable, set concepts but emerge in a haphazard fashion, often flying at the lawyers from many different directions, including from clients, partners, subordinates, formal and informal discovery, public information (including the press), and even anonymously. The information comes in with varying degrees of credibility and reliability. When the complications of group functioning are factored in, assessing the "facts" to which a lawyer can apply moral and ethical decision making is much more complicated than the tidy hypotheticals often contained in textbooks.

Well-documented cognitive biases can distort a well-meaning person's ability to see and assess facts that give rise to moral and ethical problems: self-serving bias in assessing information; the endowment effect (giving greater weight to information we already possess); the belief perseverance phenomenon (clinging to beliefs in the face of contrary evidence); the availability heuristic (we are more likely to believe things if a similar event has happened before); and the hindsight bias (looking back to seek confirming evidence for our choices) (Coquillette et al., 2010). Psychological processing, particularly under stress, can distort the lawyer's ability to take in and process facts in a quasi-objective fashion. Coupled with role-differentiated behavior, this can push even more strongly toward ethical blindness. This dynamic occurs at multiple levels. Lawyers may be so committed to their client's point of view that they cannot fully recognize the factual uncertainties that the case may raise. Lawyers may interpret the law in a way that creates uncertainty where a third-party objective observer would see greater certitude. And lawyers may define away moral uncertainty by anchoring their conduct in a duty to clients.

Legal ethics is replete with case studies of lawyers who become sufficiently numbed that they did not recognize the wrongful character of their acts. A group of lawyers who sought to build a claim of judicial bias by setting up a sting operation against a judicial law clerk to lure the law clerk into talking about confidential deliberations of the judge. Lawyers who padded their bills to meet law firm billable hours, slowly drawn into a claim that everyone does it. It is far too easy to dismiss these examples as "bad" or unethical lawyers. An equally plausible description is that they did not set out to violate the Rules of Professional Conduct but instead pushed aside concerns, failed to fully absorb negative facts, or were caught up in a group-think. They were subject to the classic distortions discussed above.

The failure to address institutional pressures fully, the psychological aspects of decision making, and the legal, factual, and moral uncertainties that are common in complex situations leaves new lawyers unprepared to address thoughtfully issues in legal ethics. The best defense against these institutional pressures and cognitive distortions is to address them directly at the beginning of a new lawyer's career. Occasionally, these issues might get touched upon in a Professional Responsibility class. Hopefully, students will take a clinic or externship and have an opportunity to discuss these complexities if these issues arise during their clinic or externship. But the issue may not arise, and in most law schools, students are not required to take a clinic. Exploring these practical aspects of decision making in context is time consuming, nuanced, and difficult to address, particularly with law students who are largely starting out as a subordinate attorney assigned work by a more senior and seasoned lawyer.

CONCLUSION: THE CHALLENGE OF
"VALUES TALK" IN LEGAL ETHICS EDUCATION

Since law is often viewed as mediating social, cultural, and religious differences, for some there is a hesitancy to discuss values that fall outside narrow economic or legal consequences of choices. All the issues discussed above might be framed from a virtue ethics lens, which would provide a single, theoretical framing. But virtue ethics is hardly universally embraced by legal academics, much less the practicing bar. A broader focus upon discussing values is more widely used, although some students push back demanding precision in the discussion or frame values (beyond legal values) as inherently subjective. Yet, learning to "talk values" is essential even if resisted by some students who have fully embraced a "just the law" mindset by the time they reach a professional responsibility class.

The Carnegie Report urged a more systematic focus upon the formation of professional identity that develops the public purposes for which the profession stands (Sullivan et al., 2007b). Commentators have urged a framing that will instill deeper meaning in being a lawyer: embrace the lawyer-statesman model, focusing upon good judgment and public-oriented attitude toward law (Kronman, 1995); focus on peace-making, problem-solving lawyers (Glendon, 1996). Prof. Neil Hamilton's extensive work in analyzing professionalism frames professionalism as having five components: continued growth in personal conscience over one's career, compliance with the ethics of duty; an ethics of aspiration; a commitment to hold other lawyers accountable to the minimum standards; and acting as a fiduciary—devoting time to the public good (including pro bono) and continued reflective engagement on balancing income and wealth in light of other principles of professionalism (Hamilton, 2008).

There is truth in all of these models. Like the wave and particle theories in physics, these models of lawyering can exist side-by-side, with lawyers choosing the model that best reconciles the internal and external values that must coexist to be an emotionally healthy, ethical lawyer. In the end, the greatest challenge to teaching legal ethics is insufficient space, time, and skill to teach and learn to talk values in a client-centered, rules-oriented profession.

REFERENCES

Abel, R. (1989). *American lawyers*. Oxford University Press.

American Bar Association. (1992). *Legal education and professional development—An educational continuum, report on the task force on law schools and the profession: Narrowing the gap*. American Bar Association (known as the MacCrate Report).

American Bar Association. (2020a). *ABA Standards and Rules of Procedure for Approval of Law Schools*. American Bar Association.

American Bar Association. (2020b). *Model rules of professional conduct*. American Bar Association.

Chafee, Z., & Morison, S. E. (Eds.) (1933). *Records of the Suffolk County Court, 1671–1680* (Vols. 29–30). Colonial Society of Massachusetts.

Christensen, B. F. (1980). The unauthorized practice of law: Do good fences really make good neighbors—or even good sense? *American Bar Foundation Research Journal*, *5*(2), 159–218.

Coquillette, D. R., Cassidy, R. M., & McMorrow, J. A. (2010). *Lawyers and fundamental moral responsibility* (2d ed.). LexisNexis.

Coquillette, D. R., & Kimball, B. A. (2015). *On the battlefield of merit: Harvard Law School—the first century*. Harvard University Press.

Coquillette, D. R., & McMorrow, J. A. (2011). Zacharias's prophecy: The federalization of legal ethics through legislative, court & agency regulation, *San Diego L. Rev. 48*, 123–150.

Daly, M. C., Green, B. A., & Pearce, R. G. (1995). Contextualizing professional responsibility: A new curriculum for a new century. *Law & Contemp. Probs.*, *58*(3–4), 193–211.

Eldred, T. W. (2012). Prescriptions for ethical blindness: Improving advocacy for indigent defendants in criminal cases. *Rutgers Law Review*, *65*(2), 333–394.

Glendon, M. A. (1996). *A nation under lawyers: How the crisis in the legal profession is transforming American society*. Harvard University Press.

Gordon, R. L. (1990). Corporate law practice as a public calling. *Maryland Law Review*, *49*(2), 255–292.

Green, B. (2018). The challenges and rewards of teaching legal ethics. *Professional Lawyer*, *25*(2), 3–7.

Hall, K., & Holmes, V. (2009). The power of rationalization to influence lawyers' decisions to act unethically. *Legal Ethics, 11*(2), 137–153.

Hamilton, N. W. (2008). Professionalism clearly defined. *Professional Lawyer*, *18*(4), 7–30.

Horwitz, P. (2019). Coxford lecture: Honour, oaths, and the rule of law. *Canadian Journal of Law & Jurisprudence*, *32*(2), 389–411.

In re Giuliani, 146 N.Y.S.3d 266 (N.Y. App. 2021). https://www.nycourts.gov/courts/ad1/calend ar/List_Word/2021/06_Jun/24/PDF/Matter%20of%20Giuliani%20(2021-00506)%20PC.pdf.

Kronman, A. T. (1995). *The lost lawyer: Failing ideals of the legal profession*. Harvard University Press.

Luban, D. (2007). *Legal ethics and human dignity*. Cambridge University Press.

Luban, D. (2020). Fiduciary legal ethics, zeal, and moral activism. *Georgetown Journal of Legal Ethics*, *33*(2), 276–303.

Markovits, D. (2003). Legal ethics from the lawyer's point of view. *Yale Journal of Law & the Humanities*, *15*(2), 209–293.

McKirdy, C. R. (1976). Before the storm: The working lawyer in pre-revolutionary Massachusetts. *Suffolk University Law Review*, *11*(1) 46–60.

McMorrow, J. A. (2016). UK alternative business structures for legal practice: Emerging models and early lessons for the US. *Georgetown Journal of International Law*, *47*(2), 665–711.

McMorrow, J. A., & Scheuer, L. (2011). The moral responsibility of the corporate lawyer. *Catholic University Law Review*, *60*(2), 275–310.

Neal, P. C. (1967). De Toqueville and the role of the lawyer in society. *Marquette Law Review*, *50*(4), 607–617.

Preston, C., & Lawrence, H. (2015). Incentivizing lawyers to play nice: A national survey of civility standards and options for enforcement. *Michigan Journal of Law Reform, 43*(3), 701–744.

Rhode, D. L. (1995). Ethics by the pervasive method. *Journal of Legal Education, 42*(1), 31–56.

Rhode, D. L. (2018). Virtue and the law: The good moral character requirement in occupational licensing, bar regulation, and immigration proceedings. *Law and Social Inquiry, 43*(3), 1027–1058.

Schiltz, P. J. (1999). On being a happy, healthy, and ethical member of an unhappy, unhealthy, and unethical profession. *Vanderbilt Law Review, 52*(4), 871–951.

Simon, W. H. (1998). *The practice of justice: A theory of lawyers' ethics.* Harvard University Press, 1998.

Stuckey, R., & Others. (2007). *Best practices in legal education: A vision and a road map.* Clinical Legal Education Association. http://cleaweb.org/bestpractices

Sullivan, W. M., Colby, A., Wegner, J. W., Bond, L., & Shulman, L. S. (2007a). *Educating lawyers: Preparation for the profession of law summary.* Carnegie Foundation for the Advancement of Teaching.

Sullivan, W. M., Colby, A., Wegner, J. W., Bond, L., & Shulman, L. S. (2007b). *Educating lawyers: Preparation for the profession of law.* Jossey-Bass.

Tremblay, P. R. (2003). Moral activism manqué. *South Texas Law Review, 44*(1), 127–183.

Vischer, R. V. (2006). Legal advice as moral perspective. *Georgetown Journal of Legal Ethics, 19*(1), 225–273.

Wald, E. (2021). Formation without identity: Avoiding a wrong turn in the professionalism movement. *University of Missouri Kansas City Law Review, 89*(3), 685–715.

Warren, C. (1911). *A history of the American bar.* Little Brown & Co.

Wendel, W. B. (2011). Should law schools teach professional duties, professional virtues, or something else? A critique of the Carnegie report on educating lawyers. *University of Saint Thomas Law Journal, 9*(2), 497–541.

Wilkins, D. B. (1990). Legal realism for lawyers. *Harvard Law Review 104*(2), 468–524.

CHAPTER 2

MEDICAL ETHICS EDUCATION AND THE "THEORY-LIGHT" APPROACH

Greg Moorlock

University of Warwick

This chapter discusses ethics education within the context of training future doctors, with a particular focus on the "theory-light" approach that is often taken. As a UK-based educator, I reflect largely upon the British experience, but this is likely to be broadly consistent with situations internationally. I start by briefly explaining the requirements for medical ethics education in the UK and then explore the constraints under which medical ethics education operates, with a view to explaining why the theory-light approach is so commonplace. Next, I explain the theory-light approach in more detail, highlighting its key features. I then explore the history of medical ethics education within the United Kingdom, explaining how the current core curriculum came to be. I move on to explain the challenges that the theory-light approach presents and will also consider issues associated with the assessment of medical ethics. Finally, I discuss some potential ways forward for the future of medical ethics education.

Keywords: Medical Ethics, Bioethics, Ethics Education, Applied Ethics

Educating in Ethics Across the Professions: A Compendium of Research, Theory, Practice, and an Agenda for the Future, pages 23–46.

Given its nature and complexity, it is unsurprising that the field of medicine is rife with ethical issues. These vary from the everyday, such as the practical requirements of consent and confidentiality, to the most controversial cases occurring at the beginning and end of life that occasionally cause sensationalist newspaper headlines. It is important for medical schools to equip their students with the skills, knowledge, and character to be good doctors, and being a good doctor undoubtedly involves more than just being able to diagnose and treat illness. Appreciating and understanding the ethical aspects of medicine, and doing the right thing, is arguably just as important. Medical ethics is grounded in rich and complex philosophical theory, but to expect medical students and doctors to become expert philosophers would be unrealistically demanding. Moreover, it is not obvious that they need to become expert philosophers in order to become good doctors. Medical ethics is often therefore taught in a "theory-light" way, where decades of work investigating applied ethics and moral theory is distilled into something practical and understandable to people who do not have the time (or often inclination) to develop in-depth philosophical knowledge. The dominance of Beauchamp and Childress's (2001) "four principles" approach to medical ethics is a prime example of this.

In this chapter, I will first explain the theory-light approach and how it has arisen. I will then situate this within the broader context of the development of medical ethics education, highlighting where medical ethics education is today in terms of curriculum content and delivery in the UK. By using the central principle of respect for autonomy as an example, I will start to explore the challenges of teaching medical ethics, highlighting the impact of the theory-light approach. I will draw specifically upon my experiences of teaching medical ethics within a UK context, situating these within the body of literature relating to medical ethics education, but the same challenges will likely arise wherever medical ethics is taught. Finally, I will discuss future prospects for medical ethics education, identifying opportunities for progress and improvement within the field.

ETHICAL ISSUES IN MEDICINE

Medicine involves many factors that bring about ethical complexity. The doctor-patient relationship and its inherent power dynamics, the types of things that doctors need to do to patients in order to alleviate their maladies, and the types of situations that lead patients to require medical assistance in the first place create a complex web of vulnerability, possibilities of rescue and benefit, but also the potential to harm or wrong in many different ways. Fundamental and routine aspects of practicing medicine ethically, such as obtaining valid consent before undertaking procedures, can highlight this complexity. Valid consent is generally considered to consist of three elements: capacity/competence, information, and voluntariness. Behind each seemingly simple element lurks significant nuance and complexity.

When considering capacity/competence, one is asking the question of who is able to make decisions for themselves. This may be relatively straightforward for many adult patients, but nuance enters the equation when children are concerned: It is uncontroversial to say that very young children lack the ability to make decisions for themselves, but this becomes less obviously true as children become older and more mature. What must a child be able to do or demonstrate in order to be considered capable of giving consent for oneself, and is this the same as we would expect from adults? Is there a determined age when it is assumed that all people can do this? Legislation may provide some guidance, but this should be underpinned by something philosophically robust and defensible.

When the question of capacity has been dealt with, the issue of information rears its head. How much information does someone need in order to be considered sufficiently informed to make a decision autonomously? Should the doctor provide all the information that one knows about risks and potential benefits, or only the information one deems to be relevant to the decision? Or should information be based upon what the patient considers to be important, in which case, how can the doctor find this out without providing all the information? Legal judgments may again provide some guidance here, but this is, at its heart, an *ethical* issue.

Voluntariness may seem simple at first glance, but it is prone to the same complexity as the other two elements. Patients rarely make decisions in complete isolation, so how much influence from, for instance, family members, is too much influence? At what point does familial input into a patient's decision become coercive and what should be done about this if it goes too far? Even with all three elements of consent clearly specified, doctors can face ethically challenging situations: What should they do if a competent adult patient refuses to consent to a procedure that is clearly medically beneficial? In this scenario is it permissible for a doctor to try to convince a patient to change one's mind, or does respect for the patient's autonomy render this path of action impermissible? The complexity of these questions is apparent without even trying to answer them, but doctors need to be equipped with the knowledge, skills, and character to ensure they make the right judgments and navigate the requirements of consent appropriately.

Consent is just one of many examples of ethical considerations in medicine. Some ethical issues relate closely to consent (confidentiality of patient information, for example, or end of life decision making), but many others are not so closely linked (doctors' responsibilities when mistakes are made, or doctors' obligations in emergency situations outside of healthcare settings). Given the importance of getting these matters right, it is crucial that doctors have received adequate training to ensure they are equipped to do just this.

OUTLINING THE REQUIREMENTS

Undergraduate medical education in the UK is guided by the UK's regulator of the medical profession, the General Medical Council (GMC), and its "Outcomes for Graduates" (General Medical Council, 2018). Medical schools awarding medical degrees are required to ensure that graduating students meet the learning outcomes outlined by this document. Curricula within British medical schools are therefore mapped specifically to these outcomes. When reading through this document, it is immediately apparent that the list of learning outcomes goes beyond the "medical" in a narrow sense of the word. The GMC outcomes reflect the fact that being a good doctor is about more than just having scientific understanding and that an understanding of the complex social contexts in which medicine takes place is also required. Moreover, there is a remarkably strong emphasis upon the importance of doctors understanding the ethical aspects of healthcare: This includes things that one would entirely expect as part of being a medical professional, such as the importance of gaining informed consent from patients, but also goes beyond this by stating that medical students should understand key ethical debates. Medical ethics is therefore a requirement of medical curricula throughout the UK, and similar situations are found internationally (see American Medical Colleges, 1999; Association of Teachers of Ethics and Law in Australian and New Zealand Medical Schools, 2001).

WHAT ARE THE PURPOSES OF MEDICAL ETHICS EDUCATION?

Although the GMC sets out its learning outcomes with precision, and in doing so, highlights the importance of ethics, it leaves open to interpretation a more overarching description of what medical ethics education should seek to achieve and how educators should seek to achieve it. The UK situation appears to be broadly similar to other countries. Carrese et al. (2015), for example, highlight that although there is consensus about the importance of teaching medical ethics, there is no such agreement about what the specific goals of this education should be, or the methods that should be used to achieve such goals. There is some general agreement about the types of ambitions that medical ethics education could have, however. For instance, a 2005 review (Eckles et al., 2005) suggests the purposes of medical ethics education fall into two main camps: first, medical ethics education can be viewed as a way to create virtuous physicians, and second, it is alternatively a way to provide physicians the skills to handle ethical dilemmas they may confront.

Giubilini et al. (2016) separate the aims of medical ethics education into similar categories, drawing a divide between cognitive/competence objectives and attitudinal/virtue objectives. In their framing, cognitive objectives are met by imparting knowledge about values, principles, and norms in the context of medicine, with attitudinal objectives having more to do with the development of the virtues that one expects of a good doctor. The distinction can perhaps be summarized in terms of aiming to produce a certain type of doctor versus aiming to produce a doctor possessing certain knowledge and skills. As has been argued elsewhere, it is not necessarily helpful to think of these two aims as being completely independent of one another.

Campbell et al. (2007) have argued for thinking of the aims of ethics education as a pyramid with fundamental knowledge at the bottom, "habitation" in the middle, and ethical action at the top. This seems like a useful way of framing the issue, as ultimately one wants doctors who will behave ethically, rather than doctors who possess detailed knowledge about how they should act but with no corresponding character that results in knowledge being applied appropriately.

For the purposes of this chapter, I will echo the suggestions made by Campbell et al. (2007) and others (Giubilini et al., 2016) that medical ethics education should be aiming to promote formation of appropriate character and development of appropriate skills and knowledge, with the overarching aim of producing ethical behaviour in doctors. Even if these overarching aims are assumed, there is significant scope for disagreement regarding how they should be balanced against each other, the extent to which they need to be achieved, and relatedly, how best to achieve them given the constraints under which medical ethics education takes place.

TEACHING ETHICS UNDER CONSTRAINTS

If one was learning about ethics in a philosophy department, the experience would differ vastly from learning about ethics in a medical school, and with good reason. In a philosophy department, entire modules might be dedicated to utilitarianism or deontology in their various forms. Months of study may also be dedicated to concepts such as autonomy and its relationship with free will and determinism. Philosophy departments also often require students to attend compulsory modules where they consider critical thinking and formal logic. It is not controversial, though, to suggest that the aims of ethics education in philosophy departments are different from the aims of ethics education in medical schools.

Without wishing to caricature philosophy departments unfairly, it is sometimes the case that ethics is more a matter of academic interest and enquiry rather than something that will shape the day-to-day future lives and guide the actions of philosophy graduates. Ethics in medical schools is rather different, and one would reasonably expect everything that is taught to be relevant to the students in their future roles as doctors. Rather than providing students with nuanced theory to promote high-minded debate and discussion then, medical schools are aiming to provide students with *enough* knowledge of theory to be able to reason about the ethical issues they are likely to encounter as junior doctors and ultimately to do the right thing. Although the aims of ethics education in medical schools may be slightly less ambitious in terms of depth of knowledge and understanding, there remains a wide breadth of content to cover, and the requirement of less depth does not make achieving the aims any more straightforward. Rather, there are additional constraints within medical schools that have a significant impact upon how ethics is taught.

Time Constraints

Medical curricula contain a vast amount of content, and feedback from students often highlights that they find the sheer quantity of what they are expected to know to be overwhelming. This is arguably unavoidable, given the diverse range of material students need to know in order to be competent doctors, with one consequence being that different subjects within the curriculum are vying for the finite time, attention, and energies of students. High rates of burnout among medical students (Ishak et al., 2013) serve to illustrate the demands confronting them. Given the demands on their time, it is unsurprising that students may struggle to engage fully with all aspects of the curriculum. Brooks and Bell (2017) found the majority of schools responding to their research believed that students engaged with ethics teaching, but many responding schools identified negative attitudes towards ethics education. Medical students sometimes appear to be under the impression that ethics is either common sense (Rogers, 2011) or something they can worry about learning once they are qualified doctors.

It is perhaps understandable that many students may perceive ethics education as a subject that is subsidiary to core anatomy or physiology (Leo & Eagen, 2008), but some do not arrive at medical school with the aim of learning ethics. Brooks and Bell's research suggests that some students perceive ethics as lacking relevance or of being lower than other aspects of the curriculum. There are therefore two dimensions of time constraints that apply to medical ethics. Actual "classroom" time is limited, due to the quantity of content in other areas of the curriculum. Although the GMC recognizes learning about ethics as important, it is unsurprising that actual time dedicated to teaching ethics is lower than for some other curriculum areas.

The time that students can commit, or are willing to commit, to ethics is also constrained. The dominance of teaching about anatomy and biology results in little time being left in the medical curriculum, or in students' lives, for medical ethics. Students may also be mindful of how different subjects will be weighted in assessments and therefore afford less time to those that constitute a smaller part of exams. These time constraints have been noted in the literature (Brooks & Bell, 2017) and have a significant impact upon how ethics is taught within medical schools. It is unlikely to be possible to explore nuanced understandings of complex concepts and principles, and even if it was possible to do so, students may not be prepared to engage fully with this teaching due to other demands on their time and cognitive energies. It is worth noting that many medical schools do have active student-led medical ethics societies, so those who do wish to delve into ethics in more detail will often create opportunities to do so. But, this may serve to perpetuate the notion that ethics is, in some way, optional and subsidiary to other elements of the formal curriculum.

Starting Points

Students coming into undergraduate medical courses are high achievers and are generally expected to have studied and excelled in science subjects at school. Entry requirements are demanding, and only students with strong grades will be accepted. Graduate-entry medical courses are not always so demanding in the specificity of requirements of previous qualifications. Warwick Medical School, for example, requires that a student has a previous degree, but this need not be in a science subject. In reality, of course, most of the students do have previous degrees in science subjects. Among the graduate-entry programs in the UK, around 20% of students have a degree in the arts, humanities, and social sciences with the majority having degrees in biology/life sciences or physical sciences (Garrud & McManus, 2018). Although there are a small number of students coming into the medical degree program with undergraduate philosophy degrees, they are a small minority. The majority of students starting medicine will therefore have little expertise or specific knowledge of medical ethics, requiring those who teach ethics in medical school to start from the very basics, assuming students have very limited knowledge about the nature of ethics, ethical deliberation, or even critical thinking. Those who have done some background reading in medical ethics before attending medical school (often in preparation for the interviews that form part of the admissions process) will generally have been exposed to the principlist approach to ethics, which as I will discuss shortly, has some profound limitations. Starting from these basics and attempting to achieve the GMC learning outcomes within the confines of a four- or five- year course, of which ethics is only a relatively small part, again means the depth of understanding has to be compromised.

Just a Matter of Opinion?

One issue likely confronting many medical ethics educators is the sense among some students (and colleagues) that there are no right or wrong answers when it comes to ethical questions. Some students appear to be of the view that it is all just a matter of opinion (Rogers, 2011), there will be a diverse range of opinions, and we should be reluctant to dismiss some of these subjective opinions as being incorrect. While it is not necessary to get into a discussion of metaethics here, even though one may have some doubts about the nature of ethical judgments, one can assert with some confidence that some ethical positions are more defensible than others and that some answers to ethical questions will similarly be better than others. Distinguishing between better and worse ethical positions requires a level of ethical reasoning, however.

In some respects, the "doing" of ethical reasoning is the justification, as it was for my high-school math teacher who was adamant that just getting the answers to his questions right was not enough because one also has to be able to demonstrate their working. In ethics, "showing your working" relies upon a level of justification and ethical reasoning, which normally draws upon theoretically rich concepts or principles.

Combatting the view that ethics is more than just mere opinion requires teaching medical students that there is underlying theory that supports or calls into question particular ethical positions, but it is not often possible to explore this theory in any depth. A nod towards the potential for deeper understanding is one matter but to gain anything more than a superficial understanding of central ethical concepts and principles takes time that many medical students do not have.

So How Do We Teach Medical Ethics?

Due to the constraints described above, some compromises have to be made. The GMC learning outcomes make it clear that the expectations of medical students when it comes to ethics are high. They must be able to reason about ethics, evaluate concepts, and demonstrate understanding of complex ideas regarding ethically contentious areas of medicine. Yet, due to the constraints mentioned above, it is not possible or maybe even desirable to try to deliver ethics education rich in theory and nuance.

Instead, much medical ethics education relies a great deal upon simplification of complex concepts and principles into more digestible and readily understandable approaches to medical ethics. This results in medical ethics education being relatively "theory-light," meaning that the depth and range of theory used to explain or justify particular positions is extremely limited. In essence, ethics and ethical deliberation are often taught without really teaching the underlying ethical theory. As a simple example, although students are often taught basic ethical theory, such as an introduction to the "big three" approaches to theory in ethics (consequentialism, deontology, and virtue ethics), it is unlikely they would be expected to understand the fine gradations between different forms of utilitarianism. Students may learn that deontology is about duties, but it is unlikely they will be able to adequately address various formulations of Kant's categorical imperative. Giving students the basic knowledge to appreciate different ways of looking at ethical issues may be important, but in a very shallow form it is not obviously the type of knowledge that is going to assist greatly the types of nuanced ethical deliberation required of doctors.

This approach contrasts strikingly with other areas of medical curricula, where in-depth knowledge and understanding of bioscientific aspects is considered essential for students to become doctors. The question of why in-depth knowledge is required for some aspects of medicine and not for the area of medicine where the stakes are maybe the highest (one is unlikely to face disciplinary action for failing to recall the finer details of the Krebs cycle, yet one will potentially face disciplinary action for failing to act in an ethical manner) is difficult to answer conclusively. Cowley (2005) draws a useful distinction between ethics and areas of scientific knowledge on the basis that we are all familiar with ethics—in some form—in other areas of our lives, and there are ethical concepts of ordinary language. Medical students are able to deliberate about ethical issues prior to joining medical school and Cowley suggests that adding additional knowledge and vocabulary to this may lead students and doctors to ignore their own—perfectly reasonable—ethical intuitions and vocabulary. While one need not agree wholesale with Cowley's argument, the idea that someone might be able to make sound ethical judgments without in-depth knowledge of theory is itself entirely reasonable. But as briefly highlighted, knowing the right thing to do is not always sufficient: Being able to justify and articulate one's reasons for choosing one course of action over another can be just as important, particularly when explaining things to patients or colleagues.

One example of a theory-light approach to medical ethics is principlism, whereby ethical issues within medicine are often reduced to consideration of four principles that many people agree are normally relevant considerations: beneficence (understood roughly as acting for the benefit of another); non-maleficence (often interpreted in the form of "first do no harm"); respect for autonomy; and justice. Although this approach has received some criticism, it has been suggested that contemporary medical ethics education centers around this principlist approach (Donaldson, 2017). It is important to note that although use of the four principles is widespread, it is not universal. For example, I—and many others—do not tend to teach just in terms of the four principles. Nonetheless, it is an approach that students often adopt when answering questions and reasoning about ethical issues in class, due to its widespread use throughout the medical profession.

Beauchamp and Childress provide more nuance to underpin this approach than they are sometimes credited with, but nonetheless it is sometimes considered to be a somewhat reductive approach to ethical reasoning. It has been suggested, for example, that principlism becomes more of a checklist than a nuanced moral framework (Fiester, 2007), and that the theory behind principlism is seldom taught in medical schools. Nonetheless, it does have some appealing features due to its accessibility, flexibility (Donaldson, 2017), and its basis in common ground. Most importantly of all in the context of medical education, perhaps, it provides an understandable way for non-experts to assess ethical issues. Principlism is, of course, not the only example of theory-light medical ethics—and given that Beauchamp and Childress do provide theory to justify their approach, it may even be unfair to characterize it as inherently theory-light. Nonetheless, it is frequently used in an extremely theory-light way.

Although an overarching theory-light approach to teaching ethics in medical schools is now commonplace, this is only one aspect of teaching medical ethics. The medical ethics curriculum has developed over time, and in the next section I will explore how this has occurred and where points of contention remain.

THE EMERGENCE OF MODERN MEDICAL ETHICS CURRICULUM

Despite medical ethics now being almost ubiquitous in modern medical schools, medical ethics education as we might recognize it today is a relatively new development. Going back to 1967, ethics education at one medical school in London consisted of a single lecture focusing vaguely on professionalism (Shotter et al., 2013). In 1972, only 4% of medical schools in the United States taught medical ethics as a formal compulsory course; before 1970, ethics education was generally provided via osmosis, with students observing the values and behaviors of more experienced clinicians (Fox et al., 1995). Understandably, some considered this approach inadequate.

Specialized medical ethics education within the UK arguably owes its existence to the London Medical Group (LMG) and the Pond Report. Formed in 1963 as a way for "students to engage with medical humanities and the wider society," LMG ran regular events in London's teaching hospitals exploring a range of topics, including ethics, with presentations by both clinicians and non-clinicians. Other medical groups were formed across the UK and hosted similar events. After undergoing various organizational changes, LMG eventually became the Institute of Medical Ethics (IME) in 1975 (Whong-Barr, 2003, p. 76).

With the GMC's encouragement, IME convened a working group in 1984 to explore medical ethics education in the UK. The resulting Pond Report on the Teaching of Medical Ethics (Institute of Medical Ethics, 1987) considered how medical ethics should be taught and by whom. The report suggested that ethics teaching should be integrated with clinical teaching and be both explanatory and analytical. The report also recommended, controversially at the time (Ledingham, 1987), that teaching should include moral philosophy and moral theology or law. Over subsequent years, there have been dramatic improvements in medical ethics education. For example, a 1990 study found that formal medical ethics education was present in all London medical schools, although the amount of time dedicated to this varied from 2–24 hours (Burling et al., 1990). Similar things occurred in the United States, with the 1985 DeCamp Report (Culver et al., 1985) arguing that medical ethics education should be required in all US medical schools (Carrese et al., 2015).

Since these early days, medical ethics education has become an established part of medical curricula, with specialist staff possessing expertise in medical ethics often being appointed to take responsibility for this part of the curriculum (Giubilini et al., 2016). Over time, detailed consensus statements have been devised and published regarding which aspects of medical ethics should be featured in the medical curriculum, who should teach them, and to some extent, how they should be taught. In 1998, IME published its consensus statement regarding teaching medical ethics in the UK. Produced by teachers of ethics (and law) in UK medical schools—consisting mostly of clinicians, philosophers, lawyers, and theologians (Doyal & Gillon, 1998)—the document outlined, in addition to core content, the organizational aspects of teaching ethics, which were considered to be prerequisites for effective delivery of the suggested content. This included the notion that adequate teaching would require the employment of "at least one full-time senior academic in ethics and law with relevant professional and academic expertise." Additionally, the document recommended that ethics teaching should be fully integrated with the broader curriculum and taught throughout the entirety of the course. Judging by later publications, many medical schools appear to have embraced these sorts of recommendations. Campbell et al. (2007), for example, highlight several changes that have occurred in medical ethics education. These include an acceptance that it should be academically robust and informed by research and that it should be thoroughly integrated into the medical curriculum. Many other have voiced this emphasis upon integration, suggesting that it should occur both vertically and horizontally, although it is worth noting that the term "integrated" is used variably (Wong et al., 2021).

In a review of ethics curricula in undergraduate medical education, Goldie (2000) reports that many of the pioneering medical ethics educators were teachers of moral philosophy or theology, but considering the recommendations relating to integration of ethics content and the broader nature of ethical issues in medicine, it is clearly desirable for ethics to be taught in a practical and clinically relevant sense rather than as a distinct academic subject. On the one hand, ethics education should be academically robust and informed by research, perhaps suggesting that it is best taught by philosophers or similar. Yet, on the other hand, these same educators are likely to lack clinical experience and run the risk of being perceived as detached from the realities of clinical practice. There are, of course, some medical doctors who are also accomplished philosophers, although these remain relatively rare. Mattick and Bligh (2006) found that 73% of medical schools that participated in their research had a full time academic taking responsibility for medical ethics. More recently, Brooks and Bell (2017) found (with fewer participating medical schools) a lower proportion (only 55% of participating medical schools) had a full-time member of staff dedicated to teaching ethics. The authors are unable to explain the reasons for this but speculate it could be due to a lack of qualified people, a lack of people interested in the role, a lack of funding for these roles, medical schools believing that dedicated staff are not required, or a combination of these factors.

The uptake of medical ethics education has been a gradual process, characterized by inconsistent approaches and there remain questions about its overall value and effectiveness. Andre (2002) has suggested that teaching ethics is "fundamentally an act of hope" and that ethics educators seldom know the impact of their teaching. Campbell et al. (2007) state that as of 2007 there was a lack of evidence on the efficacy of ethics education. Based upon his professional experience as a barrister working with clinical negligence claims, Sokol (2016) appears somewhat skeptical about the impact of ethics education on the behavior of doctors. Nonetheless he suggests that including ethics in curricula communicates an important message about it being a fundamental part of medical practice. More recently, Souza and Vaswani (2020) found that there remains a clear lack of robust evidence concerning the efficacy of ethics education. Who should ideally teach medical ethics and how the impact of medical ethics teaching should be assessed remain points of some contention. I will return to these important matters later in this chapter.

The Current Core Curriculum

Since 1998, IME has updated what it considers to be a "Core Curriculum" for medical ethics (and law) education (Institute of Medical Ethics, 2019). This curriculum contains a list of topics considered essential or necessary for doctors at the point of qualification. Given the hugely diverse range of ethical issues doctors potentially confront, one might expect some disagreement regarding what should be included as part of an ethics core curriculum. In relation to the original 1998 core curriculum, the Consensus Statement By Teachers of Medical Ethics and Law in UK Medical Schools (1998) stated, however, there was "widespread agreement about the acceptable ethical and legal contours of good and safe medical practice and little debate about the related understanding, attitudes and skills that this requires" (p. 189). The suggested core content therefore included familiar and expected territory such as informed consent and refusal of treatment, truthfulness and trust, confidentiality, and mental health. Although there may have been little disagreement at the time of its original publication, it is notable that the 2010 update to the core curriculum stated that revisions had been made due to aspects of the original being considered dated and some of its topics being more appropriate for postgraduate study (Stirrat et al., 2010). Topics such as "cloning" and "eugenics versus patient-centered care" stand out as being rather "of their time" in the 1998 document and are not included in such explicit terms in the latest version.

Following the IME Core Curriculum is not compulsory[1], but it provides an example of the range of topics that need to be covered to ensure that the GMC learning outcomes (that are compulsory in the UK) can be met. The IME document has also been mapped against the core duties that the GMC require of doctors. Reporting the contents of the current Core Curriculum in depth is not necessary here, but it is useful to highlight briefly the variety and depth of what is expected for current UK medical students.

The requirements are diverse and cover fundamental topics such as confidentiality and decision-making as well as specific issues at the beginning and end of life, for example. This corresponds broadly with similar suggestions made by Giubilini et al. (2016) who include topics such as informed consent, confidentiality, autonomy, trust, professionalism, and conceptions of doctor-patient relationships. Within the curriculum area entitled "Foundations of medical ethics and law" there is an expectation that students will be able to recognize various approaches to ethical theory. This suggests students need to be taught about ethical theory to some degree. Additionally, students are expected to be able to evaluate concepts such as autonomy and identify when other considerations may outweigh

---

[1] There are other approaches that may be taken, albeit with potentially similar core content. Dowie and Martin (2011) is one such alternative, and one that deliberately avoids providing a list of core topics and instead aims to construct a "workable frame for learning." Although outside of the taught medical school environment, the British Medical Association (the trade union for doctors in the UK) offer a structured and checklist-style framework approach to support students in learning ethics (British Medical Association, 2020)

respecting it. This is noteworthy because achieving this learning outcome would require a reasonable understanding of the concept as well as an ability to reason robustly about ethical matters and draw upon other concepts and principles. As this core curriculum document make clear, students are expected not just to be able to describe ethics or repeat ethical guidance documents, but rather to "do" ethics, to analyse or critique concepts as well as to reason and argue. It is notable, however, that implementation of the core curriculum as fleshed out by IME has not been universal: For example, Brooks and Bell (2017) found that 73% of their respondents were teaching all of IME's recommended topics as part of their ethics curriculum.

The GMC learning outcomes and how these provide guidance in IME's core curriculum make it apparent that the expectations of medical students in relation to medical ethics are high. IME's core curriculum frequently uses high-level verbs, such as "evaluate" or "analyze," appearing in Bloom's taxonomy (Bloom, 1956). In the next section, I will explore some of the challenges that medical ethics educators confront when trying to meet these ambitious aspirations.

CHALLENGES IN MEDICAL ETHICS EDUCATION: THE COST OF THEORY-LIGHT TEACHING

Earlier, I suggested medical ethics educators often adopt a theory-light approach to teaching medical ethics due to the aims of medical ethics education and the various constraints that exist. I now will consider the implications of divorcing medical ethics teaching from its philosophically nuanced underpinnings, using autonomy as an example.

Theory and Autonomy

Autonomy is a central concept to modern-day medical ethics, and respect for autonomy is considered by some to be the dominant ethical principle guiding decision making in healthcare. Although autonomy is one of four principles within principlism, it is sometimes considered to be "first amongst equals" (Gillon, 2003). IME refers specifically to the importance of medical students being able to evaluate the notion of respect for autonomy in its Core Curriculum (2019). When one surveys medical ethics literature more broadly, it can be observed that autonomy—even when a principlist approach is not explicitly taken—is central to many discussions and guides many decisions in clinical practice. Moreover, when one looks at professional guidance for doctors, one can see respect for autonomy underpins numerous aspects, such as informed consent, refusal of treatment, and maintaining confidentiality.

Many philosophers maintain that autonomy is a complex concept and it is the subject of much academic debate, with profound disagreement concerning what constitutes autonomy. The debate goes beyond this, of course, and considers whether autonomy as it may be broadly understood even exists in a potentially deterministic world. Debates about hard determinism and compatibilism, for example, have continued for decades and seem unlikely to be resolved any time soon. As an undergraduate philosopher, I studied a twelve-week module dedicated to autonomy and another module dedicated to discussion of the possibility of free will; yet, my knowledge and understanding of these complex ideas is still obviously incomplete.

There is no need for medical students to understand autonomy to even this depth and it would certainly be impossible to dedicate this amount of time to it. What IME's core curriculum requires is that students be able to evaluate the concept and identify when competing considerations may outweigh demands for its respect. Thus, while it is important for medical students to have a working understanding of autonomy, all the constraints already discussed prevent this from being a full, or even a deep, understanding.

Autonomy within medical ethics education is normally tied very strongly to the concept of informed consent *because* it is one part of respecting the autonomy of a patient. Indeed, examining what Beauchamp and Childress say about autonomy—"Personal autonomy is, at minimum, self-rule that is free from both controlling interference by others and from limitations, such as inadequate understanding, that prevent meaningful choice" (2001, p. 58)—the links to the concept of informed consent are immediately clear. This description of autonomy seems entirely reasonable and includes the key components, but in itself does little to specify key terms such as "self-rule," "controlling interference," "inadequate understanding," or "meaningful choice." It would be necessary to drill down deeper into theory to unpack these ideas to specify adequately what autonomy looks like in medical practice. Students, however, do not generally get much opportunity to do this, and instead are left with an understanding of autonomy that unfortunately resembles "If a patient says we should do something and they are not coerced into saying that, then respect for autonomy demands that we should do it."

However, the issue here is that autonomy is accorded such prominence in modern medical ethics. It is taken to have intrinsic value, making autonomy more than something instrumentally good. Although autonomy is one of principlism's four principles, it is nonetheless accorded more decisive weight than the other three. But from where does this weight arise and what is it about autonomy that makes it worth respecting? Philosophically detailed accounts of autonomy provide a range of responses. Among other things, Kantianism holds that autonomy concerns the ability to impose the moral law onto oneself. Frankfurt (1988) thinks the concern should be aligning second-order volitions with first order desires in a way that makes these desires truly one's own. Mackenzie (2014) insists there are multiple dimensions to autonomy that require careful consideration. Introducing medical students to some of these ideas, it is unlikely that it can be done with the depth required to do any of the justificatory or even explanatory work regarding autonomy. Instead, students are taught that respect for autonomy is the grounding for informed consent and that doctors generally cannot do things without a patient's consent because to do so would be to act contrary to that patient's autonomy. In the end, complexity is stripped out of the concept and replaced with a much thinner account. But, if students are to be able to identify situations in which other considerations may outweigh respect for autonomy adequately, then it seems they need to understand its value, why it is valuable, and how other considerations that are also valuable may be in tension with this.

Recent situations arising from the Covid-19 pandemic highlight the problematic aspects of simplistic thinking when it comes to autonomy. Willingness to receive a Covid-19 vaccine is arguably a matter of personal autonomy, but it is also the case that decisions in relation to this will have impacts upon immediate others and society at large. Respect for autonomy may act as one guiding principle in decisions like this, but there are limits on the weight that it can carry, for example, the UK was going to require Covid-19 vaccinations for all frontline medical staff (BBC News, 2021), highlighting how consequentialist concerns as well as professional obligations to protect the vulnerable can outweigh personal choice over vaccination. Respect for autonomy is therefore not an absolute; instead, it requires more nuanced reasoning about the concept to establish where its lines should be drawn. Evaluating the concept requires a depth of understanding of the concept that theory-light teaching fails to provide.

The Consequences of Simplification

One undesirable upshot of teaching in this way is that students leave medical school with a simplistic understanding of immensely complex philosophical concepts. This is not problematic in itself, as there is arguably no need for newly qualified doctors to have a much more complex understanding of philosophical theory. If a desired end point of medical ethics education is to produce doctors who act ethically and can reason about ethical issues, then a truly deep understanding of rich theory does not seem necessary. Many ethical issues can be addressed adequately without delving into the philosophy of autonomy and, in fact, the philosophy of autonomy may make it more difficult to make the sorts of relatively prompt ethical decisions that doctors frequently have to make. It seems unlikely that when confronted with a complex situation, a doctor can go away and think in depth for a few weeks about the nature of autonomy and come up with a robustly defensible solution; instead, a doctor may have to make a decision about how to proceed then and there. And, of course, disagreement and uncertainty in the philosophical literature only muddies the water. What happens if one doctor embraces a broadly Frankfurtian account of autonomy and another endorses relational autonomy and these two accounts yield different conclusions? It seems that, on some level, doctors actually need simplicity and practicality rather than complexity, uncertainty, and disagreement concerning ethical principles and concepts.

Lawlor has suggested that teaching theory to medical students is problematic because "the students may understand the information they are given, but what they have understood is of little or no value because it is merely a caricature of a theory" (2007, p. 370). This can be observed regularly in medical schools as students learn the principles and even how to apply them in a simplistic way, but do not develop an understanding of the nuances inherent in them. This level of superficiality is problematic if the ignored depth is ethically relevant—and it frequently is. In essence, thin understandings of rich concepts take on an almost dogmatic status and detachment from theory yields detachment from value. Medical students may be able to state *that* doctors should respect autonomy, but many will be hard pushed to explain *why* doctors should respect autonomy or even to explain what autonomy means with any depth. Without the "why," it seems today's medical students will struggle to justify fully decisions they will make in medical practice with respect to autonomy.

Because ethics is taught to medical students in a relatively understandable and superficial way, there is a risk that doctors will end up thinking what they were taught about ethics is all there is to know, without appreciating the complexity or nuance that lies behind claims they often take to be uncontroversial. On the one hand, it is crucial that doctors feel capable of making ethical decisions for themselves. So, it is key that a message of "you can all do ethics" is communicated through medical ethics education. But, on the other hand, there is a risk that this message downplays the complexity of ethics to an extent where some students begin to view ethics as a matter of "common sense" or basic balancing of burdens and benefits. Anyone who has studied autonomy in depth will understand that robust philosophical analysis of this concept is anything but common sense, is often counter-intuitive, and requires familiarity with a substantial body of literature. One consequence of doctors thinking that ethics is just common sense or that their undergraduate ethics training is sufficient to deal with complex ethical issues may result in over-confidence and an unwillingness to seek additional expert ethics advice.

I have outlined some downsides of this theory-light approach to teaching medical ethics. Unfortunately, I can see no straightforward, perfect solution to the problem as it is inherent to the theory-light approach to teaching medical ethics that is made necessary by the constraints outlined earlier. Acknowledging the limitations of theory-light teaching may at least provide a starting point. One effective way to deal with this particular challenge may simply be for medical ethics educators to be more explicit about the different levels of theory when it comes to ethics. This may ensure that complex ethical issues are not simplified beyond reasonable recognition and ensure that medical students and doctors are not left thinking that philosophically thin, theory-light principles can do all the necessary justificatory work in ethics.

ASSESSMENT IN AND OF MEDICAL ETHICS EDUCATION

A further challenge in medical ethics education is that of appropriate assessment. What constitutes appropriate assessment depends upon various factors, including the stage of the course students are in as well as the agreed aims of medical ethics education. Wong et al. (2021) found that a wide array of assessment modalities are used for assessing medical ethics. This includes, among others, multiple-choice questions, short-answer questions, essays/research papers, some form of observation, and even self-assessment. A significant issue applicable to all these modalities is ensuring that sufficient weight is accorded to them. This could be considered as making sure that the ethical components of assessment are sufficiently "high stakes." Given the profound implications of unethical conduct or failures of ethical deliberation during one's medical career, it is somewhat disappointing that assessment of medical ethics often fails to reflect these high stakes.

For example, Mattick and Bligh (2006) found that in 15 UK medical schools, failing to meet core competencies in ethics did not prevent graduation. Moreover, given the relatively low proportion of overall marks available in relation to ethics in written exams, it is entirely possible a student could get every single ethics question incorrect, compensate in other curriculum areas, and still become a qualified doctor at the end of the course. Brooks and Bell (2017) highlight that this is strictly true of any subject area in an integrated examination, but that the fewer marks available for ethics assessment make this a more significant problem. Including distinct, weight-bearing ethics assessments at specified stages of courses may improve the situation, but it remains to be seen whether there would be widespread support from medical schools to prevent progression for those students who are not successful in these assessments.

In addition to this, it is not obvious that current assessment methods are assessing the most relevant or important things. Wong et al. (2021) also describe the pros and cons of different assessment methods, and it is apparent that, as one might expect, each form of assessment exhibits significant limitations or downsides. Brooks and Bell (2017) found that most UK medical schools in their study were using multiple choice/single best answer questions, with about one third of their participants using short answer questions. Wong et al. (2021) suggest that although these types of questions are objective and reliable, they are limited in terms of what they can assess (Wong et al. suggest they can only assess knowledge) and they do not provide enough data to interpret students' ethical deliberation accurately. Mattick and Bligh (2006) found that most medical schools aimed, through their ethics education, to instill ethical conduct in their medical students. If this remains the case today, there is a striking disconnect between the aims of medical education and what is actually being assessed. This disconnect highlights a key challenge for medical ethics educators: How can they be sure that ethics education is actually helping to produce the desired outcomes? While knowledge, understanding, and even ability to reflect and reason can be assessed, it is not necessarily the case that positive results in these aspects will translate to good, ethical conduct in future.

It is apparent from existing literature that there is little evidence regarding the effectiveness of medical ethics education overall or which aspects of medical ethics education may prove to be most effective (Souza & Vaswani, 2020). Brooks' and Bell's relatively recent research highlights that teaching faculty believed their students were prepared for clinical practice, but it is fair to say these perceptions may not match reality in this respect, and other, more recent research would support skepticism regarding this belief (Machin et al., 2020). The lack of systematic evidence in these regards does lend support to Andre's (2002) earlier claim that ethics education is an act of hope.

This creates a difficult position: It is important that assessment of ethics is weight-bearing and it is problematic that students could fail every component of ethics assessment and still qualify, yet there are concerns regarding the lack of evidence relating to assessment *in* medical ethics and assessment *of* medical ethics. More evidence would be extremely valuable, but may require medical schools to experiment with different forms of assessment, which itself is a challenging proposition given the *overall* high stakes of medical exams.

PROSPECTS FOR THE FUTURE:
ETHICS EDUCATORS OF THE FUTURE

An area of important consideration for the future of medical ethics education is what constitutes an ideal medical ethics educator and where these people will come from.

Mattick and Bligh (2006) discuss the issues of staffing, staff training, and succession planning, suggesting that a frequent reliance upon a single person to have responsibility for overseeing (and sometimes delivering) medical ethics education raises questions about how these people may eventually be replaced. At the time Mattick and Bligh conducted their research, there were concerns about a lack of up-and-coming ethics educators, and it is not clear that a solution has been devised in the intervening years. Complicating matters, in the UK there is no single recognised training pathway to become a medical ethics educator.

This reintroduces the questions raised earlier in this chapter about what constitutes an appropriate formation for an ethics educator, given that "pure philosophers" and "pure clinicians" may both have significant limitations. With the lack of empirical evidence concerning what makes a good ethics educator, research addressing this issue would be extremely valuable for determining how to best equip those who will teach medical ethics in the future.

Balancing Theory and Practice

Two things appear obviously true in relation to ethics educators: Learning about ethics solely from "ivory tower" philosophers who have no nuanced understandings of life within the medical profession is unlikely to be ideal. Similarly, learning about ethics solely from doctors with little or no understanding of the theory that underpins ethical reasoning is also unlikely to be ideal. The question, then, is how to best combine the strengths of each and minimize their weaknesses.

With some degree of success, experience has taught me how to have a foot in both the medical and philosophical worlds (despite only being formally trained in the latter) and this may point to potential options worthy of further exploration. First, although I undertook a PhD in bioethics and used largely philosophical methods, I did this in a medical school. My study included some empirical work, and I spent time embedded in a hospital's transplant unit speaking to patients and staff. This experience provided some insight into the workings of medicine on a practical level, and upon reflection, has proven to be important as it informs aspects of how I teach medical ethics. Although this experience occurred several years ago, I continue to draw upon it for real-life examples in my teaching today. Second, serving as an ethicist on clinical ethics committees has ensured that I remain close to clinical practice. This experience has provided valuable insight into the current pressures confronting medical professionals, the types of issues they encounter, and the ways they reason about medical ethics. There are still times in discussions during teaching when I feel hindered by a lack of medical knowledge, so I am far from "the complete medical ethics educator." But, I have no doubt these two aspects of my experience have improved my knowledge and understanding of the context in which medical ethics occurs and therefore have helped my teaching.

Having a more clearly defined (and evidence-based) training pathway for future medical ethics educators may help address concerns about succession planning. It may also ensure there is a sufficient stream of sufficiently trained and experienced ethics educators to meet demand.

The Future of Integrating Ethics into the Curriculum

An additional consideration for the future of medical ethics education remains the issue of integrating ethics into other courses.

The suggestion that ethics should be integrated into other courses is nothing new, but how best to integrate it remains open to debate and there are some trade-offs involved. On the one hand, it is important to try to create a sense that "ethics is everywhere" and that many aspects of medical practice have complex and important ethical underpinnings. On the other hand, it is also important to create a sense that ethics is something slightly different that often requires separate consideration from other aspects of the curriculum and isn't resolved by clinical facts alone.

Integrating ethics into other courses is perhaps particularly difficult in pre-clinical years, where ethics teaching may be focused upon the more fundamental and foundational aspects of ethics to give students the basic knowledge for further much more applied learning as they gain more clinical experience. One approach that we have found success with during clinical years has been to ask students to present challenging cases they have experienced and to reflect upon the ethical aspects. Importantly, these discussions are usually facilitated by an experienced clinician and an expert ethicist and they allow students to draw out an understanding of both the "messiness" of real world ethics as well as the complexity and diversity of perspectives regarding the ethical issues they have encountered. The dual-facilitator approach supports this teaching well, brings different types of expertise into discussions, and avoids ethics being taught by *either* a philosopher *or* a doctor.

This type of approach may also be extremely valuable when it comes to ensuring that ethics education does not end when a student completes medical school. Machin et al. (2020) found that foundation doctors in the UK (doctors within the first two years of qualifying) struggle with the ethical issues they encounter. With the participants in their research stating a preference for the use of case studies, seminars, and workshops, Machin et al. propose a curriculum of continuing ethics education including those experiences for newly qualified doctors. Having an expert ethicist participate in these sessions can help to feed theoretical robustness into discussions and draw important links between key concepts and principles, while the presence of a clinically orientated facilitator ensures that practical wisdom and clinical experience can also be drawn upon to support discussions.

In addition, recent interest in "interprofessional ethics"—the recognition that doctors are required to work in multi-disciplinary teams consisting of other health and social care professionals (Knight & Papanikitas, 2021; Machin et al., 2019)—Machin et al. suggest having students from different professions learn ethics together. This approach not only reflects an additional level of integrating ethics education into the curriculum—across the health and social care professions—but also can better prepare students for delivering collaborative care.

One final aspect of integrating ethics into the curriculum that may prove valuable is an increased emphasis upon critical thinking and reasoning skills throughout the curriculum. Given the importance of these two skills to ethics, it may make sense for much of this teaching to be ethics-focused. But, with the application of these two skills valuable in many aspects of medicine, enhancing these skills in medical students would facilitate more precise discussions during sessions of the type described above, encourage them to consider the justifications for their ethical positions, and to explore the building blocks of their arguments in greater detail, particularly the building blocks that may be controversial or likely to cause other people to disagree with them.

An increased emphasis upon critical thinking and reasoning skills within medical ethics curriculum is useful from different perspectives. First, it is important that doctors be able to reason for themselves—and not just about ethics—to navigate the types of ethical issues they regularly encounter. Second, it is important that doctors be able to engage critically with the views of their patients and colleagues and to capable of exploring and understanding other people's reasoning.

Somewhat contradictorily, these aspects of integrating ethics in the curriculum are fairly distinctive, yet they highlight different ways in which medical ethics education can be joined up with other aspects of education, be that in terms of integrating the philosophical with the clinical, theoretical skills with practical scenarios, or situating ethical education within teams. Each aspect offers advantages and all of them help to emphasise the practical and embedded nature of ethical issues in medicine.

CONCLUSION

I started this chapter by introducing the theory-light approach to medical ethics, explaining how it has arisen from various constraints on medical ethics education. I then proceeded to explain how medical ethics in the UK has developed over the years and has established itself as a core part of the broader medical curriculum. I have also outlined challenges medical ethics educators confront, particularly in relation to the consequences of the theory-light approach, and separately, assessment. Lastly, I suggested some things medical ethics educators may wish to consider, moving forward.

Medical ethics education has to strike several difficult balances, but it is reassuring how much traction ethics has gained within medical curricula internationally. The solutions to some of the challenges confronting medical ethics educators are not obvious and it may be that they will persist for a long time. Yet it does seem as though things have moved and will continue to move in the right direction.

REFERENCES

Andre, J. (2002). *Bioethics as practice*. University of North Carolina Press.

Association of American Medical Colleges. (1999). Learning objectives for medical student education—Guidelines for medical schools: Report 1 of the Medical School Objectives Project. *Academic Medicine, 74*, 13–18.

Association of Teachers of Ethics and Law in Australian and New Zealand Medical Schools. (2001). An ethics core curriculum for Australasian medical schools. *Medical Journal of Australia, 175*(4), 205–10.

BBC News. (2021). *Covid-19: Vaccines to be compulsory for frontline NHS staff in England* [webpage]. https://www.bbc.co.uk/news/health-59215282

Beauchamp, T. L., &. Childress, J. F. (2001). *Principles of biomedical ethics* (5th ed.). Oxford University Press.

Bloom, B. S. (1956). *Taxonomy of educational objectives, Handbook I: The cognitive domain*. David McKay Co. Inc.

British Medical Association. (2020). *Ethics toolkit for medical students* [webpage]. https://www.bma.org.uk/advice-and-support/ethics/medical-students/ethics-toolkit-for-medical-students

Brooks, L., & Bell, D. (2017). Teaching, learning and assessment of medical ethics at the UK medical schools. *Journal of Medical Ethics, 43*(9), 606–612.

Burling, S. J., Lumley, J. S., McCarthy, L. S., Mytton, J. A., Nolan, J. A., Sissou, P., Williams, D. G., & Wright, L. J. (1990). Review of the teaching of medical ethics in London medical schools. *Journal of Medical Ethics, 16*(4), 206–209.

Campbell, A. V., Chin, J., & Voo, T. C. (2007). How can we know that ethics education produces ethical doctors? *Medical Teacher, 29*(5), 431–436.

Carrese, J. A., Malek, J., Watson, K., Lehmann, L. S., Green, M. J., McCullough, L. B., Geller, G., Braddock, C. H., & Doukas, D. J. (2015). The essential role of medical ethics education in achieving professionalism: The Romanell report. *Academic Medicine, 90*(6), 744–752.

Consensus Statement by Teachers of Medical Ethics and Law in the UK Medical Schools (1998). Teaching medical ethics and law within medical education: A model for the UK core curriculum. *Journal of Medical Ethics,* 188–192.

Cowley, C. (2005). The dangers of medical ethics. *Journal of Medical Ethics, 31*(2), 739–742.

Culver, C. M., Clouser, K. D., Gert, B., Brody, H., Fletcher, J., Jonsen, A., Kopelman, L., Lynn. J. Siegler, M., & Wikler, D. (1985). Basic curricular goals in medical ethics. *New England Journal of Medicine, 312*(4), 253–256.

Donaldson, C. M. (2017). Using Kantian ethics in medical ethics education. *Medical Science Educator, 27*(4), 841–845.

Dowie, A., & Martin, A. (2011) *AMEE guides in medical education, Guide No. 53: Ethics and law in the medical curriculum.* Association for Medical Education in Europe.

Doyal, L., & Gillon, R. (1998). Medical ethics and law as a core subject in medical education. *British Medical Journal, 316*(7145), 1623–1624.

Eckles, R. E., Meslin, E. M., Gaffney, M., Helft P. R. (2005). Medical ethics education: Where are we? Where should we be going? A review. *Academic Medicine, 80*(12), 1143–52.

Fiester, A. (2007). Why the clinical ethics we teach fails patients. *Academic Medicine, 82*(7), 684–689.

Fox, E., Arnold, R., & Brody, B. (1995). Medical ethics education: Past, present, and Future. *Academic Medicine, 70,* 761–769.

Frankfurt, H. G. (1988). Freedom of the will and the concept of a person. In M. F. Goodman (Ed.), *What is a person? Contemporary issues in biomedicine, ethics, and society* (pp. 127–144). Humana Press. https://doi.org/10.1007/978-1-4612-3950-5_6

Garrud, P., & McManus, I. C. (2018). Impact of accelerated, graduate-entry medicine course: a comparison of profile, success and specialty destination between graduate entrants to accelerated or standard medicine course in UK. *BMC Medical Education, 18*(1) 1–16.

General Medical Council. (2018). *Outcomes for graduates.* https://www.gmc-uk.org/-/media/documents/dc11326-outcomes-for-graduates-2018_pdf-75040796.pdf

Gillon, R. (2003). Ethics needs principles—Four can encompass the rest—And respect for autonomy should be "first among equals." *Journal of Medical Ethics, 29*(5), 307–312.

Giubilini, A., Milnes, S., & Savulescu, J. (2016). The medical ethics curriculum in medical schools: Present and future. *Journal of Clinical Ethics, 27*(5), 129–145.

Goldie, J. (2000). Review of ethics curricula in undergraduate medical education. *Medical Education, 34*(2), 108–119.

Institute of Medical Ethics. (1987). *Report of a working party on the teaching of medical ethics* (The Pond Report). IME Publications.

Institute of Medical Ethics. (2019). *Core curriculum for undergraduate medical ethics and law.* https://ime-uk.org/wp-content/uploads/2020/10/IME_revised_ethics_and_law__curriculum_Learning_outcomes_2019.pdf

Ishak, W., Nikravesh, R., Lederer, S., Perry, R., Dotun, O., & Berstein, C. (2013). Burnout in medical students: A systematic review. *The Clinical Teacher, 10*(4) 242–245.

Knight, S., & Papanikitas A. (2021) Teaching and learning ethics in healthcare. In D. Nestel, G. Reedy, L. McKenna, & S. Gough (Eds.), *Clinical education for the health professions* (pp. 1–19). Springer. https://doi.org/10.1007/978-981-13-6106-7_43-1

Lawlor, R. (2007). Moral theories in teaching applied ethics. *Journal of Medical Ethics, 33*(6), 370–372.

Ledingham, J. G. G. (1987). Book Review. *Journal of the Royal College of Physicians of London, 21*(4), 274.

Leo, T., & Eagen, K. (2008). Professional Education, the medical student response. *Perspectives in Biology and Medicine,15*(4), 508–16

Machin, L. L., Bellis, K. M., Dixon, C., Morgan, H., Pye, J., Spencer, P., & Williams, R. A. (2019). Interprofessional education and practice guide: Designing ethics-orientated interprofessional education for health and social care students. *Journal of Interprofessional Care, 33*(6), 608–618.

Machin, L. L., Latcham, N., Lavelle, C., Williams, R. A., & Corfield, L. (2020). Exploring the perceived medical ethics and law training needs of UK foundation doctors. *Medical Teacher, 42*(1), 92–100.

Mackenzie, C. (2014). The importance of relational autonomy and capabilities for an ethics of vulnerability. In C. Mackenzie, W. Rogers, & S. Dodds (Eds.), *Vulnerability: New essays in ethics and feminist philosophy* (pp. 33–59). Oxford University Press.

Mattick, K., & Bligh, J. (2006). Teaching and assessing medical ethics: Where are we now? *Journal of Medical Ethics, 32*(3), 181–185.

Rogers, W. (2011). In the lion's den: Teaching and assessing medical ethics. In I. Hay (Ed.). *Inspiring academics: Learning with the world's great university teachers* (pp. 104–112). Open University Press.

Shotter, E., Lloyd, M., Higgs, R., & Boyd, K. (2013). Fifty years of medical ethics: From the London Medical Group to the Institute of Medical Ethics. *Journal of Medical Ethics, 39*(11), 662–666.

Sokol, D. (2016). Teaching medical ethics: Useful or useless? *British Medical Journal, 355*, i6415

Souza, A. D., & Vaswani, V. (2020). Diversity in approach to teaching and assessing ethics education for medical undergraduate: A scoping review. *Annals of Medicine and Surgery, 56,* 178–185.

Stirrat, G. M., Johnston, C., Gillon, R., & Boyd, K. on behalf of the Medical Education Working Group of the Institute of Medical Ethics and associated signatories. (2010). Medical ethics and law for doctors of tomorrow: The 1998 Consensus Statement updated. *Journal of Medical Ethics, 36*(1), 55–60.

Whong-Barr, M. (2003). Clinical ethics teaching in Britain: A history of the London Medical Group. *New Review of Bioethics, 1*(1), 73–84.

Wong, M. K., Hong, D. Z. H., Wu, J., Ting, J. J. Q., Goh, J. L., Ong, Z. Y., Toh, R. Q. E., Chiang, C. L. L., Ng, C. W. H., Ng, J. C. K., Cheon, C. W. S., Tay, K. T., Tan, L. H. S., Ong, Y. T., Chiam, M., Chin, A. M. C., Mason, S., & Krishna, L. K. R. (2021). A systematic scoping review of undergraduate medical ethics education Programs from 1990 to 2020. *Medical Teacher*, 1–20.

CHAPTER 3

NURSING ETHICS EDUCATION

Enhancing Moral Agency for Individual and Social Good

Pamela J. Grace
Boston College

In this chapter a brief overview of the development of nursing into a profession that provides a critical human service is provided. Then, an argument outlining the ethical obligations of critical service professions serves as a foundation for describing what is needed to enable good practice. The state of the science related to ethics education for nurses (students and practitioners) is discussed, including what is and is not known about developing confidence in one's ethical decision making and advocacy to overcome environmental, systemic, and other barriers to good practice. Distinctions among nursing ethics, medical ethics, and bioethics are drawn along with acknowledgement of the need for interdisciplinary approaches to contextually complex problems and dilemmas. Finally, a critique of the current status of knowledge about nursing ethics education in the United States, with suggestions for further research, policy influences and curricular changes, is provided.

Keywords: Nursing Ethics, Moral Agency, Professional Responsibility, Nursing Ethics Education, Barriers to Ethical Practice

Educating in Ethics Across the Professions: A Compendium of Research, Theory, Practice, and an Agenda for the Future, pages 47–71.

Let whoever is in charge keep this simple question in her head (not, how can I always do this right thing myself, but) how can I provide for this right thing to be always done?

—Florence Nightingale (Notes on Nursing, 1859/1946)

INTRODUCTION

The words of Florence Nightingale signify the beginnings of the development of modern nursing from an occupation, to a vocation, and finally to the profession it is now in the United States and in many other developed countries. Notably, the development of nursing into a profession has been difficult, complex, and inextricably bound to the emancipation struggle of women more generally. A majority female profession in a male-dominated world, nursing has struggled to gain respect for the growing knowledge, skills, and importance of its members in the lives of individuals, and for society more generally (Reverby, 1987). This struggle remains, although additional reasons for it exist. Among the additional reasons are those that also pertain to medicine and allied health professions and give rise to fear about deprofessionalization (Haug, 1973; Hearn, 1982). In situations of "deprofessionalization, the professions lose the ability and right to control their own practice" (Grace, 2018a, p. 46). Deprofessionalization can be subtle and includes such things as the incursion of business and other interests into healthcare decision making in a way that limits the ability of the professional to make clinical judgments and/or enact them. As a simple example, U.S. insurance companies can dictate which drugs are included in a list (formulary) that can be prescribed by providers to those covered under that plan.

The incursion of business interests and managerialism has also pervaded education settings and is implicated in the promotion of science, technology, engineering, and mathematics (STEM) over the humanities, thus impacting the teaching of philosophical inquiry and ethics. Both are, of course, needed to maintain independent and critical review of the uses of STEM to benefit human flourishing while not stultifying independent thought (Gleason, 2020; Readings, 1996; Rolfe, 2013; Woodhouse, 2009). The nursing profession is not alone in the contemporary struggle in education generally to deemphasize the liberal arts in favor of the STEM subjects and business studies (Dutt-Ballerstadt, 2019; Gleason, 2020).

Nursing's ability to have some control over its practice, one of the generally understood criteria for a body's status as a profession, had been gaining ground but may be in jeopardy, partly as a result of pressures from business interests and managerialism but also other influences as discussed later. Arguably, the profession's ability to exercise a certain degree of self-rule (autonomy) has been fortified by the numbers of nurses who have gained advanced education. For example, in many countries nurse education is now largely at baccalaureate and graduate levels. The profession's philosophers, scholars, and theorists over the last century have worked to delineate how the specific purposes, goals, and perspectives of nursing differ from those of medicine and other healthcare professions. From these endeavors a clearer understanding of nursing purposes emerged despite controversies and disagreements within the profession. Thus, the ethical expectations of nurses are also clear and are articulated in the profession's codes of ethics as taken up later.

While health professions can be said to have mutually shared goals of promoting individual and societal health and wellbeing, the lenses through which these goals are viewed by the different professions are distinct. Ideally, these lenses coalesce the different perspectives to ensure an integrated view of persons and their healthcare needs and, thus, effective remedial actions. The perspective of nursing over the last five decades, and arguably prior, has been one of understanding that people are contextual individuals whose healthcare needs differ based not just upon a medical or psychiatric condition but also upon socioeconomic aspects of their lives. Some persons start from a place of extreme socioeconomic disadvantage that disproportionately affects their health. During the COVID-19 epidemic this problem has gained more visibility as it has become evident that race, ethnicity, and poverty all factor into the disproportionate deaths among African-Americans, other minorities, and those living on the margins of poverty (Centers for Disease Control, 2020; Finch & Finch, 2020; Washington Post, 2020)

As a result of their review of the discipline's prior works and their collaborative discussions over a two-year period, Willis and colleagues (2008), argue there is a central unifying focus for the discipline that is evident in the accumulating body of nursing literature. This focus is one of: "facilitating humanization, meaning, choice, quality of life, and healing in living and dying" (Willis et al., 2008, p. E28). Additionally, the history of nursing has been one of attending to the most disadvantaged, acting to remedy social injustices that lead to poor health, and facilitating public health (Fowler, 2017), not solely care administered in hospitals.

As of this writing the COVID-19 pandemic has rendered the worth of nursing even more visible. Nurses are in the forefront of the crisis, both in acute care settings and in public health initiatives. They innovate ways to optimize care and humanize the increasingly isolating and dehumanizing crisis environment of healthcare. In this chapter, I first briefly describe the development of nursing into what Windt (1989) categorizes as a critical service profession with ethical responsibilities to individuals and society. A critical service profession is one that is aimed at serving otherwise unmet human needs; those required for living a 'minimally decent life' as described by Powers and Faden (2006). In addition such professions aim to facilitate human flourishing. I then provide an overview of what is known about the need for ethics education, and the status of ethics education in nursing curricula. One major problem in teaching nurses to become confident in their ethical decision making is that ethics education, when it is apparent in the curricula, is often farmed out to other disciplines such as philosophy, theology, and the humanities. But in the absence of assistance from nursing faculty, including clinical faculty, if nurses are to apply this content in everyday nursing practice, they will continue to lack confidence in their decision making (Jurchak et al., 2017). A related problem is the dearth of nursing faculty who understand what practice ethics is, thus, the development of ethically astute nursing faculty should also be a priority for the profession. Finally, I describe some recent initiatives that aim to influence the integration of ethics (both nursing ethics as described shortly and the tools of ethical analysis and decision making) into nursing curricula and in nurse continuing education. Clinical and academic nurse ethicists developed these based on insights from cognitive science and available evidence about how confidence in ethical decision making is developed (Hoskins et al., 2018; Krautscheid, 2017; Lee et al., 2020; Rest & Narvaez, 1994; Reynolds, 2006). Importantly, there is evidence of an ongoing need for ethics discussions and educational opportunities to keep developing one's ethical confidence in practice (Jurchak et al., 2017; Robinson et al., 2014).

One significant challenge confronting nurse educators, and shared by faculty in a variety of disciplines concerns what Woodhouse (2009) calls "The Market Model of Education" (p. 13). Essentially, his argument is that universities are becoming more and more susceptible to the influence of market forces on what can be taught and how it can be taught. That is, the historic emphasis upon developing students and scholars to be critical inquirers is losing ground to the perspective that universities exist to "serve the needs and interests of business corporations" (p. 13). This is of course paradoxical to the project of healthcare professional ethics which, as described in more detail shortly, is critical inquiry into what is good practice and how to enact it even in the face of obstructions.

Without preparation as critical inquirers who are willing to question how what is being proposed is likely to meet practice aims, the ability to resist deprofessionalization movements will be weakened. Deprofessionalization is defined and discussed in more depth later. For example, many clinical and procedures are becoming standardized by the use of algorithms and protocols which while ensuring consistency and efficiency, tends to obscure the idea that human beings vary in their responses and can be disadvantaged by a protocol that ignores their particular needs and thus fails to attend to their optimal wellbeing. Some barriers to good care can be raised when a primary emphasis on economics and/or profits supplants a primary emphasis on human good (Austin, 2011; Schroeder, 2003). Note, I am not arguing against the need for fiscal responsibility because responsible management of resources is needed for justice in addressing healthcare needs (Powers & Faden, 2006; Rawls, 1970). Rather, I am raising the problem of prioritizing profits and expediency over the good of individuals and society as a healthcare bottom line. The implications of contemporary movements that shift the traditional focus of healthcare upon promoting human good are salient for the preparation of nursing students and their ability to address obstacles to good care as these often present to practicing nurses. Nurse educators have an ethical obligation to prepare students to be critical questioners of the status quo and received views that work against good care and to know what their supportive resources are. But it is not clear that the discipline's scholars, leaders, and educators are paying attention to these threats.

NURSING'S LONG JOURNEY TO THE STATUS OF PROFESSION

The history of nursing's advance as a practice profession is long, complex, and subject to many influences which all add to the difficulties of providing a cogent sketch of its trajectory. However, some important factors and drivers are described next as a way of contextualizing the later discussion of the status of ethics education for nursing practice. First, for every practice profession, at least for those Windt (1989) terms "critical service professions," there is a knowledge development or academic arm, what is meant by the term "discipline." The profession's scholars and researchers, informed by practice and practitioners, develop knowledge for the profession (practice) to meet its goals—the reason it exists or has come into being. Ideally, knowledge development not only proceeds in line with what is needed for practice and is informed by practice but also anticipates what will be the likely future needs for knowledge. In reality, a profession does not develop as a profession without disciplinary work that delineates its services and what is needed to provide these.

The development of nursing as a profession has progressed at various rates depending on country and circumstances, adding to the difficulties of providing a succinct or fixed timeline. Nevertheless, some important influences are highlighted below. As Donaldson and Crowley (1978) described, a discipline "is characterized by a unique perspective, a distinct way of viewing all phenomena, which ultimately defines the limits and nature of its inquiry" (p. 113). Elsewhere, I have argued that because nursing exists to meet unmet social needs—to provide a good—the profession's work is essentially ethical (Grace, 2001).

All practice professions use knowledge from other disciplines in order to fulfil their goals. For example, medicine relies on advances in physics, chemistry, and biology, among others, to inform its practice. However, the knowledge is taken and filtered through the perspectival lens of the discipline and its practice objectives or reason for being. So too is knowledge of ethics, including insights from moral theories and principles, tools of ethical analysis and so on, anchored by professional goals and perspectives (Grace, 2018a). Thus nursing ethics as a disciplinary field of inquiry does have its own substantive anchor in professional goals and perspectives. Knowledge from moral philosophy (the parent discipline of ethics) and the tools of ethics are instruments to achieve those goals. Thus the concerns of nursing ethics, medical ethics, and bioethics each have their own specific areas of interest as well as areas of overlap. While some think Bioethics should serve as the overarching discipline to address all healthcare-related ethical quandaries, the discipline of Bioethics has not concerned itself with the everyday issues of nursing practice, how nurses should be educated, nor what should be the scope and limits of nursing practice responsibilities. Bioethics would not be the appropriate discipline to do this in light of the accepted idea that professions should be, to a significant degree self-governing, if they can be legitimately ac-knowledged as professions. Next, a brief history of the development of nursing as a profession, that has a knowledge development (or disciplinary) arm, illustrates how nursing ethics is one such distinct area of inquiry.

A VERY BRIEF HISTORY OF NURSING

Important identifiable stages in the trajectory of nursing start with medieval times. During that era, there were few curative therapies, although there is evidence that interventions such as trephining (making a hole in the skull) and amputations were done with variable results. Additionally, certain herbs were known to affect the body in various ways. Some herbal remedies were helpful, others had a more dubious history. However, none were subject to formal research (Hajar, 2012). The general pattern was that the sick were either cared for at home or in sanitori-ums attached to religious institutions such as monasteries and tended to by monks and lay persons. As monasteries across Europe started to close, these sanctuaries for the sick decreased in number. However, certain churches in Germany and elsewhere carried on the tradition of caring for the sick and even provided rudi-mentary training. For example, Florence Nightingale learned of the mission work of Lutheran minister Theodor Fliedner and his wife Friederike that included train-ing a "sisterhood" of women to tend to the sick and poor. In the face of opposition from her parents, Nightingale traveled to their hospital in Kaiserwerth, Germany to receive this training and graduated in 1851 (Strachey, 1996; Woodham-Smith, 1950). What Nightingale learned there propelled her future work in developing skilled nurses to attend to soldiers injured as a result of the Crimean war and later to open the world's first training school for nurses. In 1861 Nightingale initiated the school at St. Thomas' Hospital in London, England, heralding the start of modern nursing, differentiating nursing work from medical work. Her focus was on helping persons heal by accounting for and managing the environment. She collected and used data to influence change.

Following upon this development, nursing schools attached to hospitals pro-liferated in Europe and the United States over the next several decades. In the United States the during the Civil War (1861–65), the work of women who tended to the wounded was recognized as important and also stimulated the development of training programs for nursing. For Example, "(O)ne such program was initi-ated in Pennsylvania where the Women's Hospital of Philadelphia offered a six-month nurse training course … (graduating) its first class in 1869" (Penn Nursing, 2011). Shortly thereafter, programs based upon the Nightingale model started to multiply. As Mason (2011) notes, the human devastation resulting from wars has "provided opportunities for nurses to make significant advances in both science and professional status" (p. 8). For example, during World War I (1914–18), a shortage of nurses stimulated the initiation of an Army School of Nursing linked with Vassar College, which provided an opening for some nursing education to move into universities (Mason, 2011).

Later, during World War II, the numerous biotechnological advancements, stimulated in part by the needs of the wounded, were carried over into civilian hospitals which were also proliferating because of the newly available interventions that could not be accommodated in home settings. These innovations required a more skilled and educated work force for their appropriate application in practice. As Mason (2011) notes, "the skills and knowledge that nurses needed to care for the wounded expanded and were carried into civilian nursing practice" (p. 8). At least in the United States, a significant proportion of nursing education started moving into colleges and universities and resulted in baccalaureate prepared nurses.

However, nursing in the United States continues to have different entry levels to achieving basic nursing licensure and some argue that this has caused problems for the profession in delineating its work from that of the medical profession and in having the more autonomous (self-governing) aspects of its practice respected (American Association of Colleges of Nursing (AACN), 2000). For example, nurses graduating with associate degrees (2 years full time), hospital schools of nursing diplomas (3-year equivalent) and baccalaureate degrees (4-years full time) are all entitled to take the Registration Exam and upon passing call themselves an RN. The initial depth of knowledge, skills, and competencies gained from each of these courses of study differs considerably. The varied entry levels for initial registration in the U.S. remains an area of contention that some believe has retarded the profession's ability to gain respect. However, the introduction of higher education in nursing is a promising factor that may assist the profession to mitigate this problem of respect for the profession's knowledge and skills.

The first master's program in nursing in the U.S. was offered in 1956 at Columbia University and such programs multiplied, preparing nurses to be experts in expanding specialty practice areas. Nevertheless, nurses who aspired to develop their scholarship to the doctoral level generally had to pursue these in other disciplines such as education, anthropology, sociology and so on and then make their own applications to the further development of the profession. Anecdotally, those nursing scholars educated in other disciplines in my observation over the past 30 years of academia, did have a broad outlook that is no longer possessed by many currently holding a nursing PhD. Paradoxically, these earlier nurse scholars brought their knowledge from other disciplines and applied it to the process of developing nursing. Eventually, these nursing scholars saw the need to develop theory and research-focused doctorates in nursing if nursing were to advance nursing as a profession. One unintended consequence is that as more nurses gained PhDs in nursing the focus on knowledge development for disciplinary purposes narrowed, influenced by various sources including what can be funded and pressures to achieve tenure or rise up the academic ladder (Grace et al., 2016).

Another motivator for developing nursing-focused doctorates in the U.S. was that education programs were moving from hospital associated apprenticeships to universities and universities generally wanted doctorally prepared faculty. Thus possessing theory and research-focused doctorates that were specifically nursing in orientation such as Doctor of Nursing Science (DNSc) and Doctor of Philosophy in Nursing were viewed as necessary. Boston University graduated the first DNSc in 1966 and others followed (Carter, 2013). The DNSc, like the PhD degree, is grounded in theory and focused on knowledge development for the given discipline including professional disciplines such as nursing. Initially there was debate about whether research degrees for professions should be founded on science, hence the DNSc. Later many universities decided that the PhD better described the goal of developing scholars and researchers in a profession (Carter, 2013). Since the early 1970s, there was an exponential increase initially in DNSc and PhD programs in nursing. Thus, a significant proportion of those teaching nursing in academic institutions held a research-intensive nursing doctorate, although faculty teaching clinical courses and supervising students in clinical settings are often prepared to the master's level rather than a doctoral level.

A more recent development is the proliferation of programs leading to a doctorate in nursing practice (DNP) and these now far outnumber nursing PhD programs. DNP programs are focused upon developing experts in clinical practice and clinical leadership rather than disciplinary knowledge development and research per se (American Association of Colleges of Nursing (AACN), 2020). The rapid development of this degree has been controversial within the discipline, for reasons that are beyond the scope of this chapter to review. Nevertheless, among the reasons articulated by proponents of the DNP degree why this degree should be preferable to a master's degree in nursing are: the need for nursing faculty, the numbers of hours required for nursing master's degree is more in-line with practice doctorates, the increasing complexity of the practice environment requires sophisticated management skills to ensure quality and safe patient care (AACN, 2020). Regardless of the controversy many colleges and universities are offering DNP degrees.

As practice leaders and educators those holding a DNP should be prepared to develop and support nurses' confidence in their ethical decision making which, as I argue later, is inseparable from good nursing judgment and clinical wisdom (Grace, 2018b; Haggerty & Grace, 2008). Thus, their educational preparation in ethics and ethical decision making should be of sufficient depth that they can be considered ethics resources for their students, nurses at the bedside, and interdisciplinary colleagues.

From an informal survey of select university websites advertising a DNP program, this sort of expertise is not yet an expectation in most (Grace, 2018b). It remains to be seen whether the newly accepted AACN Essentials (2021) will provide for the development of DNP expertise in ethical decision making, such that they can influence supportive work environments, provide resources for nurses to develop confidence in their ethical decision making, and as faculty infuse curricula with ethics content. Evidence of the value of persons educated at the DNP level in promoting good patient care remains scant due to the relative newness of the degree.

To clarify, a PhD in nursing prepares nurse scholars with research expertise who can identify, explore, and address the nature and substance of problems important to the profession (disciplinary specific knowledge), whereas the focus of a DNP curriculum is the preparation of clinical experts and nurse leaders. As noted in the AACN's *The Essentials of Doctoral Education for Advanced Nursing Practice* (2006), "practice-focused programs understandably place greater emphasis on practice, and less emphasis on theory, meta-theory, research methodology, and statistics than is apparent in research-focused programs" (p. 3).

With this rather surface overview of the development of nursing in the United States, one can nevertheless discern the movement into a practice-based profession. But the question remains, what is important about professions and why is it important that nursing be understood as a profession? The following section addresses this question and provides an explanation of why human service professions such as nursing are ethically important to society.

THE MEANING OF ACHIEVING PROFESSIONAL STATUS

There is no exact definition of profession that fits all circumstances and the concept of "profession" as a noun referring to certain organized groups is controversial. Certainly in the past there are valid arguments that the original professions of "ministry, medicine and law" (Grace, 2018a, p. 43) were formed out of "Guilds" and tended to be more self-serving—providing benefits and prestige for members—than primarily being about benefiting individuals and society (Carr-Saunders & Wilson, 1933; Grace, 1998). Contemporarily, however, there is general agreement that service professions which meet certain criteria have an important function in society related to human flourishing and there is an implicit or explicit social contract between the professional group and the society served. That is, the profession is accorded certain societal supports in exchange for the services rendered.

Perhaps the most recognized attempt to delineate important criteria for a group to be considered a service profession is that of Flexner (2001/1915), an educator. who was concerned about inconsistencies in medical education. His extensive study of medical education in the US and Europe led to the development of criteria he hoped would standardize medical education at a high level. Discussing human service professions, Flexner proposed that (such) professions have an extensive and specialized knowledge base, take responsibility for developing and using their knowledge, have a practice or action orientation that is used for the good of the population served, and autonomously set standards for and monitor the actions of their members.

Later commentators have also noted that an important characteristic of a profession is self-reflectivity. Being reflective about the profession and its contributions to society permits an effective adaptation to changing contexts, societal circumstances, and needs. It also facilitates the ongoing ability to fulfil the profession's reasons for existence, or its purposes. Newton's (1988) compelling assertion of profession's responsibilities is that:

> The professional must respond…if practices in his field are inadequate at any stage of the rendering of the services: if the client the ultimate consumer is unhappy; if he is happy but unknowing, badly served by shabby products or service; or if he is happy and well served by the best available product but the state of the art is not adequate to his real needs. (p. 128)

Inherent in the nature of professions, then, is the idea of a social contract as noted previously. The profession receives some societal supports (funding for education, autonomy over practice and so on). And then, in return, the profession promises to provide its services. This is an ethical exchange, in that certain "goods" are provided by a given profession and these facilitate human flourishing in some way. In the case of healthcare professions the intended goods are to promote wellness and/or relieve the suffering that accompanies illness.

Among the salient characteristics of critical human service professions—those providing services related to human flourishing—is the development of an explicit code of ethics and other guidelines, detailing what and how services are provided (Grace, 1998, 2001). The discipline's scholars, informed by clinicians, develop these guidelines which then apply to each bone fide member of the profession without exception. As exemplified *in The ANA Code of Ethics for Nurses with Interpretive Statements* (2015), the Code is:

- A succinct statement of the ethical values, obligations, duties, and professional ideals of nurses individually and collectively;
- The profession's non-negotiable standard; and
- An expression of nursing's own understanding of its commitment to society (p. viii).

Thus, the education of members of the profession should at minimum prepare them to practice in accordance with the prescriptions of the code of ethics pertaining to their country of practice. Contemporary literature highlights that professional ethics is the ethics both of everyday practice and of conflictual situations (Grace, 2018a; Milliken, 2018; Milliken & Grace, 2017). In other words, ethical implications are associated with every practice action from the most mundane such as discussing with a patient the nuances of a specialized diet to the most difficult and/or conflictual decisions such as when and how to support a patient who does not want to continue life sustaining treatments but is being pressured to do so. However, evidence suggests that many nurses, and even a significant number of nursing faculty, think that "ethics" is an esoteric topic and the province only of those with specialized education (Jurchak et al., 2017; Ulrich et al., 2010). Other faculty have a narrow understanding of ethics in healthcare as comprising the four principles Beauchamp and Childress analyzed in their multiple editions of *Prin-*

ciples of Biomedical Ethics (2019) and still others that the ANA Code of Ethics is all that is needed to teach ethics. The profession has to clear this hurdle if nurses are to continue to identify and overcome obstacles to providing good care either at the bedside or in conflictual situations that is, for nurses to possess moral agency. The profession needs to figure out how to prepare ethically astute nurses who have and sustain moral agency even when barriers to good care exist or are raised.

NURSES AS MORAL AGENTS
IN CONTEMPORARY HEALTHCARE

The question of moral agency is important in nursing. From a synthesis of philosophical and practice definitions, including Rest's (1982; 1984; Rest & Narvaez, 1994), the integrated cognitive processes underlying moral actions provided a workable definition of moral agency, which consists of: a deep understanding that all professional actions (simple to complex) have ethical implications related to whether they are intentionally focused on providing a good or not; the ability of a person to conceptualize what action in needed in a given situation—what good is to be provided; and motivation to provide that good even when barriers exist. In the nursing context, moral agency would be a nurse's understanding of what actions were warranted in a given practice situation (based on nursing goals and perspectives) along with the knowledge and skills to carry them out, including how to manage obstacles that arise. Rest's four component model of moral action, derived from research in the cognitive sciences, describes the cognitive processes involved: sensitivity to the moral content in a particular situation; the use of knowledge and reasoning to think about the likely best course of action; motivation to select and carry out the best course of action; and, implementation which requires strength of character including perseverance in the face of obstacles (Rest & Narvaez, 1994).

For nurse educators and others charged with the education of nurses, the implications concern acquiring characteristics and skills that are critical to moral agency, including: personal and professional development, acquisition of pertinent knowledge and skills related to clinical and ethical applications, and opportunities for ongoing practice of these skills. Described later is a proposed curricula structure for nursing that would address Rest's components of moral reasoning and build upon them throughout the pre-licensure program, thus developing nurse confidence in their ethical decision making. Colleagues and I also built a structure for developing more sophisticated skills in graduate students who will be responsible for the education and support of point-of-care nurses. Moreover, an important insight from the Clinical Ethics Residency for Nurses (CERN) program was that moral agency requires continued attention and fostering otherwise it can be weakened by unsupportive or toxic practice environments (Lee et al., 2020).

Nurse moral agency is necessary for the profession to continue to remain focused on achieving its goals and to hold its clinicians accountable for their actions or inaction. However, nursing curricula developers, accrediting bodies, and nurse educators all need to understand how nurse moral agency is developed and sustained. In turn, more research is needed to understand barriers and facilitators of moral agency so nursing education can account for these. The current COVID-19 pandemic has underscored the need to focus on developing and fortifying the moral agency of all healthcare professionals (Donkers et al., 2021) both for their own wellbeing and for the ethical, safe, and quality care of patients. What is clear from Rest's work is that the development of nurses who are moral agents requires more than clinical and/or ethical knowledge. Certain personal dispositions must be nurtured, knowledge of ethical language and tools must be acquired, and opportunities for guided practice that firmly "seats" the developing knowledge, skills, and confidence are needed. Moreover, continuing opportunities to be engaged in ethics discussions are also important to maintain abilities and motivation (Lee et al., 2020).

Nurses are Accountable for Their Actions

Much, if not all the daily work of nurses requires that independent judgments be made about what is best for a particular patient or groups of patients. Even when a particular action is directed by physician order, (for example, a new medication is to be administered), nurses are accountable for drawing upon their extensive knowledge base to explain what is being proposed, why it is being proposed, and ensuring that patients understand their rights to ask for more clarity and even refuse those treatments they do not desire. They are also accountable for helping patients express their particular, preferences, and perspectives. Their "primary commitment is to the patient whether an individual, family, group, community or population" (American Nurses Association, 2015, Provision 2). Nurses must also ensure that the order is based upon accurate data, is the correct dose, and does not conflict with medication orders written by other specialists. In this sense, nurses are a bit like orchestra conductors, who may not play every instrument but do need to know how to co-ordinate the work of all of the different players in order to achieve the best results.

Nurses possess an extensive knowledge base upon which to draw and are accountable for their actions. However, it is not always easy to practice well. Everyday nursing practice is rife with complexities of various sorts. In the absence of supports and mentorship, it can be especially difficult for novice nurses to enact their moral agency and be held accountable for their actions. As Hoskins et al. (2018) note in their discussion of ethics education for nurses, "(F)rom the moment a newly graduated nurse enters the clinical environment, he or she must be ready to deliver quality patient care while navigating complex relationships with patients, families, physicians, nurses, and other members of the healthcare team" (p. 3). Thus, preparing novice nurses to act as moral agents for the good of patients—which necessarily entails attention to environments that give rise to poor health or are unsupportive of patient good—is a critical component of nursing education. Additionally, remaining ethically aware and sustaining moral agency is a responsibility of the individual nurse, institutions of employment, and nurse continuing education. Arguably, the most critical role of nursing ethics education is the inculcation of an understanding that *all nursing actions have ethical aspects* with nurses either focused upon providing a good or distracted by other pressures or expediencies. At its most basic, ethical practice—good nursing practice—is the intention to provide the best possible care to patients, in a way that is sensitive to the particularities of patients' needs, the possibilities of environmental and/or contextual impediments, and the need to anticipate and minimize potential harms. A critical element for new nurses or nurses who are working in unfamiliar settings is to grasp the limits of their knowledge and seek appropriate assistance.

THE CURRENT STATUS OF ETHICS EDUCATION IN NURSING

Ethics education in nursing is far from ideal for the purposes stated above and related to what is known about the development of moral agency generally. Inadequate ethics education for nurses is not a U.S. problem alone. Prior research in nursing ethics internationally (Woods, 2005) highlights three persistent themes. First, nurses who do have some ethics content in their curriculum, are bothered by the conflicts faced but there is a tendency not to speak up or act to resolve them. Second, when nurses do speak up, whether or not they have formal ethics education, they may face resistance from colleagues (including other nurses). Third, new graduates do not speak up and often feel moral distress in conflictual situations but try to cope with the moral distress rather than try to find resolution (Woods, 2006). Similar themes persist in more recent research. In short, there is strong evidence most nurses do not have confidence in their ethical decision making (Grace et al., 2014; Milton, 2004), regardless of whether or not they have had prior ethics training or education (Grace et al., 2014; Robinson et al., 2014).

Thus, current ethics education for nurses is inconsistent and for the most part ineffective for developing confidence in ethical decision making, ability to advocate for good care, and willingness to address root causes of problematic healthcare environments. Inadequate moral agency has been shown to result in unmitigated experiences of moral distress which is detrimental to both nurses and patients (Burston & Tuckett, 2013). While definitions of moral distress differ slightly among scholars, there is general agreement that *moral distress* occurs when one is unable to do the right thing in a given situation or is uncertain how to act (Corley, 2002; Corley et al., 2005; Gallagher, 2011; Jameton, 1984). Accumulating research provides evidence that experiences of moral distress affect nurses (and others) in various ways psychological and physical, but it is also problematic for patient care and patient safety.

The link between moral agency and the unmitigated experience of moral distress is becoming clearer (Traudt et al., 2016). Moral agency facilitates action to resolve a difficult situation in several ways, but perhaps most importantly in diminishing a sense of impotence (Lee et al., 2020). Moreover, there is evidence that sustained experiences of moral distress can lead to nurse attrition from the profession. Alternatively, nurses may detach themselves from emotional engagement as repeated experiences of moral distress led to feelings of impotence (Arnold, 2020). In either case, there are implications for patient care and for meeting nursing goals (Burston & Tuckett, 2013). Arguably, moral disengagement an even more worrisome problem has been recognized as. Moral disengagement is "a process that involves justifying one's unethical actions by altering one's moral perception of those actions" (Hyatt, 2017, p. 15). As described by Bandura (1999), and in relation to nurse moral agency, one way moral disengagement manifests is denial of, or disbelief that, one has any responsibility for the unethical actions taken or the ethical actions not taken. Responsibility is assigned to someone else or to something else, for example, the institution, system, colleagues, or supervisors.

CONFUSION ABOUT PROCESS AND CONTENT OF ETHICS EDUCATION IN NATIONALLY PROPOSED GUIDELINES

A lack of research about the value of ethics education in the various levels of nursing curricula and its impact on practice contributes to current confusion (Hoskins et al., 2018). What is needed is a curriculum framework built upon what is known about effective ethics education in general and the effectiveness in nursing practice in particular. Today there is no agreement and in fact an emphasis upon ethics education in national curricula is losing ground. For example, AACN which is responsible for developing guidelines for essential content of nursing baccalaureate, master's, and DNP curricula evidences a lack of understanding about areas of distinction and mutuality between nursing ethics and bioethics (see definitions at the end of the chapter). What is most worrisome is the implication that nursing leaders, scholars, and educators do not understand the centrality of ethics to nursing care. Compounding these problems is the lack of nurse educators who are knowledgeable about the more sophisticated skills of ethical analysis and can translate these into ethical decision making in more complex nursing practice problems. This could be a substantive role for DNPs and could be incorporated into their curricula along with a practicum supervised by clinical ethics experts (Grace, 2018b). It is clear, from the literature and anecdotally from my interactions with other ethics faculty and from my own experience, that there is a serious shortage of nursing faculty who understand what is needed to develop nurse moral agency. An understanding of bioethical principles alone, while important, is insufficient for everyday practice.

Indeed, nursing ethics should be foundational for all nursing education and the language and skills of ethical reasoning should be emphasized and built upon throughout nursing curricula. The development of more complex skills of ethical analysis in conflictual situations are important adjuncts to the foundational skill set. Nurses need to be able to anticipate emerging problems—also known as preventive ethics—and articulate the nuances of a patient's situation using ethical language as pertinent. This is especially important when no one else is privy to the details of a patient's story or is hearing their preferences, values, and desires. At the graduate level, nurses should be prepared to support the ethical confidence of those they supervise and teach (Grace, 2018b). Additionally, they should be able to act as ethics resources and collaborators with nursing and interdisciplinary colleagues.

The revised AACN Essentials covering Baccalaureate, Masters, and Doctor of Nursing Practice curricula were accepted in April 2021 (AACN, 2021). These do not yet emphasize the importance of understanding how integral ethics is to everyday nursing practice—implying the widespread lack of understanding that nursing ethics is simply about good nursing practice and how to anticipate and overcome barriers. Yes, the skills of what is perhaps viewed as the more "esoteric" discipline of ethics, such as insights from moral theories, principles, and skills of ethical analysis are also important to develop but are instrumental to the fundamental project of providing good care.

Between 2017 and 2019, the Ethics Education Subcommittee (EES) of the American Nurses Association Ethics Advisory Board (ANA-EAB) developed a framework replete with examples and strategies for educators to use both in pre-licensure programs and graduate programs. Details of the framework are in press currently in the *Journal of Nursing Education*. The framework, discussed in more detail later, utilizes nursing goals and perspectives as foundations as well as Rest's four processes as structure for content and strategies that facilitate the development of student moral agency.

Ethics Preparation and Nurse Educators

For the most part, nurse educators hold a minimum of a Master's degree in nursing, although in the future many will have doctorates in nursing practice. Some nurse educators also hold a PhD, or equivalent research-intensive doctorate in nursing or another discipline. In either case, they are responsible for providing most of the basic and continuing nursing content for nursing students, including ethics. They may also be employed to provide continuing education for experienced nurses either in a hospital or academic setting. Almost all State Boards of Nursing require continuing education annually or biannually for nurses to renew their RN license providing leverage for in-service ethics content.

Besides a set of university liberal arts and science core course which all students at the baccalaureate level complete (although as noted earlier appropriate humanities courses may become scarce), most courses in the nursing-specific curricula are taught by nurses with advanced education and experience in nursing practice. These educators should be prepared to help students apply their growing knowledge base in a practice setting, both demonstrating and supporting nurse ethical comportment and an understanding of everyday ethics. The development of a DNP ethics track could prepare ethics experts to augment both clinical and academic ethics resources, including ethics education initiatives. Graduates would be prepared with in-depth knowledge of the nature, scope, and limits of ethical theory and ethical principles in resolving difficult practice issues. Critically important for nurses also is the development of the sorts of collaborative communication skills that facilitate clear articulation of a patient's physical, psychological, and contextual circumstances.

Some graduate (as well as some undergraduate) nursing programs do offer courses in bio or medical ethics taught by philosophers, theologians, and other non-clinicians. While such courses offer important content, and have been demonstrated to improve critical thinking, assistance is needed for nurses to apply their learning to their everyday practices (Pierce & Smith, 2008). Bio and medical ethics courses tend to focus on moral theory and moral principles and their use for resolving intractable bioethical dilemmas such as who of three people in need should get the one donor heart. However, more is needed for nurses to apply the content to everyday practice. Moreover, such courses can lead to loss of focus on using nursing goals and perspectives to underpin ethical decision making (Grace & Milliken, 2016). What is clear is that to teach and apply ethics in nursing practice, a deep understanding of both the scope and limits of nursing ethics as well as its relationship to the knowledge and skills used in clinical bioethics, are needed. Logically, either nurse educators have sophisticated skills of ethical analysis and decision making or they must partner with someone who has this knowledge and these skills.

Ideally, nurse educators should be prepared both to develop ethical comportment and moral agency in their charges and to understand the nuances of more complex situations requiring ethical decision making. Yet many graduate nursing programs neither have specific nursing ethics courses that situate their practice in the idea of professional responsibility and how to develop this in their charges, nor more theoretical ethics courses that hone their ability to provide leadership in conflictual situations.

Indeed, as graduate nursing programs have become more specialized, the focus has tended toward content knowledge for the particular specialized practice (adult, pediatric, women's health, anesthesia, and so on). For example, the importance of advanced physiology, pharmacology, and physical assessment is emphasized sometimes at the expense of foundational nursing knowledge. Yet, these other knowledge bases are only instruments that permit nursing perspective on a person's needs, preferences, and goals to be actualized. Thus, nurse educators themselves may lack the ability to develop ethical confidence in their students or other nurses (Laabs, 2015; Skela-Savič & Kiger, 2015).

RECOMMENDATIONS FOR NURSING ETHICS EDUCATION: PROCESS AND CONTENT

Given the discussion so far, it is evident that a more consistent approach is needed for the development and sustenance of moral confidence and moral agency in nursing. We are starting to accumulate a body of evidence about the sorts of pedagogical strategies that are needed and what works (Cannaerts et al., 2014; Jurchak et al., 2017; Lee et al., 2020; Nolan & Market, 2002; Park et al., 2012; Song, 2018). Together with what is also known about moral development and cognitive processes, a way forward is possible but will require a sustained effort to overcome distractors and detractors.

From my perspective as a nurse educator for the past several decades, one first has to dispel the myth that ethics in nursing is an esoteric topic involving moral theory, derived principles, and difficult analyses. Crucially, ethics in nursing has to be understood as having to do with all of our practice actions. We are responsible for focusing on nursing goals using nursing perspectives because we have the wellbeing of others in our hands. As educators, our educative actions concern preparing "good nurses," meaning nurses who have moral agency, can practice well, and work toward overcoming obstacles. At the graduate level, preparation should include developing nurse clinicians, leaders, and educators also to understand and be able to teach or support ethical decision making in complex, conflictual, and dilemma types of situations. Although true dilemmas, by definition, are not susceptible to resolution, most situations in healthcare that are called dilemmas (no preferable choice available) are not true dilemmas because preferable courses of action are identifiable with more fact-gathering or analysis.

Development of moral agency, for a specific purpose such as nursing practice, is a process. It requires a sequence of personal developments that results in a deep understanding of why a professional is accountable. This could be called "professional socialization" and its development can be enhanced by role modeling and open discussions in a moral safe space which permits personal growth via the perspectives of others and critical inquiry (Walker, 1993). The tools and strategies of clinical ethics and bioethics are important adjuncts and permit clear articulation of problems but need skilled assistance to translate into practice situations. Attention has to be given to helping students develop both an intellectual understanding of the intrinsically ethical nature of the work and to incorporate this understanding into their everyday work. Ideally, in every course—whether didactic or practical—nursing faculty draw attention to the fact that what is being learned is for the purpose of providing good care. Students also need ongoing opportunities for guided discussions of both everyday issues and practice dilemmas in a morally safe space where they can learn from their colleagues and faculty.

Insights for Nurse Education from CERN

The clinical ethics residency for nurses (CERN) was a funded program developed by Dr. Ellen Robinson as principal investigator (PI), Dr. Martha Jurchak and I as Co-PI's, the Reverend Angelika Zollfrank as faculty, and Dr. Susan Lee as evaluator. Consisting of an eight-hour per month program over a 10-month period for point-of-care and advanced practice nurses, CERN was available for three years. The curriculum used Rest's processes as scaffolding, nursing goals, perspectives and the ANA Code of Ethics as foundations, the American Society of Bioethics and the Humanities (ASBH) (2009) *Guidelines for Improving Competencies in Clinical Ethics Consultation: An Education Guide)* as a content guide, and principles of adult learning to inform the multi-modal nature. CERN also included opportunities for self and group-reflection, communication strategies, didactic content, guided simulations of situations, cases and real-time practice applications. Details are available elsewhere (Grace et al., 2014; Jurchak et al., 2017; Lee et al., 2020; Robinson et al., 2014). Each day's learnings were evaluated in several ways. At the beginning of each education day, participants shared how they had used the previous month's activities in their practice setting. During the simulation sessions, participants evaluated their own and each other's performance. At the end of each day, they completed an evaluation form. On the final day, called the "integration day," participants presented an essay addressing several questions that documented changes in their practice and how they had used what they learned over the year to support others and improve practice. The content analysis of these essays (N=65) identified several themes. The primary theme was that participants had "developed a moral compass to navigate the many gray areas of decision making that confront them in daily practice" (Lee et al., 2020, p.28). Additional themes included gaining confidence in the "ability to advocate for good patient care; [and] to support and empower colleagues, patients, and families" (p. 28). Applying the knowledge and skills gained to their everyday practice and to support colleagues, participants noted the value of this type of multimodal method for their development and "experienced personal and professional transformation" (p. 28). Significantly, many noted that they realized their development as moral agents needed to be an ongoing intentional process. A statistically significant finding from three years of end-of-course evaluation data was that moral distress had decreased from the levels they were experiencing at the start of the program (Robinson et al., 2014). The success of this multimodal education to increase nurse confidence in their decision, support and fortify those from other more limited or compartmentalized studies of the effects of ethics education.

As noted earlier, with insights from CERN and elsewhere, a current working group—the Ethics Education Subcommittee of the American Nurses Association Ethics Advisory Board which consists of nursing ethics scholars and clinical ethicists—has developed from Rest's framework a set of education guidelines that cover each level of nursing curricula. Included in this framework are a variety of ways to evaluate students' acquisition of ethics-related knowledge and skills and importantly their development of moral agency.

Rest's Cognitive Processes

As a reminder Rest's (1984) processes are descriptive and based on research evidence from cognitive science and elsewhere. He noted there may actually be more than these four processes and the processes themselves are *interactive, recursive, and non-hierarchical*. In one article he calls them "components of morality" to emphasize their non-hierarchical nature (1982, p. 29). However, for purposes of nursing practice, ethical sensitivity about nursing's responsibilities has to be nurtured first in order for the other processes to be engaged. The processes are enumerated below for clarity but do not indicate order.

The first component is the development of ethical awareness about one's professional responsibilities which entails understanding how personal and professional values interact and can be managed. The second component involves bringing to bear different types of knowledge acquired, including experiential, to analyze aspects of a situation and what courses of action are possible. For moral action in nursing practice, a variety of sources of knowledge is needed, including experiential. For example, knowledge from the psychosocial and physiological sciences as well as familiarity with the language of ethics and ethical decision making techniques are all necessary. The third component concerns the process of determining which of several actions is the best in the presenting circumstances. Rest terms this "deciding what one actually intends to do" (p. 33). The fourth component is carrying through the action or "executing and implementing what one intends to do" (p. 34). Perhaps most foundationally nurses need to understand the ethical implications of all their practice actions from the most mundane to the most complex and conflictual. They also need to know the limits of their abilities to resolve a difficult situation and which resources they can access as support.

Several means of evaluating these different facets are contained in the EES curricula framework. Existing evaluation tools have been developed from both quantitative and qualitative evidence, including observation. Potential evaluation techniques for different levels of the curricula are incorporate into the framework. One recent promising tool which demonstrated sound psychometric properties, the Ethical Awareness Scale (EAS) (Milliken et al., 2018), has been successfully replicated (Milliken et al., 2019). Although developed for use with nurses working in intensive care settings, the tool will permit measuring the development of ethical awareness of professional responsibilities in individual nurses before and after an educational program. With modifications, it has promises for use in other settings,

CONCLUSION

The development of nurse moral agency is critical for good nursing practice because nursing as a profession exists to meet an unmet societal need. Many obstacles can work against good practice and when nurses cannot practice in accord with what they know to be required for patient good nurses can suffer moral distress. This experience, in turn, may lead to nurse attrition or distancing from patients or numbing of what ethical sensitivity was possessed. These assertions are supported both by research in moral psychology and existing and emerging studies. In either case—nurses leaving the profession or distancing themselves from engaging with patients—a problem is posed for the profession and ultimately for patients and others served by nursing work. It is indisputable that "both knowledge of nursing ethics and knowledge of the interdisciplinary field of bioethics are critical to nursing work" (Grace & Milliken, 2016, p. S13).

As noted earlier, nursing ethics is concerned with developing nurse moral agency in everyday nursing practice and in preparing nurses to articulate their perspective when dilemmas arise that require the input of multiple disciplines for their resolution. An interface between the problems of nurses' daily practice and those tackled by other applied ethics such as medical ethics, bioethics, and social ethics is inevitable as the provision of healthcare is interdisciplinary in nature and difficult conflicts often require a team for their resolution. However, nurses first need to know who they are, what they are responsible for, and what they contribute. Second, they need to understand the scope and limits of ethical precepts in analyzing or clarifying difficult situations and to use effective language to communicate to other team members the meaning of these principles for their patients' values, goals, and preferences. Currently, the teaching of ethics in nursing is inconsistent guided neither by its code of ethics nor the precepts of those determining what is essential content in all levels of nursing curricula. Evaluating outcomes is also critical as well as what works and what doesn't work to improve the practice of nursing as an ethical profession. A remedy is available, but persistence is needed to institute educational initiatives that can improve nurse moral agency nationally and internationally.

IMPORTANT DEFINITIONS USED IN THE CHAPTER.

- **Bioethics**—A relatively new area of applied ethics. bioethics cannot be considered a professional applied ethics as such; rather, it is a multidisciplinary endeavor concerned with the appropriate use and limits of biotechnology in healthcare settings (Jonsen, 1998; Kopelman, 2006). According to (Reich, 1995), it is "the study of the moral dimensions—including moral vision, decisions, conduct and policies—of the life sciences and health care, employing a variety of ethical methodologies in an interdisciplinary setting" (p. xxi). While members of various professions may consider themselves bioethicists and be involved as healthcare ethics consultants in resolving tricky issues, their role as bioethicists is not one of professional practice per se. Thus, the goal is different; it is to find the best solution to a conflictual or difficult situation.
- **Medical Ethics**—A professional (applied) ethics, medical ethics is the study of what good medical practice is, what medicine owes to society, and how physicians should conduct themselves.
- **Moral and Ethical**—While these terms tend to be taken as having separate meanings in everyday life, in the context of teaching responsibilities for professional practice they can be used synonymously. By way of explanation, the parent discipline of ethics is moral philosophy. Moral philosophy is inquiry about the good and results in theories alternatively labeled moral, ethical, or value theories without distinction. None of these theories is able to provide definite answers to complex problems in healthcare—as theories they are all subject to critique of various sorts. We do not use moral theory to determine good practice actions. Good practice actions are those designed to further a person's or group's healthcare needs. However, we do

take ideas from moral theorizing to help us gain clarity about complex situations. Thus we can say the morally appropriate practice action is also the ethically appropriate practice action. Origins of the terms moral and ethical mean similar things but derived from different languages, Latin and Greek respectively (Bahm, 1992, p. 8).

- **Nursing Ethics**—The assumption of this chapter is that nursing ethics, is a stand-alone field of inquiry, not a subset of bioethics or medical ethics. Is a professional (applied) ethics. It is "the study of what constitutes good (everyday) nursing practice, what obstacles to good nursing practice exist, and what the responsibilities of nurses are related to their professional conduct" (Grace, 2018a, p. 11). It includes the profession's conceptualizations of its broader responsibilities to society and the appropriate education of its members. Ethical appraisal of actual nursing actions (ethical comportment) is a facet of nursing ethics.

REFERENCES

American Association of Colleges of Nursing. (2000). *The Baccalaureate Degree in Nursing as minimal preparation for professional practice.* Accessed December 20, 2020 from: https://www.aacnnursing.org/news-information/position-statements-white-papers/bacc-degree-prep#:~:text=As%20such%2C%20registered%20nurses%20at,program%20in%20nursing%20(BSN).

American Association of Colleges of Nursing. (2006). *The essentials of doctoral education for advanced nursing practice.* Accessed January 2, 2021 from: https://www.aacnnursing.org/DNP/PositionStatement

American Association of Colleges of Nursing. (2008). *The essentials of baccalaureate education for professional nursing practice.* Accessed January 2, 2021 from: https://www.aacnnursing.org/portals/42/publications/baccessentials08.pdf

American Association of Colleges of Nursing. (2020). *DNP fact sheet.* Accessed August 7, 2021 from: https://www.aacnnursing.org/News-Information/Fact-Sheets/DNP-Fact-Sheet

American Association of Colleges of Nursing. (2021). *The essentials: Core competencies for professional nursing education.* Accessed August 4, 2021 from: https://www.aacnnursing.org/Portals/42/AcademicNursing/pdf/Essentials-2021.pdf

American Nurses Association. (2015). *Code of ethics for nurses with interpretive statements.* Author.

American Society for Bioethics and Humanities. (2009). *Improving competencies in clinical education: An education guide.* Author.

Arnold, T. C. (2020). *Moral distress in emergency and critical care nurses: A metaethnography. Nursing Ethics, July 23* (Epub ahead of print). doi: 10.1177/0969733020935952.

Austin, W. J. (2011). The incommensurability of nursing as a practice and the customer service model: An evolutionary threat to the discipline. *Nursing Philosophy, 12*(3), 158–166.

Bahm, A. J. (1992). *Why be moral?* (2nd ed.). World Books.

Bandura, A. (1999). Moral disengagement in the perpetration of inhumanities. *Personality and Social Psychology Review, 3*(3), 193–209. doi:10.1207/s15327957pspr0303_3

Beauchamp, T. L., & Childress, J. (2019). *Principles of biomedical ethics* (8th Ed.). Oxford University Press.

Burston, A. S., & Tuckett, A. G. (2013). Moral distress in nursing: Contributing factors, outcomes and interventions. *Nursing Ethics, 20*(3), 312–324.

Cannaerts, N., Gastmans, C., & Casterlé, B. D. D. (2014). Contribution of ethics education to the ethical competence of nursing students: Educators' and students' perceptions. *Nursing Ethics, 21*(8), 861–878.

Carr-Saunders, A. M., & Wilson, P. A. (1933). *The professions*. The Clarendon Press.

Carter, M. (2013). The evolution of doctoral education in nursing. In S. DeNisco (Ed.), *Advanced practice nursing: Evolving roles for the transformation of the profession* (pp. 27–36). Jones and Bartlett.

Centers for Disease Control. (2020). *Covid-19: Health equity considerations and racial and ethnic minority groups*. Accessed October, 2020 from: https://www.cdc.gov/coronavirus/2019-ncov/community/health-equity/race-ethnicity.html

Corley, M. C. (2002). Nurse moral distress: A proposed theory and research agenda. *Nursing Ethics, 9*(6), 636–650.

Corley, M. C., Minick, P., Elswick, R. K., & Jacobs, M. (2005). Nurse moral distress and ethical work environment. *Nursing Ethics, 12*(4), 381–390.

Donaldson, S. K., & Crowley, D. M. (1978). The discipline of nursing. *Nursing Outlook, 26*(2), 113–120.

Donkers, M. A., Gilissen, V. J. H. S., Candel, M. J. J. M, van Dijk, N. M., Kling, H., Heijnen-Panis, R., Pragt, E., van der Horst, I., Pronk, S. A., & van Mook, W. N. K. A. (2021). Moral distress and ethical climate in intensive care medicine during CO-VID-19: A nationwide study. *BMC Medical Ethics, 22*(73). https://doi.org/10.1186/s12910-021-00641-3

Dutt-Ballerstadt, R. (2019). Academic prioritization or killing the liberal arts? *Inside Higher Ed.* https://www.insidehighered.com/advice/2019/03/01/shrinking-liberal-arts-programs-raise-alarm-bells-among-faculty

Finch, W. H., & Finch, M. E. (2020). Poverty and Covid-19: Rates of incidence and deaths in the United States during the first 10 weeks of the pandemic. *Frontiers in Sociology, 5*(47). https://doi.org/10.3389/fsoc.2020.00047

Flexner, A. (1915/2001). Is social work a profession. *Research on Social Work Practice, 11*(2). Reprinted from: *Is social work a profession? In National Conference of Charities and Corrections*. Proceedings of the National Conference of Charities and Corrections at the Forty-second annual session held in Baltimore, Maryland, May 12–19, 1915. Hildmann.

Fowler, M. D. (2017). Why the history of nursing ethics matters. *Nursing Ethics, 24*(3), 292–304.

Gallagher, A. (2011). Moral distress and moral courage in everyday nursing practice. *Online Journal of Issues in Nursing, 16*(2). DOI: 10.3912/OJIN.Vol16No02PPT03

Gleason, D. W. (2020). The humanities meet STEM: Five approaches for humanists. *Arts and Humanities in Higher Education, 19*(2), 186–206. https://doi.org/10.1177/1474022218800673

Grace, P. J. (1998). *A philosophical analysis of the concept 'advocacy': Implications for professional–patient relationships* (unpublished doctoral dissertation). University of Tennessee-Knoxville. Available from: http://proquest.umi.com/. Publication Number AAT9923287, ProQuest Document ID No. 734421751.

Grace, P. J. (2001). Professional advocacy: Widening the scope of accountability. *Nursing Philosophy, 2*(1), 151–162.

Grace, P. J. (2018a). *Nursing ethics and professional responsibility in advanced practice* (3rd ed.). Jones & Bartlett.

Grace, P. (2018b). Enhancing nurse moral agency: The leadership promise of doctor of nursing practice preparation. *OJIN: The Online Journal of Issues in Nursing, 23(*1). https://www.doi.org/10.3912/OJIN.Vol23No01Man04

Grace, P. J. (In press). An argument for the distinct nature of nursing ethics. In M. Deem & J. Lingler (Eds.), *Nursing ethics: Normative foundations, advanced concepts, and emerging issues*. Oxford University Press.

Grace, P., & Milliken, A. (2016). Educating nurses for ethical practice in contemporary health care environments. *Hastings Center Report, 46*, S13–S17. doi:10.1002/hast.625

Grace, P. J., Robinson, E. M., Jurchak, M., Zollfrank, A. A., & Lee, S. M. (2014). Clinical ethics residency for nurses: An education model to decrease moral distress and strengthen nurse retention in acute care. JONA: *The Journal of Nursing Administration, 44*(12), 640–646.

Grace, P. J., Willis, D. G., Roy, C., & Jones, D. A. (2016). Profession at the crossroads: A dialog concerning the preparation of nursing scholars and leaders. *Nursing Outlook, 64*(1), 61–70. doi: 10.1016/j.outlook.2015.10.002. Epub 2015 Oct 22. PMID: 26581973.

Haggerty, L. A., & Grace, P. J. (2008). Clinical wisdom: The essential component of "good" nursing care. *Journal of Professional Nursing, 24*(4), 235–240.

Hajar, R. (2012). The air of history (Part II): Medicine in the Middle Ages. *Heart Views: The Official Journal of the Gulf Heart Association, 13*(4), 158–162. https://doi.org/10.4103/1995-705X.105744

Haug, M. R. (1973). Deprofessionalization: An alternative hypothesis for the future. *Sociological Review Monograph 20,* 195–217.

Hearn, J. (1982). Notes on patriarchy, professionalization and the semi-professions. *Sociology. 16*, 184–198.

Hoskins, K., Grady, C., & Ulrich, C. M. (2018). Ethics education in nursing: Instruction for future generations of nurses. OJIN: *The Online Journal of Issues in Nursing, 23*(1). https://www.doi.org/10.3912/OJIN.Vol23No01Man03

Hyatt, J. (2017). Recognizing moral disengagement and its impact on patient safety. *Journal of Nursing Regulation, 7*(4), 15–21.

Jameton, A. (1984). *Nursing practice: The ethical issues*. Prentice-Hall.

Jonsen, A. R. (1998). *The birth of bioethics*. Oxford University Press.

Jurchak, M., Grace, P. J., Lee, S., Zollfrank, A., & Robinson, E. (2017). Developing abilities to navigate through the grey zones in complex environments: Nurses reasons for applying to a clinical ethics residency for nurses. *Journal of Nursing Scholarship, 49*(4), 445–455. doi: 10.1111/jnu.12297. Epub 2017 Jun 12.

Kopelman, L. M. (2006). Bioethics as a second-order discipline: Who is not a bioethicist? *The Journal of Medicine and Philosophy, 31*(6), 601–628.

Krautscheid, L. C. (2017). Embedding microethical dilemmas in high-fidelity simulation scenarios: Preparing nursing students for ethical practice. *The Journal of Nursing Education, 56*(1), 55–58. doi:10.3928/01484834-20161219

Laabs, C. A. (2015). Toward a consensus in ethics education for the doctor of nursing practice. *Nursing Education Perspectives, 36*(4), 249–251.

Lee, S., Robinson, E. M., Grace, P. J., Zollfrank, A., & Jurchak, M. (2020). Developing a moral compass: Themes from the clinical ethics residency for nurses' final essays. *Nursing Ethics, 27*(1), 28–39.

Mason, D. J. (2011). The nursing profession: Development, challenges and opportunities. In D. J. Mason, S. L. Isaacs, & D. C. Colby (Eds.). *The nursing profession: Development, challenges and opportunities* (pp. 3–79). Jossey-Bass.

Milliken, A. (2018). Nurse ethical sensitivity: An integrative review. *Nursing Ethics, 25*(3), 278–303. doi:10.1177/0969733016646155

Milliken, A., & Grace, P. (2017). Nurse ethical awareness: Understanding the nature of everyday practice. *Nursing Ethics, 24*(5), 517–524. doi:10.1177/0969733015615172

Milliken, A., Ludlow, L., DeSanto-Madeya, S., & Grace, P. (2018). The development and psychometric validation of the ethical awareness scale. *Journal of Advanced Nursing, 74*(8), 2005–2016.

Milliken, A., Ludlow, L., & Grace, P. (2019). Ethical awareness scale: Replication testing, invariance analysis, and implications. *AJOB Empirical Bioethics, 10*(4), 231–240.

Milton, C. L. (2004). Ethics content in nursing education: Pondering with the possible. *Nursing Science Quarterly, 17*(4), 308–311.

Newton, L. (1988). Lawgiving for professional life: Reflections on the place of the professional code. In A. Flores (Ed.), *Professional ideals* (pp. 47–56). Wadsworth.

Nightingale, F. (1859/1946). *Notes on nursing: What it is and what it is not.* Lippincott.

Nolan, P. W., & Markert, D. (2002). Ethical reasoning observed: a longitudinal study of nursing students. *Nursing Ethics, 9*(3), 243–258.

Park, M., Kjervik, D., Crandell, J., & Oermann, M. H. (2012). The relationship of ethics education to moral sensitivity and moral reasoning skills of nursing students. *Nursing Ethics, 19*(4), 568–580.

Penn Nursing. (2011). *Nursing, history, and health care project.* Accessed November 20, 2020 from: https://www.nursing.upenn.edu/nhhc/nursing-through-time/1870-1899/

Pierce, A. G., & Smith, J. A. (2008). The ethics curriculum for doctor of nursing practice programs. *Journal of Professional Nursing, 24*(5), 270–74.

Powers, M., & Faden, R. (2006). *Social justice.* Oxford University Press.

Rawls, J. (1970). *A theory of justice.* Belknap/Harvard University Press.

Readings, B. (1996). *The university in ruins.* Harvard University Press.

Reich, W. T. (1995). Introduction. In W. T. Reich (Ed.), *The encyclopedia of bioethics* (p. xxi). Simon Schuster.

Rest, J. R. (1982). A psychologist looks at the teaching of ethics. *The Hastings Center Report, 12*(1), 29–36. https://www.jstor.org/stable/3560621

Rest, J. R. (1984). Research on moral development: Implications for training counseling psychologists. *The Counseling Psychologist, 12*(3), 19–29.

Rest, J. R., & Narvaez, D. (Eds.). (1994). *Moral development in the professions: Psychology and applied ethics.* Erlbaum Associates.

Reverby, S. (1987). A caring dilemma: Womanhood and nursing in historical perspective. *Nursing Research, 36*(1), 5–11.

Reynolds, S. J. (2006). A neurocognitive model of the ethical decision making process: Implications for study and practice. *Journal of Applied Psychology, 91*(4), 737–748. https://doi.org/10.1037/0021-9010.91.4.737

Robinson, E., Jurchak, M., Zollfrank, A., Lee, S., Frost, D., & Grace, P. J. (2014). Enhancing moral agency: Clinical ethics residency for nurses, *Hastings Center Report*, *44*(5), 12–20. DOI: 10.1002/hast.353

Rolfe, G. (2013). *The university in dissent: Scholarship in the corporate university.* Routledge.

Schroeder, C. (2003). The tyranny of profit: Concentration of wealth, corporate globalization, and the failed US health care system. *Advances in Nursing* Science, *26*(3), 173–184.

Skela-Savič, B., & Kiger, A. (2015). Self-assessment of clinical nurse mentors as dimensions of professional development and the capability of developing ethical values at nursing students: A correlational research study. *Nurse Education Today*, *35*(10), 1044–1051.

Song, J. (2018). Ethics education in nursing: Challenges for nurse educators. *Kai Tiaki Nursing Research, 9(*1), 12.

Strachey, L. (1996). *Florence Nightingale.* Penguin.(Reproduced for Nursing Standard— extract reprinted from Lytton Strachey, Eminent Victorians (1918).

Traudt, T., Liaschenko, J., & Peden-McAlpine, C. (2016). Moral agency, moral imagination, and moral community: Antidotes to moral distress. *Journal of Clinical Ethics*, *27*(3), 201–213.

Ulrich, C. M., Taylor, C., Soeken, K., O'Donnell, P., Farrar, A., Danis, M., & Grady, C. (2010). Everyday ethics: ethical issues and stress in nursing practice. *Journal of Advanced* Nursing, *66*(11), 2510–2519.

Walker, M. U. (1993). Keeping moral space open: New images of ethics consulting. *Hastings Center Report, 23*(2), 33–40.

Washington Post. (2020). The Coronavirus is infecting and killing Black Americans at an alarmingly high rate. Available online at: https://www.washingtonpost.com/nation/2020/04/07/coronavirus-is- infecting-killing-black-americans-an-alarmingly-high-rate-post-analysis-shows/?arc404=true

Willis. D. G., Grace, P. J., & Roy, C. (2008). A central unifying focus for the discipline: Facilitating humanization, meaning, choice, quality of life, and healing in living and dying. *Advances in Nursing Science, 31*(1), E28–E40.

Windt, P. Y. (1989). Introductory essay. In P. Y. Windt, P. C. Appleby, M. P. Battin, L. P. Francis & B. M. Landesman (Eds.), *Ethical issues in the professions* (pp. 1–24). Prentice Hall.

Woodham-Smith, C. (1950). *Florence Nightingale.* Constable.

Woodhouse, H. (2009). *Selling out: Academic freedom and the corporate market.* McGill University Press.

Woods, M. (2005). Nursing ethics education: Are we really delivering the good(s)? *Nursing Ethics, 12*(1), 5–18. doi: 10.1191/0969733005ne754oa.

SECTION 2

EDUCATING IN ETHICS PROFESSIONS WITH A FOCUS UPON THE COMMUNITY/ENTITY SERVED

Chapter 4: Engineering Ethics

The survival of dignified life on earth depends, in large part, not only upon technological knowledge but also upon the moral integrity and responsibility of engineers....Today, the development of moral judgment and ethical action is an essential part of professional practice.

—Jose-Félix Lozano

Chapter 5: Urban Planning Ethics

Planning has been described as an 'organization of hope.' Even so, the intensification of environmental and urban challenges today has led many planners to experience frustration, disappointment, and even despair. There is a general perception of powerlessness in the planning profession.... planning ethics is an indispensable source of help in professional perplexities and a vital precondition of social hope.

—Jeffrey C. K. Hui

Chapter 6: Business Ethics

For students to derive the most from business ethics education, business ethics educators must ensure their efforts reflect those issues that students need to understand and be geared to the more realistic, immediate, and personal issues that students are likely to encounter throughout their careers. While this point is not new, it still seems to be an afterthought in too many teaching business ethics efforts.

—Ronald R. Sims

CHAPTER 4

TEACHING ETHICS FOR THE ENGINEERING PROFESSION

Theory, Practice, and Future Agenda

José-Félix Lozano
Universidad Politécnica de Valencia

In today's technological society, the engineer's role is central and the consequences of engineering work for society and the planet are increasing. The survival of dignified life on earth depends in large part, not only on technological knowledge but also on the integrity and responsibility of engineers. This chapter proposes three ideas: 1) ethics is an essential part of engineering practice, and consequently, it should be a fundamental part of engineering education; 2) by its nature (positivistic, materialistic, etc.), engineering education tends fosters skills and assumes epistemic perspectives which make it difficult to teach ethics to engineers; and, 3) classroom engineering education should focus upon developing ethical sensitivity and judgment among future engineers. This chapter closes with a general conclusion and five recommendations for an engineering ethics pedagogy that will improve professional practice and, ultimately, contribute to the construction of a more dignified society.

Keywords: Engineering Ethics, Ethical Responsibility, Applied Ethics, Teaching Engineering Ethics

Educating in Ethics Across the Professions: A Compendium of Research, Theory, Practice, and an Agenda for the Future, pages 75–91.

INTRODUCTION: THE NEED FOR ETHICS AMONG
ENGINEERING PROFESSIONALS

Looking at the past and thinking about the future, two major situations where ethics is crucial in science, technology, and engineering can be identified. In the past, cases of irresponsibility in science, technology, and engineering have damaged people and the environment. Looking to the future, the potential risks related to scientific and technological progress are significant.

The Challenger explosion (1986), the Bhopal disaster (1986), the Fukushima accident (2011), and the VW "Dieselgate" (2015) incident exemplify incredible scientific and technological advances and their dangers. Every incident results in immediate and loud appeals for professional responsibility.

At the same time, issues related to scientific advances and technological developments make ethics increasingly relevant and urgent. Advances in nanotechnology, biomedical engineering, robotics, digitalization, biotechnology, geo-engineering, etc., expose humanity to risks that were unimaginable a few decades earlier, resulting in situations where engineers know what they *could* do but not what they *should* do.

Science and technology professionals possess enormous power as well as the potential to shape and transform the environment, human beings (bioengineering), and belief systems (Johnson, 2010). This power and potential means that these professions have immense responsibilities. The traditional divisions between the cultures of science, technology, and humanities have broken down (Snow, 1959), with Weber's (1919) notion that science should be a value-free discipline now a distant memory. Today, the development of ethical judgment and ethical conduct is an essential part of professional practice.

Over 20 years ago, the U.S.-based association responsible for the accreditation of the engineering degrees worldwide, the Accreditation Board for Engineering and Technology (ABET), explicitly acknowledged the need to integrate ethics training in engineering studies when it stated "engineering programs must demonstrate that graduates have...an understanding of ethical and professional responsibility...[and] the education necessary to understand the impact of engineering solutions in a social and global context" (Herkert et al., 2002, p. 12).

This chapter's first section discusses the necessity for, the difficulties involved in, and ways to develop better engineering ethics teaching. Its second section offers a brief presentation of the history and evolution of engineering ethics, analyzing the epistemic challenges and practical difficulties involved in integrating ethics into engineering education. The third section focuses upon the objectives of an engineering ethics education: ethical awareness and ethical reasoning. The chapter's fourth section concludes this discussion by offering five suggestions for teaching engineering ethics effectively.

ENGINEERING ETHICS: DEFINITION AND HISTORY

The profession of engineering is less than 200 years old. The first people to be described as "engineers" were soldiers in the fifteenth century. However, military engineers were soldiers who operated siege towers, catapults, artillery, and other "war engines" not individuals possessing high levels of scientific knowledge and creative skills (Davis, 1995). It was not until 1828 that engineering was institutionalized in the form of the British Institution of Civil Engineering at a time when engineering was understood as the ability to harness and exploit the power offered by nature (Mitcham, 2009).

The *Encyclopedia Britannica* defines engineering as "the application of science to the optimum conversion of the resources of nature to the uses of humankind" (Smith, 2020, p. 1). ABET defines engineering similarly as "the profession in which knowledge of mathematics and natural sciences obtained through study, experience, and practice is applied judiciously to develop ways of using, economically, the materials and forces of nature for the benefit of mankind" (Walesh, 2012, p. 3), while Schlossberger's *The Ethical Engineer*, defines engineering as "the safe advancement of the progress of the human community, in collaboration with nature, through practical knowledge used systematically with clarity and cleanliness in decision-making practice" (1993, p. 44). These definitions assume two characteristics which Martin and Schinzinger (1996) considered fundamental to engineering: The creation of useful and safe technological products, and respect for the autonomy of clients and the public.

These definitions also have three ethical implications: 1) the products developed by engineering professional should be useful and should satisfy human needs; 2) safety and risk control should be key objectives—the professional who puts his or her collaborators or clients at risk is not a good professional; and, 3) the professional engineer should respect the free will of one's clients and society as a whole. Utility, safety, and respect for autonomy are essential engineering values.

The roots of the ethical responsibilities of professions are found in the Hammurabi Code (circa 1754 BC) which establishes sanctions for individuals whose malpractice causes damage. However, it was not until the seventeenth century when engineering became established as a profession that engineering ethics emerged. Considering a practice as a "profession" has some relevant implications, as a profession is a dignified occupation which exhibits three attributes—knowledge, organization, and the ethics of professional service (Lawson, 2004).

Two of these attributes pose ethical challenges to professionals. The first is related to the power derived from highly specialized knowledge. The knowledge gap between the client and the professional requires the latter to make decisions in the interests of the former. Knowledge asymmetries demand a high level of professional integrity to avoid abuses of power and paternalism on the part of the engineer professional for which what might be called an "ethics of professional service" is essential. Every profession has an essential mission—an "internal good" (*telos*)—which legitimates professional practice and should always rule every professional decision (MacIntyre, 1981). For example, the engineering profession aims to promote society's material well-being by identifying social ends and the ethical imperative of the specific professional service (Bowen, 2014).

To identify its social ends and ethical imperative, engineering ethics utilizes Martin and Schinzinger's definition, namely, "the analysis of moral cases and decisions faced by individuals and organizations in the field of engineering; and also the study of issues related to moral ideals, nature, politics and relations of individuals and corporations involved in technological activities" (1996, p. 2). Engineering ethics includes not only the responsibilities and rights to be respected by those engaged in engineering but also the desirable ideals and the personal commitment of the engineering professional.

According to Mitcham (2009), four phases constitute the historical development of engineering ethics:

- 1500 to 1900 when engineering was closely associated with the military: In 1828, Thomas Telford proposed the first official definition of (non-military) civil engineering: "Civil Engineering is the art of directing the great Sources of Power in Nature for the use and convenience of man" which stressed the idea of practical knowledge at the service of human interest and human progress (cited by Mitcham, 2020). In this first phase, ethics was implicit and related to loyalty.
- 1900 to the 1930s when the ethical duties of the engineering profession were made explicit and demanded loyalty to the profession: During the first three decades of the twentieth century, the first professional ethics codes were formulated. The explicit values and principles guiding the engineer's conduct were understood as the means to promote professional development and prestige. Loyalty to the group was the paramount value: "[P]rofessional engineering—insofar as it articulated loyalty as a primary value—tended to promote a kind of self-imposed tutelage to its most immediate employer" (Mitcham, 2009, p. 39). One example of this conception of ethics is found in the American Institute of Electrical Engineers Code of Ethics adopted in 1912 as well as the codes of ethics of the American Society of Mechanical Engineers and the American Society of Civil Engineers adopted in 1914.
- 1930s to the end of World War II when technical perfection became the main and almost the only objective of engineering: An obsession with efficiency generated a mindset which still predominates and separates engineering from the society it is meant to serve. In this phase, the principle of economic maximization complemented the principle of efficiency. Questions about social interest became secondary to the pursuit of economic profit and efficiency which, in turn, created a tension between democracy and technology and reconfigured society's perception of engineers (Mitcham, 2009). According to Bowen: "The prioritization by engineers of

technical ingenuity over ethical responsibility has become mirrored in public perception: engineers are often perceived as being primarily technically inventive nerds or geeks" (2014, p. 1).

- 1950s to the present which has seen a slow evolution of the social awareness among engineer professionals of the social impact of their work and their corresponding social responsibilities: The prevailing traits during this phase have been concern over the safety, health, and welfare of the whole of society. In the final few decades of the twentieth century, there was a tendency to abandon the big social technology issues in favor of a focus upon smaller ones. Mitcham describes this as "[t]he ethics of technology became environmental ethics, biomedical ethics, computer ethics, information ethics, engineering ethics, research ethics, nanoethics, neuroethics, and more. In each of these technological regionalizations there were further micro issues of risk, safety, privacy, participation, and more" (2020, p. 594). Stressing responsibility for society and the environment is core to the codes of the more influential engineering professional associations such as the Council for Professional Development, ABET, the American Association of Engineering Societies (AAES), the National Society of Professional Engineers (NSPE), and the Institute of Electrical and Electronics Engineers (IEEE). At the end of the twentieth century, engineering ethics was introduced as an academic subject into the curriculum. In 2000, ABET published the Criteria for Accrediting Programs in Engineering in the United States which listed 11 learning outcomes for graduate engineers, one of which (Criterion 3f) called explicitly for "an understanding of professional and ethical responsibility" (Accreditation Board for Engineering and Technology Inc, 1999).

Today, the crucial role of ethics in technology and engineering is generally accepted in relation not only to avoid destruction but also build a better future (Jasanoff, 2016). In addition, there is a recognition of the growing power of science and technology, the implied risks of destruction of humanity, and the potential for tackling grand challenges such as climate change and managing innovations such as genetic manipulation (Blok, 2014). Currently, the integration with engineering of neuroscience and artificial intelligence is making ethics in engineering more urgent. For instance, the development of innovative neuroscientific technologies has driven discoveries related to better visualization and understanding of the brain in relation to health and disease but at the same time carries the potential risk of altering the cognitive nature of the human being. For instance, brain technology can alter both the physical body and the individual's essential identity. There are similar examples related to the development of artificial intelligence engineering. The capacity to work with large volumes of data in the space of seconds opens the door to a surveillance society and its associated threats to both privacy and democracy (Véliz, 2020), demanding new ethical orientations (Floridi et al., 2018).

In develop nations, engineering is often considered to be confined to the high-tech industries. However, it can contribute hugely to relieving extreme poverty, upholding human rights, and maintaining peace (Bowen, 2014). In light of the potentially tremendous and unprecedented impacts of the outcomes of science and innovation, there is a practical and urgent need to integrate universal ethical principles in engineering and technology (Lozano & Monsonís-Payá, 2020).

INTEGRATING ETHICS IN ENGINEERING: EPISTEMIC CHALLENGES AND PRACTICAL DIFFICULTIES

Starting with Schlossberger's (1993) and the ABET's (Walesh, 2012) definitions, some essentials features of engineering can be identified: It is science-based, systematic, synthetic and creative, goal-oriented, dynamic, and people-oriented. The first five features are essentially positivist, materialist, and naturalistic in approach, focused upon calculative strategic rationality. The sixth feature, people-oriented, has an idealistic and social component in which dialogic rationality provide the means to legitimate ends. For this reason, as Figueiredo observes, the "epistemology of engineering" should be considered "in light of the four key questions of the philosophy of knowledge: the ontological, the epistemological, the methodological, and the axiological questions" (2008, p. 95).

Although the dominant scientific-technical approach in engineering is essential, it presents important challenges for integrating ethics into engineering training and practice. These difficulties can be categorized at the levels of epistemology and professional practice.

At the level of epistemology, the essential features of engineering epistemology are materialist and positivist. The knowledge generated and used in engineering is essentially analytical and mathematical. It involves breaking down complex problems into the smallest possible units, applying physical, chemical, and mathematical knowledge, and intervening to achieve the desired objective. Its underlying worldview is also positivist and materialist, meaning that everything must be measurable, weighed, and manipulated. The basic premise is that the world is an external entity that can be known objectively through observation and experimentation, where only one objective truth is possible. The relationship with the object of knowledge is instrumental from the subject to the object which aims at maximizing efficiency and effectiveness which always introduces an economic dimension. Precision, efficiency, and maximization are essential performance criteria. In essence: "The discourses of science continue to permeate in engineering and the latter is often viewed in popular images, and in the minds of many engineers and laypersons, as applied science" (Kant & Kerr, 2019, p 687).

This highlights one of the central aspects of this epistemology: The interest of knowledge. Engineering is a profession Habermas (1968) would identify as featuring the manipulative practical interest of knowledge. The implicit assumption is that scientific knowledge enables people to (and they should) control and manipulate the world for their own interests.

In contrast is the idea that knowledge that exists for humanistic and idealistic purposes, ethics knowledge aims to understand human beliefs and actions, and to evaluate them based upon abstract ideas of fair-unfair/good-bad to extend human freedom, what Habermas (1968) would call "emancipatory interests." The object of ethics knowledge is to understand better human-to-human relationships and their impact upon the environment and future generations (Jonas, 1979; Lenk, 1997) as well as to resolve problems and disagreements based upon rational dialogue (Scanlon, 1998). This idea makes it difficult to integrate the social and human knowledge also essential for engineering practice with natural science knowledge (Figueiredo, 2008) (Figure 4.1).

At the level of professional practice, the materials with which engineers work are mainly inert, although there is a long history in specialties such as agronomic engineering which features working with plants and animals as well as biomedical engineering advances which feature interventions upon humans. One implication for engineering ethics is that while the dominant trend in engineering education is towards working on inert material which assumes that during their professional training, engineering students develop the skills they will need to deal with objects based upon the instrumental means-end rationale. This does come at a cost: Students do not develop the skills they need to respond effectively to social perceptions and human interactions. A second implication for engineering ethics is the relationship between the engineer's work and its beneficiaries. In most cases, the relationship with consumers of engineering output is indirect and distant because engineers develop processes and artifacts which are used by and affect people who are distant in space and time. Whereas doctors, lawyers, and teachers have a direct and immediate relationship with the beneficiaries of their professional services, for the most part engineering professionals do not, which affects their awareness and responsibility (Monzon, 1999). In addition, motiva-

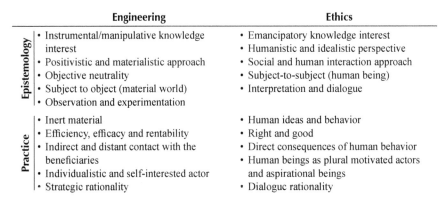

	Engineering	Ethics
Epistemology	• Instrumental/manipulative knowledge interest • Positivistic and materialistic approach • Objective neutrality • Subject to object (material world) • Observation and experimentation	• Emancipatory knowledge interest • Humanistic and idealistic perspective • Social and human interaction approach • Subject-to-subject (human being) • Interpretation and dialogue
Practice	• Inert material • Efficiency, efficacy and rentability • Indirect and distant contact with the beneficiaries • Individualistic and self-interested actor • Strategic rationality	• Human ideas and behavior • Right and good • Direct consequences of human behavior • Human beings as plural motivated actors and aspirational beings • Dialogue rationality

FIGURE 4.1. The Essential Epistemological and Practical Differences Between Engineering and Ethics

tion underlies the integration of human behavior and engineering practice. In this notion, the human being is conceived as *homo economicus*, a calculating individual who strives to maximize one's utility where cooperation and altruism are irrelevant. Mitcham (2020) argues that the links between the engineering profession and the idea of maximizing utility presented by Bentham and other utilitarian philosophers have a long tradition. The professional views oneself as a rational being who solves problems in a material world (Bucciarelli, 2008).

In contrast, the practice of ethics focuses upon how human beings treat one another. Its main task is to assist human beings to identify, judge, and guide human conduct based upon rational justification concerning what is right and wrong as well as good and bad. Professional codes of ethics, ethics committees, and ethics regulations provide principles and standards to guide how individuals should conduct themselves. A practice-based ethics orientation assumes the individual human is complex, motivated by a variety of emotions and ideas. Making decisions concerning what is right and wrong as well as good and bad about professional practice must also be based upon rational argumentation (Habermas, 1983; Kant, 1785) while integrating the emotional dimension (Cortina, 2007; Damasio, 1994; Lozano, 2020) and accounting for the concrete social and natural context not just following the dictates of formal logic and mathematical calculations (Conill, 2006).

Instrumental engineering knowledge undoubtedly has advanced the human ability to control the forces of nature and provides efficient solutions to multiple demands and human needs. However, it has been less effective at advancing social and human aims and objectives. But, engineers must consider them. Due in part to the logic of technical praxis and the epistemological presuppositions discussed above, this latter requirement has largely been ignored.

These two views of engineering knowledge and its practice are neither incompatible nor exclusive but complementary—two sides of the same coin. This complementary view is important for effective integration of ethics into engineering teaching. In what follows, what this complementary view suggests is that teaching engineering ethics should simultaneously be philosophically rigorous and focused upon real engineering problems. The first step towards effective teaching is a solid integration of engineering ethics within the curriculum as a specific and essential topic not as something that is "nice to have."

TEACHING ETHICS TO ENGINEERING
PROFESSIONALS: KEY ELEMENTS

As noted in this chapter's Introduction, the need for ethics training in engineering has been accepted, defended, and disseminated by several international institutions. The turning point in this regard was the ABET's (1999) list of accreditation criteria (Ventura, 2003). In particular, the list calls for "an understanding of professional and ethical responsibility" (Criterion 3.h) and "the broad education necessary to understand the impact of engineering solutions in a global and societal context" while highlighting "a knowledge of contemporary issues" (Criterion 3.j). This made professional ethics, at least theoretically, a substantial component of engineering education in the United States and globally. However, there is less unanimity about the effectiveness of the training initiatives implemented so far (Bucciarelli, 2008).

Mitcham and Englehardt (2019) highlight how initiatives related to developing the academic topic of ethics in engineering and how to teach ethics effectively in higher education are not new. In 1980, the Hastings Center published *Ethics Teaching in Higher Education* (Callahan & Bok, 1980) which stipulates that all ethics programs should have five objectives: to stimulate the ethical imagination; to recognize ethical dilemmas as early as possible; to analyze ethical principles and concepts in their proper context, to stimulate a sense of responsibility; and, to identify ways to manage ethical ambiguity and disagreement effectively. Harris et al. (1996) later wrote "Engineering Ethics: What? Why? How? And When?" in which they proposed a comprehensive set of learning outcomes for engineering ethics education: a) to stimulate the ethical imagination; b) to help students recognize ethical issues; c) to help students analyze key ethical concepts and principles; d) to help students deal with ambiguity; e) to encourage students to take ethics seriously; f) to increase student sensitivity to ethical issues; g) to increase students' knowledge of relevant standards; h) to improve ethical judgment; and, i) to increase ethical will-power. For his part, Hersh (2016) states the goal of ethics training in engineering is to increase ethical sensitivity, to increase knowledge about the most relevant standards of conduct, and to improve ethical judgment and will-power. In essence, the purpose of engineering ethics education is to enhance ethical judgment and develop the professional's ethical autonomy. These outcomes require introducing students to two activities aimed at increasing ethical awareness and sensitivity as well as ethical reasoning.

To increase ethical awareness and sensitivity, the first activity is to convince engineering students that ethics is an essential component of their future professional practice. While "professional education may entail fragmentation, which has the potential to narrow ethical perceptions and to lead to questionable ethical reasoning and practices" (Guntzburger et al., 2019, p. 912), the first aim of ethics education should be to overcome this narrow perspective. Along the same line, "[w]ithout awareness of ethical issues, ethics makes little sense, and one cannot do anything about the things that one does not know about" (Lennerfors, et al., 2020, p. 2). With professionals confronting multiple ethical dilemmas, problems, and challenges, issues such as conflicts of interest, confidentiality, discrimination and harassment, cultural conflicts, and corruption emerge frequently and cannot be solved from a purely technical perspective. One of the traditional ways to increase awareness is introduce the students to major scandals such as the Challenger, Union Carbide, Ford Pinto, and similar incidents. Experience derived from 20 years of teaching engineering ethics suggests this is effective for three reasons: first, students realize the magnitude of the damage that can be caused by irresponsible behavior; second, such cases show how important (and difficult) it is to "see" beyond the boundaries of a specific work field; and third, it demonstrates to students the problems involved in complex decision making in organizations. However, confronting students with negatives such as "engineering disasters" is not sufficient. As already mentioned, students need to be convinced they will confront ethical dilemmas in their everyday engineering practice which can be achieved by inviting professional engineers to make presentations as regular aspect of classroom teaching. The reflections, ideas, and emotions involved in making ethical decisions related to everyday life demonstrate to students how ethics is not just for "heroes" (Basart & Serra, 2013; Lennerfors et al., 2020).

To increase awareness and encourage development of ethical reasoning, analysis of professional ethics codes is effective. However, experience suggests this activity relates ethics primarily to professional practice. Many students will be unfamiliar with the text of ethics codes. Reading, analyzing, and reflecting upon codified duties and rules gives them an idea of the ethical dilemmas they will confront in the future (Lozano, 2006). Moreover, the long tradition of ethics codes in professional practice increases awareness of the enduring relevance of ethics issues in engineering work. Miñano and colleagues confirm this notion, concluding that "the use of professional deontological codes is a powerful method to teach professional ethics at an introductory level" (Miñano et al., 2017, p. 280). The final strategy for increasing ethical awareness is workplace experience. Nudelman and English (2019) suggest that work experience provides students with the opportunity to identify and reflect on the ethical challenges that arise in the workplace.

Enhancing ethical reasoning assumes that all human beings have the capacity to reflect upon their actions and the only way to decide what the right thing to do is to use the reasoning capacity (Kant, 1784). The capacity to make ethical judgments is specific to humans and is the condition of possibility for making autonomous decisions and engaging in responsible conduct. How ethical judgment develops has been the subject of research for many years (Kohlberg, 1981) and this research indicates that reasoning requires a rigorous theoretical framework. Students, in general, and engineers, in particular, tend to understand ethics norms as personal, relativistic, and arbitrary often voicing in classrooms the subjective notion that "everyone has his own ideas, and no idea is better than any other." However, subjectivism is misconceived and generates relativism as well as the idea that ethical principles and standards have no stronger foundation than personal belief. To overcome this acritical and dangerous assumption, it is necessary to explain to students the traditions, authors, concepts, and ideas contained in ethics using rigorous and solid argumentation. Virtue ethics, utilitarianism, deontology, ethics of discourse, etc., are well-established theories which offer concrete orientations to decision making. Knowledge about these theories is not simply an academic exercise but is required for responsible decision making and professional conduct. Presenting diverse ethical theories with philosophical rigor is the best way to promote ethical conduct and avoid accusations indoctrination.

One way those who teach engineering ethics can foster the capacity for ethical judgment is to analyze and discuss ethical problems and dilemmas in engineering practice (Lozano et al., 2006). Inviting students to defend their positions assists in developing ethical judgment as does participation in open, rational dialogue, encouraging students to practice essential skills such as listening, respecting others, paying attention to their arguments, reviewing those arguments critically, offering robust and precise explanations, and accepting discrepancies (Cortina et al., 2008; Habermas, 1983). Public debate enables dominant narratives to be questioned and cultivates self-critical perspectives concerning the dogmas and mental models that govern business and organizations (Werhane et al., 2010). Analyzing documentaries and other films, using case studies, writing essays, and debating ethical controversies offer good pedagogical strategies to foster the development of each student's ethical judgment.

Ethical awareness and sensitivity as well as ethical reasoning must be considered together and included in engineering ethics courses. The influence of the emotional dimension upon ethical decision making is well-established, and several researchers have demonstrated how emotional content in case-based ethical training has a stronger effect than impersonal dilemmas (Haidt, 2001; Jones, 1991; Lozano, 2020; Thiel et al., 2012).

In addition, case studies (Pinkus et al., 2015), role-play (Seiler et al., 2011), ethical dilemmas (Lozano et al., 2006), and innovative strategies for teaching engineering ethics through drama (Birch & Lennerfors, 2020) convey the complexity and practical guidance students needed to increase sensitivity and judgment as well as to demonstrate higher levels of ethical conduct (Kohlberg, 1981). These strategies integrate advances in neuroethics with practical decision making and demonstrate how the separation between reason and emotions is inaccurate, unrealistic, and impossible (Damasio, 1994).

One way to evaluate the effectiveness of engineering ethics teaching is to employ Rest et al.'s (1997) defining issues test (DIT). Based upon Kohlberg's (1981) theory of moral development, DIT evaluates progress in: 1) identification of ethical dilemmas (recognizing); 2) ethical evaluation (judgment); 3) deciding whether to act ethically or unethically (intention); and, 4) performing the ethical conduct. Miñano and colleagues proposed a model and scoring system to assess the development of ethical judgment in engineering students. They conclude that teaching engineering ethics through dilemmas and engineering codes of ethics improves the capacity of students to identify ethical issues, analyze sensitive ethics situations, and assess ethical decision making. Especially relevant is the impact of analyzing professional ethical codes of conduct to increase ethical awareness and identify ethical dilemmas (Miñano et al., 2017, p. 282).

Lastly, engineering ethics education must be an essential part of the engineering education curriculum, not an elective course or optional topic. As already mentioned, the ethical dimension of professional practice must not be viewed as secondary; instead, it is crucial for excellent professional practice. As Harris et al. note: "students should be introduced to ethics as many times and in as places inside and outside the curriculum as possible" (1996, p. 95). In "Ethics across the Curriculum: Prospects for Broader (and Deeper) Teaching and Learning in Research and Engineering Ethics," Mitcham and Englehardt provided an extensive review of the history of ethics across the curriculum in the United States. They conclude: "Establishing an ethics across the curriculum (EAC) program at any university is difficult, for the simple reason that any cross-disciplinary activity is difficult." (2019, p. 1736). They add that this difficulty is compounded by three factors related to the successful integration of ethics in the engineering curriculum: grassroots faculty interests; administrative receptivity; and, interdisciplinary leadership. Along similar lines, Taebi and Kastenberg's (2019) proposal for a graduate course in engineering ethics in a cooperation between TU Delft University and UC-Berkeley University confronted two obstacles—one academic and one institutional. The implicit and extended perception of interdisciplinary research (specifically engineering ethics which combines hard science with humanities) as second-rate academic work constitutes a major obstacle. The institutional lack of formal recognition and economic support for initiatives beyond traditional discipline boundaries also presents an obstacle.

CONCLUSIONS AND RECOMMENDATIONS

Engineering ethics is an essential part of engineering practice. Teaching this topic in engineering faculties can effectively improve student awareness of both ethical dilemmas and ethical decision making. The goal is not to train engineer heroes (Basart & Serra, 2013) but engineers who are aware of the relevance of the professional context for making ethical decisions (Lozano, 2020). The latter is essential for the development of future engineers who are responsible and ethically competent. Their training requires action at two levels: ethics curriculum and faculty ethos.

The first refers to the structure and content of the engineering ethics curriculum which can be structured in three blocks and includes both a theoretical framework and conceptual basis. In the absence of conceptual clarity and a theoretical framework, rigorous analysis of engineering cases and dilemmas is impossible. The second focuses upon ethics dilemmas in engineering, including conflicts of interest, corruption, security and safety, environmental impact, impact on vulnerable communities, cultural conflicts in organizations, harassment, discrimination, among others. The goal is to increase ethical awareness and encourage reflection upon ethical solutions to real engineering dilemmas. The third focuses upon presenting and proposing solutions to ethical dilemmas which engineering students are likely to confront in their professional practice. This requires cultivating in students an awareness of existing "ethics instruments"—for example, codes of ethics, ethics auditing models, corporate social responsibility initiatives, ethics training—and how these can orient and guide engineering practice and demonstrate how it is possible to manage the ethical dimension of engineering work.

Time should be allocated for discussing innovative solutions and reflecting upon current significant social and environmental challenges including climate change, poverty, global security, privacy, human rights, etc. The goal is that students will understand how engineers can contribute to the resolution of these challenges.

Faculty ethos refers to the idea that the knowledge, techniques, and values transmitted in the classroom are not the only factors that influence the training of responsible and ethical professionals. In addition, policies, culture, organizational processes, and symbols influence it. For this training to be effective, institutional ethos—the culture transmitted (the synthesis of language, image, instruments, practices, etc., identifying what is to be down and how to do it) and which influences student expectations—must be consistent with the content of ethics presented in the classroom (Lozano, 2012, p. 221).

Looking to the future, these proposals suggest an agenda of five recommendations for effective engineering ethics education:

1. **Theoretical rigor**. What professionals think often guides what they do. With awareness and knowing function as essential pillars of thinking, promoting ethical conduct in engineering students requires, first, clarifying the concept of ethics and ethical theories and, second, providing provide concrete reasons for conducting oneself in certain ways. Clarity, rigor, coherence, and rationality are attributes of both ethics and the natural sciences; both should be evident in the classroom. Lack of philosophical rigor only contributes to or affirms to skepticism, relativism, and indifferentism.

2. **Orientation to professional engineering practice**. Ethics emerges from daily professional practice but teaching engineering ethics requires providing the knowledge and cultivating each student's intellectual capacity to contend with ethical dilemmas. Analyzing cases, inviting experts to make presentations, and introducing professional codes and international standards can assist in promoting this orientation, demonstrating how ethics is an essential and inevitable dimension of professional practice.

3. **Innovative pedagogies**. Since Aristotle wrote about ethics 2,500 years ago, the objective of ethics has been to assist people to act ethically. As anthropology, philosophy, and psychology demonstrate, human conduct is influenced by many factors: reasons, feelings, beliefs, intuitions, etc. (Damasio, 1994; Dubljevic & Racine, 2014; Greene, 2013; Haidt, 2001; Kahneman, 2011). As a result, motivating students to conduct themselves ethically requires all these factors to be mobilized. Case studies, ethical dilemmas, analysis of movies, drama, service-learning projects, and role-playing provide innovative and effective ways to increase students' ethical awareness and judgement.

4. **Interdisciplinary cooperation**. Professional engineering practice is complex and dynamic, one requiring vast technical, social, and cultural

knowledge as well as the capacity to integrate and balance all these dimensions. Professional practice is neither isolated nor does it develop in a scientific vacuum. Instead, it requires interdependence, interdisciplinary work, and cooperation. This also applies to the teaching of engineering ethics which requires constructive interdisciplinary work among educators representing different scientific areas and philosophies.

5. **Institutional acknowledgement and support.** Formal support from faculty governing bodies is essential, first, because it provides the material resources and the time necessary to develop engineering ethics teaching and research and, second, because it provides the area with institutional support and legitimacy. Including any topic in an academic curriculum sends the message to society and future professionals that this is necessary and important knowledge and skills.

These five recommendations offer the promise of more effective engineering ethics pedagogy that will improve professional practice and, ultimately, contribute to the construction of a more dignified society.

ACKNOWLEDGEMENTS

I want to thank three excellent colleagues and highly qualified experts who reviewed the chapter and made valuable critics and comments. Sincerely thanks to Dr Joé T. Martineau (HEC-Montreal), Dr Thomas Taro Lennerfors (Uppsala University) and Dr Cristóbal Miralles (Universidad Politécnica de Valencia).

A big thanks to Prof. Richard Jacobs for his impressive work and coordination effort. The patience and endurance for guiding this book in uncertain pandemic times are admirable. His critical comments and suggestions made a huge contribution to focus and clarify some parts of the chapter.

REFERENCES

Accreditation Board for Engineering and Technology Inc. (1999). Criteria for accrediting engineering programs. *Cycle*, (25). http://www.abet.org/Linked Documents-UPDATE/Criteria and PP/C001 08-09 CAC Criteria 11-8-07.pdf

Basart, J. M., & Serra, M. (2013). Engineering ethics beyond engineers' ethics. *Science and Engineering Ethics*, *19*, 179–187. https://doi.org/10.1007/s11948-011-9293-z

Birch, P., & Lennerfors, T. (2020). Teaching engineering ethics with drama. In *2020 IEEE frontiers in education conference (FIE)* (pp. 1–5). IEEE. https://doi.org/10.1109/FIE44824.2020.9274160

Blok, V. (2014). Look who's talking: Responsible innovation, the paradox of dialogue and the voice of the other in communication and negotiation processes. *Journal of Responsible Innovation*, *1*(2), 171–190. https://doi.org/10.1080/23299460.2014.924239

Bowen, W. R. (2014). *Engineering ethics: Challenges and opportunities* (Vol. 9783319040). https://doi.org/10.1007/978-3-319-04096-7

Bucciarelli, L. L. (2008). Ethics and engineering education. *European Journal of Engineering Education*, *33*(2), 141–149. https://doi.org/10.1080/03043790801979856

Callahan, D., & Bok, S. (1980). *Ethics teaching in higher education.* The Hasting Center.

Conill, J. (2006). *Ética hermenéutica.* Tecnos.

Cortina, A. (2007). *Ética de la razón cordial. Educar en la ciudadanía.* Ediciones Nobel.

Cortina, A., Conill, J., García-Marzá, D. (Eds.). (2008). *Public reason and applied ethics: The ways of practical reason in a pluralist society.* Ashgate Publishing.

Damasio, A. (1994). *Descartes´error. Emotion, reason, and the human brain.* Penguin Books.

Davis, M. (1995). An historical preface to engineering ethics. *Science and Engineering Ethics, 1*(1), 33–48. https://doi.org/10.1007/BF02628696

Dubljevic, V., & Racine, E. (2014). The ADC of moral judgment: opening the black box of moral intuitions with heuristics about agents, deeds, and consequences. *AJOB Neuroscience, 5*(4), 3–20.

Figueiredo, A. D. de. (2008). *Toward an epistemology of engineering* (pp. 94–95). Proceedings Workshop on Philosophy & Engineering (WPE 2008), Royal Engineering Academy, London, November 2008. https://doi.org/10.5840/symposion2016313

Floridi, L., Cowls, J., Beltrametti, M., Chatila, R., Chazerand, P., Dignum, V., Luetge, C., Madelin, R., Pagallo, U., Rossi, F., Schafer B., Valcke, P., & Vayena E. (2018). AI4People—An ethical framework for a good AI society: Opportunities, risks, principles, and recommendations. *Minds and Machines, 28*(December), 1–24. https://doi.org/10.12932/AP0443.32.4.2014

Greene, J. (2013). *Moral tribes. Emotion, reason, and the gap between us and them.* Penguin Books.

Guntzburger, Y., Pauchant, T. C., & Tanguy, P. A. (2019). Empowering engineering students in ethical risk management: An experimental study. *Science and Engineering Ethics, 25*(3), 911–937. https://doi.org/10.1007/s11948-018-0044-2

Habermas, J. (1968). *Erkenntnis und interesse* [Knowledge and human interests]. Felix Meiner Verlag.

Habermas, J. (1983). *Moralbewusstsein und kommunikatives handeln* [Moral consciousness and communicative action]. Shurkamp.

Haidt, J. (2001). The emotional dog and its rational tail: A social intuitiionist approach to moral judgement. *Psychological Review, 108*(4), 814834. https://doi.org/10.1037//0033-295X.

Harris, C. E., Davis, M., Pritchard, M. S., & Rabins, M. J. (1996). Engineering ethics: What? Why? How? And When? *Journal of Engineering Education, 85*(2), 93 96. https://doi.org/10.1002/j.2168-9830.1996.tb00216.x

Herkert, J., Pritchard, M., & Rabins, M. (2002). Continuing and emerging issues in engineering ethics education. *The Bridge, 32*(3). http://www.nae.edu/Publications/TheBridge/Archives/EngineeringEthics7377/ContinuingandEmergingIssuesinEngineeringEthicsEducation.aspx?layoutChange=LowGraphics%5Cnhttp://ethics.iit.edu/eelibrary/taxonomy/term/6911

Hersh, M. A. (2016). Engineers and the other: the role of narrative ethics. *AI and Society.* https://doi.org/10.1007/s00146-015-0594-7

Jasanoff, S. (2016). *The ethics of invention.* W. W. Norton and Company.

Johnson, D. G. (2010). The role of ethics in science and engineering. *Trends in Biotechnology, 28*(12), 589–590. https://doi.org/10.1016/j.tibtech.2010.08.003

Jonas, H. (1979). *Das Prinzip Verantwortung. Versuch einer Ethik für die technologische Zivilisation* [The responsibility principle. Proposal of an ethics for the technical civilization]. Shurkamp.

Jones, T. M. (1991). Ethical decision making by individuals in organizations: An issue-contingent model. *Academy of Management Review, 16*(2), 366–395.

Kahneman, D. (2011). *Thinking, fast and slow.* Penguin Books.

Kant, I. (1784). *Beantwortung der Frage: Was ist Aufklärung* [An answer to the question what is Enlightment]. (1994). Vandenhoeck and Ruprecht.

Kant, I. (1785). *Grundlegung zur Metaphysik der Sitten* [Foundations of the metaphysics of morals]. Shurkamp.

Kant, V., & Kerr, E. (2019). Taking stock of engineering epistemology: Multidisciplinary perspectives. *Philosophy and Technology, 32*(4), 685–726. https://doi.org/10.1007/s13347-018-0331-5

Kohlberg, L. (1981). *The philosophy of moral development: moral stages and the idea of justice.* Harper & Row,.

Lawson, W. D. (2004). Professionalism: The golden years. *Journal of Professional Issues in Engineering Education and Practice, 130*(1), 26–36. https://doi.org/10.1061/(ASCE)1052-3928(2004)130

Lenk, H. (1997). *Einführung in die angewandte Ethik. Verantwortlichkeit und Gewissen* [Introduction to applied ethics. Responsibility and conscience]. Kohlhammer.

Lennerfors, T. T., Laaksoharju, M., Davis, M., Birch, P., & Fors, P. (2020). A pragmatic approach for teaching ethics to engineers and computer scientists. *Proceedings - Frontiers in Education Conference, FIE, 2020-Octob.* https://doi.org/10.1109/FIE44824.2020.9274029

Lozano, J-F., & Monsonís-Payá, I. (2020). Civic ethics as a normative framework for responsible research and innovation. *Journal of Responsible Innovation,* 1–17. https://doi.org/10.1080/23299460.2020.1816024

Lozano, J.-F. (2006). Developing an ethical code for engineers: The discursive approach. *Science and Engineering Ethics, 12*(2). https://doi.org/10.1007/s11948-006-0024-9

Lozano, J.-F. (2012). Educating responsible managers. The role of university ethos. *Journal of Academic Ethics.* https://doi.org/10.1007/s10805-012-9166-3

Lozano, J.-F. (2020). Understanding unethical decision-making in organizations and proposals for its avoidance: The contribution of neuroscience. In E. Martineau & Joé T., Racine (Eds.), *Organizational Neuroethics* (pp. 147–165). Springer International Publishing. https://doi.org/10.1007/978-3-030-27177-0

Lozano, J.-F., Palau-Salvador, G., Gozálvez, V., & Boni, A. (2006). The use of moral dilemmas for teaching agricultural engineers. *Science and Engineering Ethics, 12*(2). https://doi.org/10.1007/s11948-006-0031-x

MacIntyre, A. (1981). *After virtue. A study in moral theory.* Notre Dame University Press.

Martin, M. W., & Schinzinger, R. (1996). *Ethics in engineering* (3rdf ed.). McGraw-Hill.

Miñano, R., Uruburu, Á., Moreno-Romero, A., & Pérez-López, D. (2017). Strategies for teaching professional ethics to IT engineering degree students and evaluating the result. *Science and Engineering Ethics, 23*(1), 263–286. https://doi.org/10.1007/s11948-015-9746-x

Mitcham, C. (2009). A historico-ethical perspective on engineering education: From use and convenience to policy engagement. *Engineering Studies, 1*(1), 35–53. https://doi.org/10.1080/19378620902725166

Mitcham, C. (2020). The ethics of technology: From thinking big to small—and big again. *Axiomathes*, *30*(6), 589–596. https://doi.org/10.1007/s10516-020-09505-8

Mitcham, C., & Englehardt, E. E. (2019). Ethics across the curriculum: Prospects for broader (and deeper) teaching and learning in research and engineering ethics. *Science and Engineering Ethics*, *25*(6), 1735–1762. https://doi.org/10.1007/s11948-016-9797-7

Monzon, J. E. (1999). Teaching ethical issues in biomedical engineering *. *TEMPUS Publication*, *15*(4), 276–281.

Nudelman, G., & English, J. (2019). Ethical dilemmas experienced by engineering students during their vacation work. *Journal of Professional Issues in Engineering Education and Practice, 145*(2), 1–8. https://doi.org/10.1061/(ASCE)EI.1943-5541.0000406

Pinkus, R. L., Gloeckner, C., & Fortunato, A. (2015). The role of professional knowledge in case-based reasoning in practical ethics. *Science and Engineering Ethics*. https://doi.org/10.1007/s11948-015-9645-1

Rest, J., Thoma, S., & Edwards, L. (1997). Designing and validating a measure of moral judgment: Stage preference and stage consistency approaches. *Journal of Educational Psychology*, *89*(1), 5–28. https://doi.org/10.1037/0022-0663.89.1.5

Scanlon, M. T. (1998). *What we owe to each other*. The Belknap Press of Harvard University Press.

Schlossberger, E. (1993). *The ethical engineer*. Temple University Press.

Seiler, S. N., Brummel, B. J., Anderson, K. L., Kim, K. J., Wee, S., Gunsalus, C. K., & Loui, M. C. (2011). Outcomes assessment of role-play scenarios for teaching responsible conduct of research. *Accountability in Research*, *18*(4). https://doi.org/10.1080/08989621.2011.584760

Smith, J. R. (2020). Engineering. In *Enciclopaedia Britannica*. https://doi.org/10.1201/9780203966167.ch13

Snow, C. P. (1959). *Las dos culturas y la revolución científica* [The two cultures and the scientific revolution]. Editorial Sur.

Taebi, B., & Kastenberg, W. E. (2019). Teaching engineering ethics to PhD students: A Berkeley–Delft initiative: Commentary on "Ethics Across the Curriculum: Prospects for broader (and deeper) teaching and learning in research and engineering ethics." *Science and Engineering Ethics*, *25*(6), 1763–1770. https://doi.org/10.1007/s11948-016-9809-7

Thiel, C. E., Bagdasarov, Z., Harkrider, L., Johnson, J. F., & Mumford, M. D. (2012). Leader ethical decision-making in organizations: Strategies for sensemaking. *Journal of Business Ethics*, *107*(1), 49–64. https://doi.org/10.1007/s10551-012-1299-1

Véliz, C. (2020). *Privacy is power. Why and how you should take back control of your data*. Penguin Books.

Ventura, J. (2003). Accreditation criteria for engineering programs—Implementing EC-2000 criteria. *ASEE Annual Conference Proceedings*, 3911–3918.

Walesh, S. G. (2012). *Engineering your future: The professional practice of engineering* (3rd ed.). American Society of Civil Engineers. https://doi.org/10.1002/9781118160459

Weber, M. (1919). *Wissenschaft als Beruf. Politik als Beruf* [Science as vocation. Politics as vocation]. J.C.B. Mohr.

Werhane, P. H., Hartman, L. Archer, C. Englehardt, E. E., & Pritchard, M. (2010). *Obstacles to ethical decision-making: Mental models, Milgram and the problem of obedience*. Cambridge: Cambridge University Press.

CHAPTER 5

URBAN PLANNING ETHICS

Teaching a Practice of Hope

Jeffrey K. H. Chan
Singapore University of Technology and Design

Planning has been described as an "organization of hope." Even so, the intensification of environmental and urban challenges today has led many planners to experience frustration, disappointment, and even despair. There is a general perception of powerlessness in the planning profession. What can be done to address this predicament in planning? And how might the practice of ethics produce hope? This chapter discusses professional ethics in planning beyond the frame of professional conduct, and underscores the need to reconsider how to teach this subject for the purpose of imbuing hope. Three different pedagogies for teaching professional ethics in planning are described; (1) broadening the scope of professional ethics; (2) empowering planners by expanding their ethical imagination; and, (3) rendering ethics communicative.

Keywords: Urban Planning; Professional Ethics; Ethics of Hope; Ethical Imagination; Urban Planning Pedagogy

Educating in Ethics Across the Professions: A Compendium of Research, Theory, Practice, and an Agenda for the Future, pages 93–113.

Now, a younger generation doesn't dream, it hopes; it hopes that we will survive, that there will be water for all, that we will be able to feed everyone, that we will not destroy ourselves.

—Dunne and Raby (2013, p. 9)

INTRODUCTION: CONTEMPORARY CHALLENGES OF URBAN PLANNING

Despite their variegated roles in different public or private organizations, planners are committed to the "organization of hope" (Baum, 1997, p. 288; Campbell et al., 2014, p. 45). Hope is the ability to believe the future will be substantively different from—better and freer than—the past (Rorty, 1999, p. 120). To translate belief into reality, hope has to be organized and shaped through planning with others (Inch et al., 2020), where planners and stakeholders envision and lay out new possibilities and make changes that can promote justice (Forester et al., 2008, pp. 537–538). Especially for the economically and socially marginalized and vulnerable, the institution of planning may be the last "organization of hope" that they can count on to improve their lives. Even if in a limited way, planning can shape more beneficent or virtuous institutions that in turn lead to more just outcomes for many people.

Improving the lives of people through planning has become urgent. By one estimate, the global population will be urbanized by 2090 (Batty, 2018, p. 26). Beyond the immediate need to provide affordable and sanitary housing to the billions who are projected to dwell in cities, planners also have to wrestle with the environmental cost of urbanization. The usual focus of planners is land-use within city limits will have to expand accordingly—and quickly—to include regional arable lands, forested areas, and other key ecosystems that support the urban environment (Rees, 2018, p. 57). How to limit the environmental impacts of cities while protecting the ecological capacities of the natural environment, or finding new ways for the city to accommodate and collaborate with nature, will be vital for better changes by planning (Beauregard, 2018, p. 61).

In tandem, planners are increasingly practicing in what Rydin (2013) describes as growth-dependent cities: Cities that rely on economic growth as the sole driver of urban change and prioritize economic growth at the expense of neglecting other equally important developments, for example, the urban commons that may be low in economic value but generate high social values (Petrescu & Petcou, 2019). When planners work with the real-estate market to drive urban change (Stein, 2019), visions for what count as improvements are severely constricted. One unintentional consequences is the reinforcement of urban inequities (Marcuse, 1976; Marcuse, 2014, p. 16). While planners today need to make improvements, they have to question present approaches for making these changes and ask exactly for whom these changes are in fact improvements. The COVID-19 pandemic has further compounded these challenges by overturning a great many planning precepts overnight. The assumptions behind planning that guide how and where people live, work, play, and move about in cities will require a systematic rethinking in the post-pandemic age (Batty, 2020).

Against these challenges and more, one might think with Hoch that planners will "make plans to respond to (these) situations" (2009, p. 227). While plans are surely being made in many places to ensure greater sustainability and equity in post-pandemic cities, plans are nevertheless made amid an eroding morale in the profession of planning that, even before the pandemic, has been characterized by frustration, disappointment, and even despair (Taşan-Kok & Oranje, 2018a, p. 1). Especially for public planners, frustrations and disappointments arise from the contradictory pressures of aligning to the goals of the growth-dependent city while addressing the different problems caused by this approach—for instance, problems of congestion, pollution, or the availability of affordable housing—that the market is neither interested nor able to solve (Hoch, 1994, p. 8). At the same time, planners are expected to be technical experts within a bureaucratic environment; despite this expectation, public planners remain committed to fight for the citizens' rights to the city by ensuring greater equity and access to urban resources (Taşan-Kok et al., 2016, p. 623). Despair can descend swiftly upon planners when they realize they neither have the tools nor the power to do all that is good and, at the same time, be blamed for their inability to make the improvements they deem necessary (Beauregard, 2020, p. 78).

PLANNING ETHICS IN PROFESSIONAL PRACTICE

Caught between conflicting interests and obligations amid a rapidly changing and uncertain environment of planning, ethical dilemmas arise. Many different types of dilemmas arise in planning, from relying on pragmatically effective but unethical expedients to the more quotidian concern of ensuring true and accurate information (Brooks, 2002, pp. 70–72). Another common ethical conflict arises from the dilemma of identifying with either the community served or aligning with the local authority interest (Thomas & Healey, 1991, p. 181). Other dilemmas include the conflict between personal and professional values as well as upholding professional or scientific recommendations under political pressure (Lauria & Long, 2019, p. 402; Wachs, 1989). When certified planners in the United States (US) were confronted with these dilemmas, they acknowledged the influence of the Code of Ethics of the American Institute of Certified Planners (AICP), but they did not consciously consider it during the decision-making process (Lauria & Long, 2019, p. 400). They confronted pressures to ignore the AICP Code due to concerns regarding job security (p. 402).

Despite the lack of a unified public interest, planners are nevertheless still guided by what they deem to be in the interest of the city and its residents as an organic entity (Beauregard, 2020, p. 69). However, value pluralism and cultural diversity often render this organic sense of public interest elusive, which in turn can accentuate ethical conflict. Planners must ask whose value they prioritize in a democratic polity, and why, for example, which principle or ethical judgment promotes equity and justice? Sandercock (2000) delineates the conundrum of planners practicing in culturally diverse cities. On one hand, they are motivated to reconcile differences to improve solidarity. But on the other hand, they are also required to recognize these differences and respect different spatial needs. A fair recognition of cultural differences should lead not to the equality of treatment for all but to different treatments based upon particular difference and cultural need (Agyeman & Erickson, 2012, p. 362). Yet, discerning when to maintain equity and when to seek differential treatment requires ethical judgment (Campbell, 2006).

Should democratic political values then guide ethical judgment (Beauregard, 2020, p. 74)—values such as equity and justice that presumably, even a pluralist public would endorse? Hardly, because even reasonable individuals can have different notion of what equity means and they may rely upon arguments of fairness to advance their special interests (Brand, 2015, p. 254). Instead, political pluralism all but guarantees that there will be different interpretations of what appears to be incontestable values (McAuliffe & Rogers, 2019, p. 304). And while the AICP Code broadly suggests a need to consider the rights of others, concern for long-range consequences and deals fairly and even-handedly—among other considerations—requires planners to exercise independent judgment (Weitz, 2015, p. 2). But little or no guidance, or precise instruction, are provided about how planners are to formulate this judgment.

When confronting complex ethical challenges with no easy answers to the question concerning how to enable ethical judgments in professional practice, planners have little recourse beyond complying to political fiat (or norms) (Flyvbjerg, 2002). Moreover, without a commitment to foster the knowledge that undergirds ethical judgment, frustration, disappointment, and even despair become increasingly likely in the profession. One possible redress is to promote the teaching of urban planning ethics, which then offers the hope of future planners to make ethical judgments.

AIMS, CONTRIBUTIONS, QUESTIONS, AND THE ORGANIZATION OF THIS CHAPTER

The overall aim of this chapter is to consider how to advance the teaching of urban planning ethics *as ethical*. This chapter continues an established line of study in planning ethics, which began with a focus upon "professional ethics" in the 1970s and evolved into "ethics in planning" in the 1980s, before culminating into a broader conception of "planning ethics" in the 1990s (Wachs, 1995, p. xiii). Subsequently, Hendler (2002) updated "planning ethics," which is comprised of the ethics of everyday (professional) behavior, the ethics of administrative discretion, the ethics of plans and policies, the ethics of planning techniques, and the ethics of (normative) planning theory. This expansive development of planning ethics notwithstanding, this chapter argues for the need to revisit professional ethics in planning while anticipating that present and future planners will confront ethical issues on the critical frontlines of professional practice, but courses devoted to ethics in planning schools are "uncommon" (see Kaufman, 1993, p. 107). Furthermore, growing evidence indicates that professional ethics, either applied in the workplace or taught in schools, is not keeping up with challenges planners confront, whether in the U.S. (Lauria & Long, 2019, p. 402) or generally elsewhere in the world (Taşan-Kok & Oranje, 2018b, p. 309). Ineluctably, the question, "What should professional ethics (in planning) comprise?," has lost neither its relevance nor urgency (Verma, 1996, p. 449).

In revisiting professional ethics in planning, this chapter presses beyond this history in the attempt to bring to bear the theoretical resources of contemporary planning ethics to advance professional ethics in planning which, in turn raises the question of what and how to teach the planner. This chapter is organized to address two questions: How can professional ethics be constituted to produce hope? And, how may one teach this approach to ethics to students in planning studies?

Professional ethics in planning has largely revolved around the question of "What ought I do?" (Brooks, 2002, p. 68). A certified planner in the U.S., for instance, will review the AICP Code, especially taking note of what should not be done, before addressing an ethical dilemma in professional practice. This planner will subsequently evaluate the gap—if any—between the situation and what the Code stipulates ideally comes close to what Rawls calls a "reflective equilibrium" (1999, p. 18). In this process, the planner goes back and forth between the Code's stipulations and the ethical demands of the situation until she has defined some convergences between the Code and these ethical demands (Beatley, 1994, p. 29). In this state of reflective equilibrium, the planner knows which stipulation has shaped her judgment and, conversely, how her judgment has been revised to meet the Code's stipulations. This is a process where planners "would try to test their prospective decision against some set of moral standards before deciding what to do" (Kaufman, 1993, p. 112).

At least for planning, this focus upon "What ought I do?" is necessary but not sufficient. This is because the question "What may I hope?" is equally critical for planners (Kant, 1992, p. 538). Planning is projective, only undertaken in the hope of ameliorating the human condition. In this way, planners produce plans characterized by what Pieper calls the "not yet"—plans that simultaneously encapsulate the absence of realization and an orientation toward fulfilment (1997, p. 93). Invariably, plans encapsulate steps to be taken toward their fulfilment; they presume the hope of realization. Conceived this way, the question "What ought I do?" is inseparable from "What may I hope?" in planning. This connection does not point merely to the integrity between means and ends, seen for instance where planners cannot hope to attain the ends (or goals) of a fair and just city when they engage in unjust means for doing so. Instead, this also concerns how hope can begin to engender conviction as well as how conviction in practice shapes action. This is reflected when a planner creates a plan that encapsulate her objects of hope and then takes successive steps to realize these hopes. Restating planning ethics this way—connecting professional hope and practical action—changes the horizon in which planning can be taught and practiced.

What then may count as a professional ethics in this practice of hope? Three suggestions for rethinking professional ethics in planning will be explicated later, but are briefly outlined here. First, the need to broaden the scope of professional ethics in planning. Notably, professional ethics in planning has been observed to comprise of at least two primary bodies of knowledge: that which revolves around the peculiar ethical problems of city and regional planning—for instance, when planning interventions that benefit certain groups end up exacerbating structural injustice for others—and that which concerns professional conduct common in all public and policy fields, such as issues of corruption and whistle-blowing (Howe, 1990, p. 125). The latter, which is concerned with the "narrower questions of professional conduct," has been emphasized (Beatley, 1994, p. 8). In formulating ethical planning as a practice of hope, there is also a need to focus upon the former. As Taşan-Kok and Oranje (2018a) observe, the ethical challenges planners encounter in practice, when allowed to fester, can exacerbate helplessness and corrode their self-respect. Mapping and then addressing these peculiar ethical challenges represents a positive step toward redressing the frustration and even despair observed in professional practice. Instead of framing these peculiar ethical challenges as hindrances to ethical practice, they become targets for amelioration, which is constitutive to planning as a practice of hope.

Second, this professional ethics should allow planners to do more, rather than less. Ethics is aspirational (Damon & Colby, 2015, p. 56), which can trigger the planner's imagination to envision new possibilities and responsibilities. Instead of burdening the planner or causing emotional distress due to cognitive dissonance, this professional ethics should enable planners to become "more adept at systematically analyzing difficult situations, addressing the moral content of competing claims, and arriving at sounder and more defensible bases for informed ethical judgments" (Lang & Hendler, 1990, pp. 56–57). Professional ethics informs the planner what he or she should not do, but it should also and, in tandem, inspire this planner to do more, and better. In other words, professional ethics should be developed to expand the ethical imagination in order to empower planners in new ways.

And third, as a body of knowledge that presumes a broader consideration of others and their interests, professional ethics provide a platform for communicating with different publics—provoking new debates and enlarging the appreciation of the impacts of urban planning (Healey, 2012, p. 70). If the important ideals of planning—planning for a more liveable, fairer, and healthier city cannot be achieved though physical (or spatial) planning alone (Albrechts, 2018, p. 287)—must also depend upon cooperation and behavioral change on the part of the citizens as well, then the democratic task of convincing different people and recruiting them to the cause of planners becomes paramount for successful planning (Taşan-Kok et al., 2016, p. 631). Convincing people how and why an urban planning project can benefit them not only takes the persuasion of projective benefits and possibilities, but also requires the capability of mending ethical divides and conflicts.

What planners do and how planning is a normative practice will be subsequently discussed. Next, the discussion will summarize the current state of ethics in planning. Drawing from the seminal framework of Wachs (1985) and Hendler (2001), the discussion will survey some more recent contributions in planning ethics. This summative discussion identifies gaps and openings that constitute the background to discuss how to teach professional ethics.

WHAT PLANNERS DO (AND WHERE
AND HOW THEY DO THIS)

"What do planners do?" is not a straightforward question if only because planning comprises of a diversity of specializations and activities conducted in different spheres of professional practice (Sungu-Eryilmaz, 2018, p. 132). Planners today no longer work exclusively in the municipal bureaucracy, but also practice in various non-profits overseeing a diverse range of urban concerns in both public and private sector (Friedmann, 2011, p. 144). In one study, American planners were found to be employed as designers and research analysts as well as program and project managers overseeing different scales and sectors of the city—from economic development to community planning to environmental planning (Sungu-Eryilmaz, 2018, p. 128).

At least three attributes identify what planners do. First and foremost, planners make plans: they produce reports, pictures, and visions of future landscapes, and in doing so, shape attention; they do this by persuading the different stakeholders of these plans and mediating between them by listening and negotiating with them (Hoch, 1994, p. 108). At least for urban planners, they generally do not make or implement the objects and spaces that they plan (Beauregard, 2015, p. 7). Instead, they produce proposals and reports of these objects and spaces on behalf of the different public interests that are undergirded by a shared interest for better ways of living in the city. Nevertheless, these plans redistribute social costs and benefits albeit unevenly (Beatley, 1994, p. 87). How to ensure equity between those who gain and those who lose due to these plans remains a constant challenge for planners.

Second, planners deliberate, analyze, and reflect upon the consequences of their plans before acting on them. Rationality—the anticipation of consequences of contemplated action (Protzen & Harris, 2010, p. 153)—and orderliness—the orderly functioning of cities and regions (Beauregard, 2015, p. 27)—characterize the planning activity. To facilitate planning, planners rely upon Geographic Information System (GIS), scale models, census data, neighborhood surveys to craft and support their proposals (p. 29). In doing this, planners converge the introspective and the empirical and focus upon the context of the real sites and places (p. 11). Even so, techniques and methods of planning often generate data and insights that can violate privacy or the right to be free from manipulation (Lo Piccolo & Thomas, 2008). How to ensure safety and minimal risk, both during planning and when plans are implemented, represents another challenge for planners.

Third, the practice of planning first presumes but then also creates choices (Beauregard, 2015, p. 26). After all, to plan is to offer different choices regarding how to act. These choices represent different kinds of hope for the future. Choosing *which future that one hopes for*—jointly with others alongside their counsels as well as cacophonies and conflicts—remains a hallmark of urban planning in liberal democracies (Hoch, 2009, p. 223). Nevertheless, making a choice for the future tends to foreclose other choices. How should planners justify selecting any particular future while foreclosing others? In sum, these considerations make planning a normative practice. What planners do involves carefully weighing a variety of ethical considerations.

THE STATE OF PLANNING ETHICS: A CHRONOLOGICAL SUMMARY

About two decades ago, a long-time researcher and teacher of planning ethics, Sue Hendler (1960–2009) wrote: "Every year I teach a planning ethics course, and every year I search for new course materials. There hasn't been much to choose from" (2002, p. 9). Unfortunately, this state of affairs has hardly changed (Campbell, 2012, p. 381).

The consensus is that planning ethics began formally with the publication of Marcuse's (1976) seminal article, "Professional ethics and beyond: Values in planning" (Hendler, 1995, p. xvii), which called for the rediscovery of planning's reformist roots amid the intensification of planning as a rational, scientific, and technocratic discipline (Klosterman, 1978, p. 38; Rittel & Webber, 1973, p. 162–163). During this period, planners were recognized not only as technical experts preoccupied with the rigor of their scientific methods and techniques, but also as practitioners who must consider the normative goals of planning (Klosterman, 1978). In recognizing this dilemma, planners needed to question what they were doing and whose interest they actually served, and in their practice, to aim to improve the status quo instead of maintaining it. Significant follow-up research in this period included Howe and Kaufman's (1979) first systematic and empirical study of the ethics of contemporary American planners as well as Kaufman's (1981) systematic reflection about how to teach planning ethics.

Subsequently, this awareness of the normative underpinnings of planning activities evolved into a more systematic appreciation of "ethics in planning." This evolution observed in the publication of Wachs's (1985) anthology comprising of contributions not only from within the discipline of city and regional planning, but also and significantly with contributions from outside the discipline by well-known moral philosophers and public administration experts. Wachs's contributions to the development of planning ethics are twofold. First, his anthology is the earliest book-length recognition that planning ethics could benefit from a multidisciplinary study. The anthology recognizes ethical issues peculiar to the discipline of city and regional planning; at the same time, it also recognizes expertise from other disciplines can contribute to expanding the horizon of ethics in planning. Second, when summarizing the multidisciplinary nature of "ethics in planning," Wachs created four systematic different sub-areas to facilitate further work in this domain: "the ethics of everyday behavior," "the ethics of administrative discretion," "the ethics of planning techniques," and finally, "the ethics of plans and policies." The significance of these contributions cannot be overstated. For almost four decades, these sub-areas have organized teaching and research in planning ethics, and they still remain canonical and current to this day.

One decade later, Hendler (1995) offered a subsequent update by reformulating "ethics in planning" to "planning ethics." Like Wachs (1985), her anthology also comprises different perspectives and voices regarding planning ethics. But unlike Wachs's multidisciplinary orientation, Hendler's anthology appears to have turned inward with most, if not all of the contributions coming from researchers or practitioners from the discipline of city and regional planning, which could be read as the first sign of a nascent domain securing a more confident foothold within the discipline of city and regional planning; just as likely, it could be reflective of an incipient specialization and consolidation of planning ethics. Whatever the case, nearly a third of this anthology is dedicated to ethics in planning education. Hendler's (2001, 2002) subsequent updates to planning ethics included a fifth sub-area, "the ethics of (normative) planning theory," which concerns normative theories that can guide ethical planning practice and research.

Since Wachs (1985) and Hendler (1995), there has been no systematic update of planning ethics. Campbell's (2006) later work in situated ethical judgment has introduced the virtue of justice into planning ethics. Even so, the present state of planning ethics, despite its vital importance for a rapidly urbanizing world, can be characterized as uneven and perhaps even sporadic. But curiously, interest in matters that once concerned planning ethics has grown in recent years outside of the discipline of city and regional planning. Practitioners and researchers from disciplines as disparate as architecture and urban design (Mostafavi, 2017; Sennett, 2018) as well as policy and urban studies (Barrett et al., 2021; Chan, 2019) have tilled the fertile intersection between the city and ethics. Observing the ethical challenges of a rapidly urbanizing world, interest in matters concerning planning ethics is not anticipated to wane, and will likely grow from this point forward.

At this point, three salient trends of research in contemporary planning ethics can be observed: research regarding professional ethics; the need for pedagogical research in teaching planning ethics; and, normative planning theory. Each trend will be briefly discussed here.

First, ever since Howe and Kaufman's (1979) study of the ethics of American planners, a sustained line of empirical studies—notably focused upon American planners—has been undertaken. In recent years, this line has taken the form of a professional guidebook in navigating the ethical dilemmas of planning using the AICP Code (Weitz, 2015), a sustained series of empirical investigations into planners' ethics, and the influences and impacts of the AICP Code on planners (Lauria & Long, 2019). Despite the influence of the AICP Code for all U.S. certified planners, some notable gaps have been found. For example, Weitz (2015, p. 4) concedes that not everything that is ethical or unethical can be articulated in rules, and that some "ingenuity and opportunity for critical thinking" (p. 6) should be allowed in the formulation of the planner's ethical judgments. On the other hand, Lauria and Long's study suggests the AICP Code should be revised to make it more relevant, applicable, and useful for the practitioners. Planners were found to have ignored, if not also eschewed, the Code for reasons of job security (2019, p. 402). Planners were also found to confront the prospect of political retribution if they chose *not* to ignore the Code (p. 403). If these findings are generalizable, then the culture of some planning organizations in both the public and private sector can be inferred to be opposed to ethical conduct. This troubling possibility is supported by the findings of Taşan-Kok and Oranje (2018a), which documented the helplessness and frustration of young planners as they confronted ethical disjointedness and even betrayal when the realities of power relations in professional practice arose.

Second, how to teach ethics has been an area of perennial concern since the inception of planning ethics (Kaufman, 1981). Similar to many other professions, planners view education as the formative phase of professionalization, where learning about ethics is integral for future professional accountability and competency. The role of ethics was further ratified in 1989 when the Planning Accreditation Board (PAB)—which sets criteria and procedures for accrediting graduate level planning programs in the US—elevated ethics to a more prominent place in the curricula of planning programs (Kaufman, 1993, p. 108). Since Kaufman, there have been few publications, if any, that offer systematic guidance about how to teach planning ethics. In the decades since Kaufman's contribution to the pedagogy of planning ethics, only Hoch (1995) and Thomas (2012) come close to thinking about how to teach planning ethics. And, while the most recent contribution by Taşan-Kok and Oranje (2018a) returns to ethical concerns of the young planner, this study is more diagnostic than pedagogical. It reveals a wide chasm separating the ethical knowledge that young planners learned in school and the kind of ethical realities that arise in practice (see Oranje et al., 2018, p. 82). Howeverr, this valuable study did not offer practical guidance about how to teach ethics beyond recommending a closer and tighter connection between education and practice (Taşan-Kok & Oranje, 2018b, pp. 302–306).

Another related approach for teaching ethics in planning is service-learning, which attempts to integrate meaningful community service with instruction and reflection so that students, as well as those they serve, are transformed (Angotti et al., 2011, p. 2). Even so, systematic knowledge of planning ethics is not an explicit goal of service-learning and teaching, and while students may contribute to transformative improvements in the communities where they serve, they still may not know the underlying ethical principles that drive these improvements. Controversies surrounding which improvement to prioritize can become intractable. Should systematic knowledge in planning ethics matter here? To resolve many of these intractable controversies, Rein and Schön (1994) argue that it is necessary to reframe them or to question the underlying structures of belief, perception, and appreciation behind these controversies. In turn, reframing presupposes reflecting-in-action, where the planner, among other know-how, relies on knowledge of ethical principles and frames to clarify these controversies (p. 37). In other words, community service-learning can complement planning ethics, but it is no substitute for systematic education in planning ethics.

Therefore, when it comes to teaching ethics in planning education, much work remains to be done. While a professional training guidebook such as Weitz's (2015) could be used as a stop-gap measure, it cannot substitute for the invention of formative and creative pedagogies designed to teach ethics in the classroom as Kaufman (1993) detailed. And while service-learning can immerse students in communities where improvements can be made, it is not a substitute for systematic instruction in planning ethics. How to activate students' ethical compasses, expand their ethical imagination and awareness, and prepare them for an ethically charged practice through the gradual familiarization of real dilemmas encountered in practice, remain an urgent agenda for pedagogical research in planning ethics.

Lastly, at least since Howe (1990), what planners define as ethical issues is shaped by their choices of which normative moral theory to adopt. In other words, these theories not only define how to decide upon what is good and right in planning, but they also influence ways of reasoning and justifying ethical choices. Acknowledging this normative dimension in any pluralistic society also means that different stakeholders are likely to rely upon their preferred ethical theories—formal or otherwise—to define and appraise planning issues. In turn, the absence of any universalist normative theory for planning is likely to leave ethical considerations relative to the way they have been defined (Campbell & Marshall, 1999, p. 472).

What or who then is to arbitrate "the ethics of ethics" (Hösle, 2004, p. 80)? Two different approaches have been conceived to address this question. In one approach, planners need to go deeper into meta-ethics: To consider the nature and meaning of value-based judgments that planners employ (Winkler & Duminy, 2016, p. 112). Another approach suggests that there is no rational way for securing ethical agreements today (MacIntyre, 2007, p. 6). The historical context or the local situation appears to shape ideas regarding what planners consider right and wrong (McClymont, 2019, p. 294). Even so, there appears no unanimous way of securing ethical agreements despite the recognition that normativity matters. The fractious reality of conflicting ethical tenets observed in any pluralistic society then marks normative theory as a relevant and pressing topic for planning ethics.

The next section offers three suggestions for rethinking the teaching of professional ethics in planning: (1) broadening the scope of professional ethics in planning; (2) expanding the ethical imagination of students and empowering them with knowledge of ethics; and, (3) rendering ethics communicative. While these suggestions directly underscore the need to innovate in the teaching of planning ethics, they also build upon the emerging trend of professional ethics and normative theory identified earlier in this section.

BROADENING THE SCOPE OF PROFESSIONAL ETHICS

Students usually first encounters professional ethics during their planning studies. Taught either by scholars of planning theory, or increasingly by certified planning practitioners, acquainting students with professional ethics entails at least basic knowledge of the AICP Code (or equivalent outside of the U.S.), methods of applying this knowledge to commonly encountered ethical problems in practice (Weitz, 2015), and ideally, an overview of how discourse of planning ethics has evolved within the broader framework of planning theory.

Beauregard (2020, p. 116) suggests that the future of planning theory "looks bleak" in part due to changing academic expectations in planning studies and a general lack of enthusiasm for planning theory within the planning profession. In turn, this is likely to mean that planning ethics will become increasingly "professionalized" with more attention given to appropriate professional conduct and relatively less scrutiny of the broad but significant ethical issues and problems brought about by the practice of urban planning. In all likelihood, trainers in professional continuing education programs accredited by the AICP will increasingly take on the responsibility of teaching ethics. Therefore, is there a way to concede to the rise of professionalizing planning ethics without committing to its narrower focus?

In planning ethics, both the broader and narrower concerns of ethics matter. However, professional ethics tends to focus upon the narrower questions of professional conduct at the expense of neglecting the peculiar ethical issues of city and regional planning. To formulate this differently, the peculiar issues of planning ethics are usually not encountered in the same space as issues of professional conduct. For instance, focusing upon how to handle a disagreement or conflict with one's supervisor is a typical, but important, aspect of professional conduct (Weitz, 2015, pp. 9–10). But when this ethically significant scenario is abstracted into a checklist "what to do" and "what not to do," planners tend to miss out on the significance of peculiar ethical conflicts in planning.

For example, how should a planner deal with a disagreement if structural injustice constitutes the pivot of conflict with her supervisor? As Beauregard noted, structural injustice refers to the systemic social processes that discriminate against certain groups by subjecting them to conditions of dominance and deprivation while enabling other groups to enjoy a wide range of life-enhancing opportunities and resources (2018, p. 161). Some form of structural injustice is usually endemic in the background of every planner's practice amid non-ideal conditions. And assuming that the supervisor is sympathetic to those impacted by structural injustice yet thinks, contrary to the planner, this is not a problem requiring intervention but rather, a condition to be accepted. In Hoch's words, the planner perceives an ethical opportunity while her supervisor sees professional risks (1995, p. 294). What should be done?

The AICP Code requires the planner at least to exercise independent judgment while also treating other professionals fairly—including one's supervisor—in thinking about how to proceed. To have experienced disagreement or conflict here already suggests some evidence of independent judgment. But further mastery of the AICP Code offers neither "substantive guidance" beyond knowing exactly which principles are applicable nor does it reveal the nature of this judgment (Beatley, 1994, p. 8).

Without prejudicing an abstract conflict in practice, a planner should align one's actions with one's hopes. If the planner's hope is to address this structural injustice—even if one's interventions are far too meagre to make any significant change—this planner should then refuse the supervisor's view regarding this matter. While almost certainly there will be practical or job-related consequences for doing this, acting commensurate with this hope immediately procures two concrete outcomes. First, the planner will have acted in a way that can prevent the kind of corrosive helplessness Taşan-Kok and Oranje (2018a) document. In other words, this planner will have demonstrated ethical agency by exerting some control over her choices (Damon & Colby, 2015, p. 65). Second, and paraphrasing Beauregard (2015, p. 160), correcting injustice *must be seen to have been done*— even if the attempt may turn out to be consequentially insignificant. This planner will have been seen to have tried to address structural injustice, and this on its own, is consequential. Even when actual actions are insignificant, to be seen doing the right thing can nevertheless focus public and bureaucratic attention, galvanize new convictions, and perhaps also mobilize future actions against structural injustice. After all, how people view planners treat others and how planners *see to the ways people are treated* are central to the growth of any ethically conscious society (Thomas, 2012, p. 404).

In the absence of specific details, it is important not to over-emphasize what exactly the planner ought to do in this situation. Instead, when teaching professional ethics, the more important point entails bringing to light the peculiar ethical challenges of city and regional planning. These peculiar ethical challenges include issues that are specific to urbanization or issues arising from the professional practice of planning. The pedagogical purpose behind bringing these challenges to light is twofold. The primary purpose is to rebalance the present narrower focus upon professional conduct which adds context for reinterpreting the AICP Code. This reinterpretation can improve the resolution in an ethically contentious scenario. The more significant purpose, however, is to accustom students to the wide range of seemingly intractable challenges in their chosen vocation and, in this way, to cultivate their intellectual stamina for these challenges while building their orientation for considering ethical matters at the same time.

Kaufman might refer to this as activating the student's own "ethical compass" (1993, p. 113). But what good is a "compass" if students are unaware of how far they can go and where they want to go, both of which are predicated on their intellectual stamina and ethical orientation? Expanding professional ethics beyond questions of "What ought I do?" to include the peculiar ethical challenges in planning changes the way professional ethics can be taught.

EXPANDING ETHICAL IMAGINATION AND EMPOWERING STUDENTS

There is perhaps no way to avoid the impression that professional ethics has to do with rules, which are stipulations that state what should not be done. This is clearly seen at least in the rules of conduct of the AICP Code, which hold planners legally accountable for any violation. For this reason, professional ethics in planning can appear to restrict more than it can inspire and empower.

But ethics does not consist of only rules in the absence of ideals (Gert, 1998, p. ix), and it is vital to give space to ideals especially when rules are inapplicable or have to be violated for the sake of other important ethical goals. In other words, ideals are closely connected to the ethical imagination that is required to perceive possibilities beyond what rules stipulate. Imagining what is possible becomes more plausible if planners are able to articulate their ideals and when rendering these ideals, new possibilities become present which, in turn, offer new scenarios where ethical exceptions could be made. Providing space to the ideals of planning can counteract the perception that professional ethics is a burden that restricts the scope of discretion or else are abstract ideals that can never be attained in practice and therefore generating dissonance and angst. Weighing in on ethically charged planning situations with ideals can allow a planner to do more, rather than less.

Kaufman is correct to suggest that an important way of stimulating the ethical imagination of students is first and foremost, to become more aware of the ethical dimensions of planning (1993, p. 113). Many contentious planning issues are usually not cast in ethical terms (p. 111). As a matter of fact, "ethics" is a rather uncommon term in the planning literature. More commonly used are terms such as, "fairness," "equity," or "values." But, as Beatley argues, "values" do not immediately translate into "ethics" (1994, p. 18). Instead, deliberation involves making and defending ethical choices, which encapsulate some of these values. For example, a student might intuitively understand that an unfair distribution of benefits by planning is, prima facie, wrong. However, this student is unlikely to articulate in what ways that decision is prima facie wrong or which ethical principles and standards could be used to support her intuitive judgment. In turn, this student cannot articulate under what conditions this decision might be possibly accepted as the right one.

At this point, it is necessary to empower students through ethics, which can liberate their mind to deliberate about possible ethical choices. Students are free when knowledge of ethics simultaneously questions the fetters of their prior ethical assumptions while enabling new choices that can expand the "ethical gaze" when contemplating deep ethical quandaries (Beauregard, 2020, p. 72).

But how might a teacher facilitate this process?

Kaufman argues for the need to equip students with the new language of concepts and frameworks from moral philosophy. With this new language, students can begin making connections between how contentious planning issues are being framed and reported, and why—and in what ways—they are considered ethical issues (1993, p. 111). Another suggestion, which underpins the practice of hope in this chapter, is to bring ethical ideals to bear on the discussion of contentious planning conflicts. Ethical ideals help students visualize the objects of hope in planning and articulating them can further clarify what planners should do. In this process, students find themselves neither at the mercy of what rules proscribe nor at the whims of their social and professional norms. Instead, they can rely upon their imagination to frame and shape new ethical possibilities. In turn, students move from the frame of "rigorous ethical analysis," where the parameters to ethical conflicts are accepted as given, to questioning these parameters through their new frames, which may present the original issue in an entirely different light (Hendler, 2001, p. 11477).

RENDERING ETHICS COMMUNICATIVE

Planning schools are influential in molding their students (Thomas, 2012, p. 402) and are likely to be *the* venue that offer the first, and possibly also the last opportunity where students can "step back" and deliberate about perplexing ethical issues with others. For this reason, planning ethics should be conducted in a classroom climate characterized by free and open dialogue, where all points of view are treated as equally legitimate and worthy of respect (Klosterman, 1995, p. 256). Even so, planning ethics often illuminate controversial issues that sharpen differences between students who attach different weights to ethical principles, or hold diametrically different values and ethical principles from each other (Kaufman, 1993, p. 113). It is the rare class in planning ethics where ethical disagreements are subdued and concord is prized.

When ethical disagreements are respectfully expressed and rigorously debated, tolerance and philosophical intelligence can be synthesized. In fact, to identify genuine areas of ethical disagreement in planning, and further, to understand exactly why students disagree, how their disagreements are justified, and by which standards or principles is a boon both for teachers and the students. However, because this class is likely the last time students will systematically discuss ethical matters before professional practice, to end only with an enlightened understanding of ethical disagreements is not only dissatisfying but also, and more seriously, undermining the communicative promise of ethics. Though laudable for clarifying ethical disagreements, the process of sharpening one's ethical understanding by whetting it against others in the form of witty counterarguments or else trading respectful philosophical barbs, does not equip students with either the skills of bridging value gaps or persuading others of the significance of their values and ethical principles and why they are crucial to the enterprise of planning in a pluralistic society.

The absence of rendering ethics more communicative in the classroom becomes all the more salient when, at least according to the AICP Code, planners ought to aspire to educate the public about planning issues. As a matter of fact, to meet the AICP ethical obligations to "all persons," planners need to cultivate cultural competence in order to recognize, understand, and engage difference, diversity, and cultural as well as ethical heterogeneity in creative and productive ways (Agyeman & Erickson, 2012, p. 358).

This implies not only that a planner should be able to describe the substantive matters of a planning issue to the public but also to explain what ought to be done and why the plans should be implemented. Furthermore, a planner should be able to communicate ethical issues to others who differ. Taken together, these competencies require communicating normative values to stakeholders who are likely to be indifferent or who may even be opposed to the values assumed in these plans. In doing this, the planner is not merely living up to the aspirational AICP Code; rather, she understands the success of a planning project also depends on its reception by other stakeholders who will be impacted by the plan. To achieve the good promised by the plan requires persuading stakeholders to see and consider accepting her point of view (Ley, 1952, p. 201).

How then should the pedagogy of planning ethics be augmented to improve the prospect of communicativeness in ethics? To say the least, the common disposition of "jostling"—which begins to describe how students argue in order to identify and clarify areas of ethical disagreements, or else, the formation of a maieutic process comprised of conflicting viewpoints for the purpose of inducing new ethical insights—is necessary in professional ethics pedagogy. But this mode of "jostling" should not dominate classroom discussions. Instead, the teacher should also cultivate dispositions of "translating" and "bridge-building," especially when "jostling" tries to overpower every discussion on ethical matters in the classroom.

First, "translating" is distinguished from "jostling" by the activity of reformulating ethical propositions and arguments instead of trying to win an argument. The teacher may wish to identify students in the classroom who are clearly following the discussion, but who chose to remain pensive. Cultivating these "translators" begins by prompting them with a question, for instance, "How might one reformulate what has been argued so far such there are fewer distortions yet still reconnect to our objective of not only identifying areas of ethical disagreements, but also the hope of attaining a common ground for advancing on this issue?" The role of "translators" is to first clear the air by reformulating what has been argued through a new perspective, then through the new meanings generated by this perspective, to draw in new participants into the discussion. Constructive translations do not distort the meanings of original arguments; yet, they are able to challenge the biases in these arguments, and in this process, expand the prior horizon of ethical discussions.

Second, "bridge-building" is the activity of identifying new connections that can reconcile opposing arguments. "Bridge-building" is not just mediation to mitigate argumentative conflicts. Instead, it is a creative act: To offer a third argument that can reconcile two diametrically different arguments or to question the common but perhaps erroneous assumptions shared by these opposing arguments. "Bridge-building" does not engage in the assault-and-defence style of "jostling," but rather, builds new connections and pathways always for the purpose of moving ethical discussions from the stalemate of "agreeing to disagree." "Bridge-builders" in the classroom are rare, but the disposition behind "bridge-building" can be invaluable to demonstrate the cooperative, rather than the conflictive, dimension of ethics.

CONCLUSION

In an article that predates early discussions on planning ethics, Fromm posed this fundamental question: "What are the principles that plan our planning?" (1972, p. 68). In this chapter, at least one answer has become clear: These principles are embodied in the decisions, actions, and interactions of planners. These principles are introduced, deliberated, and refined in that short but formative period when students learn about planning ethics before professional practice. Enacting these principles in practice through the frame of ethics produces hope—not only for the planning profession, but also for the cities and societies that planners serve. Acknowledging this approach makes the task of teaching planning ethics all the more critical and urgent—especially before the environmental and urban challenges of the 21st century, which have only been exacerbated by the COVID-19 pandemic.

Nevertheless, anticipating the need to revise professional ethics in planning (Lauria & Long, 2019), this chapter has focused upon advancing professional ethics by teaching it in three different ways that can produce hope. First, the scope of professional ethics can be broadened beyond issues of professional conduct to include the peculiar ethical challenges of city and regional planning. Second, planners can be empowered through the expansion of their ethical imagination, where they are able to do more with students' knowledge of ethics beyond applying ethical rules and codes. And third, to cultivate planners who are not only competent in clarifying and evaluating areas of ethical disagreement but also are capable of mending ethical conflicts and communicating ethical values to stakeholders. Through these propositions, this chapter demonstrates the possibility and importance of beginning to address the frustration, disappointment and even despair that Taşan-Kok and Oranje (2018a) observed by improving ethics pedagogy.

But to accomplish this also presupposes the presence of formative institutions for planning ethics. While there will always be the professional commitment to keep planning practitioners abreast of the state-of-the-art knowledge in ethics, this commitment will be nonetheless undermined if professional attention is singularly devoted to matters of professional code of conduct. As noted earlier in this chapter, many professional perplexities are rooted in deeper social inequities. On the other hand, planning theory—which encompasses planning ethics—is no longer an important focus in most, if not all planning schools (Beauregard, 2020, p. 116). Increasingly deprived of both teachers and students (many of whom will become future practitioners) who can advance planning ethics as a substantive area of focus, ethics is likely not to be prioritized despite its growing relevance and significance for an unequal and precarious world today. Those who teach planning ethics will keep the hope alive if they proceed to reform professional training programs in the direction of a broader notion of planning ethics beyond professional conduct. For students in planning schools who are inspired by hope, they can mobilize themselves to demand a greater curricular commitment to planning ethics beyond the minimum required today. After all, planning ethics is an indispensable source of help in relieving professional perplexities and a vital precondition of social hope.

REFERENCES

Agyeman, J., & Erickson, J.S. (2012). Culture, recognition, and the negotiation of difference: Some thoughts on cultural competency in planning education. *Journal of Planning Education and Research, 32*(3), 358–366.

Albrechts, L. (2018). A quest for a critical debate and new ideas. In T. Taşan-Kok & M. Oranje (Eds.), *From student to planner: Young practitioners' reflections on contemporary ethical challenges* (pp. 287–295). Routledge.

Angotti, T., Doble, C. S., & Horrigan, P. (2011). Introduction. At the boundaries: The shifting sites of service learning in design and planning. In T. Angotti, C. S. Doble, & P. Horrigan (Eds.), *Service-learning in design and planning: Educating at the boundaries* (pp. 1–16). New Village Press.

Barrett, B. F. D., Horne, R., & Fien, J. (2021). *Ethical cities*. Routledge.

Batty, M. (2018). *Inventing future cities*. The MIT Press.

Batty, M. (2020). The Coronavirus crisis: What will the post-pandemic city look like? *Environment & Planning B: Urban Analytics and City Science, 47*(4), 547–552.

Baum, H. S. (1997). *The organization of hope: Communities planning themselves*. SUNY Press.

Beatley, T. (1994). *Ethical land use: Principles of policy and planning*. The John Hopkins University Press.

Beauregard, R. A. (2015). *Planning matter: Acting with things*. The University of Chicago Press.

Beauregard, R. A. (2018). *Cities in the urban age: A dissent*. The University of Chicago Press.

Beauregard, R. A. (2020). *Advanced introduction to planning theory*. Edward Elgar Publishing.

Brand, A. L. (2015). The politics of defining and building equity in the Twenty-First Century. *Journal of Planning Education and Research, 35*(3), 249–264.

Brooks, M. P. (2002). *Planning theory for practitioners*. The American Planning Association.

Campbell, H. (2006). Just planning: The art of situated ethical judgment. *Journal of Planning Education and Research, 26*(1), 92–106.

Campbell, H. (2012). "Planning ethics" and rediscovering the idea of planning. *Planning Theory, 11*(4), 379–399.

Campbell, H., & Marshall, R. (1999). Ethical frameworks and planning theory. *International Journal of Urban and Regional Research, 23*(3), 464–478.

Campbell, H., Tait, M., & Watkins, C. (2014). Is there space for *better* planning in a neoliberal world? Implications for planning practice and theory. *Journal of Planning Education and Research, 34*(1), 45–59.

Chan, J. K. H. (2019). *Urban ethics in the Anthropocene*. Palgrave.

Damon, W., & Colby, A. (2015). *The power of ideals: The real story of moral choices*. Oxford University Press.

Dunne, A., & Raby, F. (2013). *Speculative everything: Design, fiction, and social dreaming*. The MIT Press.

Flyvbjerg, B. (2002). Bringing power to planning research: One researcher's praxis story. *Journal of Planning Education and Research, 21*(4), 353–366.

Forester, J., Reardon, K., Rumbach, A., Bycer, E., & Kasbekar, P. (2008). Introduction: Making a difference in response to Hurricane Katrina Planning, hope, and struggle in the wake of Katrina; Ken Reardon on the New Orleans Planning Initiative Challenges of disaster response, or what the textbooks don't teach us politics, Inspiration and vocation: An education in New Orleans An international student's perceptions of Hurricane Katrina. *Planning Theory & Practice, 9*(4), 517–564.

Friedmann, J. (2011). *Insurgencies: Essays in planning theory*. Routledge.

Fromm, E. (1972). Humanistic planning. *Journal of the American Institute of Planners, 38*(2), 67–71.

Gert, B. (1998). *Morality: Its nature and justification*. Oxford University Press.

Healey, P. (2012). Performing place governance collaboratively: Planning as a communicative process. In F. Fischer & H. Gottweis (Eds.), *The argumentative turn revisited: Public policy as communicative practice* (pp. 58–82). Duke University Press.

Hendler, S. (Ed.). (1995). *Planning Ethics: A reader in planning theory, practice and education*. Center for Urban Policy Research.

Hendler, S. (2001). Planning ethics. In N. J. Smelser & P. B. Baltes (Eds.), *International encyclopedia of the social and behavioral sciences* (pp. 11474–11479). Elsevier.

Hendler, S. (2002). It's the right to do—or is it? Contemporary issues in planning ethics. *Plan Canada, 42*(2), 9–11.

Hoch, C. (1994). *What planners do: Power, politics and persuasion*. The American Planning Association.

Hoch, C. (1995). Teaching ethics and planning theory. In S. Hendler (Ed.), *Planning ethics: A reader in planning theory, practice and education* (pp. 280–300). Center for Urban Policy Research.

Hoch, C. (2009). Planning craft: How planners compose plans. *Planning Theory, 8*(3), 219–241.

Hösle, V. (2004). *Morals and politics. Translated by Steven Randall*. University of Notre Dame Press.

Howe, E. (1990). Normative ethics in planning. *Journal of Planning Literature*, *5*(2), 123–150.

Howe, E., & Kaufman, J. L. (1979). The ethics of contemporary American planners. *Journal of the American Planning Association*, *45*(3), 243–255.

Inch, A., Slade, J., & Crookes, L. (2020). Exploring planning as a technology of hope. *Journal of Planning Education and Research*. https://doi.org/10.1177/0739456X20928400

Kant, I. (1992). *Lectures on logic* (J. M. Young Trans., Ed.). Cambridge University Press.

Kaufman, J. L. (1981). Teaching planning ethics. *Journal of Planning Education and Research*, *1*(1), 29–35.

Kaufman, J. L. (1993). Reflections on teaching three versions of a planning ethics course. *Journal of Planning Education and Research*, *12*(2), 107–115.

Klosterman, R. E. (1978). Foundations for normative planning. *Journal of the American Institute of Planners*, *44*(1), 37–46.

Klosterman, R. E. (1995). Introduction. In S. Hendler (Ed.), *Planning Ethics: A reader in planning theory, practice and education* (pp. 246–260). Center for Urban Policy Research.

Lang, R., & Hendler, S. (1990). Environmental ethics: Ethics and professional planners. In D. Macniven (Ed.), *Moral expertise: Studies in practical and professional ethics* (pp. 52–70). Routledge.

Lauria, M., & Long, M. F. (2017). Planning experience and planners' ethics. *Journal of the American Planning Association*, *83*(2), 202–220.

Lauria, M., & Long, M. F. (2019). Ethical dilemmas in professional planning practice in the United States. *Journal of the American Planning Association*, *85*(4), 393–404.

Leys, W. A. R. (1952). *Ethics for policy decisions: The art of asking deliberative questions.* Prentice-Hall.

Lo Piccolo, F., & Thomas, H. (2008). Research ethics in planning: A framework for discussion. *Planning Theory*, *7*(1), 7–23.

MacIntyre, A. (2007). *After virtue: A study in moral theory* (3rd ed.). University of Notre Dame Press.

Marcuse, P. (1976). Professional ethics and beyond: Values in planning. *Journal of the American Institute of Planners*, *42*(3), 264–274.

Marcuse, P. (2014). A just code of ethics for planners: A priority for Planners Network. *Progressive Planning*, *198*, 16–19.

McAuliffe, C., & Rogers, D. (2019). The politics of value in urban development: Valuing conflict in agonistic pluralism. *Planning Theory*, *18*(3), 300–318.

McClymont, K. (2019). Articulating virtue: Planning ethics within and beyond post politics. *Planning Theory*, *18*(3), 282–299.

Mostafavi, M. (Ed.). (2017). *Ethics of the urban: The city and the spaces of the political.* Lars Muller Publishers.

Oranje, M., Venter, S., & Ferreira, A. (2018). Good intentions, deep frustrations, and upward mobility: Just another young planner's day in South Africa. In T. Taşan-Kok, & M. Oranje (Eds.), *From student to planner: Young practitioners' reflections on contemporary ethical challenges* (pp. 74–87). Routledge.

Petrescu, D., & Petcou, C. (2019). Designing, sustaining and defending resilient urban commons: The story of R-Urban. In S. Bloemen & T. de Groot (Eds.), *Our commons: Political ideas for a new Europe* (pp. 63–69). The Institute of Network Cultures.

Pieper, J. (1997). *Faith, hope, love*. Ignatius Press.

Protzen, J. P., & Harris, D. J. (2010). *The universe of design: Horst Rittel's theories of design and planning*. Routledge.

Rawls, J. (1999). *A theory of justice*. (rev. ed.). Harvard University Press.

Rees, W. E. (2018). Planning in the Anthropocene. In M. Gunder, A. Madanipour, & V. Watson (Eds.), *The Routledge handbook of planning theory* (pp. 53–66). Routledge.

Rein, M., & Schön, D. A. (1994). *Frame reflection: Toward the resolution of intractable policy controversies*. Basic Books.

Rittel, H. W. J., & Webber, M. M. (1973). Dilemmas in a general theory of planning. *Policy Sciences*, *4*(2), 155–169.

Rorty, R. (1999). *Philosophy and social hope*. Penguin.

Rydin, Y. (2013). *The future of planning: Beyond growth dependence*. Policy Press.

Sandercock, L. (2000). When strangers become neighbours: Managing cities of difference. *Planning Theory & Practice*, *1*(1), 13–30.

Sennett, R. (2018). *Building and dwelling: Ethics for the city*. Allen Lane.

Stein, S. (2019). *Capital city: Gentrification and the real estate state*. Verso.

Sungu-Eryilmaz, Y. (2018). In search of a place: Young planners' reflections on planning and practice. In T. Taşan-Kok & M. Oranje (Eds.), *From student to planner: Young practitioners' reflections on contemporary ethical challenges* (pp. 126–136). Routledge.

Taşan-Kok, T., Bertolin, L., Oliveira e Costa, S., Lothan, H., Carvalho, H., Desmet, M., De Blust, S., Devos, T., Kimyon, D., Zoete, J. A., & Ahmad, P. (2016). "Float like a butterfly, sting like a bee": Giving voice to planning practitioners. *Planning Theory & Practice*, *17*(4), 621–651.

Taşan-Kok, T., & Oranje, M. (2018a). Why it is important to give values to young practitioners. In T. Taşan-Kok & M. Oranje (Eds.), *From student to planner: Young practitioners' reflections on contemporary ethical challenges* (pp. 1–11). Routledge.

Taşan-Kok, T., & Oranje, M. (2018b). Editors' reflections and conclusions. In T. Taşan-Kok & M. Oranje (Eds.), *From student to planner: Young practitioners' reflections on contemporary ethical challenges* (pp. 296–311). Routledge.

Thomas, H. (2012). Values and the planning school. *Planning Theory*, *11*(4), 400–417.

Thomas, H., & Healey, P. (1991). Tackling ethical issues. In H. Thomas & P. Healey (Eds.), *Dilemmas of planning practice: Ethics, legitimacy and the validation of knowledge* (pp. 176–185). Avebury Technical.

Verma, N. (1996). Commentary: The systemic nature of professional ethics. In S. J. Mandelbaum, L. Mazza & R. W. Burchell (Eds.), *Explorations in planning theory* (pp. 448–455). Center for Urban Policy Research.

Wachs, M. (Ed.). (1985). *Ethics in planning*. Center for Urban Policy Research.

Wachs, M. (1989). When planners lie with numbers. *Journal of the American Planning Association*, *55*(4), 476–479.

Wachs, M. (1995). Foreword. In S. Hendler (Ed.), *Planning Ethics: A reader in planning theory, practice and education* (pp. xii-xv). Center for Urban Policy Research.

Weitz, J. (2015). *The ethical planning practitioner*. The American Planning Association.

Winkler, T., & Duminy, J. (2016). Planning to change the world? Questioning the normative ethics of planning theories. *Planning Theory*, *15*(2), 111–129.

CHAPTER 6

TEACHING BUSINESS ETHICS IN THE UNITED STATES

Understanding How We Got to Where We Are

Ronald R. Sims
William and Mary

This chapter offers a look at the rich history of teaching business ethics, which includes a number of important issues. The chapter first provides a brief but detailed look at the evolution of teaching business ethics in the U.S. The chapter next discusses those issues (e.g., Can ethics be taught? Who should teach business ethics? The goals of teaching business ethics? How best to teach business ethics? and How to assess the impact of efforts to teach business ethics?). The chapter concludes with a brief discussion regarding several suggestions business ethics eduators must be attentive to in the years to come.

Keywords: History of Teaching Business Ethics, Issues in Teaching Business Ethics

At first sight, it appears the teaching of business ethics has been around a little under 40 years, but in reality it has been around for hundreds and perhaps thousands of years. There is still disagreement about when teaching business ethics actually

Educating in Ethics Across the Professions: A Compendium of Research, Theory, Practice, and an Agenda for the Future, pages 115–137.
Copyright © 2023 by Information Age Publishing
www.infoagepub.com

began, for example, in the United States. In a book about teaching business ethics in various countries, the chapter about the U.S. begins its story in the late 1970s (Mahoney, 1990, p. 23). Further, Benson (1982) asserted that "when American business schools were started in the early twentieth century, curiously little was said about business ethics" (p. 22). In contrast to such views, Daniel (1998) notes that "ethics courses were attempted, however briefly" at Harvard in 1916 and New York University in 1919, when "some prominent articles advocating ethics in the business curriculum appeared during this time" (p. 73, 272). Khurana argued that business school deans in the early twentieth century struggled with the problem of "how to teach business ethics" (2007, p. 188; see also Abend, 2013). Khurana suggested that the first attempt at formal, academic discussion of business ethics in the United States began with the introduction of business schools in the late 1800s and early 1900s. Despite what may seem to be a lack of agreement about when teaching business ethics began in the U.S., there is sufficient evidence a focus upon teaching business ethics and hotly debated issues concerning it began with the establishment of the very first business school.

This chapter first looks at the history of teaching business ethics. Next, the focus turns to the issues in teaching business ethics debated over the years. The chapter concludes with a discussion of an agenda for the future offering some food for thought for those who teach and will be teaching business ethics.

TEACHING BUSINESS ETHICS: FROM THE BEGINNING TO NOW

Despite the existing critics of teaching of business ethics in the late nineteenth and early twentieth centuries, some scholars suggested that one way for advocates of business schools to strengthen their case that business should be (and could be) taught, was to link it to moral and social objectives as well as "service to society" (Abend, 2008, pp. 139–151). For example, Joseph Wharton's 1881 "Plan of the Wharton School of Finance and Economy"—the nation's first business school—stated:

> The general tendency of instruction should be such as to inculcate and impress upon students…[t]he immorality and practical inexpediency of seeking to acquire wealth by winning it from another rather than by earning it through some sort of service to one's fellow-men. (Education of Business Men, 1891, p. 33)

1900–1920

In 1903, the *Wall Street Journal* summarized this expectation: Business schools' "highest use will be, first, in the training of the consciences of their students in habits of spontaneous morality." Such schools were needed because "[w]e want a race of young men who have been trained in the idea that success is not the only test by which life shall be judged." Thus, business schools would instill ethics into business, make students aware of their obligations, and advance "the highest ideals of truth and honesty" (*Wall Street Journal*, 1903, p.1; see Abend, 2013). In short, there was an expectation during the founding of business schools that they had a responsibility to teach students business ethics, and several schools quickly put some time into doing so.

Depending upon the research or perspectives of various scholars, there were numerous examples of efforts to teach business ethics with the creation of new business schools in the late nineteenth and early twenty century. For example, the University of California's College of Commerce launched the "Barbara Weinstock Lectureship on the Morals of Trade" in 1904. Per the University of California's Register, Harris Weinstock, a prosperous retailer in Sacramento, California, created the lectureship on May 14, 1902, with an endowment of $5000. Its purpose was to be the education of young men "to the belief that success in business is more probably and more lasting if conducted upon a high ethical plane, and that true success lies in developing character rather than in heaping up gold" (Abend, 2013, p. 179). The lecture was part of the regular courses of instruction (University of California, 1904, pp. 103–104; University of California, 1915, p. 159).

Weinstock saw a direct relationship between knowledge and ethics, and believed the moral progress of business could be furthered "by inviting the best thoughts of some of the country's best minds on the subject of The Morals of Trade" (p. vi). The Weinstock lectures were intended not only for University of California students or students of its College of Commerce but also "the many already engaged in business who have not had the benefit of a college training" (Abend, 2013, p. 180; University of California, 1907).

As early as 1905 New York University (NYU) offered a "special course of lectures on business ethics" concerning subjects such as "Morality in Wall Street" and "Commercial Morality: A Study of Certain of the Conditions and Influence by which it is determined" (*Wall Street Journal*, p. 5). In 1908, the Sheffield Scientific School at Yale University offered a series of lectures on business ethics, called the "Page Lecture Series," which included chapters about the ethics of production, competition, credit and banking, public service, as well as corporate and other trusts (Sheffield Scientific School, 1910). Subsequent lectures included Industry and Progress (1911), Trade-Morals (1914), and Ethics in Service (1915) (Abend, 2013). Senior students received instruction in "Commercial Ethics," a course of five lectures (the Page lectures) which dealt with "the ethical side of business life, and were given by "men of experience" in mercantile, financial, and legal pursuits" according to the 1914–1915 *Catalogue of Yale University* (Yale University, 1914, p. 354).

In 1912–1913, NYU offered "a specific course in Business Ethics" and hired a "Professor of Business Ethics"—the Episcopal minister Lyman Powell (see Bond, 1915; Powell, 1925). At Harvard University, the preceding Dean Edwin Gay and Arch Shaw co-taught a course titled "Social Factors in Business Enterprise" from 1915 to 1916.

1920s

In 1928, Wallace B. Donham, Dean of Harvard University's business school from 1919 to 1942, instituted a "Professorship of Business Ethics" in 1928 (Abend, 2016; Copeland, 1958). Donham introduced a course titled "Business Ethics" and hired an "Assistant Professor of Business Ethics" (Piper et al., 1993). In reality, this idea was not new. Around the same time, the University of Chicago and the University of Wisconsin offered classes about business ethics (Reed, 1916; Tufts, 1919). "(T)he logic of the situation is irresistible" Powell (1913) forecasted in 1912, adding "(w)ithin the next five years every important university in the United States will have established a department of business ethics" (p. 8). Powell's forecast notwithstanding, in 1925–1926 out of 38 members of the American Association of Collegiate Schools of Business (AACSB) only seven universities (e.g., Boston University, Chicago, North Carolina, Indiana, Northwestern, Kansas, and Stanford) required a course in "social control, including ethics" (Heilman et al., 1928). In reality, "a number of schools did develop formal instruction about the ethical aspects of business conduct which (varied) from a few lectures to a fully developed course" (Bossard & Dewhurst, 1931, p. 410).

Besides classes and lectures, several high-status business schools and the AACSB emphasized the significance of ethics and social responsibility. At Michigan, for example, one "objective (was) to emphasize to the student, and incidentally to the business community at large, the social function of the business administrator" (Griffin, 1928, p.161). According to a 1920s survey titled, "Collegiate Education in Business," more than 85 percent of business school deans, faculty, and university presidents said that "introducing persons with a social point of view into business" was one of the "appropriate aims or purposes of collegiate education for business" (Heilman et al., 1928, p. 31). For some, this was the very point of a business school, its *raison d'etre*" (Heilman, 1930, p. 21) by which business schools could "justify themselves as serviceable and necessary parts of our general scheme of publication education" (Wooster, 1919, p. 53). With this in mind, Abend (2016) asks the important question: "Else, why should business be taught at universities, alongside philosophy, physics, theology, and medicine" (p. 57)?

In the late 1920s and in response to a gift from the William A. Vawter Foundation, Northwestern University's School of Commerce set out to establish a lectureship in business ethics. The series of lectures would focus on various phases of business ethics (Northwestern University Alumni News, 1928). It would be the first attempt on the part of any school of commerce to include business ethics as part of its curriculum. The subject of the 1929 Vawter lectures was the ethical problems of modern finance. The lectures were delivered by several "men eminent in education and banking" (*Bankers Magazine,* 1930, p. 796). These lectures continued up through 1936 (Abend, 2013).

Efforts to teach business ethics to students in the U.S. in the first decades of the twentieth century were driven by the belief that business schools (and universities) could and should exert a positive influence on educating people. Abend

(2013) has suggested business education advocates and leaders typically did not present ethics as being an incidental afterthought, an add-on to the core features and business school objectives. Instead, moral and social objectives gave business schools *raison d'etre*; that was one of the main reasons given to explain why there should be business schools at universities at all.

1950s

Prior to the development of business ethics as an area of inquiry and pedagogy, individual courses concerning moral issues in business, as well as lectures and articles about ethics in business appeared here and there. Bishop (1992) and Paul (1987) noted that efforts in the 1950s by the Ford and Carnegie Foundations and the AACSB focused upon evaluating business school curricula and their role in addressing the need for a shared set of values in the business community.

1960s

The many social unrest movements in the U.S. during the 1960s and 1970s led to attacks on business and accompanying responses from business (DeGeorge, 1982). The 1960s saw the introduction in business schools of courses in social issues in management and corporate social responsibility. However, these were largely *ad hoc* and even if at the forefront of the academic movement, their direction lacked a cohesive approach. According to Baghdadi, "In response to the growing importance of business's commitment to its "social responsibility business ethics courses were added to the curricular of many colleges and universities forsaking their former esoteric course offerings of theoretical ethics of Plato, Aristotle and other noted forefathers of philosophical theorems of ethical behavior" (n.d., p. 4).

1970s

The 1970s saw business ethics emerging as a field of academic inquiry, with a few business ethics courses being taught (DeGeorge, 2007). With a grant from the National Endowment for the Humanities, Norman Bowie chaired a committee in the late 1970s to develop a model curriculum for business-ethics courses. About the same time, Richard DeGeorge developed a course in business ethics and circulated a 90-page course curriculum to 900 interested professors in business schools and philosophy departments. In 1979, the first texts in business ethics appeared (for example, Bowie's *Ethical Theory and Business* (1979) and Donaldson and Werhane's, *Ethical Issues in Business: A Philosophical Perspective* (1979)). The books found a ready market, and courses were introduced in philosophy departments and business schools. Competing texts and courses increased rapidly (DeGeorge, 1982).

In the 1970s, teaching and research regarding business ethics were being influenced by philosophers who developed the macro/normative foundations for business ethics. A number of business professors were also developing micro/ descriptive research to understand organizational ethics (Ferrell & Ferrell, n.d.). Ethical decision-making models evolved from research that linked normative and descriptive models, and these increasingly found their way into efforts to teach business ethics. DeGeorge notes that "Many of the philosophers who were especially active in starting the field moved into distinguished chairs in business schools, usually in departments of management and slowly gave way to empiricists in the social sciences" (1982, p. 352). Additionally, an increasing number of business professors began writing about the criticality of adopting a policy of ethical behavior in the commercial business arena. During the early 1970s, the discussions and decisions to include business ethics in a curriculum was still being debated (Baghdadi, n.d.).

1980s

By the early 1980s, business ethics instruction at universities and colleges was more widespread. The results of a survey published in 1982 indicated that, "[o]f the 655 schools that responded, 317 said that a business ethics course was being offered" (Hoffman & Moore, 1982, p. 81). In the late 1980s, Harvard Business School (HBS) created a "Leadership, Values, and Decision-Making" module for first year MBA students and in 2004 established a core course, "Leadership and Corporate Accountability," the first required primary ethics course in HBS history (Baghdadi, n.d.). Teaching business ethics to undergraduate and MBA students increased in the 1980s and 1990s as an increasing number of business schools experimented with various ways to bring to fruition specialized classes, courses, and business ethics programs. In addition, efforts increased efforts to: 1) teach or train professors of business (for example, about ethical theory) so they could play a more active role in teaching business ethics and 2) encourage faculty to conduct high quality research to help develop the discipline of business ethics.

1990s

In the late 1990s, a number of major ethical scandals (e.g., Enron) found business schools being blamed for failing to do a better job of educating ethical and responsible leaders. In response to this blame, teaching ethics became a key component in more business schools across the U.S. and the rest of the world. Through the increased use of case studies and simulations, business schools focused increasingly upon real-world examples in business ethics courses. Doing so, business schools attempted to teach students how to practice and look at ethical behavior by taking a critical dive into the consequences of an issue or dilemma: who will benefit and who will be harmed as well as whose rights are exercised and whose rights are denied.

In the 1990s, an important alternative in the U.S. for teaching business ethics as corporate social responsibility (CSR) gained increased attention in business and business schools. By the early 2000s, CSR had become an essential strategy for many organizations and soon CSR had morphed into a variety of titles to include corporate citizenship and sustainability (Weygandt, et al., 2015). As one would expect, business schools in the U.S. developed an increasing number of courses that focused on teaching CSR (and in some instances with less attention on teaching business ethics or simply merging CSR and business ethics together or removing some traditionally critical components of business ethics and replacing them with CSR concepts like sustainability).

AASCB encouraged business schools to teach CSR in their programs (AACSB, 2004). Additionally, organizations like the Institute of Management Accountants (IMA) stated that "management accountants in organizations of all sizes and ownership patterns should listen to and be prepared to lead their organizations as the sustainability conversation evolves" (Verschmoor, 2016, p. 16). Responding to the AACSB, other professional business organizations, and companies, business schools began implementing socially responsible initiatives with the goal of educating future leaders, managers, and workers who would ultimately struggle with environmental, social, and economic systems throughout their careers (Stubbs & Schapper, 2011). AACSB (2012) then created a series of conferences and workshops directed at business schools that focused upon the integration of social responsibility in their programs.

2000s

In the early 2000s, teaching business ethics became commonplace in a variety of forms including ethics courses, ethics components of traditional functional courses, and different types of service learning projects designed to promote behavioral, managerial, and/or cognitive competence (Williams & Dewett, 2005). Nonetheless, critics of teaching business ethics remained vocal concerning whether or not business ethics could be taught, the utility and goals of teaching business ethics, and whether or not business ethics is better taught outside of the business school (BusinessWeek Online, 2003).

During the first two decades of the 21st century and partly in response to critics of efforts to teach business ethics to students, business schools and researchers produced an abundance of: 1) theories concerning what should be included in teaching business ethics; 2) the best pedagogical approaches to teach business ethics; 3) the preparation of students prior to taking ethics courses; 4) who should shoulder the responsibility of educating tomorrow's leaders regarding the subject of ethical business behavior; and, 5) how best to evaluate or assess the impact of efforts to teach business ethics. In addition, a major focus of business ethics educators concerned the challenge of adapting to very rapidly changing environments due to technological developments.

In the early 2000s, the millennials and Z generations who were native digitals growing up in the digital age instead of acquiring digital knowledge as adults (Palfrey & Gasser, 2011) entered the world of business school education. In response to the recognition that technological developments affected the evolution of learning styles from verbal to visual to virtual (Proserpio & Goia, 2002), business ethics educators focused upon adopting new teaching methods to connect with students (Wankel, 2009). With research (see Montiel et al., 2020) demonstrating that for the millennial and Z generations, learning is more effective when using interactive learning, demonstration, and social networking than using traditional lectures, there are increased calls for business schools to recognize the implications of the shift to progressive learning styles and to correspondingly use more technology in efforts to teach business ethics (Sholihin et al., 2020).

The burgeoning trend toward online education in the early 2000s saw some preliminary focus on teaching business ethics online (Collins, et al., 2014). Further growth in teaching business ethics over the past decade has been attributed to technological advancements in online learning and the use of virtual tools or contents for teaching activities (Schlierer & Brinkmann, 2017). Similar to face-to-face teaching of business ethics efforts online courses also focused upon pedagogical design, delivery, student engagement, and assessment.

Historically, the incorporation of ethics into the curricula of business schools has been progressive and has taken various forms. During the past two decades, teaching business ethics became an integral component of business school curriculum (Raman, et al., 2019). Academic endeavors in teaching business ethics have been gradual as business schools and scholars increasingly have disparately focused on establishing linkages between core theories and their real-life applications, contrasting between domain specific and inclusive assessments, and emphasizing outdated or developing new teaching techniques. With limited consensus about these concerns (for example, as the pedagogy that comprehensively addresses the various concerns emerging when teaching business ethics), disparate attempts at addressing them continue to highlight numerous factors that influence the efficacy of a given specific pedagogy or teaching business ethics in general, with no solution currently in sight.

A CLOSER LOOK AT THE ISSUES OVER THE YEARS AND NOW

Across the decades, historical perspectives suggesting how to teach business ethics, what to teach, who should teach, and even whether to teach it at all can be found in the literature (Kvalnes, et al., 2018) and, arguably over more than an entire century (Hudson, 1912). The debate concerning these issues has been heated and generally remain unresolved today (Walsh, 2019).

Can Ethics Be Taught?

From the first lectures or courses, there has been a debate as to whether or not business ethic can be taught. In support of the view that ethics can't be taught, the *Wall Street Journal* published an editorial in the late 1980s (Kristol, 1987) suggesting that ethics could not be taught, which as one would expect, overlaps with can business ethics be taught? Velasquez et al. (1987) challenged the *Wall Street Journal* denouncing ethics courses (Hodges, 2016). Citing psychologist Lawrence Kohlberg's (2001) research, Velasquez et al. (1987) summarized the three levels of moral development, identifying education as one of the factors that can stimulate progression through these levels to improve a person's ability to learn ethical reasoning.

With little agreement regarding whether or not business ethics could be taught, there was an increased effort to take a closer look at how professors were teaching ethics. Stark (1993) indicated that the unethical behavior exhibited high profile scandals (e.g., Enron) was not the result of an absence of business ethics curriculum since "over 500 business-ethics courses are currently taught on American campuses; fully 90% of the nation's business schools now provide some kind of training in the area" (p. 38).

Weber (1990) reviewed four studies and found three of the four indicating a positive shift in ethical reasoning as a result of ethics education. Even though published research found ethics education improving ethical attitude, others demonstrated a negative relationship (Stephens & Stephens, 2008). The conflicting research results and debate about whether or not business ethics "can or cannot be taught" remains unresolved (Walsh, 2019). However, despite the conflicting research results and debate, the AACSB recently noted that it is not only possible—but necessary—to teach business ethics by exposing students to the principles of responsible business as an essential element of any business education (Berk & Custin, 2020). The authors contended that ethics can (and must) be taught by business schools so students will grasp the foundations of theoretical and practical knowledge while also reflecting upon and further developing their personal values and decision-making processes or skills.

Who Should Teach Business Ethics?

Historically, Klein (1988) brought the issue of "Who should teach business ethics?" front and center in his article titled "The One Necessary Condition for a Successful Business Ethics Course: The Teacher Must Be a Philosopher." In that article, Klein asked

> …why are Business Ethics courses all over the country (and the world) being taught by academics who have PhDs in Management, Economics, Psychology, Communications, MBAs, J.D.s, or even bachelor degrees with no formal philosophical training at all. Is it that society-at-large has no understanding of, and/or respect for, the expertise of philosophers—all of whom are trained in ethics, some of whom specialize in it? Or, more fundamentally, is it that we just do not believe that there is such a thing as 'ethics expertise' at all? (p. 562)

Like others, Klein believed that professors of business did not possess the ability to appeal to a broad range of deeply philosophical foundations, state-of-the art examples and counterexamples, and imaginative hypotheticals lacking those abilities was only the tip of the iceberg.

McGowan (2005) argued "it is less important that a business ethics course and its teacher be housed in the philosophy department or the business school-though there are practical matters to consider-than that the course be taught from a philosophical perspective by a person with an education, formal or informal, in philosophy, and especially in ethics" (p.1). McGowan suggested the problem of who should teach ethics is several millennia old and argued trained ethicists who stand outside the perspective of the discipline can teach ethics to those within the discipline (for example, through mentoring or direct supervision).

Over the last two to three decades an increasing number of business ethics courses have been taught by those who did not come from or have a background in philosophy. Part of this shift in "who should or does teach business ethics" can be attributed to AACSB International's 2004 Ethics Education Task Report which identified the domain of business ethics in colleges of business as "ethical leadership, ethical decision-making, corporate governance, and business and society" (AACSB International, 2004). The identification of such a domain moved the focus of teaching business ethics away from what Klein (1988) called "teaching philosophical perspectives" (e.g., utilitarianism, rights theories, and justice theories) in the business ethics classroom to what Ferrell and Ferrell (2005) would call "to understand and describe how ethical decisions are made and the environment that influences ethical decision making" (p. 2).

What Are the Goals of Teaching Business Ethics?

Historically, the goals or objectives of teaching business ethics received considerable attention and evidenced disagreement by researchers and business ethics educators. Several scholars have suggested that identifying strategic goals and objectives must be the first step in any efforts to teach business ethics effectively (Ryan & Bisson, 2011). However, reaching agreement about the goals of teaching business ethics has not been an easy task. For example, although scholars have identified various goals and objectives over the past four decades, business educators are not unanimous about those goals and objectives (Gates, et al., 2018).

In a review of the objectives of ethics education, Agle and Crossley (2011) found 35 different objectives that have been identified over the years as the aims of a business ethics education. Their study suggested that the four most frequently mentioned teaching business ethics objectives included ethical decision-making skills; moral awareness; understanding of one's values and principles; and, comprehending the place of business in society. In addition to these aims, other frequently mentioned objectives continue to include: the development of rhetorical skills to become effective advocates for ethical positions; the development of moral courage; advancing to moral leadership; and, the attainment of moral character.

Others have suggested the goals or objectives of teaching business ethics must focus upon relevancy. That is, teaching business ethics efforts should begin with connecting business ethics to each student's life. For example, ethics education must be relevant to the student for it to transfer into workplace practice (Ritter, 2006). Felton and Sims (2005) argued that teaching business ethics concerns assisting students to bring to consciousness their personal set of values, while also recognizing how their values may conflict with those values of the business world. Gentile argues that the goals of teaching business ethics is to help students expand their skills or ability to voice their values more often and more effectively (as cited in Moehring, 2020, p. 8).

Should Business Ethics be Taught as Standalone Courses or Integrated Across the Curriculum?

Since AACSB does not mandate or recommend a specific approach to teaching ethics, schools of business must decide what is best for their students (AACSB, 2013). Not surprisingly, there is as much support for a dedicated standalone business ethics course as there is against it.

Henderson (1988) suggested a standalone course was necessary because the rules in business are constantly changing and it was difficult for students to understand how business should be conducted. Strong and Hoffman (1990) argued that ethics courses explore theoretical frameworks, which helps students understand how reasoning works. DeGeorge (1987) stated that if business schools offer a separate ethics course, it will create "the impression that ethics is separate from business" (p. 507). Sims and Brinkmann (2003) also noted a separate ethics course might separate ethics from business, maintaining that "Business ethics (should not be) taught and perceived in a vacuum, but in relation to its business curriculum environment and to other courses" (p. 69). In contrast, Ritter (2006) argued that standalone courses are disconnected from real-world applications, and ethics must be integrated throughout the curriculum. Saul had previously suggested that if business ethics is to succeed, ethical considerations must be woven into every aspect of the "decision making repertoire as economic ones" (1981, p. 273), a view Felton and Sims (2005) supported, stating "ethics is embedded in all business decision-making. A given decision may be described as marketing, production, or financial decision, but ethical dimensions are intertwined in the decision" (p. 381).

Suggesting a "both/and approach," Swanson and Fisher (2008) argued for a combination of standalone classes and integration to realize various objectives and goals for teaching business ethics. Researchers continue to study integration (Scrivens, 2019), with Russell (2006) calling this "the greatest challenge that business schools face" (p. 4). The definition of "integrated" varies, covering everything from general statements about intent to specific statements providing detailed evidence of integrative activities (Christensen et al., 2007). However, the integration of business ethics can be a complex and difficult process and how it is implemented or delivered needs to be carefully considered from a pedagogical perspective (Rusinko, 2010), for example, using case studies or experiential learning (see Christensen et al., 2007; Rusinko, 2010).

What Pedagogies Should be used to Teach Business Ethics?

Despite all the studies regarding teaching business ethics to date, the pedagogical approaches to this day vary widely across schools (Lee, 2014) and among scholars, and there is no clear consensus in the literature on which pedagogies are the most effective (Kvalnes et al., 2018). According to Hosmer (2000), there are traditionally two alternative approaches to teaching business ethics. The first stresses background knowledge and analytical procedures clearly needed for rigorous ethical evaluation. This theory/policy method of instruction is often called the "philosophical approach" to teaching business ethics (Donaldson, et al., 2008), which consists of acquainting students with the leading theories of philosophical ethics (from authors ranging from Socrates and Aristotle to Kant and Rawls and Nozick)—generally in excerpt or summary form, and then exploring how these theories may be applied to resolve various ethical problems or corporate policy issues such as advertising, deception, environmental damage, sexual harassment, etc., arising in the business work environment (Hasnas, 2013).

The second approach called "the atheoretical approach" focuses much more upon the strategic and functional problems of business organizations (Hasnas, 2013). Students analyze detailed real world (or hypothetical) cases that present difficult ethical issues and propose various courses. No attempt is made to apply any particular ethical theory, but various factors that bear on the decision are weighed against one another. Thus, the students might discuss how the proposed courses of action would affect the business's prospects for financial success, what impact they would have upon different stakeholders, whether they would enhance or undermine the business's reputation, etc. This casuistic process is often accompanied by heuristic devices such as the *New York Times* test—would you want an account of your action to appear on the front page of the *New York Times*?—or the mirror test—could you look at yourself in the mirror if you took the proposed action (Hasnas, 2013)? One specific example of the atheoretical approach might find the business ethics educator emphasizing personal, professional, and organizational morality, asking students to compare and contrast their personal code of ethics with that of a professional or organizational code and to confront the tensions inherent in the process.

Kulshreshtha (2005) has suggested a blending of a business's economic incentives and objectives with ethical motivations. Others have suggested that course content can be derived from philosophy, sociology, political science, psychology, and organization behavior (Brady & Hart, 2007). Some have emphasized laws and regulations, while yet others emphasized ethical theories (Bruton, 2004), and Catholic social justice (Costa & Ramus, 2012), as well as religion and spirituality (Pava, 2007). Course design can be influenced by psychology and learning theory (Weber, 2007), as well as integrated coping-modeling and problem-solving techniques (Simola, 2010).

More specific pedagogical approaches, like case studies (see Bridgman, 2010), have been advocated to achieve teaching business ethics' goals (Sharma & Tewari,

2017). These include lectures, videotapes, CD-ROMs, board games, simulations, and scenario-based examples (Markula Center for Applied Ethics, 2016); Brown and Duguid (2000) suggest sharing stories; others have suggested using drama and literature (Freeman et al., 2015), while still others have argued for the use of audiovisual approaches (e.g., films and videotapes) to teach business ethics (Fisher et al., 2015). Izzo et al. (2006) recommended the use of interactive or experiential business ethics teaching—including behavioral simulations and games (Jagger & Sloan, 2016) and role-play (Knapp, 2011).

How to Assess the Impact of Teaching Business Efforts?

As noted earlier, the standards promulgated by the AACSB require that students learn ethics as part of a business degree. Hartman and Werhane (2009) recently noted that notwithstanding the choice of delivery process, a business school must ensure that it is able to demonstrate the students' achievement of learning with regard to ethics—a bar that was raised, or arguably simply modified, in 2003 by the AACSB.

Business ethics educators have historically wrestled with how to ensure they are able to demonstrate student achievement of learning with regard to business ethics. Not surprisingly, assessing the impact of teaching business ethics has focused upon facilitating feedback to improve such efforts (Sims, 2002). One of the first to review the business ethics education literature, Weber (1990) concluded that, in general, such courses lead to some improvement in students' ethical awareness and moral reasoning. Over the past few decades, others have confirmed the positive impact of teaching business ethics (May et al., 2014; Mayhew & Murphy, 2009). However, despite the studies that suggest ethics can be taught, other research has found minimal to no effect from teaching business ethics (Simha et al., 2012).

Regardless of the contradictory evidence regarding whether business ethics can be taught or not or the different goals and outcomes, it is important that we spend more time focusing upon finding an answer to the question, "How can we best teach business ethics?" To answer this question, business ethics educators should conduct more longitudinal studies that explore various groups and cultures and the long-term effects of different pedagogical approaches. In addition, attention should be directed to the various ethical student outcomes (e.g., ethical awareness, sensitivity, decision-making in real-world or practical situations, courage, leadership, or effectiveness in "giving voice to one's values) and the overall impact of a course or business schools teaching business ethics initiatives. Further, business ethics educators will need to continue to accept the reality that the assessment of student learning in teaching business ethics efforts is not a luxury but a necessity in every business school given the reality of an increased interest in assessment and accountability.

TEACHING BUSINESS ETHICS:
AN AGENDA AND FOOD FOR THOUGHT

An important takeaway from this chapter is that business ethics educators must move beyond the debate of whether or not business ethics can and should be taught, even though it may be difficult in some situations to do so. With this in mind, I suggest spending "*NO*" more time and energy looking for answers to questions like: "Should business schools teach ethics?" and "Can business schools teach ethics?" Like many issues, there will always be a continuum of beliefs which, in reality, do nothing more than distract from the efforts to teach business ethics (for example, Cohen & Bennie, 2006; Parks-Leduc et al., 2021; Ryan & Bisson, 2011; Stephens & Stephens, 2008; Walsh, 2019). Instead of debating whether or not business ethics "can be taught," one way to stimulate constructive discussion is to rephrase the question as "If business ethics can be taught, then how can business ethics educators' best teach it?" Simply put, business ethics educators must transition from instruction to facilitating learning on the target or student group's terms.

Confront the Relevancy Challenge Head-On

Looking to the future, business ethics educators should re-double their efforts to confront head-on the relevancy challenge in teaching business ethics. The best place to start is to be attentive to the need to ensure learning activities are grounded in the "real world." For students to derive the most from business ethics education, business ethics educators must ensure their efforts reflect those issues that students need to understand and be geared to the more realistic, immediate, and personal issues students are likely to encounter throughout their careers.

While this point is not new, it still seems to be an afterthought in too many teaching business ethics efforts. The challenge of relevance is to achieve a direct connection between personal choices and real problems and issues. This dilemma provides both a theoretical and experiential framework students can apply in evaluating a situation and choosing, for example, between conflicting ethical demands. In such learning dilemmas, any student' analysis should rely upon self-reflection (e.g., evaluation of one's values), the power of reason to raise important questions of ethicality, and guidelines for actions and logically defensible responses.

Ethics educators agree students should be positioned to confront the kinds of ethical dilemmas real business face, which in turn should raise their awareness, for example, about the importance of good decision making and stimulate the realities of their future work lives. Work lives that focus upon the reality that businesspeople often don't garner a great reputation when it comes to exhibiting ethical behavior. Headlines about pharmaceutical price gouging, car companies cheating on emissions testing, fraudulent accounts being hoisted upon clients, ethical scandals related poor working conditions, and many others, reveal the challenges students will confront and provide ample opportunities for business schools to confront the relevancy challenge. Irrespective of the pedagogical approach used, integrating ethical responsibility into the business curriculum needs to relate to specific management tasks, such as finance, organizational behavior, entrepreneurship, and strategic management, among others, so that students will be better prepared to operationalize them in leading and managing businesses (Jurowski & Liburd, 2001; Rusinko, 2010).

Attend To and Manage the Learning Process

In addition, business ethics educators must also be aware of the ongoing changes in themselves and particularly students during this period of great change. As business ethics educators facilitate learning, growth, and development in students during these times of change, they should strive to become more effective classroom leaders, planners, presenters, and facilitators. This means regularly reexamining their choice of pedagogy and assumptions about the learning process. Rather than only using the teaching style with which they may be most comfortable and familiar, business ethics educators should learn to implement new techniques and approaches to respond to continuous changes in both students and innovations in teaching business ethics.

Business ethics educators should teach business ethics in a manner attractive to the individual learning styles of students and which fosters student development. The management system should be based upon on a valid model of the learning process (e.g., Kolb's, 1984) experiential learning model, Kilpatrick's (1983) levels of learning, and conducive to new technologically driven pedagogical approaches to teach business ethics (e.g., mobile apps and Web 2.0 tools). Although these techniques tend to be highly sophisticated and creative applications, business ethics educators should constantly ask themselves if they are enhancing student learning. This includes providing for the differences in learning styles that are characteristic of both individuals and subject matters like business ethics.

In assessing the performance or merits of a teaching business ethics approach any approach to teaching business ethics should look for a diversity of approaches. For example, are a range of pedagogical approaches used? Are a variety of teaching materials incorporated? Are opportunities for individual study and group collaboration provided? Are lectures, cases, discussions, experiential learning pedagogies and techniques interspersed? Are the different mindset/attention/focus/limitations of the 2000+ generations recognized and approached? Likewise concerning the generational shift in recent years: Are millennials, for example, interested in having serious conversations about ethics, particularly CSR?

Institutionalize Outcomes Assessment

Business ethics educators should make every effort to institutionalize outcomes assessment in any teaching business ethics effort by taking the time to come to agreement concerning the purpose and/or goal and how to assess the outcomes before the effort begins. This point cannot be overemphasized.

A number of methods have been proposed over the years to assess the effectiveness of teaching business ethics (Sholihin et al., 2020; Sims, 2002, 2004). Similar to an agreement concerning the purpose and/or goals of teaching business ethics, agreeing upon a common method of assessment for measuring student performance, for example, against shared standards or core competencies in business ethics, also will generate conflicts among business ethics educators. Addressing and resolving such conflicts is especially important since agreement about assessment instruments can ultimately lead to a common goal for business ethics and operationalization of the goal in terms of specific performance indicators.

In any business school, the assessment of outcomes is often equated with measuring performance on examinations. Indeed, if the instructor has presented a highly structured unit on statistics or accounting, a pencil and paper test may well be an appropriate choice to assess how the degree to which the learning objectives have been met. If the learning objective is to develop the ability to make well-informed ethical judgments, howecver, assessment is more complex than simply measuring the ability to master a body of factual knowledge.

When teaching business ethics, the question becomes "Does the incorporation of ethics into the business curriculum make a difference in the ethical behavior of students and what they will or do in actual real world or business situations?" For this reason, the goal of assessment is to produce reliable data that can be used to aid in the evaluation of efficiency and effectiveness. In much the same manner as an audit, assessment data provide feedback regarding what has gone before and suggests what should come next.

One popular assessment strategy includes four different levels of assessment: A student's reactions and learning as well as change in behavior and results (e.g., does the students' application of concepts like ethical principles to a real world scenario improve over time?) (Kilpatrick, 1983). In this system, assessment unfolds at any of the levels of teaching business ethics: planning, designing, and implementation and includes micro teaching design (MTD), teaching the course (TC), and teaching business ethics (e.g., at the area or business school level) (ABP).

At the MTD level, business ethics education focuses on the process and products of the exercises, activities, and pedagogical methods. For some business ethics education efforts, not every MTD (perhaps none) will be rigorously assessed. In some instances, simple observation may be all that is needed to indicate achievement of objectives at this level or a need, for example, to modify procedures or activities.

At the TC level, assessment focuses upon the process and outcomes of individual business ethics education components. This requires aggregating data from the MTD level, or separately at the TC level, such as administering pre- and post-tests to analyze individual effects.

At the ABP level, assessment focuses upon the process and outcomes of the total teaching business ethics initiative. Assessment can be performed by aggregating data from previous assessments or, making observations prior to and following a teaching business ethics initiative. Typically, assessment at the ABP level has the purpose of measuring program effects on the total organization or system (e.g., business school), and continues for months or years after students have graduated and moved on to the world of work identify these effects. At this level, where evidence of effects is more mediated and distal than at lower levels, the teaching business ethics assessment is more difficult to conduct and is usually more complex in design.

Moving forward, business schools must attend to institutionalizing outcomes assessment at different levels, which can assist business schools and business ethics educators to think systematically about educational purposes and expectations, as well as how best to achieve them in the years to come.

CONCLUSION

In concluding this chapter, business ethics educators must continue to look at business ethics in fresh ways. How do the different areas within business look at ethics? How does business ethics look from the point of view of students?

Equally important, we must continue to build frameworks upon which business ethics "can be taught." This important element of the curriculum cannot be left to specialists (e.g., philosophers and trained ethicists), qualified as they may be. Those whose responsibility includes teaching business ethics need to articulate what they do, why they do it (e.g., the goals or objectives), and how they will assess whether or not the intended outcomes have been achieved.

If more business schools seriously consider the importance of teaching business ethics, they will help build effective environments for teaching and learning business ethics, and the rewards—for the schools and their students—will provide a cornerstone upon which future examinations of the history of teaching business ethics can be undertaken.

It is the author's hope that future researchers will find business schools having accepted responsibility to form future ethical leaders and managers, not for the sake of improving the bottom line (triple or otherwise) or to avoid scandal. Instead, it will be to assist students to understand the importance of ethics and instill in them a set of values by the time they move into the world of work.

REFERENCES

AACSB. (2012). *B-Schools and sustainability.* Association to Advance Colleges and Schools of Business. http://www.aacsb.edu/sustainability/index.html

AACSB. (2013). *Mission.* https://www.ascb.edu/about/default.asp

AACSB International. (2004). *Ethics education in business schools.* https://www.aacsb.edu/~/media/AACSB/Publications/research-reports/ethics-education.ashx

Abend, G. (2008). *A genealogy of business ethics*. PhD Dissertation, Department of Sociology, Evanston, IL: Northwestern University.

Abend, G. (2013). The origins of business ethics in American universities, 1902–1936. *Business Ethics Quarterly, 23*(2), 171–205.

Abend, G. (2016). How to tell the history of business ethics. *Journal for Business, Economics & Ethics, 17*(1), 42–76.

Agle, B. R., & Crossley, T. (2011). *Business ethics education, why bother? Objectives, pedagogies, and a call to action*. Proceedings of the Conference on Leveraging Change—The New Pillars of Accounting Education, Toronto (November).

Baghdadi, S. A. (n.d.). The evolution of business ethics studies. *Al-Nasser University Journal*. http://www.al-edu.com/wp-content/uploads/download-manager-files/The%20Evolution%20of%20Business%20Ethics%20Studies.pdf

Bankers Magazine. (1930, November). The ethical problems of modern finance. *Bankers Magazine, 121*(5), 796.

Benson, G. C. S. (1982). *Business ethics in America*. Lexington Books.

Berk, A., & Custin, R. E. (2020, October 16). *Instilling responsibility in the business leaders of tomorrow*. https://www.aacsb.edu/insights/2020/october/instilling-social-responsibility-in-the-business-leaders-of-tomorrow

Bishop, T. R. (1992). Integrating business ethics into an undergraduate curriculum. *Journal of Business Ethics, 11*(4), 291–299.

Bond, J. H. (1915). *The teaching of professional ethics in the schools of law, medicine, journalism and commerce in the United States*. PhD dissertation, University of Wisconsin, Madison, WI.

Bossard, J. H. S., & Dewhurst, J. F. (1931). *University education for business*. University of Pennsylvania Press.

Bowie, N. E. (1979). *Ethical theory and business*. Prentice-Hall.

Brady, F. N., & Hart, D. (2007). An exploration into the develop mental psychology of ethical theory with implications for business practice and pedagogy. *Journal of Business Ethics, 76*(4), 397–412.

Bridgman, T. (2010). Beyond the manager's moral dilemma: Rethinking the 'ideal-type' business ethics case. *Journal of Business Ethics, 94*(2), 311–322.

Brown, J. S., & Duguid, P. (2000). *The social life of organization*. Harvard Business School Press.

Bruton, S. V. (2004). Teaching the golden rule. *Journal of Business Ethics, 49*(2), 179–187.

BusinessWeek Online. (2003). *MBAs need more than ethics101*. http://www.businessweek.com/bschools/content/jan2003/bs20030121_5068.html

Christensen, L. E., Peirce, L., Hartman, Hoffman, W., & Carrier, J. (2007). Ethics, CSR, and sustainability education in the *Financial Times* top 50 global business schools: Baseline data and future research directions. *Journal of Business Ethics, 73*(4), 347–368.

Cohen, J. R., & Bennie, N. M. (2006). The applicability of a contingent facators model to accounting ethics research. *Journal of Business Ethics, 68*(1), 1–18.

Collins, D., Zambrrano, R., & Weber, J. (2014). Teaching business ethic online: Perspectives on course design, delivery, student engagement, and assessment. *Journal of Business Ethics, 125*(3), 513–529.

Copeland, M. T. (1958). *And mark an era: The story of the business school*. Little, Brown and Company.

Costa, E., & Ramus, T. (2012). The Italian Economia Aziendale and Catholic social teaching: How to apply the common good principle at the managerial level. *Journal of Business Ethics*, *106*(1), 103–116.

Daniel, C. A. (1998). *MBA: The first century*. Bucknell University Press.

DeGeorge, R. (1982). *A history of business ethics* (5th ed.). Macmillan.

DeGeorge, R. T. (1987). Ethical theory for business professors. *Journal of Business Ethics*, *6*(7), 507–508.

DeGeorge, R. T. (2007). *A history of business ethics*. https://www.bbvaopenmind.com/en/articles/a-history-of-business-ethics/

DeGeorge, R. (2015, November 17). *A history of business ethics*. https://www.scu.edu/ethics/focus-areas/business-ethics/resources/a-history-of-business-ethics/

Donaldson, T., & Werhane, P. W. (1979*). Ethical issues in business: A philosophical approach* (1st ed.). Prentice-Hall.

Donaldson, T., Werhane, P. W., & Van Zandt, J. (2008). *Ethical issues in business: A philosophical approach* (8th ed.). Pearson.

Education of Business Men. (1891). *An address before the convention of the American Aankers' Association at Saratoga, September 3, 1890, by Edmund J. James.* Plan of the Wharton School of Finance and Economy. Proceeding of the Association Relative to the Address of Professor James, and upon the Founding of Schools of Finance and Economy. New York: W.B. Greene. https://www.worldcat.org/title/education-of-business-men-an-address-before-the-convention-of-the-american-bankers-association-at-saratoga-september-3-1890/oclc/916530883?referer=di&ht=edition

Felton, E. L., & Sims, R. R. (2005). Teaching business ethics: Targeted outputs. *Journal of Business Ethics*, *60*(4), 377–391.

Ferrell, O. C., & Ferrell, L. (n.d.). *Historical developments of business ethics: Then and now.* https://danielsethics.mgt.unm.edu/pdf/Historical%20Development%20of%20Business%20Ethics.pdf

Ferrell, O. C., & Ferrell, L. (2005). *What your mother never taught you: How to teach business ethics*. https://danielsethics.mgt.unm.edu/pdf/How%20to%20Teach%20Business%20Ethics.pdf

Fisher, J., Grant, B., & Palmer, D. (2015). Bad teacher? Using films as texts when teaching business ethics: Exploring the issues. *International Journal of Business and Management*, *10*(8), 14–22.

Freeman, R. L., Dunham, L., Fairchild, G., & Parmar, B. (2015). Leveraging the creative arts in business ethics teaching. *Journal of Business Ethics, 131*(3), 519–526.

Gates, D., Agle, B. R., & Williams, R. N. (2018). Teaching business ethics: Current practice and future directions. In E. Heath, B. Kaldis, & A. Marcoux (Eds.), *The Routledge companion to business ethics* (1st ed., pp. 60–76). Routledge.

Griffin, C. E. (1928). The aims of the school of business administration. *Michigan Alumnus*, *35*(8), 159–162.

Hartman, L. P., & Werhane, P. H. (2009). A modular approach to business ethics integration: At the intersection of the *stand-alone* and the *integrated* approaches. *Journal of Business Ethics*, *90*(S3), 295–300.

Hasnas, J. (2013). Teaching business ethics: The principles approach. *Journal of Business Ethics, Education, 10*, 275–304.

Heilman, R. E. (1930). Introductory-Ethical standards in business and in business education. In *The ethical problems of modern finance. Lectures delivered in 1929 on the William A. Vawter foundation on business ethics, Northwestern University School of Commerce* (pp. 3–27). Ronald Press Company.

Heilman, R. E., Kiekhofer, W. J., Ruggles, C. O., Sharfman, I. L., & Marshall, L. C. (1928). Collegiate education for business. *Journal of Business of the University of Chicago, 1*(1), 1–59.

Henderson, V. E. (1988). An ethics roundtable: Can business ethics be taught? *Management Review, 77*(8), 52–54.

Hodges, A. B. (2016). *Ethics: Can it be taught?* https://apps.dtic.mil/dtic/tr/fulltext/u2/1007246.pdf

Hoffman, W. F., & Moore, J. M. M. (1982). Results of a business ethics curriculum survey conducted by the center for business ethics [at Bentley College]. *Journal of Business Ethics, 1*(2), 81–83.

Hosmer, L. T. (2000). Standard format for the case analysis of moral problems. *Teaching Business Ethics, 4*(2), 169–180.

Hudson, W. (1912). Aim and content of the first college in ethics. *The Journal of Philosophy, Psychology, and Scientific Methods, 9*(17), 455–459.

Izzo, G., Langford, B., & Vitell, S. (2006). Investigating the efficacy of interactive ethics education: A difference in pedagogical emphasis. *Journal of Marketing Theory and Practice, 14*(3), 239–248.

Jagger, S., & Sloan, D. (2016). *A virtual reality game to educate tomorrow's ethical managers.* British Academy of Management Conference Proceedings 2016: Thriving in Turbulent Times (September). http://nrt.nothumbria.ac.uk/policies/html

Jurowski, C., & Liburd, J. (2001). A multi-cultural and multi-disciplinary approach to integrating the principles of sustainable development into human resource management curricula in hospitality and tourism. *Journal of Hospitality and Tourism Education, 13*(5), 36–50.

Khurana, R. (2007). *From higher aims to hired hands.* Princeton University Press.

Kilpatrick, D. L. (1983). Four steps to measuring training effectiveness. *Personnel Administrator, 28*(11), 19–25.

Klein, E. R. (1988). The one necessary condition for a successful business ethics course" The teacher must be a philosopher. *Business Ethics Quarterly, 8*(3), 561–574.

Knapp, J. C. (2011). Rethinking ethics training: New perspectives to enhance effectiveness. In R. R. Sims & W. I. Sauser, Jr. (Eds.), *Experiences in teaching business ethics* (pp. 231–245). Information Age Publishing, Inc.

Kohlberg, L. (2001). *Kohlberg's three stages theories of development.* http://www.integratedsociopsychology.net/stages-moral_development.html

Kolb, D. A. (1984). *Experiential learning: Experience as the source of learning and development.* Prentice-Hall.

Kristol, I. (1987, September 15). Ethics, anyone? Or morals? *The Wall Street Journal*, 32.

Kulshreshtha, P. (2005). Business ethics versus economic incentives: Contemporary issues and dilemmas. *Journal of Business Ethics, 60*(4), 393–410.

Kvalnes, O., Brinkmann, J., & Sims, R. R. (2018). *Learning outcomes of role-play in business ethics education.* Working paper. BI Norwegian Business School.

Mahoney, J. (1990). *Teaching business ethics in the UK, Europe and the USA.* The Athlone Press.

Markula Center for Applied Ethics. (2016). *Ethics cases.* https://www.scu.edu/ethics/ethics-resources/ethics-cases/

May, D. R., Luth, M. T., & Schwoerer, C. E. (2014). The influence of business ethics education on moral efficacy, moral meaningfulness, and moral courage: A quasi-experimental study. *Journal of Business Ethics, 124(*1), 67–80.

Mayhew, B., & Murphy, P. (2009). The impact of ethics education on reporting behavior. *Journal of Business Ethics, 86*(3), 397–416.

McGowan, R. J. (2005). *Teaching business ethics from a philosophy department perspective.* https://www.butler.edu/las/resources/ethics

Moehring, C. (2020, September 24). *Season 2, episode 3: Interview with Mary Gentile discussing the future of business ethics.* https://walton.uark.edu/business-integrity/blog/mary-gentile.php

Montiel, I., Delgado, J., Natalia, C., de Mandojana, O., & Antolin, R. (2020). New ways of teaching: Using technology and mobile apps to educate on societal grand challenges. *Journal of Business Ethics, 161*(2), 243–251.

Northwestern University Alumni News. (1928, April). Gift to endow business ethics course. *Northwestern University Alumni News.*

Palfrey, J. G., & Glaser, U. (2011). *Born digital: Understanding the first generation of digital natives.* Basic Books.

Parks-Leduc, L., Mulligan, L., & Raymond, M. A. (2021). Can ethics be taught? Examining the impact of distributed ethical training and individual characteristics on ethical decision-making. *Academy of Management Learning & Education, 20*(1). https://doi.org/10.5465/amle.2018.0157

Paul, K. (1987). Business environment and business ethics in management thought. In K. Paul (Ed.), *Business environment and business ethics: The social, moral, and political dimensions of management.* Ballinger Publishing.

Pava, M. (2007). Spirituality in (and out) of the classroom: A pragmatic approach. *Journal of Business Ethics, 73*(3), 287–299.

Piper, T. R., Gentile, M. C., & Parks, S. D. (1993). *Can ethics be taught? Perspectives, challenges, and approaches at Harvard Business School.* Harvard Business School.

Powell, L. P. (1913, October 4). Teaching industrial efficiency at school. *California Outlook,* 8.

Powell, L. P. (1925). *The human touch.* G.P. Putnam's Sons.

Proserpio, L., & Goia, D. A. (2007). Teaching the virtual generation. *The Academy of Management Learning and Education, 6*(1), 69–90.

Raman, G. V., Garig, S., & Thapliyal, S. (2019). Integrative live case: A contemporary business ethics pedagogy. *Journal of Business Ethics, 155*(4), 1009–1022.

Reed, H. B. (1916). *The morals of monopoly and competition* [PhD dissertation]. University of Chicago.

Ritter, B. A. (2006). Can business ethics be trained? A study of the ethical decision-making process in business students. *Journal of Business Ethics, 68(*2), 153–164.

Rusinko, C. A. (2010). Integrating sustainability in higher education: A generic matrix. *International Journal of Sustainability in Higher Education, 11*(3), 250–259.

Russell, J. (2006). Breaking into the mainstream. Ethical corporation special report-corporate social responsibility and education. In L. E. Christensen, L. Peirce, L., L. Hartman, W. Hoffman, & J. Carrier. (2007). Ethics, CSR, and sustainability education in the *Financial Times* top 50 global business schools: Baseline data and future research directions. *Journal of Business Ethics, 73*(4), 347–368).

Ryan, T. G., & Bisson, J. (2011). Can ethics be taught? *International Journal of Business and Social Science, 2*(12), 44–52.

Saul, G. K. (1981). Business ethics: Where are we going? *The Academy of Management Review, 6*(2), 269–276.

Schlierer, H., & Brinkmann, J. (2017). The use of online resources for teaching business ethics: A pilot project, a framework, and recommendations. *Journal of Business Ethics Education, 14*, 261–284.

Scrivens, M. J. (2019). *Teaching ethics: Business school deans' perceptions regarding the presentation of ethics within the business curriculum.* https://urresearch.rochester.edu/institutionalPublicationPublicView.action?institutionalItemVersionId=35011

Sharma, E., & Tewari, R. (2017). *Multiple stakeholder views on the relevance of teaching business ethics.* https://ahduni.edu.in/research-working-paper/multiple-stakeholder-views-on-the-relevance-of-teaching-business-ethics

Sheffield Scientific School. (1910). *Every-day ethics: Addresses delivered in the Page Lecture Series, 1909, before the senior class of the Sheffield Scientific School, Yale University.* Yale University Press.

Sholihin, M., Sari, R. C., Yuniarti, N., & Illyana, S. (2020). A new way of teaching business ethics: The evaluation of virtual reality-based learning media. *The International Journal of Management Education, 18*(3), 1–13. https://www.ncbi.nlm.nih.gov/pmc/articles/PMC7574845/

Simha, A., Armstrong, J. P., & Albert, J. F. (2012). Attitudes and behaviors of academic dishonesty and cheating—Do ethics education and ethics training affect either attitudes or behaviors? *Journal of Business Ethics Education, 9*, 129–144.

Simola, S. K. (2010). Use of a "coping-modeling, problem-solving" program in business ethics education. *Journal of Business Ethics, 96*(3), 383–401.

Sims, R. R. (2002). *Teaching business ethics for effective learning.* Quorum Books.

Sims, R. R. (2004). Business ethics teaching: Using conversational learning to build an effective classroom learning environment. *Journal of Business Ethics, 49*(2), 201–211.

Sims, R. R., & Brinkmann, J. (2003). Business ethics curriculum design: Suggestions and illustrations. *Teaching Business Ethics, 7*(1), 69–86.

Stark, A. (1993, May–June). What's the matter with business ethics? *Harvard Business Review, 71*(3), 1–8.

Stephens, V. R., & Stephens, A. S. (2008). An examination of accounting majors' ethical decisions before and after an ethics course requirement. *Journal of College Teaching & Learning, 5*(4) 49–55.

Strong, V. K., & Hoffman, A. N. (1990). There is relevance in the classroom: Analysis of present methods of teaching business ethics. *Journal of Business Ethics, 9*(7), 603–607.

Stubbs, W., & Schapper, J. (2011).Two approaches to curriculum development for educating for sustainability and CSR. *International Journal of Sustainability in Higher Education, 12*(3), 259—268.

Swanson, D., & Fisher, D. (Eds.). (2008). *Advancing business ethics education.* Information Age Publishing.

Tufts, J. H. (1919). *The ethics of cooperation.* Houghton Mifflin.

University of California. (1904). *Register 1903–1904.* The University Press.

University of California. (1907). *The University of California Chronicle. An official record* (Vol. IX). The University Press.

University of California. (1915). *Circular of information concerning the colleges of letters and science, commerce, agriculture, mechanics, mining, civil engineering, and chemistry, the schools of architecture, education and jurisprudence, and the first and second years of the medical school, 1915–1916.* University of California Press.

Velasquez, M., Andre, C., Shanks, T., & Meyer, M. J. (1987). *Can ethics be taught?* https://www.scu.edu/ethics/ethics-resources/ethical-decision-making/can-ethics-be-taught/

Verschmoor, C. C. (2016, October). Global surveys measure nonfinancial reporting. *Strategic Finance*, 16–18.

Wall Street Journal. (1905, April 25). Morality of Wall Street, p. 5.

Walsh, D. (2019, December 16). *Can ethics be taught?* https://mitsloan.mit.edu/ideas-made-to-matter/can-ethics-be-taught

Wankel, C. (2009). Management education using social media. *Organization Management Journal*, *6*(4), 1–12.

Weber, J. (1990). Measuring the impact of teaching ethics to future managers: A review, assessment, and recommendations. *Journal of Business Ethics*, *9*(3), 183–190.

Weber, J. A. (2007). Business ethics training: Insights from learning theory. *Journal of Business Ethics*, *70*(1), 61–85.

Weygandt, J. J., Kimmel, P. D., & Kieso, D. E. (2015). *Managerial accounting: Tools for business decision making* (7th ed.). Wiley.

Williams, S. D., & Dewett, T. (2005). Yes, you can teach business ethics: A review and research agenda. *Journal of Leadership and Organization Studies*, *12*(2), 109–120.

Wooster, H. A. (1919). University Schools of business and a new business ethics. *Journal of Political Economy*, *27*(1), 47–63.

Yale University. (1914). *Catalogue of Yale University. 1914–1915.* Published by the University.

SECTION 3

EDUCATING IN ETHICS: PROFESSIONS WITH A FOCUS UPON THE PRESERVING/SUSTAINING THE SOCIETY SERVED

Chapter 7: Public Administration Ethics

Ethical awareness and reflection are crucial for those in public service by helping them to define and act on core values and beliefs to advance the public interest. Those who act with insufficient regard to core values and professional ethics put at risk their careers, the reputation of their organizations or jurisdictions, and the common good.

—*Jonathan P. West*

Chapter 8: Military Ethics

Genuine dilemmas are situations where the right answer is difficult to determine due to apparently conflicting values. But, while many may appear to be dilemmas, they actually turn out to be simple tests of integrity, where the right thing to do is obvious, but it may come at a personal price (doing the right thing can hurt sometimes, such as taking the unpopular but correct course of action).

—*David Whethem & Andrew Corbett*

CHAPTER 7

EVOLVING ETHICS EDUCATION IN PUBLIC ADMINISTRATION

Past and Present

Jonathan P. West
University of Miami

This chapter examines ethics and ethics education initiatives in the context of public administration. The role of U.S. government reforms in the past 150 years is briefly tracked with its implications for ethics. The evolution of ethics in the public administration profession is then discussed. The analysis explores the contemporary period by examining issues germane to the purposes, substance, delivery modes, and contested issues of ethics education and training. Drawing upon existing literature, survey data, and examination of MPA ethics course syllabi, attention is directed to current trends, pedagogy, curricular content, and competencies related to public administration ethics instruction and training. The summary and conclusion include specific lessons learned.

Keywords: Ethics, Public Administration, MPA, History, Contested Issues

Educating in Ethics Across the Professions: A Compendium of Research, Theory, Practice, and an Agenda for the Future, pages 141–167.
Copyright © 2023 by Information Age Publishing
www.infoagepub.com
All rights of reproduction in any form reserved.

INTRODUCTION

Ethics shape and define the nature of the public administration profession. Administrators and employees who are informed by ethics are more likely to know the right thing to do, to act on those values, to justify their actions based on professional and moral criteria, and to protect themselves against charges of ethical wrongdoing (Carter, 1996; Jurkiewicz & Nichols, 2002; Menzel, 1997; West & Berman, 2006). Ethical awareness and reflection are crucial for those in public service by helping them to define and act upon core values and beliefs to advance the public interest. Those who act with insufficient regard to core values and professional ethics put at risk their careers, the reputation of their organizations or jurisdictions, and the common good (Bowman & West, 2022; Dobel, 2019; Newell, 2015).

Attention-grabbing scandals and ethics violations involving elected and appointed officials have brought a resurgent interest in ethics (Seitelman, 2020). Revelations of illegal and unethical conduct in the public sector have created a public trust deficit and a profession attacked by antigovernment rhetoric and highlighting government failures and misdeeds (Light, 2020; Rosenthal & Trost, 2012; Vinzant, 2019). Responses to these ethical lapses often come in two forms: laws and codes that define and forbid wrongdoing, and education or training efforts to help managers and employees do the right thing. While laws and codes emphasize the need for proper conduct and provide a deterrent to those who might engage in illegal or unethical behavior, they are increasingly regarded as insufficient for ensuring a proper ethical environment. Education and training are growing in importance to ensure that public servants recognize the ideals of public service that are the hallmark of ethics (Jacobs, 2019; Lewis & Gilman, 2012; Menzel, 2012). A robust ethics strategy includes elements of both approaches.

The purpose of this chapter is to examine ethics education in the past and present in the U.S. public administration context.[1] It begins by briefly reviewing American political reforms in the past 150 years that reflect enduring values and provide continuity between the old and new concerns about government performance and ethics. The evolution of professional ethics in American public administration during the same time period is then examined, the analysis moving forward to the present by exploring five contested issues in ethics education and training. Current practices in public affairs ethics education are then considered focusing upon how and why the subject is taught in higher education courses based on review of course syllabi. The final section provides a summary and conclusion to the chapter with specific lessons learned.

MACRO HISTORICAL DEVELOPMENTS

Two useful frameworks help in tracing the history of government reforms and the emphasis upon ethics in American public administration. One is from Paul Light's 1997 book, *The Tides of Reform*, that identifies four reform tides—scientific management, war on waste, watchful eye, and liberation management—that ebb and flow though American public administration. The second is from Imane Hijal-Moghragbi and Meghna Sabharwal's 2018 article in *Public Integrity* on the evolution of ethics in public administration. The latter is divided into six historical eras—the progressive era, the New Deal and Post-World War period, the civil rights era, the post-Watergate era, the reinventing government period, and the current new governance era. These frameworks aid in summarizing how government reform policies and the education of public service professionals have changed from "doing things right" to balancing this by "doing right things."[2]

Scientific Management Era

During this period, reforms like the Pendleton Act of 1883 sought to professionalize public administration, eventually transforming governance from the spoils system to one that is merit-based. Bureaucratic values like the 3 E's of efficiency, effectiveness and economy were emphasized, and democratic values connected citizen involvement and efficient government (Mosher, 1968; Schachter, 2007). The political/administrative dichotomy was accepted. Hierarchy, division of labor, specialization, standardization, and clear lines of authority as well as Frederick Taylor's ideas of scientific management describe bureaucratic organizations and operations that sought to improve government performance (Shjafritz & Hyde, 2016, pp. 36–38).

Management principles summarized by the acronym POSDCORB—planning, organizing staffing, directing, coordinating, reporting and budgeting—and more business-like practices were also advocated. Reforms recommended by two presidential study commissions in the 1930s (Brownlow Commission) and 1940s (Hoover Commission) reflected the philosophy and focus of scientific management that had implications for public administration performance and ethics. Moral judgments were fueling reform efforts to curb political influence and corruption of political party machines. Key participants during this era were experts and key products were well-defined structures, specific rules, and management controls to reduce costs and promote efficiency. By the end of World War 1 and the country's unfortunate decline into the Great Depression, public administrators recognized the need to exercise greater judgment in decision making, rather than strict adherence to economic efficiency guidelines in government management. This enhanced bureaucratic discretion brought increased attention to public service ethics.

New Deal and Post World War Two Era

This era continued with the emphasis upon efficiency, regulations, and characterizations of the bureaucrat's role primarily as one of compliance and neutral competence. The debate between Carl Friedrich and Herman Finer disputed ways to promote administrative responsibility and ethical behavior. Friedrich (1940) argued that greater attention should be given to a public servant's moral responsibility, while Finer (1941) put more emphasis upon the importance of accountability to elected leaders, a recurring matter of contention since that time.

Civil Rights Era

Civil rights in the 1960s and 1970s challenged the notion of the value-neutral bureaucrat who implemented standardized service to all citizens, using social equity arguments that support customizing services to meet the needs of different societal groups. To ensure social equity in governing, particularly following the civil rights movement, public administrators began to exercise even greater administrative discretion when making decisions, bringing increased interest to administrative ethics. Critics proposed de-bureaucratization as a corrective to the existing over-sized, inefficient, unresponsive bureaucratic structures and processes.

Post-Watergate Era

The period of the mid-1970s and 1980s presented new challenges of a rapidly changing society, both in size and diversity. The Watergate scandal exemplified the need for attention to the development of public service ethics and the need to rebuild public trust in government—demonstrated by the 1978 Ethics in Government Act which created the Office of Government Ethics (OGE), charged with responsibility for oversight and training on ethics and was empowered to create Designated Agency Ethics Officials in every department and agency. Public service ethics was also promoted when the U.S. Department of Justice created its Public Integrity Section in 1976 (U.S. Government Accountability Office, 2001, p. 2), which was later charged with supervising administration of the Independent Counsel Act until its expiration in 1999 (p. 11). Oversight of the federal effort to combat corruption continues to be provided by the Public Integrity Section through the prosecution of elected and appointed officials at all levels of government (U.S. Department of Justice, n.d.; Svara & West, 2018).

Citizen access to information was given priority after the abuses of the Watergate scandal 1972–1974 (Brownell, 2020) and the disclosure by Daniel Ellsberg of the Pentagon Papers in 1971 about U.S. involvement in Vietnam (Branch, 2009; Rudenstein, 1996). There were other whistleblowers during this period who followed the law, were protected by the Office of Special Counsel, and exposed misuse of government authority and funds. This era's emphasis coincides with Light's (1997) "Watchful Eye" reforms stressing fairness, rights and transparency. Sunshine requirements also reflect the watchful eye philosophy.

Light's war-on-waste reform theme also overlaps with these concerns, emphasizing cost control, improved performance through strategic planning, and applying business principles. Audits, investigations, inspectors general, congressional investigations, and media scrutiny were relied upon to control overspending and detect graft, waste, and abuse. The implications for ethics involved the need to uncover wrongdoing, investigate scandals and protect whistleblowers. Close supervision, rigorous oversight, and tight internal controls were implemented as part of the war on waste. "Right behavior" was based upon law and codes, but there was also emphasis upon the ethical values of public service.

The Reinventing Government Era

The period of the late 1980s and 1990s reintroduced business values, methods and processes into government to improve service provision and bolster trust in government. Key values in this era were efficiency, productivity, customer service, and government accountability for performance. Enactment of the 1993 Government Performance and Results Act reflects the concerns in this period for higher performance. Those advocating New Public Management (NPM) offered a different paradigm for improving operations of public organizations as business enterprises expected to be responsive to performance standards established by managers. NPM emphasized the need for more fair and responsive government that highlights new moral values of inclusiveness and benevolence.

Loosening internal controls and enhancing managerial flexibility was expected to improve both accountability and transparency. Light refers to this tide as "liberation management" with its emphasis upon reduced planning, regulation, and procedures as well as its stress upon evaluations, outcomes and results. Greater employee empowerment, reengineering, work teams, and other process improvements were to further the goal of debureaucratization and move in the direction of organizational liberation. Critics contended that the NPM models raised ethical issues, undermined the public ethos, sacrificed equity norms, were excessively concerned about efficiency (rather than democratic accountability), abandoned neutral competency, and increased the likelihood of ethical wrongdoing with relaxed regulations (Ferlie, 2017; Frederickson, 1980; Lynn, 2008).

New Governance Era

Hijal-Moghragbi and Sabharwal's final era is the current one, titled the "New Governance" which refers to the move from bureaucracy to new service delivery modes or network arrangements that cut across public, private and nonprofit sectors. Collaboration among those in the three sectors could enable better-coordinated efforts, make it easier to acquire and allocate resources and help to solve problems that could not be achieved by one sector operating alone. This has implications for ethics, the authors note, by combining an ethos supporting public service virtues with private sector entrepreneurial values and processes. Nonetheless, the "public-private" enterprises that this model advocated led to a spate of ethical issues and corruption cases at the federal, state and local level (Radu & Hamlin, 2005). Much like contracting out during NPM, the inability of government to be as sophisticated as their private sector counterparts has led to ethical lapses, abuse, and corruption. New governance advocates do not view moving from vertical hierarchies to flatter horizontal ones as sacrificing traditional virtues based on democratic governance. Light (2020) does not have a comparable final reform era, although elements of liberation management remain. He broadly labels the post-World War 11 period the "Tide of Tinkering" because of the decline of large-scale reforms and the rise of small-scale changes.

After examining government reform eras, Light concluded that efficiency "appears at or near the top in virtually every reform report of the past one hundred years" (1997, p. 21). However, Hijal-Moghrabi and Sabharwal's analysis showed that while efficiency was valued in all eras, it was interpreted somewhat differently as social and economic conditions changed and competing values gained attention. Their analysis highlights the changing connotations of efficiency with ethical implications surrounding efforts to eliminate corruption and reduce waste, control government bureaucracy, advance social equity, maximize outputs, and enable organizations to adapt with resilience (2018, p. 466). Preconceptions and values also colored assessments of efficiency, ethics, and government performance (Downs & Larkey, 1986). The values reflected in the eras and reform tides with their implications for efficiency, ethics, and government performance don't "fade" away. Rather, they evolve and co-exist.

With this broad historical backdrop, attention now shifts to related developments occurring over time within the public administration profession that reflect growing interest in ethics and ethics education. This is important because paralleling macro-governmental reform eras with their implications for ethics described above are meso-level developments among professional nonprofit organizations.

MESO DEVELOPMENTS IN PROFESSIONAL ASSOCIATIONS

The focus here is upon two professional associations and their efforts to foster ethics—the American Society for Public Administration (ASPA) and the Network of Schools of Public Affairs and Administration (NASPAA).

American Society for Public Administration

ASPA was organized in 1939 at the height of the New Deal to help address the concerns of government management and promote public service as an honorable profession. ASPA's first president, William Mosher, emphasized the importance of ethics as the foundation for a "profession of public service" (1938, p. 336). While he supported a code of ethics based upon themes of public interest, relationships with other officials and the public, personal integrity, and a commitment to providing impartial service to all of the public (p. 330), it wasn't until the 1970s that ethics received more than sporadic examination in ASPA and public administration journals (Cooper, 1994; Svara & West, 2018).

In response to Watergate and the increased emphasis on social equity, ASPA formed the Professional Standards and Ethics Committee in 1974 (Svara, 2022, p. 81). Still, the Committee reflected a negative attitude toward codes of ethics, developing a workbook—*Applying Professional Standards and Ethics*—published in 1979 that helped ASPA members conduct self-analysis of their ethical values and responsibilities. The workbook stated that "Although it is possible to develop a long list of 'thou shalts' and 'thou shalt nots,' as many professions have done, ultimate responsibility for standards and ethics falls on the individual" (Mertins, 1979, p. 1).

ASPA's first set of moral principles was adopted in 1981 with subsequent modifications resulting in a code of ethics in 1984, 1994, 2013. In 2014, ASPA established Standards Implementation Committee (King et al., 2019; Plant, 2013). The upgraded 2013 code includes eight aspirational principles that include: advance the public interest, uphold the constitution and the law, promote democratic participation, strengthen social equity, fully inform and advise, demonstrate personal integrity, promote ethical organizations, and advance professional excellence. As King and his colleagues observe, the eight principles, "address ethics standards of both 'bureaucratic and democratic ethos,' which the extant research has shown to be an important framework in the MPA ethics curriculum" (2019, p. 7).

Network of Schools of Public Affairs and Administration

As administrators sought to fulfill their service to the public fairly, the subject of ethics increasingly became recognized and incorporated into education and training. Ethics courses began to appear in MPA programs in the 1960s, 1970s, and 1980s prompted in part by initiatives of the National Association of Schools of Public Affairs and Administration (NASPAA)—now known as the Network of Schools of Public Affairs and Administration. Graduate programs in public administration and affairs were established to accomplish the goal of adequately preparing students for the profession. It became apparent the diverse context of these programs was too varied (Menzel, 1998). Established in 1970 by deans and directors from various institutions that offered public administration and affairs (PA/A) programs with the intent to create a uniform educational context, NASPAA encouraged public administration programs to "enhance the student's values, knowledge and skills to act ethically and effectively" (Menzel, 1998). In 1986, NASPAA established its accreditation process and, in 1989, adopted Standard 3.21 that "largely settled the question of whether ethics should be taught in graduate public administration/affairs" (Yoder & Denhardt, 1994, p. 200). Even though the standard fell short of requiring the addition of a core course on ethics, programs could satisfy the standard by discussing ethics throughout the curriculum. It could be argued that the NASPAA approach denigrates ethics instruction because it suggests that any professor of public administration can teach ethics.

Other Driving Forces Promoting Ethics Education

Jeremy Plant and Bing Ran (2009, pp. 225–226) explain the four key factors that spurred development of public administration ethics:

- the growth of scholarly research and writing on ethics and ethics education in public administration (e.g., John Rohr's, *Ethics for Bureaucrats* [1978] and Terry Cooper's *The Responsible Administrator* [2012], followed by five new editions)

- a series of conferences concerning ethics education held in Washington, D.C., Park City, Utah, and Tampa, Florida (the latter resulting in a 1998 book edited by James Bowman and Don Menzel, *Teaching Ethics and Values in Public Administration Programs: Innovations, Strategies and Issues*
- NASPAA sponsorship of the *Journal of Public Affairs Education (JPAE)* in 1994. Between 1995 and 2018 the journal has published nearly two dozen articles on teaching ethics (Raadschelders et al., 2019, p. 57)
- scholars conducting research concerning ethical issues in public and private sector human resource management (e.g. Bowman et al., 2004; Budd & Scoville, 2005; Greenwood, 2013; Miller, 1996; Pinnington et al., 2007; Schumann, 2001).

James Svara and Jonathan West (2018) identify other important developments documenting the growth of interest in public administration ethics including:

- Publication of a 1981 compilation of articles in *Public Personnel Management* journal (edited by James Bowman, 1981).
- Don Menzel examined the cumulative number of articles on ethics in three time periods—1970 to 1989, 1990 to 1998, and 2005 to 2014, showing the movement from a conceptual research focus to empirical articles (Menzel, 2005, 2015; Menzel & Carson, 1999).
- The 1996–1997 publication of the *Public Integrity Annual* by the Council of State Governments (CSG) and ASPA.
- In 1997, Menzel, Bowman, and others organized the "Section on Ethics"— since 2015 known as the Section on Ethics and Integrity in Governance (SEIgov). At the annual ASPA conference in 1998, the Section was officially formed and planned to launch a quarterly journal, *Public Integrity*. Four years later the journal's publisher switched from CSG/ASPA to Westview Press and then to M.E. Sharpe (subsequently subsumed by Taylor & Francis/Routledge in 2014).
- In 2003, Jeroen Maesschalck and Carole Jurkiewicz organized the first ASPA-European Group on Public Administration. Jurkiewicz followed James Bowman as editor of *Public Integrity* in 2014. She was followed in turn by Michael Potter in 2019 and Amanda Olejarski in 2020.

Jeremy Plant (2013) identified four other factors that stimulated ethics education in the 1960s through the 1980s: growing concern with the role of public managers and social equity, increasing interest among junior scholars in ethics, declining trust in government, and graduate program responses to incentives by professional associations to give attention to ethics in the curriculum.

Given this background of macro and meso developments and driving forces shaping the heritage of public administration, ethics, and ethics education, the next section explores selected contemporary contested issues in public affairs education and training.

FIVE CURRENT CONTESTED ISSUES

The What, Why and How of Ethics Instruction

Ethics education is controversial because there is little agreement on what to teach and how to teach it (Menzel, 2016*)*. In 1986, April Hejka-Ekins conducted a survey investigating the state of the art of ethics education in NASPAA graduate programs in public administration. She found that improving the moral judgment of students was the primary goal (more so than affecting their character or conduct), educators stress both the bureaucratic and democratic ethos, and they think the bureaucratic ethos characterizes the field, but they give greater attention to the democratic standards. To cultivate moral judgments, she reports the approach was either a utilitarian (weigh the probable consequences) or a deontological framework (uphold the moral principles at stake) or both.

One decade later, Don Menzel (1997) re-examined ethics pedagogy in NAS-PAA graduate PA/A programs by surveying MPA alumni to determine factors influencing MPA graduates' ethical outlook and behavior. He found the most important factors in rank order were: (1) discussion of ethics and values in ethics courses, (2) discussion of ethics and values in MPA coursework as a whole, (3) interaction with students in their MPA program, (4) discussion of codes of ethics and professional standards of conduct, (5) membership in a professional association, and (6) interaction with faculty outside the classroom. Menzel found the six most widely used instructional methodologies were (in rank order): lectures (71%), case studies (55%), research papers (48%), small group discussion (44%), decision-making scenarios (34%), and self-assessments (10%).

Regarding the effectiveness of ethics education, eight of ten respondents to Menzel's survey had experienced a job-related ethical dilemma and a plurality indicated their ethics education had helped them resolve the dilemma. Case studies and decision-making scenarios were especially helpful.[3] Overall, most of the alumni from the schools surveyed said that ethics education had made a difference in their professional lives. Five years later, Jurkiewicz and Nichols (2002) surveyed public administrators and found those who had completed a semester-long ethics course were able to distinguish ethical conflicts from other conflicts more often than those without formal ethics education. They were also more likely to refuse to behave unethically when directed to do so by a superior. Not all survey-based studies were as sanguine about the effectiveness of ethics education (e.g., Hug & Rowe, 1996; Kaptiein et al., 2005). Indeed, the impact of ethics training is still unknown. The only research that suggests an empirically valid impact is that of Jurkiewicz and Nichols, but their study is both limited and a more subjective assessment than empirical analysis.

One pedagogical method of ethics instruction is to introduce students to ethics in the abstract. Various decision-making models could illuminate whether a decision or action is ethical, but one is especially helpful because its broad scope—adding to that previously mentioned by Hedjka Ekins (1986)—reduces the chances of an incomplete assessment: the ethical triangle. Based upon an understanding of the three approaches to ethical standards, students can comprehend the duties unique to public administration (Svara, 2014). This framework encompasses three schools of thought based on: 1) expected results of an action (consequentialism or teleology), 2) application of ethical rules (deontology or duty ethics) and 3) personal character (virtue ethics). Inclusive yet succinct, the ethics triangle recognizes that the three schools of thought are complementary and interdependent (Svara, 2014; Garofalo & Geureas, 1999; Bowman & West, 2022). Other ethical frameworks can be broadly categorized by approaches under the rubric of consequences, principles, and virtues (see Kline & Aristigueta, 2020).

Pre-service and in-service public administration students should consider results, respect rules, and develop virtues to justify their decisions and actions. Contested issues can be analyzed in classes using the ethics triangle to produce more interesting—and often conflicting—findings. Each school of thought in the approach may advise a different course of action. When that occurs, the student at least has the satisfaction that the problem has been fully examined (Bowman & West, 2022).

Greater Attention to Behavioral Ethics

While teaching ethics in public administration often involves the use of rational decision- making models like the ethics triangle, behavioral ethics recognizes some of its shortcomings. The father of this behavioral approach, David Hume (1998 [1751]), argued that behavior is the result of the emotive not logical reasoning.[4] Focusing upon insights from psychology, sociology, and neurosciences, behavioral ethics helps to make philosophical models more practical. It challenges dubious assumptions about logical decision-making suggesting that orthodox models cannot adequately explain or predict how people will actually behave. Bounded ethicality may lead otherwise ethical decision makers to make questionable choices. The contributions of behavioral science to public administration and of behavioral ethics to public administration education have been slow to penetrate the field.

A review of the present status of behavioral decision science to research and practice of public service ethics indicates it has had modest impact (Bowman, 2018). Examination of half a dozen core textbooks used in public administration ethics courses found that while one did include behavioral ethics five did not (however, a recent edition of one of the latter books now has now added the behavioral approach), and a leading 16-chapter anthology also contained only one contribution on the topic. Nonetheless, there are some promising signs that the findings from behavioral science and attention to behavioral ethics are receiving increased attention in public administration. Recently, *Public Administration Review* published a lead article providing a comprehensive overview of behavioral public administration (Battaglio, et al., 2019). A special issue of *Public Integrity* considering the past, present, and future of ethics research dealt with the emergence of behavioral ethics (Bowman, 2018). Then, in 2018, the peer-reviewed, interdisciplinary *Journal of Behavioral Public Administration* was launched (Jilke et al., 2018).

With these developments, it is expected public service ethics instructors will see value in adding course material on crucial components of behaviorism to demonstrate how individuals frequently are not rational actors when confronting ethical dilemmas and how psychological tendencies, emotions, and situational factors can influence behavior. Concepts such as bounded rationality, System 1 and System 2 thinking, motivated reasoning, framing effects, and a plethora of conscious and unconscious stubborn biases can help explain decision making and have implications for ethical behavior (Bazerman & Tenbrunsel, 2011; Bowman & West, 2022; Kahneman, 2011). However, there may be some hesitancy to include consideration of these blindspots in ethics courses, partially explained by instructors' uncertainty about how to incorporate behavioral ethics into their courses or the view that behavioral psychology departments in their institution might provide students with this content. However, instructors, scholars, and practitioners are encouraged to capitalize on the considerable potential for inquiry, education, and practice from this interesting field. The ethics course should include discussion concerning how to overcome blindspots and other behavioral shortcomings such as snap decisions.

Single Standalone Class and/or Teaching Ethics across the Curriculum

Whether ethics should be taught as a stand-alone course, offered across the curriculum, or offered in both forms to be debated (Bowman & Menzel, 1998; Griffith, et al., 2014, Jurkiewicz, 2013; King, et al., 2019; Plant, 2013; Willey, et al., 2012). Various professional accreditation bodies have permitted individual institutions to choose their teaching approach (Bowman & Menzel, 1998; Sanders & Hoffman, 2010; Willey, et al., 2012). While both approaches are used; however, concerns have been raised about the effectiveness of non-stand-alone approaches (Bowman & Menzel, 1998; Cooper & Menzel, 2013; Jurkiewicz, 2013). NASPAA Accreditation standards provide no specific requirements on methods of instruction (Plant, 2013) and since 2009 have not included an explicit reference to ethics in its core competencies (Svara, 2022, p. 187).

Over the years, the stand-alone ethics approach has increased from less than one quarter in 1980 (21%) to nearly three quarters in 2011 (74%) (Jurkiewicz, 2013; Menzel, 1997, 1998; Worthley & Grumet, 1983), but there is some limited-sample, qualitative evidence that the separate ethics course is regressing at universities (Scurr, 2016).[5] Dalton Lee (1989) discussed the barriers to teaching public service ethics, many of which continue to be relevant more than three decades later regardless of which pedagogical strategy is followed. These include the lack of available teaching tools, clarity in both the field and among PA profession about ethics, faculty and student interest, connecting teaching ethics and ethical behavior, qualified instructors, financial resources, NASPAA guidelines regarding teaching ethics, and too many required courses already.[6]

Both pedagogical approaches confront challenges, with special obstacles confronting the embedded approach given the high transaction costs required to integrate ethics in all core courses, the possible diluting of ethical concepts and issues, and concerns that instructors may lack adequate knowledge of ethical theory (Plant, 2013). Nonetheless, some faculty believe that teaching ethics across the curriculum is more effective and valuable than introducing ethics to students in a stand-alone course (Menzel, 1998).

Bowman et al. (2001) urged educators to review ethical standards of conduct by examining the content of 12 general public administration textbooks. They found that all included some coverage, although limited, of four pillars of ethics: value awareness; reasoning skills; the role of law; and, strategy implementation. While the findings demonstrate the presence of basic ethics instruction in the curriculum, ethics may not be consistently covered in sufficient depth across the curriculum (p. 195).

Building upon the work of Hoeppel and Wadsworth (1992) and applying it to ethics, April Hejka-Ekins (1998), discusses the steps necessary to infuse ethics in courses throughout the curriculum in ways that address the barriers identified by Lee (1989). The basic steps include identifying key stakeholders (faculty, department chair, dean), holding a strategy session (gaining project team input and buy in), conducting a needs assessment (identifying ethical dilemmas in the subfields and ways to address them), developing a plan (building a rationale and strategy for teaching ethics, gathering bibliographic references and case resources, training faculty), building capacity for faculty (workshops, incentives), and evaluating the plan (considering the ways the barriers identified by Lee can be addressed in the steps of the Hoeppel and Wadsworth approach to curriculum infusion). Hejka-Ekins does not view the issue of ethics infusion as an either/or choice between a stand-alone vs. ethic-across-the-curriculum option and the above steps could be followed under either pedagogical approach.

If the decision is to integrate ethics across the curriculum in courses like human resource management, project management, and policy making (as recently suggested by Raadschelders & Chitiga, 2021), an important unanswered question concerns the competence of instructors. This question is addressed regarding the human resource management course in an article by McBeth et al. (2021) showing instructors how to use case studies to spur discussion and elicit theoretical insights on issues like hiring processes, insider information, implicit bias, whistleblowing, and other HR topics with ethical dimensions. A similar pedagogical approach could be used in other core courses in the MPA curriculum if the instructors are willing and able to incorporate ethics effectively into their course design. To this end, James Svara (2014, chapter 11) examines ethical issues in each of the core curricular areas and identifies ethical problems and challenges that could be examined in each course.

Ethics Education and Current Events

Since teaching ethics is difficult and the best way to teach it is subject of debate (Facer & Bradbury, 2005), instructors need to consider carefully content selection and ways to engage students' moral imagination. Such decisions can influence, encourage, and enable present and future public service professionals to act ethically. A contentious issue is the extent to which class content should focus upon contemporary developments by relying on examples from news stories and popular culture. One way instructors can capture student interest in public service ethics is to center the instruction upon current topics in the news. For example, carefully considering the nation's and world's experience with the COVID-19 crisis can spark discussion of public health choices facing government and nonprofit administrators (e.g., rationing health care services, variable impacts of coronavirus on minority communities) and cultivate new insights by examining them through the lens of different ethical theories. This approach helps show students how institutions and their leaders are responding to the ethical challenges in real time.

Topics for debate, case studies, group work, and research are plentiful—consider issues surrounding the Black Lives Matter movement, police use of force and ethical policing, climate changes and its impacts, the use of misuse of political powers, whistleblowing problems, implicit bias, white-collar crime and how to control it, and technological developments (drones, robots, surveillance activities) with their positive and negative implications. These and other complicated current issues often involve the exercise of administrative discretion provide opportunities to demonstrate the applicability of theoretical models to real-time events and offer useful examples of dilemmas and behaviors. Engaging students through discussion of current events can get them to unpack administrative issues through an ethics lens. A 2020 Call for Papers on Ethics Education in Public Administration by the *Journal of Public Affairs Education* resulted in 27 proposals, a few exploring ethics education in relation to such challenging contemporary events or societal changes (e.g., ethics education during COVID-19, ethics training post-pandemic, ethics training for law enforcement).

The ethics literature also provides numerous examples of instructors' experience using movies, videos, documentaries, television series, Ted Talks, and other forms of visual media to demonstrate the pervasiveness of ethics in our daily lives and how analytical frameworks can help students to understand and explain events or the actions of decision makers. For example, Seth Meyer's 2020 article in *Public Integrity* describes how he builds his course on Administrative Ethics around a case study of the TV series, "The Good Place." Meyers provides an extensive list of other articles that use visual media to highlight moral dilemmas and provide context for applying ethical theories, including TV shows like Parks and Recreation (Borry, 2018), Grey's Anatomy (Fariña, 2009), the Office (Del Campo et al., 2010), and a variety of movies like Schindler's List (Dubnick, 2000) or Captain America: Civil Wars (Bharath, 2019; see Dubnick, 2000 and Jurkiewicz

& Giacalone, 2000, for movie lists highlighting ethical issues, public administration, and the use of film in the classroom).

The Elusive Value of Ethics Training

Ethics violations have led many organizations to offer ethics training to employees and managers. Debates are ongoing about the content, style, frequency and effectiveness of training (Menzel, 2015). Often viewed as a "lower order of instruction" than the more theoretical approach to professional responsibility emphasized in university courses (Berman, et al., 2022; Plant, 2013), normative ethics and tools like the ethics triangle are not often included in training. The purpose is often to ensure that personnel are aware of important laws, codes, and policies (e.g., gift taking, conflict of interest) and steps to comply with them. These training sessions can be required or voluntary, online or in-person, general or tailored to the needs of a specific function (e.g., health care, law enforcement). Information about laws, rules, and policies related to such things as government travel, misuse of government office, post-government employment, working with contractors, sexual harassment, hiring, and so forth may be discussed as part of compliance training. A broader approach, though less frequently found, is integrity training which goes beyond a compliance focus to engage trainees creatively with positive inducements and decision tools that assist in dealing with challenging ethical dilemmas, applying moral principles, and aspiring to higher ethical standards (Menzel, 2015).

Ethics training is likely to be most effective when it is tailored and integrated into how the organization is run (West et al., 2013). A few local government studies support this point, for example, West and Berman (2004) found that about two thirds of U.S. cities with populations over 50,000 use some form of ethics training. While such training is mandatory in about one third of cities, the mean duration of the training is only about one-half day per year. The results indicate that targeted ethics training focused upon agency-specific applications and practices rather than emphasizing general awareness is integrated with broader management efforts. Ethics trainings is correlated with critical organizational variables—organizational culture, labor-management relations, and employee productivity. A key finding is that moral leadership by senior managers influences or even drives all other activities. Findings also indicate that the presence of a code of conduct is not as important in contributing to increased commitment by staff as monitoring adherence to the code combined with ethics training.

By 2012, an International City/County Management Association State of the Profession Survey found slightly more than half of responding local governments offered ethics training. More recent research by Bruce Perlman and colleagues (2021) reported on a national survey of ethics training in local governments finding that topical coverage emphasized compliance-related content (low-road ethics) more than integrity-based content (high-road ethics). In an earlier but related study, Feldheim and Wang (2003–2004) surveyed 100 largest local governments finding that more than a third regularly offered ethics workshops. Research surveying chiefs of police in 100 U.S. cities found support for the value of training that reinforces departmental policies, encourages reporting of unethical actions and helps to identify ethical issues for discussion (Wyatt-Nichol & Franks, 2009). Menzel (2012) and Bowman et al. (2010) provide more examples of training offered in local, state, and federal governments. Determining the long-term effectiveness of this training is often difficult and is more likely to be effective if reinforced by other management tools, including role modeling, conduct codes, oaths, appraisal, feedback, and continuous messaging that ethical conduct matters (Berman et al., 2022).

In public administration, a general reading of the state of ethics education is "We believe ethics education and training has an impact, but we are not sure." It may be that business—especially large corporations with greater financial resources to make an in-depth assessment—have been more successful in evaluating the effectiveness of ethics training. Corporations like Lockheed-Martin, Merck Pharmaceuticals, Toshiba, and Royal Dutch Shell found their codes of conduct provided only a foundation for broader issues. Ethics training in business, echoing the findings above regarding the experience in government, needs to be supplemented with regular discussion of ethics issues, whistleblower protection, and effective actions taken against those who violate their trust. This conclusion is supported by many university studies as well as the bi-annual National Business Ethics Survey by the Ethics Resource Center. Yet, both sectors are still stymied in effectively evaluating the long-term impact of ethics training.

The preceding discussion is limited to five contentious issues. However, several others are important as well, including but not limited to: the instructional challenges of online vs. in-person classes; teaching ethics to a diverse workforce in a changing workplace; the role of codes, oaths, cases, and laws in ethics instruction; ethics education strategies for developing countries; and, competing approaches for developing ethical competency (more information on competency development is briefly provided in the next section). To know what is really happening in graduate public administration ethics courses in the United States, we now turn to an examination of ethics course syllabi.

A SNAPSHOT EXAMINATION OF 51 COURSE SYLLABI

In order to understand better what is actually taught and how it is taught in public administration ethics courses, the focus now shifts to examination of 51 course syllabi.[7] Following a brief discussion of the sample and some background information regarding the course instructors, the findings are presented.

The study sample included 51 stand-alone course syllabi collected by the author in 2017 from 43 public and 8 private U.S. universities. Three of the private schools were religious institutions and 42 of the 51 were from NASPAA accredited programs. Among those teaching the courses, 88 percent of instructors had Ph.D.s, 6 percent had JDs, and 6 percent did not specify the academic degrees of the instructor. In terms of instructor's academic rank, 45 percent are full professors, 25 percent are associate professors, 4 percent are assistant professors, 18 percent are instructors/lecturers or teaching assistants, and 8 percent did not specify the academic rank of the teacher. Regarding the instructor's gender, 68 percent are male, 28 percent are female, and in 4 percent of the syllabi it was not possible to discern their gender.

Regarding the teaching style adopted among those in the sample, 44 percent used a combination of lecture/seminar, 16 percent used seminar, 18 percent were online, 4 percent were hybrid (online/in-person), and 18 percent did not specify the teaching style.

There was marked similarity in the required textbooks used. Three-fourths (39) out of 51 instructors used one of five textbooks (76.5%), 31 (60.8%) used one of three textbooks, and 25 used one of two textbooks (49%). The five most frequently used texts were: Terry Cooper, *The Responsible Administrator: An Approach to Ethics for the Administrative Role* (13 users); James Svara, *The Ethics Primer: For Public Administrators in Government and Nonprofit Organizations* (12 users); James Bowman and Jonathan West, *Public Service Ethics: Individual and Institutional Responsibilities* (6 users); Rosemary O'Leary, *The Ethics of Dissent: Managing Guerrilla Government* (4 users); and Sissela Bok, *Lying: Moral Choice in Public and Private Life* (4 users).[8]

In addition to or in place of textbooks instructors use other publications. Articles from ten journals or media outlets were among the reading assignments shown in the course syllabi. Based upon the total times each publication was used for reading assignments, the five most frequently used were: *Public Administration Review* (98), *Public Integrity* (93), *Nonprofit and Voluntary Sector Quarterly* (12), *New York Times* (11), and *Administration & Society* (7). Other journals listed on syllabi include: *American Review of Public Administration* (6), *Journal of Business Ethics* (4), *Criminal Justice Ethics* (3), *Ethics and Behavior* (3), and *CQ Researchers* (3).

Thus, where specific journal articles were used for required reading assignments, 44 percent of all assignments were drawn from either *Public Administration Review* or *Public Integrity*. However, the overwhelming majority of 51 course syllabi did not include any journal articles in their reading assignments. Those that did assign journal articles tended to rely heavily on these scholarly research outlets (e.g., one instructor used 23 journal and news articles).

An important chapter in Terry Cooper and Don Menzel's (2013) edited book, *Achieving Ethical Competence for Public Service Leadership*, was written by Carole Jurkiewicz titled, "Advancing Ethical Competence Through Pedagogy." In this chapter, she identified five key ethical competencies: understanding moral philosophy and moral arguments, ability to distinguish moral issues separate from other issues, ability to logically reason regarding resolution of ethical problems, students' enhanced understanding of their own and others' ethical frameworks, and ability to perform ethically despite pressures. Table 7.1 from Jurkiewicz's chapter identifies elements or topics of an ethics course that could be linked to the five factors of ethical competence.

Data from the 51 course syllabi were coded using the Jurkiewicz-posited links between course content topics and the five factors of ethical competence (Table 7.2). Results identify the percentage of coverage of each of the factors among the courses examined. While the range of coverage of the five factors is from a high of 33.6 percent (Understanding Moral Philosophy and Moral Arguments) to a low of 25 percent (Students Enhanced Understanding of Their Own and Others' Ethical

TABLE 7.1.   Elements of An Ethics Course Linked to the Five Factors of Ethical Competence

Topic	A	B	C	D	E
Introduction to public service ethics	X	X			
Philosophical Modeling	X	X	X	X	
Ethics and law	X	X	X		
Ethical decision making	X	X	X		X
Ethics code		X		X	
Ethics policy		X		x	
Whistleblowing		X	X	X	X
Ethical vs. unethical behavior	X	X		X	
Lying		X		X	
Ethics in crises		X	X	X	
The cost of ethics (Ethinomics)	X	X	X	X	
Situational ethics	X	X	X	X	
Ethics and politics		X		X	X
Power and ethics	X	X		X	X
Ethical leadership		X	X	X	X
Organizational evil	X	X		X	X
Moral dilemmas	X	X	X	X	X
Virtues	X	X		X	
Ethics audit		X	X		X
Ethical wills		X		X	
Ethics measures	X	X	X	X	X

Key:
A: Understanding moral philosophy and moral arguments
B: Ability to distinguish moral issues separate from other issues
C: Ability to logically reason regarding resolution of ethical problems
D: Students' enhanced understanding of own and others' ethical frameworks
E: Ability to perform ethically despite pressures

Adapted from Jurkiewicz, C. L. (2013)

TABLE 7.2.   Percentage of Class Time Taken Up by Each of the Five Factors of Ethical Competence

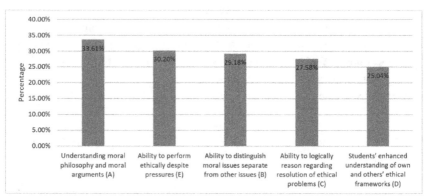

Frameworks), each of the factors received substantial coverage. From this analysis, it appears instructors of these courses are including content that contributes to competency development in Jurkieweicz's five areas.

The percent of specific topics addressed shows that seven topics were addressed in a majority of the courses examined. These include: introduction to public service ethics (80.4%), moral dilemmas (74.5%), ethical decision-making (56.9%), ethics codes (54.9%), ethical leadership (54.9%), philosophical modeling (52,9%), and obedience/duty (52.9%). Between 45 and 49 percent of courses also addressed: virtues (49.0%), whistleblowing (47.1%), and ethics and law (45.1%). A lower percent of courses also addressed: ethics and politics (35.3%) as well as ethical vs. unethical behavior (27.5%).[9]

Regarding assessment criteria used in determining student performance, the syllabi identify a range of grading factors. The five most frequently used assessment approaches are: class participation (38), case study analysis (30), final exam (27), midterm exam (22), and oral presentations (22).[10]

To summarize, the syllabi indicate that the bulk of the ethics instructors are Ph.D.-trained, senior faculty, and predominantly male. Most teach in a lecture/seminar format and select textbooks from a half-dozen published works. Scholarly journals are seldom included as required reading; when used, articles in *PAR* and *Public Integrity* are most often assigned. The coverage of ethical competencies is fairly evenly distributed across five factors identified in the literature, together reflecting broad topical coverage. Assessment strategies rely heavily upon class participation, case studies, exams and written papers.

SUMMARY AND CONCLUSIONS

This chapter highlighted the macro U.S. government reforms over the past century and a half and their ethical implications. It analyzed the evolution of the meso public administration profession's interest in ethics and ethics instruction over the bulk of this period. While interest in ethics has increased over time among American government policy makers and within the public administration profession, contentious issues remain to be resolved surrounding ethics education. Those highlighted here concerning the nature, extent and delivery of ethics instruction; the challenge to incorporate the latest findings from behavioral ethics; the stand-alone course versus or with ethics-across-the-curriculum approach; the effective inclusion of current events to engage student interest and demonstrate the relevance of ethical theory; and, the uncertain impacts of ethics training on managerial or employee behavior. Some of these issues have been debated for several decades and remain contentious; others have recently emerged and will receive increased attention in the future.

While many of the issues confronting ethics education in public administration may be mirrored in other fields and disciplines, the unique public service context with its emphasis upon both the democratic ethos and bureaucratic values makes it distinctly different. It is also distinctive in that almost every federal, state, and local government has an enforceable code of ethics or standards of conduct which public administrators are required to follow. The immediate impact of codes for the vast majority of public administrators is that ethical lapses have significant real-world consequences—through criminal law and administrative regulations and penalties, and in some cases civil law liability. Another distinguishing feature of public service at the federal and state level and in all three branches of government is oath taking. This transpires when, upon assuming office, public officials swear an oath as evidence of dedication, commitment, and duty to the constitution. In this way, stating and acting upon such public pledges plays an important role in upholding democratic values and reinforcing the bond between the populace and public officials (Bowman & West, 2019, 2021a, 2021b).

Given that each profession—like public administration—has its distinctive or unique ways of approaching ethics education, this volume makes it possible to examine what might be transferable from one context or field to another. The selections in this volume also make possible a synthesis of lessons that should reveal what each profession can learn from the others to further enrich our understanding of this fascinating area of ethics education and training.

What can ethics educators in other disciplines or fields learn from the experience of public administration educators concerning the teaching of ethics?[11]

Some lessons or "provocative" responses to this question as they concern American ethics reforms and ethics instruction from public administration include:

- Actions to improve individual and institutional performance need to achieve balance among conflicting values such as efficiency and ethics.
- Nudges from professional associations can increase the salience, sophistication, and effectiveness of ethics education.

- Work is needed by ethics instructors to draw more broadly on cross-disciplinary scholarly research to capture the insights from their own and related fields (e.g., philosophy, psychology, law, business, behavioral science) and to enrich ethics education.
- Course design needs to reflect the importance of government context—policies, processes and pedagogical practices—and democratic norms that can influence the content, delivery systems, and success of ethics education initiatives.
- Ethical competency development and assessment, including self-assessment, is an increasingly important topic deserving on-going attention from ethics instructors and researchers. Helpful in this regard is the ASPA publication *Implementing the ASPA Code of Ethics: Workbook and Assessment Guide* (American Society for Public Administration, 2016).
- Curricular revisions may be required to reflect the shift from government provision of services to new governance with many indirect and cross-sector service providers that raises numerous ethical issues that need inclusion in the ethics curriculum.
- Strategic plans are needed to recruit new, younger, diverse faculty members with an interest in teaching ethics to replace many of the faculty nearing retirement who have been responsible for ethics instruction for years.

It is expected that lessons from ethics educators in other disciplines and fields will spark new insights that will further enhance ethics instruction in public administration. The volume in which this chapter is included will help ensure that a cross-fertilization of ideas takes place that hopefully will lead to more effective ethics education in multiple professions.

ENDNOTES

1. While this chapter focuses primarily on ethics education in graduate programs in the United States it is important to recognize that it is only a segment of important ethics education and training efforts. Some of these efforts are outside of the public administration community in departments of political science, philosophy, psychology, and sociology. However, the majority of the work of providing ethics education and training comes from non-academic programs, such as, professional groups and governments at all levels in the U.S. and around the world. A few examples illustrate the range of such efforts: The Office of Government Ethics provides annual ethics training to all senior U.S. officials, as well as, entry and regular training all other employees (civilian and military) of the executive branch; the International City-County Management Association has provided ethics training to local officials for the past 30 years; The Council of Government Ethics Laws was a coordinating body for state and local ethics officials and developed several training mod-

ules that continue to be used; the World Bank, the IMF, the Council of Europe, the Asia Development Banks all invested resources on ethics education, and training as part of their loan and grant making activities; and the UN Convention against Corruption has been ratified by more than 187 countries and bodies and focuses on preventive measures including ethics training.

2. One concern with the newer approach to "doing right things" is that it drifts into doing policy. For example, in social equity the narrow public administration focus would be on hiring, promoting, and retaining people without prejudice, the "right thing" is to advance the policy focus of ensuring fair representation of groups in the administration. The question is whether this kind of discretion is ethical within a democratic context. Should nonelected officials be making grand policy?

3. A helpful example of using case studies to teach moral reasoning can be found in Himmelreich and Cohen (2021). Examination of case law is also a useful way to encourage students to think broadly and deeply about ethics in public administration (see Szypszak, 2021).

4. Contemporary scholars like Jonathan Haidt (2012) conclude that emotional reactions precede moral judgments. For consideration of integrating emotive competencies in public administration education see Awasthi and Mastracci (2021).

5. As of 2002, a mandatory ethics course was offered in 23 percent of accredited and non-accredited MPA programs; 39% offered elective courses (Jurkiewicz & Giacalone, 2002, p. 57; Jurkiewicz & Nichols, 2002, p. 103).

6. In many programs the number of required courses is much smaller than the number of elective courses.

7. A presentation of results from this research on ethics syllabi was made at the annual NASPAA meeting in Washington, D.C. in 2017.

8. Other books used in courses include: *Defining Moments: When Managers Must Choose Between Right and Right; Ethics in City Hall: Discussion and Analysis for Public Administration*; *Ethics Management for Public Administrators*; *Managing in the Public Sector: A Case Book of Ethics and Leadership*; Ethics *for Public Managers*; *Blind Spots: Why We Fail to Do What's Right and What to Do About* it; *Ethics and Politics: Cases and Comments*; *Unmasking Administrative Evil*; *Justice: What is the Right Thing to Do?*; and *Administrative Law for Public Managers: Essentials of Public Policy and Administration.* Clearly, instructors have a wide range of text materials to draw on; however, a few books clearly dominate the course adoptions.

9. Ten topics from the Jurkiewicz list were found in less than 20 percent of courses, including the following: lying, behavior of ethics, ethics training in organizations, organizational evil, power and ethics, ethics policy,

distributive/procedural justice, change/social change, ethics in crises and ethics measures. None of the syllabi included: the cost of ethics, situational ethics, ethics audits and ethical wills. While some of these topics may receive little or no attention on the syllabus, they may be covered within the chapters or articles assigned.

10. Other approaches less frequently used (13 or fewer) include: research paper, ethical paper, term/final paper, regular homework, chapter/book reviews, current event analysis, regular writing posts, short essay, quiz, study questions, discussion leaders, create ethics code, penalizing irregular participation, praxis paper, analysis paper, diversity paper, and blog post. Compared to classes on other subjects, the greater assessment weight in these ethics offerings was given to participation, cases, and various forms of research papers.

11. This question draws on a theme at the heart of a symposium edited by Richard Jacobs addressing the question, "What might public administration ethics educators have to suggest to business administration ethics educators concerning the teaching of ethics?" published as a special edition in the *Journal of Management Systems* (2015).

REFERENCES

American Society for Public Administration. (2016). *Implementing the ASPA code of ethics: Workbook and assessment guide*. ASPA. https://www.aspanet.org/ASPADocs/Membership/Ethics_Assessment_Guide.pdf

Awasthi, P., & Mastracci, S. (2021). Integrating emotive competencies in public affairs education. *Journal of Public Affairs Education*. https://doi.org/10.1080/15236803.2021.1947072

Battaglio, P., Belardinelli, P., Belle, N., & Cantarelli, P. (2019). Behavioral public administration ad fronts: A Synthesis of research on bounded rationality, cognitive biases, and nudging in public administration. *Public Administration Review, 79*(3), 304–320.

Bazerman, M., & Tenbrunsel, A. (2011). *Blindspots: Why we fail to do what's right and what to do about it.* Princeton University Press.

Berman, E., Bowman, J., West, J., & Van Wart, M. (2022). *Human resource management in public service: Paradoxes, processes, and problems.* Sage.

Bharath, D. M. (2019). Ethical decision making and the avengers: Lessons from the screen to the classroom. *Public Integrity,* 1–4. https://doi-org/10.1080/10999922.2019.1600352

Borry, E. L. (2018). Teaching public ethics with TV: Parks and Recreation as a source of case studies. *Public Integrity, 20*(3), 300–315. https://doi-org.access.library.miami.edu/10.1080/10999922.2017.1371998

Bowman, J. (1981). Introduction to special issue. *Public Personnel Management, 10*(1), 1–2.

Bowman, J. (2018). Thinking about thinking: Beyond decision-making rationalism and the emergence of behavioral ethics. *Public Integrity, 20*(Supplement 1), 89–105.

Bowman, J., Berman, E., & West, J. (2001). The profession of public administration: An ethics edge in introductory textbooks? *Public Administration Review, 61*(2), 194–205.

Bowman, J., & Menzel, D. (1998). *Teaching ethics and values in public administration programs: Innovations, strategies and issues.* SUNY Press.

Bowman, J., & West, J. (2019). Pointless or powerful: The case for oaths of office. *Administration & Society.* https://doi.org/10.1177/0095399719890836

Bowman, J., & West, J. (2021a). Oaths of office in American states: Problems and prospects. *Public Personnel Management, 50*(1), 109–133.

Bowman, J., & West, J. (2021b). Classical rationalism and contemporary realism: Oaths of office an empty formality or empowering function? *Public Integrity.* http://doi.org/10.10800/10999922.2021.1902035

Bowman, J., & West, J. (2022). *Public service ethics: Individual and institutional responsibilities.* CQ Press.

Bowman, J., West, J., & Beck, M. (2010). *Achieving competencies in public service: The professional edge.* M. E. Sharpe.

Bowman, J., West, J., Berman, E., & Van Wart, M. (2004). *The professional edge: Competencies in public service.* Routledge.

Branch, T. (2009). The odd couple. Washington Monthly. In A. Gumann, & D. Thompson (Eds.), *Ethics & politics: Cases & comments* (pp. 193–202). Nelson Hall.

Brownell, K. (2020). *Watergate, the bipartisan struggle for media access, and the growth of cable television.* Cambridge University Press. http://Cambridge.org/core/jourals/modern-america_american+history/article/watergate_the_bipartisan_strugle_for_media_access

Budd, J., & Scoville, J. (Eds.). (2005). *The ethics of human resources and industrial relations.* Labor and Employment Relations Association. LERA.

Carter, S. (1996). *Integrity.* HarperCollins.

Cooper, T. (1994). *The handbook of administrative ethics* (revised and expanded). Marcel Dekker.

Cooper, T. (2012). *The responsible administrator: An approach to ethics for the administrative role.* Kennikat Press.

Cooper, T., & Menzel, D. (Eds.). (2013). *Achieving ethical competencies for public service leadership.* M.E. Sharpe.

Dobel, P. (2019). *Public leadership ethics: A management approach.* Routledge.

Downs, G., & Larkey, P. (1986). *The search for government efficiency.* Temple University Press.

Dubnick, M. (2000). Movies and morals: Energizing ethical thinking among professionals. *Journal of Public Affairs Education, 6*(3), 147–159.

Facer, R., & Bradbury, M. (2005). Practical strategies for increasing ethical behavior in the workplace. In S. E. Condrey (Ed.), *Handbook of human resource management in government* (pp. 257–271). Jossey-Bass Publishers.

Fariña, J. (2009). A model for teaching bioethics and human rights through cinema and popular TV series: A methodological approach. *Counselling Psychology Quarterly, 22*(1), 105–117. https://doi-org.access.library.miami.edu/10.1080/09515070902853946

Feldheim, M., & Wang, X. (2003–2004). Ethics and public trust: Results from a national survey. *Public Integrity, 6*(1), 63–75.

Ferlie, E. (2017). The new public management and public management studies. *Oxford research encyclopedia.* http://doi.org/10.1093/acrefore/9780190224851.013.129

Finer, H. (1941). Administrative responsibility in democratic government. *Public Administration Review, 1,* 336–50.

Frederickson, H. G. (1980). *New public administration.* University of Alabama Press.

Friedrich, C. (1940). Public policy and the nature of administrative responsibility. In C. Friedrich (Ed.) *Public policy* (pp. 5–6, 19–20). Harvard University Press.

Greenwood, M. (2013). Ethical analysis of HRM: A review and research agenda. *Journal of Business Ethics, 114,* 355–366.

Griffith, S., Domenech, R., Anderson, M., & Austin, J. (2014). *Training and Education in Professional Psychology, 8*(4), 248–252.

Haidt, J. (2012). *The reflective mind: Why good people are divided by politics and religion.* Pantheon Books.

Hejka-Ekins, A. (1986). Teaching ethics in public administration. *Public Administration Review, 48*(5), 885–891.

Heika-Ekins, A. (1998). Teaching ethics across the public administration curriculum. *Journal of Public Affairs Education, 4*(1), 45–50.

Hijal-Moghrabi, I., & Sabharwal, M. (2018). Ethics in American public administration: A response to a changing reality. *Public Integrity, 20*(50), 459–477.

Himmelreich, J., & Cohen, J. (2021). Teaching moral reasoning: Why and how to use the trolley problem. *Journal of Public Affairs Education.* https://doi.org/10.1080/1523 6803.2021.1966591

Hoeppel, J., & Wadsworth, E. (1992). *Prevention across the curriculum: Leadership in education in advance prevention.* Northeastern Illinois University.

Hug, R., & Rowe, L. (1996). *City manager perceptions of the International City/County Management Association code of ethics and guidelines.* Southeastern Conference on Public Administration, Miami, FL, United States.

Hume, D. (1998 [1751]). *An enquiry concerning the principles of morals: A critical edition* (T.L. Beauchamp, Ed.). Clarendon Press.

Jacobs, R. (2015). An audacious, arrogant, and/or ignorant question? *Journal of Management Systems,* 1041–2808.

Jacobs, R. (2019). *Teaching public administration ethics: A 20-year Public Integrity retrospective. Public Integrity.* https://think.taylorandfranciscom/teaching-public-administration-ethics/#?utm_source=CPB&utm_mediu=cms&utm_campaign=JOAO7838

Jilke, S., Meier, K., & Van Ryzin, G. (2018). *Journal of Behavioral Administration, 1*(1), 1–3. http://doi.org/10.30636/jbpa.11.9

Jurkiewicz, C. (2013). Advancing ethical competency through pedagogy. In T. Cooper, & D. Menzel (Eds.), *Achieving ethical competence for public service leadership.* M. E. Sharpe.

Jurkiewicz, C., & Giacalone, R. A. (2000). Through the lens clearly: Using films to demonstrate ethical decision-making in the public service. *Journal of Public Affairs Education, 6*(4), 257–265.

Jurkiewicz, C. L., & Giacalone, R. A. (2002). Learning through teaching: demonstrating ethical applications through a training session and manual development exercise. *Journal of Public Affairs Education, 8*(1), 57–70. https://doi-org.access.library.miami.edu/10.1080/15236803.2002.12023533

Jurkiewicz, C., & Nichols, K. (2002). Ethics education in the MPA curriculum: What difference does it make? *Journal of Public Affairs Edu*cation, *8*(2), 103–114.

Kahneman, D. (2011). *Thinking fast and slow*. Farrar, Straus and Giroux.

Kaptiein, M., Huberts, L., Avelino, S., & Lasthuizen, K. (2005). Demonstrating ethical leadership by measuring ethics. *Public Integrity, 7*(4), 299–311.

King, S., Agyapong, E., & Robert, G. (2019). ASPA code of ethics as a framework for teaching ethics in public affairs and administration: A conceptual content analysis of MPA ethics course syllabi. *Journal of Public Affairs Education, 27*(2), 176–197.

Kline, A., & Aristigueta, M. (2020). Ethical decision making. In C. Jurkiewicz, S. Gilman & C. Lewis (Eds.), *Global corruption and ethics management: Translating theory into action* (pp. 143–150). Rowman & Littlefield.

Lee, D. (1989). The challenge of teaching PA ethics. *The Political Science Teacher,* Fall, 1–4.

Lewis, C., & Gilman, S. (2012). *The ethics challenge in public service: A problem solving guide*. Jossey-Bass.

Light, P. (1997). *The tides of reform: Making government work, 1945–1995*. Yale University Press.

Light, P. (2020). Catch-22 government: Federal performance in peril. In J. Perry (Ed.), *Public service and good governance for the twenty-first century* (pp. 14–42). University of Pennsylvania Press.

Lynn, L. (2008). *New public management comes to America*. Harris School of Public Policy Studies, University of Chicago Working Papers.

McBeth, M., Brewer, A., & Lund, J. (2021). Ethics in the public human resource management course: An integrated and case approach to decision making. *Journal of Public Affairs Education*. https://doi.ort/10.1080/15236803.2021,1938485

Menzel, D. (1997). Teaching ethics and values in public administration: Are we making a difference? *Public Administration Review, 57*(3), 224–230.

Menzel, D. (1998). To act ethically: The what, why, and how of ethics pedagogy. *Journal of Public Affairs Education, 4*(1), 11–18.

Menzel, D. (2005). Research on ethics and integrity in governance: A review and assessment. *Public Integrity, 7*(2), 147–168.

Menzel, D. (2012). *Ethics management for public administrators.* M. E. Sharpe.

Menzel, D. (2015). Research on ethics and integrity in public administration: Moving forward, looking back. *Public Integrity, 18*, 343–370.

Menzel, D. (2016). *Ethics management for public administrators: Building organizations of integrity.* Routledge.

Menzel, D., & Carson, K. (1999). A review and assessment of empirical research on public administration ethics: Implications for scholars and managers, *Public Integrity, 1*(3), 239–264.

Mertins, H. (1979). *Professional standards and ethics: A workbook for public administrators.* ASPA.

Meyer, S. (2020). Everything is fine! Using "The Good Place" to teach administrative ethics. *Journal of Public Affairs Education*. https://doi.org.access.library.miami.edu/10.1080/15236803.2020.1782102

Miller, P. (1996). *Strategy and the ethical management of human resources*. Wiley Online Library. Wiley.http://onlinelibrary.wiley.com/doi/abs/10.1111/j1748-8583.1996.tb00393.x

Mosher, F. (1968). *Democracy and the public service*. Oxford University Press.

Mosher, W. (1938). Public administration: The profession of public service. *American Political Science Review, 32*(2), 3322–342.

Newell, T. (2015). *To serve with honor: Doing the right thing in government*. Loftland Press.

O'Leary, R. (2006). *The ethics of dissent: Managing guerrilla government*. CQ Press.

Perlman, B., Reddick, C., Demir, T., & Ogilby, S. (2021). What do local governments teach about in ethics training? Compliance versus integrity. *Journal of Public Affairs Education*. http://doi.org/10.1080/15236803.2021.1972742

Pinnington, A., Macklin, R., & Campbell, T. (Eds.). (2007). *Human resource management: Ethics and employment*. Oxford University Press.

Plant, J. (2013). Ethical competence and professionalism in public administration. In T. Cooper & D. Menzel (Eds.), *Achieving ethical competency for public service* (pp. 189–217). M. E. Sharpe.

Plant, J., & Ran, B. (2009). Education for ethics and human resource management. *Public Integrity, 11*(3), 21–228.

Raadschelders, J., & Chitiga, M. (2021). Ethics education in the study of public administration: Anchoring to civility, civics, social justice, and understanding government in democracy. *Journal of Public Affairs Education*. https://doi10.1080/15236803.2021.1054468

Raadschelders, J., Whetsell, T., Diamand, A.-M., & Kieninger, K. (2019). *Journal of Public Affairs Education* at 25: Topics, trends, and authors. *Journal of Public Affairs Education, 25*(1), 51–72. https://doi-org.access.library.miami.edu/10.1080/15236803.2018.1546506

Radu, B., & Hamlin, R. (2005). *Corruption and ethical issues retarding public-private partnership*. http://researchgate.net/publication/265195973_Corruption_and_ethical_issues_regarding-public-private_partnership

Rohr, J. (1978). *Ethics for bureaucrats: An essay on law and values*. Marcel Dekker.

Rosenthal, L., & Trost, C. (2012). *In steep: The precipitous rise of the Tea Party*. University of California Press.

Sanders, S., & Hoffman, K. (2010). Ethics education in social work: Comparing outcomes of graduate social work students. *Journal of Social Work Education, 46*(1), 7–22.

Schachter, H. (2007). Does Frederick Taylor's ghost still haunt the halls of government? A look at the concept of government efficiency in our time. *Public Administration Review, 67*, 5 800–810.

Scurr, C. (2016). *Ethics as a program of study requirement in public administration graduate programs*. SECOPA Conference, Miami, FL, United States.

Seitelman, B. (2020). *Recent scandals prompt new wave of ethics reform proposals*. Multistate. https://www.multistate.us/insider/2020/8/25/recent-political-scandals-prompt-new-wave-of-ethics-reform-proposals

Shjafritz, J., & Hyde, A. H. (Eds.). (2016). *Classics of public administration* (6th ed.). Wadsworth.

Svara, J. (2014). *The ethics primer: For public administrators in government and nonprofit organizations*. Bartlett & Jones.

Svara, J., & West, J. (2018). *A tribute to Public Integrity and ASPA's Section on Ethics and Integrity in Governance: Background for the 20th anniversary symp*osium. Section on Ethics and Integrity in Governance Monograph Series #1.

Szypszak, C. (2021). Case law as raw material for teaching ethics in public administration. *Journal of Public Affairs Education.* http://doi.org/10.1080/15236803.2021.1935193

Taylor, F. (1912/2007). Scientific management. In J. Shjafritz, & A. Hyde (Eds.), *Classics of public administration* (6th ed, pp. 36–38). Wadsworth.

Thompson, W., & Leidein, J. (2008). *Ethics in city hall: Discussion and analysis for public administration.* Bartlett & Jones.

U.S. Department of Justice. (n.d.). *Public integrity section.* https://www.justice.gov/criminal/pin

U.S. Government Accountability Office. (2001). *Report to the Chairman, Committee on the Judiciary, House of Representatives: DOJ's Public Integrity Section—Case management policies followed, but closing some matters took too long* [report]. GAO. https://www.gao.gov/assets/gao-01-122.pdf

Vinzant, P. (2019, December 7). Combating administrative evil. American Society for Public Administration. *PA Times.* https://patimes.org/combating-administrative-evil/

West, J., Beh, I., & Sabharwal, M. (2013). Charting ethics in Asia-Pacific HRH: Does east meet west, ethically? *Review of Public Personnel Administration, 33*(2), 185–204.

West, J., & Berman, E. (2004). Ethics training in U.S. cities: Content, pedagogy, and impact. *Public Integrity, 6*(3), 189–206.

West, J., & Berman, E. (2006). *The ethics edge.* International City/County Management Association.

Willey, S. L., Mansfield, N., & Sherman, M. (2012). Integrating ethics across the curriculum: A pilot study to assess students' ethical reasoning. *Journal of Legal Studies Education, 29*(2), 263–296.

Worthley, J., & Grumet, B. (1983). Ethics and public administration: Teaching what "can't be taught." *American Review of Public Administration, 17*(Spring), 54–67. https://journals.sagepub.com/doi/10.1177/027507408301700106

Wyatt-Nichol, H., & Franks, G. (2009). Ethics training in law enforcement agencies. *Public Integrity, 22*(1), 39–50.

Yoder, D., & Denhardt, K. (1994). Ethics education in public administration and affairs. Preparing graduates for workplace moral dilemmas. In T. Cooper (Ed.), *Handbook of administrative ethics* (2nd ed., pp. 59–78). Marcel Dekker. Revised and expanded.

CHAPTER 8

PROFESSIONAL MILITARY ETHICS EDUCATION

David Whetham and Andrew Corbett
King's College London

Many people assume that legal compliance is the same as ethical behavior. Rules, whether they be legal ones or institutional ones, are understandably important in a military environment, but the rules can only take military personnel so far. This is why militaries around the world are also values-based institutions rather than just rules-based ones drawing attention to the important difference between ethics and compliance. Simply following rules will take military personnel so far but knowing what the right thing to do when the rules are unclear is essential. This chapter charts the evolution of Professional Military Ethics Education in the UK and demonstrates its scope before focusing in on the very real challenges confronting military personnel today. Professional Military Ethics Education has evolved over time in an attempt to meet the challenges of the contemporary military environment. When done well, professional military ethics education equips military personnel with the necessary skills and awareness to make the right decisions even in the most challenging of circumstances.

Educating in Ethics Across the Professions: A Compendium of Research, Theory, Practice, and an Agenda for the Future, pages 169–182.
Copyright © 2023 by Information Age Publishing
www.infoagepub.com

Keywords: Military Ethics; Military Ethics Pedagogy; Ethics Education; Professional Military Education; Professional Ethics Education; Professional Military Ethics Education

This chapter charts the evolution of Professional Military Ethics Education (PMEE) in the UK and demonstrates its scope before focusing in on the very real challenges confronting military personnel today. PMEE has evolved over time in an attempt to meet the challenges of the contemporary military environment. The contents consider: why PMEE matters; what military ethics is; the history and development of PMEE pedagogy; and, some recurring and emerging themes in PMEE. The chapter concludes by describing how when PMEE is done well, it equips military personnel with the necessary skills and awareness to make the right decisions even in the most challenging of circumstances.

WHY DOES PROFESSIONAL
MILITARY ETHICS EDUCATION MATTER?

Each of the professions in this volume is governed in large part by its own ethic. For members of the armed forces, this is uniquely demanding because military forces are empowered to use lethal force under certain circumstances, and the control of those circumstances is more than a simple legal judgment. Furthermore, the personnel most immediately involved are often the most junior and least experienced. By its very nature the profession of arms operates under extremely demanding legal and ethical constraints and these are as integral to its operations as the complex technologies it uses to achieve political ends.

It is a core assumption of military ethics that all legitimate use of military force is directed in the pursuit of states' authorised political objectives; anything else is just illicit violence, meaning not everything can be considered a legitimate military target. One role of senior military personnel is to assure themselves through detailed engagement with and understanding of their political direction, that any proposed military action is indeed legitimate. This requires a particular skill set. On the other hand, the instantaneous decision to use lethal force (or not) in more immediate circumstances often falls to very much younger and less experienced personnel. This requires a related, but different skill set. Both must be accommodated in the ethical education of military personnel.

This challenge, combined with the vast range of other ethical issues that confront those in service in contemporary armed forces, means that professional military ethics education (PMEE) is a subject that is demonstrating increasing prominence within institutions charged with providing training and education for professional military personnel around the world. This chapter will make reference to the global military profession but will refer to specifics in the UK system; available space precludes detailed comparison with other states' PMEE, but the authors' experience suggests that the general principles appear broadly generic among Western militaries, and in many cases, beyond.

WHAT *IS* MILITARY ETHICS?

While closely related, the law of armed conflict is not synonymous with military ethics. The laws of armed conflict (LOAC), or international humanitarian law, were first codified in the 1906 Geneva Conventions and have been revised and updated by subsequent conventions and protocols. There is a legal requirement for all military personnel to receive regular LOAC training and all senior commanders are supported in-house by appropriately qualified legal advisors. Obviously, ethics and the law are closely related, but not synonymous. In shorthand, LOAC defines what cannot be done and, by extension, circumscribes what can be done. But, LOAC cannot differentiate what "should" be done in a given circumstance. This is a much more nuanced and less categoric judgment, which must be made within the constraints imposed by LOAC, but to a set of moral criteria which might not be legally binding. In the control of the use of lethal force, this decision tests the integrity of the service personnel involved, and often places them on the edge of exquisitely nuanced moral judgment; it is for this situation that professional military education seeks to prepare personnel.

Military ethics also covers other areas, and it can be useful to divide these up into separate (but overlapping) parts: the *Individual in the Profession*; the *Profession at Work*, and; the *Profession and Society* (NATO, 2008).[1] The first of these parts focuses upon the military virtues and standards expected of professional military personnel such as courage, integrity, and loyalty (see below), and how they might be applied appropriately in specific situations. The second, the *Profession at Work*, is more focused upon the rules and principles that guide and govern the work of military personnel at all levels of responsibility. This can cover issues relating to the management of scarce resources and defense planning, but is most often associated with the rules and norms that determine when and against whom it is appropriate to use force on an individual level (*jus in bello*) all the way up to the actual decision to use military force taken at the level of governments and states (*jus ad bellum*). The latter two areas are often associated with the Just War Tradition—a "fund of practical moral wisdom" that has evolved over millennia to reflect the changing character of war. The third part, the *Profession and Society*, is concerned with the relationship between the state and its servants, how and where the military fits into this relationship, the responsibilities and duties on both sides (sometimes referred to as "the military covenant"), how the values of the military relate to wider social values, and the limits (professional, legal and personal) of military obedience. This latter area receives the least attention in many Western military syllabi, but is often the most important as it underpins the extraordinary rights afforded to military personnel when they act on behalf of their state.

---

[1] For example, this is the approach taken in NATO's Partnership Action Plan on Defence Institution Building: Reference Curriculum (Kingston, Ontario: Canadian Defence Academy, 2008).

PMEE PEDAGOGY: HISTORY AND DEVELOPMENT

Traditionally, military ethics was not a subject formally taught to military officers. When Robinson (2008) cites "institutional osmosis" as responsible for much of the values exhibited by the British Armed Forces, this is a valid observation to the extent that they tended be "caught rather than taught." While not always done explicitly, or even consciously, military ethics training and education is still often implicit and taught through example and environment. For example, even today, the "military institutional way of rewarding the behavior it wishes to see at the individual level is through the use of citation and awards" (Whetham, 2020a).

Beyond this type of signalling, most of the heavy lifting in military ethics inculcation has historically been achieved by focusing upon on character. Initial selection, career progression, and promotion all, to a greater or lesser extent, hinge upon assessments of character. The military institution attempts to ensure that those they promote into positions of authority have the character to be able rise to the challenge of any new position. This virtue ethics approach concentrates upon the importance of character and how it can be nurtured by the right types of behavior. While the formal articulation of these is a fairly modern occurrence, today, all professional militaries (and often the individual branches within those militaries) now identify specific values that underpin this virtue ethics approach, representing the institutional articulation of expected behavior. For example, the values for the Australian Defence Force are professionalism, service, courage, respect, integrity, and excellence (Australian Defence Force, 2021). The Royal Navy core values are: commitment, courage, discipline, respect for others, integrity, and loyalty (Royal Navy, 2016), while the British Army's values are almost identical (British Army, 2015), and the Royal Air Force core values include respect, integrity, service, and excellence (Royal Air Force, 2019).

The idea is that by articulating such statements, inculcating them at basic training, and continually referring back to them, such values are internalised through conscious training and unconscious institutional diffusion, that is, "This is what we should do." The values are more than a checklist: Service personnel are the "products" of an ongoing and coherent education that enables them to inhabit all of these virtues, or competences, without necessarily being conscious of it. That said, the competencies or virtues can also be explicitly synthesised to support an archetypal "identity" to which service personnel might aspire. Using the terms of virtue ethics, the more one does the right thing, the more it becomes habit and, therefore, part of the stable disposition that informs one's character. The hope is that, by "fostering such behaviors, and promoting those who consistently demonstrate them, people will be able to do the right thing when the situation demands it" (Whetham, 2020a).

However, military ethics today is recognized as a subject that is too important to be left implicit and one that needs to be about more than simply focusing upon character development, important though that is. It is understood that to reflect the professional requirements of military personnel at different ranks and responsibilities successfully, the content of different foundational and continuing professional courses must consciously engage with the normative challenges that are likely to arise. Inevitably how they do this (and how successful they are) will vary, depending upon the desired outcome from each cohort. These varied outcomes require related, but distinct, ethical competences which evolve as service personnel become more senior.

Recent research has considerably expanded our understanding of the concept of "ethical competence" and, by extension, this chapter seeks to synthesise that understanding with modern evolution of PMEE pedagogy. There are two views regarding the nature of ethical competence, one focused upon the character of the individual moral actor, and one focused upon the activities they conduct (De Schrijver & Maesschalck, 2013). In the past, PMEE focused upon the activities that were being conducted; "they first identify work activities that are central for accomplishing specific work and then transform those activities into personal attributes" (Sandberg, 1994). Thus, training could, by repetition, instill a series of reactions to a given set of circumstances which would encourage the appropriate moral response. Modern ethical education, however, seeks to develop the individual's values and character—their knowledge, skills, and abilities or attributes—such that they are prepared to make intuitive moral interpretation in novel situations with which they have never been confronted. Modern PMEE is more about judgment than a trained response to particular stimuli.

De Schrijver and Maesschalck elaborate upon this concept of ethical competence, drawing heavily on Rest's four components of moral competence—moral awareness, moral judgment," moral motivation, and moral character—and they distinguish three types of stimulus (De Schrijver & Maesschalck, 2013). Once again, these distinctions can be mapped fairly neatly across into the evolution of PMEE. The first is a stimulus that demands behavior in accordance with rules and procedures. An historical example of this was the Captain reading the articles of war to the Ship's Companies on board HM Ships at least once per month, usually after Church. These articles were derived from the Laws of Oleron, introduced by Eleanor of Aquitaine in the 12th century, incorporated in the Admiralty "Black Book" in 1336 and their regular repetition was not rescinded until the 1950s. Second are stimuli that guide individuals to consider the consequences of their actions for others, such as focused discussion with more experienced personnel. The third stimuli are arguments considering the consequences of actions for oneself, such as discussions with experienced personnel on moral injury, LOAC, disciplinary processes, and Rules of Engagement (simplified rules that explain the legal position but also the additional policy constraints that ensure that the military instrument remains within political control—e.g., Allied Joint Doctrine 2017) (NATO, 2017). While the third category could be construed as encouraging self-interested and overly selfish thinking, it is balanced out by the other types of reflection required. The combination of the second and third stimuli form a consequentialist approach which informs the pedagogy of contemporary UK PMEE, considered below.

Moral awareness suggests that the moral actors (in this case the service personnel) develop sensitivity to ethical dilemma situations. Genuine dilemmas are where the right response is difficult to determine due to apparently conflicting values. But many situations may appear to be dilemmas, but actually turn out to be simple tests of integrity, where the right thing to do is obvious, but it may come at a personal price (doing the right thing can hurt sometimes, such as taking the unpopular but correct course of action) (Coleman, 2009). Once moral awareness is established, moral judgment is deployed, that is, the ability to judge what course of action is morally right. Blind adherence to the military codes or ethos can be problematic here (see below). A key test of the success of ethical education is whether it fosters an understanding of the distinction between what is morally right and what is expedient with a focus upon individual integrity is critical in this process. For example, a fictitious discussion scenario where the "students"—while going through a colleague's effects after his death—uncover video evidence of prisoner abuse by a colleague, demands consideration of this dilemma of loyalty, integrity, and the moral "rightness" in a visceral way that is impossible to convey here, but is consistently a challenging and thought-provoking session.

Having established this moral awareness and judgment, the motivation to take the morally right course of action if it is not expedient or contradictory to some aspect of a code of loyalty is probably the most challenging component of moral competence. This is not achieved in any ingrained sense through the repetition of rules like the Laws of Oleron; the right choice here would simply be made in order to prevent punishment, which might be effective in the moment, but it is not in that sense morally informed. It would be better to have educated students to develop rounded moral characters, to have themselves become moral actors who are fully aware of their own judgment and motivated to take the right course of action, because it is the right thing to do. Achieving this requires not a pedagogy of how to teach, but consideration of the andragogy of how adults learn, enabling students to influence their own learning processes (Gravells, 2014).

Military basic training has historically tended to be repetitious, designed to ingrain instinctive responses to previously experienced stimuli. As noted above, when combined with the implicit "lessons" derived from the service or unit ethos, history, and traditions, what it is to be a "good" member of the forces was taught as much by example as by any kind of formal instruction (Robinson, 2007). This style of instruction provided a basic level of moral awareness; but, in focusing upon inherited, codified, and top-down instructions, the training itself tended to inhibit development of individual moral judgment. This may have been for a number of historical and cultural reasons and expectations, rather than necessarily an appreciation of what could be achieved with the right methods. However, for context, a 2013 UK report suggested that almost 40% of new army recruits had a reading age of only 11 (Sellgren, 2013).

In order to instil sufficient moral judgment to enable trainees to develop full moral competence, a different attitude and approach was required. Basic training in the UK, for instance, now can involve the use of decks of playing cards printed with ethical dilemmas, as well as the normal suits and numbers. These range from the geostrategic—"Can a country use whatever tactics and weaponry are necessary if it is on the brink of being defeated (7 of hearts)?"—to the far more immediate and personal—"Should you always report someone who has broken the rules?" and "Does it matter if you don't think the rule is important (5 of spades)?" The cards can be carried in a pocket in almost any circumstances and used as an informal means of ongoing exposure to ethical dilemmas in small group discussion, or for playing whist (an early form of bridge). Each card also carries a unique QR code which links the reader to a more detailed on-line consideration of the specific issue. A phone or tablet application version of the playing cards is also in the works, for those who are more tech-focused than tactile (Centre for Military Ethics, 2015). The benefit of the peer-to-peer engagement of this type of exercise is difficult to over-estimate. While not quite realistic learning tasks, the absence of more senior leadership in this informal environment enables junior personnel to explore demanding moral questions, before they are confronted with them in reality (Jochems et al., 2003).

Such activities are a means of engaging personnel more intimately in their own development (Centre for Military Ethics, 2019) and is essential in ethics education. Active learning is any learning process where students are invited to engage in the learning process, in contrast to more traditional learning where they are passive recipients of information conveyed by experts. Typically, these learning processes involve students working together during classes, but importantly, extends beyond formal instruction and structured learning. Moreover, adding small active learning strategies enhances the effectiveness of traditional classes by enabling positive reinforcement of learning objectives (University of Minnesota Center for Educational Innovation, 2018). Replacing unit lectures with highly interactive activities such as debates, particularly in a professionally "safe" environment with senior officers not present, enables junior personnel to explore their own views and understanding of ethical issues and guidance without worrying that their superiors are noting their responses. Clearly, such sessions must be handled by competent personnel; the risk of aberrant group-think led by opinionated individuals would otherwise be very real.

Following upon work begun in 2007, the UK Defence Academy established a Tri-Service Moral Leadership Working Group, supported by dedicated military personnel, the Chaplaincy, and ethicists from King's College London and Cranfield University. This group shaped a new curriculum designed to strengthen moral competencies appropriate to Junior and Senior Non-Commissioned Officers (NCOs). The curriculum is based upon the internalization of service "core values" combined with developing ethical thinking, decision-making, and behavior using active learning and materials selected to be of direct relevance to each cohort. The development of this course into a "Train the Trainer" model in the future, remains an aspiration, but the effect of its graduates permeating the services is greatly increasing the impact across the different services.

Today, PMEE for junior officers needs to accommodate very much the same criteria and enable them to develop moral competence before they take up their first post-training appointment. They will, after all, be responsible for the performance, including moral behavior, of their own subordinates. In this, junior officers are aided by experienced senior NCOs who will (ideally) have had both their own PMEE and experience from which they can draw when sharing their own guidance. UK officers' initial training tends to be shorter than that of many other states (between 6 months and 1 year as opposed to 4 years—which includes a bachelor's degree in the USA). Recent changes to PMEE by the UK forces involve its delivery methods: Discrete "ethics" lectures and maybe debates have been replaced by ongoing programmes or a "golden thread" of "command leadership and ethics" which reaches into every area of training and highlights the importance of ethics in pretty much every aspect of military command, decision-making, and operations.

This "golden thread" pedagogy is integral to both the Intermediate Command and Staff training usually delivered to officers at the sub-unit command level (about 6–10 years' experience) and the year-long Advanced Command and Staff Course which is attended either immediately before or shortly after unit command (Defence Academy of the UK, 2019). These professional development opportunities, representing a substantial investment in money and personnel resources, are a common feature of military careers around the world.

Over the last decade, the focus of PMEE has evolved from a top-down presentation of ethical guidance, to more visceral, peer-led, and highly participative means of education where military students exploit situational learning and active discussion to develop their personal judgment, based upon values inculcated throughout their training.

RECURRING AND EMERGING THEMES IN PMEE

There are many different areas of challenge for PMEE that we could focus upon, but two specific areas deserve the attention in this short chapter. One is an enduring challenge for military ethics though the ages, while the other is a far more contemporary challenge to the profession and the way it does its business in the 21st century.

Obedience and Military Ethics

At first look, dissent seemed to be antithetical to the entire military endeavor. Obedience and discipline are at the core of the military profession. However, being a military professional is about much more than simply following orders. Indeed, there are situations in which part of being a military professional is knowing when one shouldn't obey an order. But how does one educate a professional to do this?

Brigety and French (2019) ask: "How does one simultaneously train a person to charge the hill, to take out the machine gun nest, and to obey the lawful orders of those appointed over them, and also train them not only to be comfortable with, but indeed to embrace the necessity of speaking up with dissent when they see that something is antithetical to the mission, values, or laws that govern the organization?" The Nuremburg and Tokyo War trials definitively demonstrated that "just following orders" was not an acceptable defense for those tried with committing war crimes. But military professionalism requires more than a negative duty of simply not obeying unlawful orders—as a profession rather than simply an armed bureaucracy, it also requires a positive duty to challenge superiors in some situations. That is one of the reasons that courage is understood by military organizations around the world to have both physical and moral forms: An honest, forthright soldier will have the courage to tell even a general that he has misjudged the placement of the enemy's guns. A courageous squadron commanding officer will close out every pilots' briefing by saying they should follow the mission as briefed, "unless it doesn't look right" (Brigety & French, 2019).

Professional armed forces need to educate their personnel as individual moral actors so they are not amoral automatons, without undermining the discipline on which the forces operate. Vittoria made clear 500 years ago that manifestly wrong orders should not be obeyed and modern British military training advocates that orders should be questioned if the subordinate is concerned about their legitimacy, and should be refused if they are manifestly illegal. Inviting this kind of "reasonable challenge" is one of the best safeguards that any organisation can foster, but it is also an important corrective to certainty in wider contexts when it might be misplaced due to insufficient or inaccurate information, bias, or limited perspective (Development, Concepts and Doctrine Centre, 2016). Subordinates should be able to trust they have been given the right orders, but senior officers should also be able to trust their subordinates to correct inaccurate or erroneous understandings of a situation.

Following the UK's controversial intervention in Iraq in 2003, the Chilcot Inquiry was commissioned to learn both institutional and national lessons. While the long-awaited report was finally published in 2016 (Chilcot, 2016), it highlighted significant failures in leadership, processes, and organizational culture within the UK Ministry of Defence. The report also identified a number of factors that led to these failures, including a disturbing tendency to "groupthink" across government, where people conformed in their thinking to such an extent that the decisions they made became dysfunctional or even irrational. Key assumptions were not questioned, even when those assumptions were blatantly false.

In response, the UK articulated "Reasonable Challenge" as a form of constructive dissent which is now taught across the various professional development courses taken at each promotion stage for all three services. Astutely, and recognising the reality of hierarchical command structures, the policy document starts by addressing those who receive the challenge, rather than those that might make it. In so doing, rather than simply telling military personnel not to be bystanders and encouraging them to speak up when they see something might be wrong, the policy and practice recognizes that unless those in positions of leadership respond to appropriate challenge in the right way, no one is going to have the courage to say anything that deviates from what they believe to be the received view (MOD, 2017).

"Reasonable challenge" provides the litmus test of contemporary PMEE: How to enable and promote a sufficient degree of individual moral autonomy without detracting from military discipline. It is challenging, but achievable.

Technological Change—Will Machines Make Studying Military Ethics Obsolete?

While much public discussion of Artificial Intelligence (AI) is focused upon autonomous Terminator-like killing machines, the official UK position and that of many other states at this moment in time is that there will always be a person directly involved in any life-or-death decisions (in the loop) or at least monitoring and able to intervene (on the loop).

Presently, this may be the case. Yet, this discussion ignores the defensive uses of AI in many integrated systems where any human operator monitoring and intervening in a system would render that system too slow to be effective—there is simply no point in having human response times involved in near-light speed processes. This means autonomy is likely to creep in through defensive systems, whatever the stated position of any government, and the spread of autonomous systems is most unlikely to stop there (Whetham & Payne, 2019). Does this mean that military leadership needs to be more focused upon machine ethics and less worried about PMEE?

It may be that AI could actually make more effective ethical decisions on our behalf than we humans are capable of in most situations on a day-to-day basis. Afterall, machines cannot get tired (the single largest factor in bad ethical decision making), angry, or vengeful. Networked machines can all learn simultaneously from a single mistake almost immediately and ensure that it is never repeated (no need to learn from their own experience). While there is no doubting the importance of ensuring that appropriate ethical and legal responses are fully ingrained in any AI developments, the integration of AI into existing and future systems is very likely to be as assistance or augmentation to humans, rather than as an autonomous factor. For example, AI is already starting to transform military activities, including logistics, intelligence, surveillance, and even weapons design. AI appears to offer a powerful tool to assist in seeing through the "fog of war," those doubts and uncertainty that hamper rapid and effective decision making in the strategic environment.

Without effective and targeted PMEE, there may be overwhelming temptation to act with confidence and certainty in response to "an answer" even when caution is the appropriate course of action. Machine-bias, also known as automation bias and is demonstrated every time someone drives into a river while following their satnav (Middleton, 2019), means that when the machine tells military personnel to do something, they are likely to believe it to be correct, even when it is manifestly obvious that it is not. Any system is only as good as the information that is fed into it, and that data and the conclusions it points to can be tainted by algorithmic bias or lack of relevant diversity. However, the answers generated through AI systems are still likely to be taken as definitive, even when they are very clearly wrong from any objective position. This misplaced confidence risks removing the necessary caution from planning, something that can be extremely dangerous in a conflict situation that ultimately has the potential to escalate into a nuclear exchange (for example, the Cuban missile crisis). Service personnel must have the moral fiber to call out objections and recognize that automated systems are still fallible, and are likely to remain so for many generations at least. This is not the place for an in-depth examination of the ethics of artificial intelligence and lethal autonomous weapons systems, nor the acknowledged challenges to martial virtues through remotely piloted systems (drones) (Kirkpatrick, 2015). But, this is an increasingly demanding area of PMEE which demands ever more complex ethical intervention by service personnel. Therefore, technological change and the increasing integration of AI into military systems should, if anything, make us want to *increase* the provision of military ethics education and training rather than abandon it as no longer relevant.

How Much PMEE is Enough?

How much military ethics training or education is sufficient? A definitive empirical answer to this is obviously not possible, but even short courses in PMEE, delivered in the right way, by the right people, using the right material and methods of delivery can have very real results on the behavior of personnel deployed on operations (Warner et al., 2011). Just reminding people about good behavior makes them behave better (Ariely, 2012).

Robust research supports this observation. For example, a training package based upon movie vignettes and leader-led discussions, was delivered and administered seven to eight months into a 15-month high-intensity combat deployment in Iraq, between December 11, 2007, and January 30, 2008. Reports of unethical behavior and attitudes, in this sample, were compared with a randomly selected pre-training sample from the same brigade. The training, limited though it was, was associated with significantly lower rates of unethical conduct of soldiers and a greater willingness to report and address misconduct than in those before training or for those that did not receive it (Warner et al., 2011).

Put simply, done appropriately, PMEE works.

CONCLUSION

PMEE, if handled wrongly, can actually be a damaging thing (Robinson, 2007). It is essential to avoid the idea that PMEE is about limits and how to get around them or give people the idea that as long as they have gone through some kind of ethical decision-making process or model, whatever they decide is now acceptable because it can in some sense be justified in a Court Martial. While education is about being able to ask the right question and being able to reason towards an appropriate answer, that does not mean every answer is equally valid. Even for those issues for which right and wrong are difficult to determine, the difference between better and worse answers are still generally discernible, and PMEE should be about helping military personnel have the confidence that their decisions are the best that they can be.

On the other hand, while confidence in one's decisions is important, *moral certainty* is also something that may not be desirable. There is the Romany curse—"May you become involved in a conflict in which you know you are right"—which, of course, provides the path to crusades and the erosion of the recognition of the equality of the other side (Whetham, 2009). If moral or ethical education results in this type of reasoning, we believe that it will have failed.

Service personnel need to understand, intuitively, that military ethics is not about compliance or the subsequent justification of actions, nor are the situations with which personnel will be faced simple, neat, or tidy. Getting this balance right is at the heart of good PMEE.

REFERENCES

ADF. (2021). *Military ethics* [Ebook] (1st ed., pp. 29–30). Directorate of Information, Graphics and eResources Lessons and Doctrine Directorate. https://theforge.defence.gov.au/sites/default/files/2021-10/ADF%20Philosophical%20Doctrine%20-%20Military%20Ethics.pdf

Ariely, D. (2012). *The honest truth about dishonesty: How we lie to everyone—Especially ourselves* (1st ed., pp. 197–207). HarperCollins.

Brigety, R., & French, S. (2019). Strategic dissent in the military. In M. Skerker, D. Whetham, & D. Carrick (Eds.), *Military virtues* (pp. 70–74). Howgate Press.

British Army. (2015). A soldier's values and standards. Retrieved 18 October 2021, from https://www.army.mod.uk/who-we-are/our-people/a-soldiers-values-and-standards/

Centre for Military Ethics. (2015). *Centre for Military Ethics.* https://militaryethics.uk/en/

Centre for Military Ethics. (2019, October). *Military ethics feedback survey.* Survey Monkey. https://www.surveymonkey.com/results/SM-YZJWD5HP7/

Chilcot, J. (2016). *The report of the Iraq Inquiry* (pp. 128–135). Her Majesty's Stationery Office. https://webarchive.nationalarchives.gov.uk/ukgwa/20171123122743/http://www.iraqinquiry.org.uk/the-report/

Coleman, S. (2009). The problems of duty and loyalty. *Journal of Military Ethics, 8*(2), 105–115. doi: 10.1080/15027570903037892

Defence Academy of the UK, Intermediate Command and Staff Course Maritime. (2021). *Unpublished curriculum.* Author.

De Schrijver, A., & Maesschalck, J. (2013). *A new definition and conceptualization of ethical competence.* Retrieved 19 October 2021, from https://researchportal.vub.be/en/publications/a-new-definition-and-conceptualization-of-ethical-competence

Development, Concepts and Doctrine Centre. (2016). *Joint doctrine publication 04 understanding and decision making* [Ebook] (2nd ed.). Ministry of Defence. https://assets.publishing.service.gov.uk/government/uploads/system/uploads/attachment_data/file/584177/doctrine_uk_understanding_jdp_04.pdf

Gravells, A. (2014). *The award in education and training.* Sage.

Jochems, W., van Merriënboer, J., & Koper, R. (2003). *Integrated e-learning: Implications for pedagogy, technology and organization* (1st ed.). Routledge.

Kirkpatrick, J. (2015). Drones and the martial virtue courage. *Journal of Military Ethics*, *14*(3–4), 202–219. doi: 10.1080/15027570.2015.1106744

Middleton, L. (2019, October 2). Man drove van into fast-flowing river because sat nav told him to. *Metro*. https://metro.co.uk/2019/10/02/man-drove-van-fast-flowing-river-sat-nav-told-10851190/

MOD. (2017). *The good operation* [Ebook]. https://assets.publishing.service.gov.uk/government/uploads/system/uploads/attachment_data/file/674545/TheGoodOperation_WEB.PDF

NATO. (2008). *Partnership action plan on defence institution building: Reference curriculum*. Canadian Defence Academy.

NATO. (2017). *AJP-01 allied joint doctrine* [Ebook] (1st ed.). NATO Standardization Office. https://assets.publishing.service.gov.uk/government/uploads/system/uploads/attachment_data/file/905877/20200728-doctrine_nato_allied_joint_doctrine_ajp_01.pdf

Robinson, P. (2007). Ethics training and development in the military. *The US Army War College Quarterly: Parameters*, *37*. https://press.armywarcollege.edu/parameters/vol37/iss1/8

Robinson, P. (2008). Introduction: Ethics education in the military. In N. de Lee, D. Carrick, & P. Robinson (Eds.), *Ethics education in the military* (pp. 1–12). Ashgate.

Royal Air Force. (2019). *Ethos, core values and standards.* Ministry of Defence. https://www.raf.mod.uk/recruitment/media/3897/20200703-raf_ap1_2019_rev_3_page_spreads.pdf

Royal Navy. (2016). *Naval personnel management.* Ministry of Defence. https://www.royalnavy.mod.uk/-/media/royal-navy-responsive/documents/reference library/br-3-vol-1/chapter-21.pdf

Sandberg, J. (1994). Basis for a smart workforce. In R. Gerber & C. Lankshear (Eds.), *Training for a smart workforce* (pp. 47–72). Routledge.

Sellgren, K. (2013). *Almost 40% of army recruits have reading age of 11*, MPs warn. Retrieved 19 October 2021 from https://www.bbc.co.uk/news/education-23346693

University of Minnesota. (2018). *Center for educational innovation active learning* [Video]. https://cei.umn.edu/active-learning

Warner, C., Appenzeller, G., Mobbs, A., Parker, J., Warner, C., Grieger, T., & Hoge, C. (2011). Effectiveness of battlefield-ethics training during combat deployment: A programme assessment. *The Lancet*, *378*(9794), 915–924. doi: 10.1016/s0140-6736(11)61039-8

Whetham, D. (2009). The moral, legal and ethical dimensions of war at the Joint Services Command and Staff College. In D. Carrick, J. Connelly, & P. Robinson (Eds.), *Ethics education for irregular warfare*. Routledge.

Whetham, D. (2020a, Nov 27). *What senior leaders in defence should know about ethics and the role that they play in creating the right command climate*. Defence Academy of the United Kingdom. https://www.da.mod.uk/publications/category/181/ What-senior-leaders-in-defence-should-know-about-ethics-and-the-role-that-they-play-in-creating-the-right-command-climate

Whetham, D. (2020b, Nov 19). *Special Operations Command: Leadership and ethics review: Annex A to Chapter 3.03 of the Inspector-General of the Australian Defence Force Afghanistan Inquiry Report*. Commonwealth of Australia. https://afghanistan-inquiry.defence.gov.au/sites/default/files/2020-11/IGADF-Afghanistan-Inquiry-Public-Release-Version.pdf

Whetham, D., & Payne, K. (2019). AI: In defence of uncertainty [Blog]. https://defenceindepth.co/2019/12/09/ai-in-defence-of-uncertainty/

SECTION 4

EDUCATING IN ETHICS: RECONCEIVING
PROFESSIONAL ETHICS EDUCATION

Chapter 9: The Subject of Professional Education, Educating the Spirit in Ethics

Even if others were to excoriate the decision as well as the person making it, this individual—as a self-perfecting and self-possessed free spirit in the world—will stand tall, firm in the knowledge and self-understanding that "I did the *right* thing" and demonstrated ethical competence. Of this professional, Socrates would observe, "it is better to die for the truth than it is to live a lie, for the unexamined life is not worth living.".
—*Richard M. Jacobs (1981, 38a:41)*

Chapter 10: A Process for Envisioning Professional Ethics Education, Ethics Education—An Integral Formation for Professionals

My analysis points toward "professional formation" as the best descriptive term that captures the multi-faceted developmental growth toward the core values that applied ethics educators in the professions want to foster....It is a lifelong commitment to continued progress toward excellence and the aspirational core value of deep responsibility and care for the persons served by the profession.
—*Neil W. Hamilton*

CHAPTER 9

TEACHING APPLIED ETHICS ACROSS THE PROFESSIONS

Educating the Spirit *in* Ethics

Richard M. Jacobs
Villanova University

This chapter reflects upon the formation of ethical professionals—in particular, their character—differentiating between instruction *about* virtue and education *in* virtue (Carr, 1991). Tracing the origins of this distinction to the late-eighteenth and early- to mid- nineteenth century German romantics and their concept of education ("*Bildung*"), this chapter explores what their ambitious, philosophical desiderium suggests to those who teach applied across the professions. This concept requires educating professionals—beginning with their pre-service formation and continuing across the years of their in-service formation—*in* virtue. Then, if researchers utilize a variety of empirical and quasi-empirical methods to assess the efficacy of applied ethics education to ascertain the degree to which in-service professionals express their spirit and bring glory, first, to themselves and, second, to the profession from which they sprang.

Keywords: Applied Ethics, Ethics Education, Education in Ethics, Ethics in the Professions

Educating in Ethics Across the Professions: A Compendium of Research, Theory,
Practice, and an Agenda for the Future, pages 185–211.
Copyright © 2023 by Information Age Publishing
www.infoagepub.com

This chapter reflects upon the formation of ethical professionals—in particular, their character—taking as its starting point the literature of those who have been teaching applied ethics across the professions detailed in the preceding eight chapters. Of particular interest concerning this body of literature is not so much the pedagogical challenges and struggles those educators have confronted but the resounding similarities of those challenges and struggles across the professions especially as they attempt to facilitate students to deliberate about ethical dilemmas from the post-conventional level of ethical reasoning, namely, the social contract and universal ethical principles (Kohlberg, 1981). While many of these challenges and struggles arise from an academic culture which prizes science—the descriptive, using empirical and quasi-empirical tools—applied ethics emerges from and flourishes within an academic culture which prizes philosophy—the normative, applying principles and virtue.

That academic culture today confronts applied ethics educators with what appears to be a relatively simple and straightforward challenge: To assess the efficacy of their pedagogical efforts. While all are likely to agree that learning applied ethics should promote deliberating, making judgments, and engaging in conduct that demonstrate ethical competence (Cooper & Menzel, 2013), assessing this achievement is a much-contested matter. When science is prized, so it is believed, students who learn ethics—in a standalone course or content that's integrated across the curriculum—should demonstrate fewer, if any ethical lapses or failures in professional practice when compared to those who haven't learned applied ethics. When media reports tout egregious ethical failures on the part of professionals, many in the Academy ask "What value does ethics add to the curriculum?", the assumption being that some ethics education is taught if not required across the professions.

This chapter explores the ethical dimensions of teaching applied ethics, its premise being that what constitutes a "good" ethics educator involves more than subject knowledge expertise and competent pedagogical skills if only because the conflicts of values causing ethical dilemmas usually preclude a unitary resolution due to the positive and negative consequences associated with most resolutions (Peterson & Arthur, 2021; Simpson & Sacken, 2021). Examining how applied ethics is taught from a normative perspective, the chapter's goal is to direct attention to how those who teach applied ethics assist students to form their mind and heart, that is, to engage in "character formation" that will be tested in profession practice. With pedagogical success requiring the "good" to take root in each student's character, it's reasonable to assume evidence of success will be revealed through professional practice in ethical judgments and conduct demonstrating ethical competence. Furthermore, this can be assessed using the tools of science, namely, various quantitative and qualitative measures demonstrating the degree to which students have integrated the "head" and the "heart" with the "hand" in conduct demonstrating ethical competence (De Graff & Van Exel, 2008; Kaptein et al., 2005; Lawton, 2008; Swisher et al., 2001; Von Maravić, 2008; Zinner, 2011).

Upon completing an applied ethics course, whether students will continue act-ing upon that formation in professional practice is an entirely different matter as professional practice tests and forges character, with each professional allowing it to strengthen or weaken one's character. While that continuous formation—a self-formation—is also a pedagogical goal, it's implicit in applied ethics education as currently conceived in the Academy and needs to be effectively communicated, re-affirmed and, yes, assessed longitudinally. While this goal can also be assessed utilizing the tools of science, the continuous self-formation of ethical character and its assessment has yet to be firmly established across the professions (Walton, 2000; West & Berman, 2004; Wheeland, 2013).

To frame this discussion concerning the character formation of ethical profes-sionals, consider those shared pedagogical challenges and struggles from a nor-mative perspective informed by natural law.

Nature has bestowed upon human beings the innate capability to seek hap-piness by willing the "good" ("virtue"). Concerning this formation of will, Carr (1991) distinguished carefully between instructing students *about* the good—the mental capacity to know and understand what virtue is and requires—in contrast to educating them *in* the good—the power of will to conduct themselves virtu-ously. Carr maintained that while many educators believe they educate students in the latter, their pedagogical methods reveal them instructing students about the former, if not inculcating in them what Rohr once called "regime virtues" (1978, pp. 59–94).

Carr's was a "distinction with a difference"—instruction *about* virtue in con-trast to education *in* virtue. But, it certainly wasn't novel.

This chapter traces the origins of this distinction to the late-eighteenth and early- to mid- nineteenth century German romantics, in general, and their concept of education ("*Bildung*"), in particular. While the interest of many of their con-temporaries was decidedly scientific and utilitarian—using the tools of science to the end of using education to construct a more virtuous nation—the interest of the German romantics was a far more ambitious, philosophical desiderium: How education assists students to redeem themselves and, in turn, they would redeem the nation.

This distinction raises a matter of immense significance concerning the teach-ing of applied ethics across the professions, one that can be formulated as a ques-tion: Is applied ethics education a *means* to the end of perfecting a profession?

The early German romantics would respond with an emphatic "*Nein!*", argu-ing that education—properly understood as a continuously self-perfecting and self-possessed human being (*Bildung*)—is the *end* (Beiser, 2003). As this con-cerns teaching applied ethics, one's chosen profession does not perfect a profes-sional nor does its ethical practice bring glory to a professional. No, an ethical professional is a continuously self-perfecting and self-possessed spirit who "re-deems" oneself, first, and one's chosen profession, second, in much the same way the fledgling which returns "brings eternal glory to the nest whence [it] sprang" (Leonardo da Vinci, cited in Merezhkovsky, 1908, p. 300).

What does *Bildung* suggest about educating pre-service professionals *in* ethics, what does this require of those who teach this practical discipline, and how does it reframe its teaching?

This chapter responds to this important question, first, by contextualizing Carr's distinction using a thought experiment—instructing Federal Bureau of Investigation (FBI) agents *about* ethics. Three connotations of *Bildung* are then explicated, second, to specify the substantive purpose for educating pre-service professionals primarily *in* ethics to identify a pedagogy promoting this outcome. This chapter then discusses two challenges *Bildung* raises about teaching applied ethics, third, by considering a fourth connotation: aesthetic experience. These connotations are then used to revisit Carr's distinction by considering the training of pre-service and in-service FBI agents *in* virtue across the years and decades of their professional service. The chapter concludes by offering applied ethics educators a way they might reconceive *why* they do *what* they do by reframing applied pre-service ethics education in light of its normative purpose.

A THOUGHT EXPERIMENT IN UTILITARIAN THOUGHT: TRAINING FBI AGENTS *ABOUT* ETHICS

In most locales across the nation, the normative purpose of the law enforcement profession is "to protect and serve." These two principles frame the decision-making process as law enforcement professionals decide what those principles denote for professional practice, sometimes to the extent the good—*ethical* law enforcement—requires an officer to lay down one's life to protect and serve one's fellow citizens and property, thus exhibiting ethical competence by paying the ultimate price.

That normative purpose, oftentimes emblazoned on a law enforcement agency's emblem and prominently displayed on its shields, vehicles, office doors, and windows, enunciates the two principles that have motivated no small number of citizens to devote themselves to this profession since the U.S. Congress created the first Federal law enforcement officer on September 24, 1789—the United States Marshall—and President George Washington subsequently appointed the first 13 U.S. Marshalls (National Law Enforcement Officers Memorial Fund, n.d.). Similar to other professions and since its founding, the law enforcement profession and law enforcement have evolved and, in particular, from a politicized system to professionalism, then constitutionalism, and ultimately community policing (Kelling & Moore, 1988).

As the nation's pre-eminent law enforcement agency, how does the FBI train agents about its normative purpose and principles—its "ideals"—so these become evident in ethical competence?

Those who seek to become FBI agents first must apply and undergo a rigorous and extensive vetting process. Once accepted, recruits attend the FBI Academy located within the Marine Corps Base in Quantico, Virginia. The 20-week basic field training course—called "Hogan's Alley"—features instruction about the fundamentals of professional practice (FBI, 2017a).

One aspect of this basic field training is ethics, with agents being instructed about and required to demonstrate mastery of: the fundamental principles of ethics which place the highest value upon protecting the innocent and upholding the rule of law; the importance of protecting the public and preventing the abuse of authority that fails to protect and serve with compassion and fairness; the importance of civil rights for all; and, the need for oversight and accountability. The goal of this instruction is that FBI "special agents"—the term identifying graduates of Hogan's Alley—will "always do the right thing for the American people" (FBI, 2017b). To ensure that special agents remain in compliance by doing the right thing for the American people, the FBI has established an Office of Integrity and Compliance (FBI, 2011).

In Hogan's Alley, instruction about ethics (in Latin, *instruere*, "to build in") consists of a prescribed curriculum which instructors implement to build into agents the knowledge and understanding of the agency's normative purpose as well as how to gather data yielding sufficient positive evidence so that, as special agents, they will uphold the agency's ideals in the field where they will be making decisions about what professional practice requires. Upon graduation, the FBI holds special agents personally accountable for upholding those ideals in their professional practice.

Given its utilitarian intent, this approach to ethics training—instruction *about* ethics—resembles how applied ethics were taught to many pre-service professionals during the 20th century. Once accepted into a university-based training programs, students moved through the prescribed curriculum as faculty implemented it by providing instruction that conveyed the curriculum's content to students and then assessing its acquisition (Milner, 2005; Schachter, 2011). When asked what subject they teach, many faculty would likely have responded "I teach ethics," meaning that instruction is the primary means for building a profession's ideals and proprietary knowledge into groups of students.

This approach to training denotes a particular kind of instruction, the aim of which is to "inculcate" ethics through the use of force (from the Latin, *in-calx*, "using the heel to force upon, stamp in, tread down"). Yet "force" isn't a fixed quantity, but can range from the exertion of a small amount—for example, the pressure of gentle persuasion that Simon called "simple propaganda"—to the exertion of an immense amount—for example, an authoritarian regime demanding rigid conformity through brainwashing—which Simon called "intense propaganda" (1993, p. 126). With the pedagogical objective being to inculcate ethics, irrespective of the kind of force used, instruction *about* ethics while necessary is not education *in* ethics as the ensuing discussion concerning *Bildung* will clarify.

In addition, while this approach may communicate the profession's ideals and proprietary knowledge efficiently, the use of external force to inculcate them in students (most prominently, through readings, lectures, case study analysis, and a variety of quantitative and qualitative assessment mechanisms) isn't likely to motivate pre-service professionals to root the content of these lessons in their character, if only because the reward for doing so is derived from an extrinsic source (among others, positive feedback, good grades, graduation, and the conferral of a much-coveted degree and the desired entry-level job). Additionally, this approach oftentimes requires compliance—the "low road" of protecting oneself from professional harm by adhering to relevant laws, policies, rules, and regulations which can end in ethical minimalism (Rohr, 1978).

This divergence—instructing students *about* ethics and students educating themselves *in* ethics—brings the concept of *Bildung* front and center. How are those who teach applied ethics across the professions to facilitate student to educate themselves *in* applied ethics so that, in their future professional practice, they will express the spirit that Nature has endowed them with by bringing glory to their chosen professions as they demonstrate ethical competence (Cooper & Menzel, 2013)?

THE CONCEPT OF *BILDUNG*

Although "*Bildung*" denotes "education," its connotations aren't the utilitarian notions that for much of the past century have come to be associated in the United States with training groups of students (for the purpose of this discussion, "pre-service professionals"). In contrast, *Bildung* posits an end—a continuously self-forming human being—the connotations of which have profound implications for training pre-service professionals, in general, and teaching applied ethics, in particular. Concerning the latter, the pedagogical objective is for pre-service professionals to educate themselves *in* ethics so their professional practice as "in-service professionals" will embody their chosen profession's highest ideals as only each of them can instantiate those ideals, thus deliberating, making decisions, and conducting themselves in continuously self-perfecting ways that demonstrate increasingly sophisticated ethical competence (Cooper & Menzel, 2013).

Given this objective, what methods might ethics educators utilize to convey a profession's normative purpose and its ethical principles in such a way that pre-service professionals initiate the continuous process of educating themselves *in* ethics?

The ensuing discussion responds by directing attention to four connotations associated with *Bildung*, the first three being considered first: 1) freedom as the end; 2) the self-formation of the spirit; and, 3) educating the spirit. These connotations raise two pedagogical problems that will then be solved with the application of *Bildung's* fourth connotation: aesthetic experience. This connotation challenges ethics educators to reconceive *why* they do *what* they do by directing attention to training pre-service professionals primarily through education *in* ethics. Here, the subject taught is the student, experience provides the curriculum, and continuous self-formation *in* ethics as an in-service professional—the desiderium—is eventually achieved as the professional integrates the head and the heart with the hand of professional practice.

FREEDOM AS THE END

As *Bildung* concerns education *in* ethics, pedagogy isn't utilitarian, that is, a means toward the end of what's useful or good so that pre-service professionals will use it to perfect themselves continuously as professionals and, by extension, their chosen profession as well. Instead, *Bildung* directs pedagogy to the end of freedom—the pre-service professional liberating one's spirit from all that would constrain it from expressing itself.

Writing under the pseudonym "Novalis," the early German romantic poet, philosopher, and mystic Georg Philipp Friedrich Freiherr von Hardenberg (1772–1801) was among if not the first to identify this end, noting that "All education [*Bildung*] leads to nothing else than what one can call freedom, although this should not designate a mere concept but the ground of all existence" (quoted in Beiser, 2003, p. 293).

Clarifying what constitutes this "ground of all existence," the German romantic philosopher and poet Karl Wilhelm Friedrich Schlegel (1772–1829) argued that *Bildung* is "The highest good, and the source of everything useful..." (quoted in Beiser, 2003, p. 88). For Schlegel, freedom evidences itself in individuals, groups, and collectivities of educated individuals and, for the purposes of this discussion, in the professions. Yet, the professions don't liberate their practitioners but, in a way that's similar to Da Vinci's observation about the fledgling leaving its nest for the first time and whose freedom brings to fulfillment its idiosyncratic instantiation of its aves spirit, freedom enables professionals to become those continuously self-perfecting and self-possessed spirits who "bring eternal glory to the [profession] whence [they] sprang."

Directing pedagogy toward liberating the spirit (*Geist*), educators bid their students to liberate themselves from all that would otherwise keep them from being critical of the world. Yet, as von Hardenberg envisioned this process, they would not criticize the world as it exists "out there" but, in a way that's similar to that fledgling venturing forth for the first time from its nest, they would allow their spirit to guide them by breaking free of any extrinsic constraint so they can contemplate the world and all that constitutes it as it truly exists "in here." Quoting Novalis, von Hardenberg wrote:

> We dream of a journey through the universe. But is the universe then not in us? We do not know the depths of our spirit. Inward goes the secret path. Eternity with its worlds, the past and future, is in us or nowhere. (quoted in Beiser, 2003, p. 294)

Though not essential for navigating this "secret path"—as the pantheon of self-educated human beings across the millennia attests—an educator can prove crucial, especially one who capably assists pre-service professionals to make this turn inward to the world of the spirit. This formative experience provides the foundation for ethics educators to facilitate students to grow in freedom as they discover and explore this eternity within themselves. Then, as these students venture forth into the world of practice as in-service professionals, this experience initiates and hopefully motivates what, for them, will be the lifelong process of self-formation as a self-perfecting and self-possessed "spirits in the world" (in German, "*Geist und welt*").

THE SELF-FORMATION OF THE SPIRIT

Although von Hardenberg and Schlegel conceived of education as human perfection—an end in itself not a means to another end—the educational establishment in the United States views education an instrumental means to a desired end. As this end pertains to training professionals, education denotes instructing groups of students about the knowledge, skills, attitudes, and abilities they will need to be highly qualified and sought-after employees. To this end, the prescribed curriculum—like that of Hogan's Alley—specifies the various subjects those who provide instruction—many of them subject-matter specialists—will inculcate in students and, in turn, assess their achievement—the course objectives having been specified by the syllabus.

Engrained into the nation's consciousness for over two centuries (Dewey, 2013; Mann, 1957; Tyack & Hansot, 1982; Wilson, 1887), Hardenbury and Schlegel would observe that this notion's decidedly utilitarian intent gets two substantive pedagogical matters backwards. For those who teach applied ethics, those include: 1) the subject taught and 2) the curriculum implemented to liberate the subject's spirit.

For the German romantic philosopher of science Georg Wilhelm Friedrich Hegel (1770–1831), the subject of education is neither the curriculum nor its content but the student—a spiritual entity endowed with a rational mind. With the end being freedom of the spirit—and, for the purposes of this discussion, the pre-service professional's spirit—Hegel identified the means to that end—the curriculum—as the social and historical life process which "forms" that spirit. This curriculum doesn't consist of one's upbringing in the sense that parents, schools and their agents, or other social institutions inculcate these matters into students. Instead and precisely because human beings are embodied spirits to be freed not embodied machines to be trained, the curriculum consists of what Hegel called "experience"—which spurs students to engage in inner, self-directed activity to liberate the spirit. This self-formation emerges through a "conflict-ridden process" in the course of which each student as a spiritual being discovers one's identity or selfhood "while striving to actualize the selfhood it is in the process of discovering" (Hegel, as cited in Wood, 2003, p. 301).

As this self-formation relates to training pre-service professionals, their identity—as each currently conceives of it—has been formed to the degree they have previously reflected upon experience, representing their current stage of self-formation. Experience challenges pre-service professionals to progress beyond this stage by forming a distinctive identity—an idiosyncratic synthesis of spirit, mind, and power of will—which defines *this* particular individual as a *unique* professional and differentiates this professional from all other professionals. The end of education is for each student to be free to live as a particular instantiation of one's chosen profession—a continuously self-perfecting and self-possessed spirit in the world—an "educated" professional.

While some might liken this process to "lifelong learning" (Candy, 1991), Hegel understood it differently. For Hegel, *Bildung* doesn't focus primarily upon learning the contents of a prescribed curriculum through instruction that aims to increase a student's store of theoretical knowledge or technical skill sets. That utilitarian focus reduces education to instruction—a means to another end. In contrast, Hegel understood *Bildung* as a process of continuous self-formation directed at a singular end—education—which frees the spirit of all that constrains it and, as the spirit develops strength, the subject of education increasingly is impelled from within to engage continuously in the arduous work of continuous self-perfection. The end of this formative process is to be the unique spiritual entity one is—to instantiate itself at this time, in this situation with its particular circumstances, and in this way. Then, as the liberated spirit soars, additional fresh, serendipitous, unusual, and novel experiences will challenge professionals to actualize selfhood beyond any previously attained self-perfection and self-possession.

This process of self-formation explains why, for example, only Johann Sebastian Bach could express his distinctive genre of Baroque music, only Paul Gauguin could express his distinctive genre of symbolism, and only William Shakespeare could express his distinctive genre of blank verse. The same can be said of those professionals described in this volume's eight preceding chapters—lawyers, physicians, nurses, engineers, urban planners, business executives, public administrators, and soldiers—who have liberated and express their distinctive spirit in the practice of their chosen profession today. As this discussion unfolds, it will become increasingly clear that professionals are more akin to artists—craftsmen—than specialists—technical experts.

When the subject is the student and experience is the curriculum, ethics educators function like that fledgling's mother by nurturing students to be able to move beyond what's comfortable, providing experiences that will enable each to liberate its spirit to expand beyond any and all previously experienced horizons of experience. Freedom will evidence itself in professional practice, then, as in-service professionals continuously differentiate their idiosyncratic genre of practice as individuals who differ from every other member of their profession. Perfecting—"redeeming"—themselves, each of them individually and all of them collectively perfect—"redeem"—their chosen profession.

Educating the Spirit

Educating the spirit *in* ethics begins when applied ethics educators introduce pre-service professionals to experiences of their chosen profession's normative purpose and ethical principles. These noble ideals possess the power to fuel the spirit to desire the experience the freedom of determining what those ideals mandate for resolving the dilemmas of practice. With the pedagogical objective being that pre-service professionals become self-perfecting and self-possessed professionals, pedagogical success evidences itself as pre-service professionals respond to these experiences by identifying, deliberating about, and then making freely-willed, unconstrained ethical decisions rooted in those ideals that are now taking root in their character and bespeak their dignity as "liberated" spirits at this time.[1]

Case study analysis provides one pedagogical method to this end. Carefully examining a case—knowing and understanding its contents as well as analyzing it through the lens of a profession's ideals—will reveal students proposing a number of conflicting if not contradictory yet principled solutions. Furthermore, identifying what constitutes these "best" solutions will imply considering a variety of conflicting if not contradictory ethical principles (Svara, 2015). Importantly, questioning and thinking about these principles—each exhibiting strengths and weaknesses—will initiate the turn inward that's required for pre-service professionals to engage in "conflict-ridden process" which Hegel believed was crucial for a spiritual being to liberate itself from what otherwise would constrain it and to begin discovering and actualizing one's selfhood through discovery (as cited in Wood, 2003, p. 301).

This pedagogical method for educating pre-service professionals *in* ethics inculcates a profession's ideals in students from an intrinsic source, namely, the spirit. In addition, extrinsic rewards begin to pale when compared to the satisfaction derived from that intrinsic source for having taken the "high road" charted by deliberating about what a profession's normative purpose and ethical principles require, making the "best possible" decision, and then implementing it (Rohr, 1978). Even if others were to excoriate the decision as well as the person making it, this individual—as a self-perfecting and self-possessed free spirit in the world—will stand tall, firm in the knowledge and self-understanding that "I did the *right* thing" and demonstrated ethical competence. Of this professional, Socrates would observe, "it is better to die for the truth than it is to live a lie, for the unexamined life is not worth living" (Plato , 1981, 38a:41).

While this pedagogical method does not preclude instruction *about* ethics—for example, informing students about and assessing various ethical theories (Rachels & Rachels, 2015), decision-making modalities (Anand, 1993; MacCrimmon, 1968; Peterson, 2009), and attributes of character (Menzel, 2010)—the pedagogical challenge concerns how best to convey that information. Education *in* ethics requires that pre-service professionals exercise and strengthen their power of spir-

---

[1]Although this challenge can be motivated extrinsically, the motive is primarily intrinsic. Achieving higher levels of sophistication in professional practice, experience provides the foundation for professionals to strive for yet higher level of sophistications. This developmental, progressive movement may be likened to reaching the "horizon" once envisioned and, having arrived there, the horizon has now moved further away. The satisfaction associated with this achievement fades into the past as the spirit's innate desire seeks to engage in the more arduous and challenging work of becoming what education has made possible.

it as they experience the need for this information and, then, to gin up the desire, motivation, and commitment to learn it and root it in their character.

Of education—this process of continuous self-formation—Beiser observed:

> The paradox of German romanticism is its utter commitment and devotion to the education of humanity, and yet its recognition that it cannot and ought not do anything to achieve it. We are left, then, with a striking gap between theory and practice, which it was the very purpose of romanticism to overcome. (2003, p. 105)

Those who teach applied ethics are uniquely positioned to resolve the failure to bridge this striking gap—"knowing the good" and "doing the good"—identified historically as the "theory-practice divide." To bridge this gap requires reframing pre-service ethics education to emphasize primarily education *in* ethics.

A THOUGHT EXPERIMENT IN NORMATIVE THOUGHT: EDUCATING FBI AGENTS *IN* ETHICS

To consider what this reframing requires, recall what ethics is and implies for educating pre-service professionals *in* ethics. The ensuing discussion applies this concept in a practical way to Hogan's Alley.

What Aristotle called "practical philosophy" (1958, pp. 158–274) exists precisely because an ethical dilemma features two conflicting goods. The "best possible" decision that can be made oftentimes is a "good" or "better" decision resulting in at least one negative outcome for which an agent accepts personal and professional responsibility. For example, "to protect and serve" might require a law enforcement professional to utilize violent means—to kill a human being—to the end of demonstrating ethical competence.

As a focus of scholarly inquiry, applied ethics in the professions examines the process by which professionals incorporate the ideals specified by their chosen profession's normative purpose into the decision-making process—what Aristotle called "*phronesis*" (1958, pp. 158–274). That is, when confronting the dilemmas of professional practice, applied ethics requires professionals to integrate ethical theory—the head—with technical skill—the hand—so they not only "*know* the good" and "*will* the good" but also, and more crucially, "*do* the good"—the heart.

Phronesis doesn't exclude instruction *about* ethics—a "mild" form of force so pre-service professionals will know, understand, and be capable of applying its contents in their in-service professional practice—if only because all three are essential in professional practice. In addition, those contents have been incorporated into the curriculum precisely because generations of experience have identified those contents as requisite to best practice. Moreover, new generation doesn't need to "reinvent the wheel." In this and subsequent generations, the pedagogical challenge concerns how applied ethics educators will convey those contents in a way that pre-service professionals introduce *phronesis* into their self-formation so that, in their practice, they will make ethical decisions and conduct themselves ethically, thus demonstrating ethical competence (Cooper, 2013; Cooper & Menzel, 2013). What is absolutely critical vis-à-vis *Bildung*, however, is the binding force of those ideals, namely, the individual's spirit.

More concretely, consider again the training of FBI agents. But, this thought experiment reframes training in Hogan's Alley commensurate with *Bildung's* ideals so as to denote education *in* virtue. This method introduces agents to what will become their continuous and progressive developmental self-formation as FBI special agents who demonstrate ethical competence.

This training begins with experience and, in particular, being inspired by the FBI's purpose as specified by its mission—to protect the American people and uphold the Constitution of the United States—and its vision—to be "ahead of the threat through leadership, agility, and integration"—to the point human beings aspire to become FBI agents. That mission and vision, conveyed tersely in the FBI motto's three virtues—"Fidelity, Bravery, Integrity"—require of those who aspire to be special agents: rigorous obedience to the Constitution of the United States; respect for the dignity of all those the FBI protects; compassion; fairness; uncompromising personal and institutional integrity; accountability and responsibility for actions and decisions as well as their consequences; leadership, both personal and professional; and, diversity (FBI, n.d.).

Agents training in Hogan's Alley, it would seem, are already motivated to learn about these noble ideals as well as to will them freely to inform and guide their conduct due to the intrinsic satisfaction to be derived when, as special agents, they will enact those ideals in their professional practice thus demonstrating ethical competence. From the beginning, the binding force of those ideals has emanated from within—the individual's spirit—making each a unique instantiation of an FBI agent. In contrast, the use of extrinsic force to inculcate those ideals in an agent not only denigrates their nobility but also and, more substantively, violates each agent's spirit—the freedom each will possess one day as a special agent to deliberate and make prudential decisions about what the FBI's ideals require personally and professionally as members of the nation's pre-eminent law enforcement agency.

Describing this outcome—the end—of this process, Hegel noted:

> Only in this freedom is the will completely *with itself* because it has reference to nothing but itself, so that every relationship of *dependence* on something other than itself is thereby eliminated. (quoted in Beiser, 2003, p. 177)

As the end—"self-perfection" and "self-possession" as Hegel described education or "self-actualization" as Maslow (1954) would later call it—its achievement evidences itself in FBI special agents whose freely-willed judgments and conduct demonstrate ethical competence. As self-perfected and self-possessed professionals, for example, they don't rely solely upon external fictions—laws, codes, procedures, or even public opinion polls—to make or justify their decisions. Instead, self-perfection and self-possession represent the apex of freedom at their current level of experience while failure requires ridding themselves of "every relation-ship of dependence on something other than itself." Accepting personal and pro-fessional responsibility for their judgments and conduct as well as learning how to avoid vice in the future represent the highest possible achievement of educa-tion—FBI special agents whose freedom of spirit represents their self-chosen and freely-willed unique instantiation of spirit in the world. For Hegel, this achieve-ment is the end of education—*Bildung*—and provides its substantive purpose. In addition, this achievement is one of many because FBI special agents will need a continuous and developmental education that will challenge them to grow beyond their currently achieved levels of fidelity, bravery, and integrity.

Given this end, Plato's observation in the *Phaedo* rings true. That is, although a self-perfected and self-possessed human being can be ridiculed, maligned, and imprisoned, as Socrates was, the spirit remains free. It's those human beings who are neither self-perfecting nor self-possessed who should be pitied, as Socrates noted to his friends gathered around him just prior to his freely-willed suicide:

> The lovers of learning know that when philosophy gets hold of their soul, it is im-prisoned in and clinging to the body, and that it is forced to examine other things through it as through a cage and not by itself, and that it wallows in every kind of ignorance. Philosophy sees that the worst feature of this imprisonment is that it is due to desires, so that the prisoner himself is contributing to his own incarceration most of all. (Plato, 1981, 82e:121–122)

When education is the end not a means, the subject of education—the student who is responsive to experience—liberates one's "spirit" of any attachment that can keep it from grasping the truth that will set it free like a fledgling hesitantly but fiercely determined to bound forth from the nest for the first time.

Summarizing Hegel's discussion of *Bildung*, Wood noted how achieving this freedom of spirit is no easy task:

> *Bildung* is simultaneously a process of self-transformation and an acquisition of the power to grasp and articulate the reasons for what one believes or knows. Acquiring a genuinely rational comprehension of things goes hand in hand with a process of liberating maturation through a struggle involving selfhood and the overcoming of self-conflict. (Wood, 2003, p. 302)

In this way, *Bildung* and its early German romantic connotations directly chal-lenge the utilitarian tradition of training pre-service professionals as this became institutionalized in the United States during the twentieth century. More important for the purposes of this discussion, however, this tradition was also institutional-ized in applied ethics education across the professions. Both Schlegel and Hegel would be critical of those who would call this "education," arguing that those who believed they were educating pre-service professionals in applied ethics during those decades had substantive pedagogical matters backwards, evident in the way they made the curriculum the subject and implemented it to instruct pre-service professionals *about* ethics.

In contrast, when *Bildung* provides the guiding rationale for training professionals, the student is the subject, experience is the curriculum, and continuous self-formation as a particular instantiation of spirit in the world as a professional is the pedagogical objective. This process reframes professional training by constructing it upon a substantive rationale concerning why professionals educate themselves *in* ethics, first, as pre-service professionals through their classroom experience and, second, as in-service professionals in their professional practice through continuous professional development rooted in their experience.

Then, through continuous education *in* ethics, these professionals serve others as living exemplars of their profession's ideals whose spirit flourishes as they exhibit ethical competence when confronting the dilemmas of practice having made good, if not better decisions based upon universal principles (Kohlberg, 1981). In turn, their professional practice provides others an experience to redeem themselves, to experience their spirit's liberation, and to will to become more self-perfected and self-possessed as well as to demonstrate ethical competence in their professional practice as they educate themselves *in* virtue.

REFRAMING THE TEACHING OF APPLIED ETHICS: EDUCATION *IN* VIRTUE

When education *in* ethics provides the foundational principle for ethics training, those who teach applied ethics are positioned to bridge the theory-practice gap which Beiser believes romanticism failed to surmount because it didn't solve two pedagogical challenges: 1) how to facilitate students to liberate their mind to deliberate and 2) how to assist students to liberate their spirit to demonstrate ethical competence.

Liberating the Mind to Deliberate

Neither Schlegel or Hegel rejected developing the mind's rational powers—knowing, understanding, and applying both to one's life—that came to be associated with traditional education. But commensurate with *Bildung*, Schlegel and Hegel accorded primacy to the continuous and progressive developmental self-perfection and self-formation of the spirit. Why? Schlegel and Hegel grasped two fundamental drawbacks of traditional education and, for the purposes of this discussion, instruction *about* ethics.

Traditional instruction *about* ethics likens the mind to a passive receptacle, a container designed by Nature to hold an ever-expanding amount of static information that can be called upon to solve a variety of problems as they arise. Commensurate with this view, many if not most pre-service professionals embark upon their professional training seeking to acquire and fill their minds with that body of information. Then, demonstrating mastery of their chosen profession's knowledge base by applying it through a variety of in-class exercises, examinations, and perhaps a culminating project (e.g., portfolio, comprehensive examination, internship, residency), pre-service professionals begin the transition into the next stage of instruction—in-service professional practice—where they replicate what they learned previously.

From this perspective, traditional instruction *about* ethics doesn't liberate the student's mind to deliberate when confronting the dilemmas of professional practice currently presenting themselves. That is, prior to implementing a solution, professionals question and think about as well as judge independently what others have previously questioned, thought about, and judged to constitute ethical practice, namely, what gradually came to constitute the canon of intellectual history contained, for example, in a profession's encyclopedias, textbooks, research journal articles, and trade magazines. To construct an *ethical* profession, then, efficiency requires instructing pre-service professionals not only *about* their chosen profession's ideals but also its canonical literature.

Not rejecting this pedagogical method outright, both Schlegel and Hegel would have observed how it gets substantive matters backwards. While instruction *about* ethics is important, rather than liberating the mind and commensurate with Boyle's 1662 law[2], instruction increases external pressure upon the mind—the container—causing it to contract as, for example, principles—the "high road" of professional practice—devolve into rules—the "low road" of profession practice. In contrast, *Bildung* decreases external pressure upon the mind, thus allowing its powers—like gas inside the container—to expand its powers by slowing down the decision-making process as professionals turn inward and work with their profession's ideals and canonical literature to determine what best practice suggests in this situation and its idiosyncratic circumstances. In this way, Schlegel and Hegel would have observed, professionals instantiate their unique spirit in the world rather than simply replicate what they know and understand.

Liberating the pre-service professional's mind raises a pedagogical challenge: How will ethics educators assist pre-service professionals to bridge the gap demarcating "knowing" and "understanding" from "doing"?

Assisting the Spirit to Demonstrate Ethical Competence

Although instruction *about* ethics conveys important information, this method—"to know" and "to understand"—does not guarantee the content will be applied to the ethical dilemmas that arise in professional practice. Even though the information conveyed has been judged by experts to be relevant for successful professional practice—"to do things *right*"—a profession's ideals represent a fun-

---

[2] Boyle's law states: "The absolute pressure exerted by a given mass of an ideal gas is inversely proportional to the volume it occupies if the temperature and amount of gas remain unchanged within a closed system" (cited in Levine, 1978, p. 12). That is, the volume of any gas at a constant temperature varies directly with the absolute pressure.

damentally more substantive and significant *a priori* matter—the animating spirit of professional practice—which professionals must employ as they confront the dilemmas of practice.

How are those who educate pre-service professionals *in* virtue to assist them to liberate their spirit to be virtuous—"to do," and, in particular, "to do *right* things"? Schlegel's contemporary, the poet and philosopher Johann Christoph Friedrich von Schiller (1759–1805) offers a provocative response.

Describing a fourth connotation of *Bildung*, Schiller argued that strengthening the mind's rational powers was insufficient if only for the reason doing so failed to motivate human beings intrinsically to act according to the dictates of reason. Schiller maintained that even if students interact dynamically with the contents of the instruction they have accumulated, a different pedagogical method was necessary to inspire the mind to activate the power of will, that is, if students were to liberate their spirit from any extrinsic factor that otherwise might impinge upon if not constrain it.

To bridge the gap demarcating theory and practice, Schiller asserted that *Bildung* mandated introducing students to aesthetic experiences because, he argued, "philosophy cannot stimulate action...religion cannot convince reason, but...art has the power to inspire us to act according to reason. Because it so strongly appeals to the imagination, and because it so deeply affects our feelings, art can move people to live by the high moral ideals of a republic" (quoted in Beiser, 2003, p. 95). In Schiller's estimation, aesthetic experience—for example, reading accounts detailing a profession's exemplars as well as those who have defiled it and sullied or impugned their character in its practice—can inspire pre-service professionals *about* ethics which, in turn, generates a more powerful motive: To conduct themselves ethically.

Returning to Hogan's Alley, individual instantiations of fidelity, bravery, and integrity (and vice-versa)—exemplars of FBI heroism across the decades—would be equally if not more important than instruction in the knowledge and understanding of the best practices associated with being a special agent. Introducing those stories first, putting flesh and blood onto the FBI's purpose and virtues—would provide an inspirational motive to demonstrate that purpose and those experiences as well as foundational experience for learning the policies, procedures, and rules that govern the practice of special agents and which have emerged from the practice (or malpractice) of those exemplars.

That said, Schiller may have had another, more important outcome in mind: Pre-service professionals would educate themselves *in* ethics.

For those who teach applied ethics, incorporating aesthetic experience into the curriculum provides a means to stimulate pre-service professionals to achieve a short-term goal: To initiate their education—their self-perfection and self-formation—*in* ethics. The long-term goal is *Bildung*—the lifelong endeavor on the part of in-service professionals to perfect themselves continuously through their professional practice into "works of art" (Beiser, 2003, p. 80).

Yet, the short- and near- term goal requires incorporating aesthetic experience into professional training. This isn't only a matter of inspiring pre-service professionals to respond to their chosen profession's ideals but also a matter of introducing them to aesthetic experiences of those ideals that will inspire within their spirit the desire to be ethical. To assist pre-service professionals to begin creating a powerful, albeit unique synergy of themselves *in* ethics that lies beyond their current horizon of experience, ethics educators assist students to appreciate those ideals and to direct their powers of mind—"to know" and "to understand"—and spirit—"to do"—into a unified entity and determining how the parts will best work in concert.[3]

Inspired by aesthetic experience, self-perfection and self-formation facilitate the development of a unique instantiation of spirit evidencing itself in the form of what Shiller called a "good and beautiful spirit," that is, a continuously self-generating and self-organizing whole. Unconstrained by anything extrinsic and exuding the profession's ideals in one's in-service practice, this professional responds to ethical dilemmas because the desired end—*Bildung*—continuously disciplines and exercises this individual's spirit *in* virtue. In turn, the sprit provides the strength and unifies reason and passion as well as the ethical and natural sensibilities…all of this evidencing itself in ethical competence.

Beyond inspiring this unique synthesis of powers as an ethical professional, aesthetic experience also makes freedom synonymous with self-perfection and self-possession and, in particular, the freedom to be self-determining, aware of and yet unconstrained by any extrinsic force. For this reason, aesthetic experience and becoming a connoisseur of the "good and beautiful" in one's chosen profession requires pre-service professionals to become increasingly deliberative which, in turn, awakens the spirit within to recover the "primal harmony…torn apart by the development of civilization" (Beiser, 2003, p. 295).

Extrapolating Schiller's understanding of aesthetic experience beyond inspiring the continuous self-formation of pre-service professionals *in* ethics, it also motivates them to commence forth with confidence from pre-service training to the in-service practice of their chosen profession. Then, as in-service professionals, training continues unabated as they instantiate the profession's ideals by engaging in unconstrained, free interactions with others who continuously perfect one another and their profession, thus forming a Utopia of professionals—an aesthetic state—whose members, as self-possessed and self-perfecting spiritual beings, are united as a harmonious whole (pp. 291–292). In Schiller's estimation,

---

[3] Kohlberg (1981) would later argue that ethical development is developmental and progress, consisting of three levels and six stages. What's important to note, and of critical importance for teaching applied ethics when the pedagogical goal is to educate student in ethics, is that ethical development moves progressively from stage to stage and, furthermore, that movement is fostered as ethics educators ask questions framed by the next developmental level, similar in a way to how human beings learn to walk by taking baby steps prior to walking and learning to walk well prior to engaging in distance running.

these professionals discover their perfection not as they practice their profession but in their freedom to embody its ideals in their practice.

Stephens (2021) likens this aesthetic state to a choir, wherein members continuously adapt their conduct in response to fluctuating conditions with limited disruption to the group's performance. Researching a community choir, Stephens noted how members adapted when they believed their collective performance was becoming fragmented or falling apart. His process model demonstrates that "this aesthetic experience—the sense of fragmentation based on inputs from the bodily senses—leads to emotional triggering, meaning group members' emotions prompt changes in their attention and behavior." Distributing their attention in new ways in increasing attentiveness and awareness by focusing upon the whole—musical score and conductor—and its parts—the individual vocalist's contributions, aesthetic experience can lead to embodied forms of cognition that complement accounts of representational forms of knowledge, thus facilitating real-time adaptation in complex action group work.

This understanding of a responsible professional makes one's true interests synonymous with those of a profession and vice versa, what Beiser calls "autonomous, active and enlightened citizen[ship]" (2003, p. 285). Left unchecked, however, this understanding of responsible citizenship can be co-opted and devolve into a totalitarian ideology that eventually leads to the loss of self-perfection and self-possession. As Immanuel Kant (1724–1804) famously observed of this phenomenon, a nation's high ideals can characterize "a nation of devils" (as quoted in Beiser, 2003, p. 285) or, for the purpose of this discussion, professionals who just do their jobs and are complicit in the form of the "many" and "dirty" hands of those who perpetrate administrative evil (Adams & Balfour, 2014).

The most responsible of professionals—those whose motive is to be ethical—devote themselves to preserving, protecting, defending, and furthering themselves as well as their profession and its noble ideals by continuously moving beyond the horizon of their current experience. These professionals view work not so much as a contracted "job" providing a steady stream income as a member of an objective "profession" but more so as a covenantal "ministry" exemplifying their subjective "service" to that profession. Their professional practice demonstrates ethical competence because, educated *in* ethics, the good is firmly rooted in and expresses ethical character.

BRIDGING THE GAP: REFRAMING THE PURPOSE OF PRE-SERVICE ETHICS EDUCATION

Envisioning the training of pre-service professionals as *Bildung*, the traditional purpose for instructing pre-service professionals *about* ethics can be reframed, primarily by deemphasizing its utilitarian connotations and emphasizing a normative end, namely, education *in* ethics. As an end in itself, pre-service ethics education aims to provide pre-service professionals experiences enabling them to become continuously self-perfecting and self-possessed professionals whose ethical competence will perfect them as professionals and, in turn, their chosen professions.

This reframing of applied ethics challenges applied ethics educators to reconsider the means in light of that normative end and, in particular, the subject taught, the curriculum implemented, and the pedagogical methods utilized. This reframing then provides a substantive purpose for teaching applied ethics—*why* ethics educators do *what* they do—and identifies the significant contribution they can make to the education of future professionals and, hence, the value they can add to the training of pre-service professionals.

Concerning the Subject

This reframing directs the attention to the student—the subject ethics educators teach—and their critical role in educating pre-service professionals *in* ethics.

In *Education at the Crossroads*, Maritain (1943) identified four norms to guide pedagogy when the subject is the student.

The first norm—"foster those fundamental dispositions which enable the [student] to grow in the life of the mind" (p. 39)—directs ethics educators to bring to each student's conscious awareness their resources and potential to delight *in* ethics. These resources—especially the intrinsic desire to be an ethical professional—empowers the will which, in turn, fortifies the determination to overcome any tendency that otherwise might detract each student from educating themselves *in* ethics. Then, as the power of intellect strengthens, ethics educators turn the student inward to pursue the challenging and sometimes perplexing questions that arise from within when confronting dilemmas and to consider their solutions from multiple and conflicting perspectives.

While many students approach learning believing it should require little or no effort, effective pedagogy fosters the development of the motive for and fundamental dispositions that will enable pre-service professionals to develop the life of their mind. As ethics educators teach this subject, they encourage students to inculcate the self-discipline required to become a continuously self-perfecting and self-possessed professional.

While many ethics educators begin their course with case studies, it should be noted that those spark delight *about* ethics. In contrast, *Bildung* requires students to delight *in* ethics, thus indicating that ethics educators should begin their course by introducing students to ethical principles and, in particular, the ability to know, understand, apply, and defend as well as critique each principle. Learning to advance principled arguments equally well on both sides of a dilemma challenges students, in turn, to deliberate more judiciously about each principle as well as the dilemma's situation and idiosyncratic circumstances. Then, as students learn additional principles and develop greater cognitive complexity concerning the content of ethics, they realize there is no "best" solution, only a "good" or perhaps "better" one. This realization evidences their mind's intellectual powers strengthening, evidencing how ethics educators have assisted the subject of their pedagogy to grow in conscious awareness of their inner resources and ability to delight *in* ethics.

As noted above, this delight *in* ethics—its principles—might better be spurred by introducing students to biographies detailing the experiences of those professionals who exemplify their profession's virtues and vices. Expanding conscious awareness of the realities associated with professional practice both good and bad, students challenge themselves from within to move beyond their current state of conscious awareness of what ethics is and requires of professionals. In addition, this experience challenges students from within to contemplate what can be "good" and "bad" about professional practice. Assessing these matters against the strengths and weaknesses of a body of ethical principles introduces students to the reality of ethical practice: Commensurate with the nature of an ethical dilemma, more oftentimes than not there is no "best" option but only a "good" or "better" option to "do things right" as a professional as that's informed by one's ethical stance to "do right things" as an ethical professional (for example, see Cooper, 2012; Jacobs, 2019; Svara, 2015).

The second norm—centering each student's attention upon the aesthetic experiences being introduced and internalized—assists pre-service professionals to become aware of the internal dynamism present within that, once awakened, will liberate their artistic, creative, and imaginative powers. "Before being formed and expressed in concepts and judgments," Maritain notes, "intellectual knowledge is at first a beginning of insight, still unformulated which proceeds from the impact of the illuminating activity of the intellect on the world of images and emotions and which is but a humble and trembling movement yet invaluable, toward an intelligible content to be grasped" (p. 41). With experience providing the curriculum as well as its content, Maritain observes that educators must be "concerned with discerning and seeing, with getting vision, rather than with collecting facts and opinions." In this way, ethics educators use the content of applied ethics for students to grasp the reality of the practice of applied ethics. Directing their attention primarily to the latter, "then in the mind of the student the power of intuition will be awakened and strengthened unawares, by the very intuitivity traversing such teaching" (p. 45).

This awakening of intuition provides the necessary foundation for introducing case studies, as these will challenge students to think more artistically, creatively, and imaginatively about the contents in light of the various solutions proposed by different ethical principles. At this point, ethics educators might also introduce students to the "hermeneutical suspicion" (Ricoeur, 1973a,b), namely, suspending judgment about social phenomena because appearances can be deceptive as their meaning lies hidden beneath layers of accretions, each requiring interpretation. Thus, when introducing cases, ethics educators might challenge students to inquire into, identify, and then consider those many layers of meaning, discerning the multiple and confounding factors implicit in each and which successful administrators know they overlook at their own peril. This inspires students to be more thoughtful—clever, perhaps—before rushing to judgment.

The third norm—"the whole work of education and teaching must tend to unify, not to spread out; it must strive to foster internal unity in [a student]" (p. 45)—challenges ethics educators to equip each student's mind with an ordered understanding of ethics—its scope and sequence—that will develop prudence and wisdom. With students besieged from all sides by many diverse interests and inclinations, each constantly vying for attention, students oftentimes don't possess that internal unity, what Newman (1981) called a "comprehensive understanding" of the whole—the arrangement of its parts and how they coalesce, for better and worse. Assisting students to develop this internal unity enables them to deliberate and formulate generalizations concerning the true nature of what will confront them in professional practice and to respond with prudence and wisdom.

Ethics educators can assist students to unify their study of applied ethics by having them write a provisional statement of ethical leadership (Svara, 2015). During the course, this first, nascent effort—featuring students cobbling inchoate thoughts together perhaps as a series bullet points or short paragraphs—is continuously revised as students study those biographies, consider stories of exemplars' virtue and vices, learn the body of ethical principles, the process of deliberation, and as they formulate tentative judgments. The final product—the provisional statement of ethical leadership—yields evidence of the degree to which each student has developed the fundamental dispositions representing growth in the life of the mind, what Maritain called "the humble and trembling movement toward the intelligible content to be grasped, and the internal unity of [ethical] knowledge achieved."

Retrospectively, this exercise unleashes an experience of increasing competence and accomplishment—the horizon that students have surpassed and the new horizon of experience that currently lays beyond them. But, more importantly, the document provides a standard to judge the ethical practice of their profession one day in the future as in-service professionals. Interestingly, this scholarly yet practical product of the mind will remain a *provisional* statement because, as in-service professionals, students will continuously develop it as their professional practice challenges them to resolve new dilemmas and surpass further horizons of their experience as ethical professionals.

Lastly, the fourth norm requires assisting students to liberate their minds by emphasizing the power of reason over recall of facts. Similar to active engagement in learning (Dewey, 2013) and constructivism (Vygotsky, 1978), Maritain emphasizes that curricula "should never be passively or mechanically received, as dead information which weighs down and dulls the mind. Instead, the mind must rather be actively transformed by understanding into the very life of them, and thus strengthen the latter...." (p. 50).

Ethics educators utilize the content of ethics so students will empower themselves to construct the foundation upon which they learn to reason about and translate that content into ethical decisions and conduct demonstrating increased ethical competence. Or, as Nieuwenburg, described this process, to assist students to inculcate in themselves the dispositions "not only to act but to think, and even to perceive certain situations as embodying reasons for action." This requires ethics educators to introduce students to the modes of practical thinking involved "to foster not only virtue, but the several modes of reflection essentially bound up with it" (2003, p. 25).

Implying that ethics education continues beyond the classroom and into the workplace—where it will be tested, refined, and perfected—the power of deliberation is the primary learning pre-service professionals will take into in-service professional practice. Knowing, understanding, and applying ethical principles in the classroom—which strengthen the mind's deliberative powers—may be forgotten but can always be retrieved. But, deliberation transforms the mind by immersing pre-service students into the very life of ethics and is evidenced when, in their in-service practice, their judgments will demonstrate increasing levels of ethical competence.

Concerning the Curriculum

This reframing of pre-service training *about* ethics upends the primary concern of ethics educators over the past century: the curriculum. Viewing applied ethics as a means—instructing pre-service professionals *about* ethics—many have believed the best curriculum will increase the likelihood that professional practice will evidence ethical competence. The challenge has been to identify the contents of that curriculum.

Yet, with the profession's knowledge base continuously evolving and advancing as new theory and best practices are tested and incorporated into it, identifying the best curriculum proves to be an elusive goal that may be based upon a fantastical hope. Furthermore, developing expertise in communicating the contents of the curriculum becomes focal. Possessing an intangible love for the subject matter rather than the subject taught, ethics educators then devote themselves to communicating this enthusiasm by teaching and motivating students to master the newest most up-to-date body of content.

Enjoying wide repute as an expert rhetorician, apologist for the Roman Emperor, and renowned teacher of rhetoric sixteen hundred years ago, Aurelius Augustine called these instructors "word vendors" (1997, IV.2.93), sarcastically asking "For who would be so absurdly curious as to send his child to school to learn what the teacher thinks?" (1949, p. 185). When applied ethics is the means to the end of educated professionals demonstrating ethical competence in the practice of their chose profession, ethics educators don't lose sight of or grow blind to that *a priori* end, namely, the formation of the spirit of a continuously self-perfecting and self-possessed professional.

Bildung upends this focus by reframing the curriculum as experience. The pedagogical process begins with aesthetics, proceeds into the consideration of principles, then engages students in deliberating about the content, and concludes with making prudential and wise judgments based upon experience that has moved students beyond their present state of conscious awareness about what ethics is and requires of in-service professionals. This experience, in turn, challenges pre-service professionals from within to form themselves to think *and* conduct themselves as ethical professionals think *and* conduct themselves. As discretion will require when confronting the dilemmas of practice, this self-formation obliges those teaching ethics to focus primarily upon immersing their students in experiences *in ethics* through which they will free themselves from anything that might otherwise impinge upon and constrain their decision-making process, including the content of ethics.

Freedom, then, enables pre-service professionals to apply and reflect upon the outcomes of their experience by questioning and thinking. Then, as they make increasingly more refined and sophisticated professional judgments, conduct themselves accordingly, and reflect upon the outcomes to determine their efficacy and respond accordingly, pre-service professionals begin developing the habit of reflective practice and construct a body of "professional knowledge" (Sergiovanni, 1986, 1995). That is, they learn to translate their experience of the curriculum into ethical professional practice.

Concerning Pedagogy

When *Bildung* is the end, pre-service ethics educators aren't dispassionate instructors who implement a prescribed curriculum. Instead, possessing a profound respect for their subject's spirit which has motivated them to seek to learn about their chosen profession's noble ideals, theories, and best practices, ethics educators respect the subjects they teach and devote themselves to provide an education *in* ethics so that, in turn, their subjects will practice their professions as continuously self-perfecting and self-possessed ethical professionals. This vision mandates those who teach applied ethics to reframe pedagogy.

When the subject is the student and experience the curriculum, the "genius" of pedagogy evidences itself not as a "performance art" (Sarason, 1999), but as ethical professionals, namely, the ability to educate students *in* ethics and with all else being subsidiary to and supporting this end. Genius evidences itself in their creative, artistic, and imaginative use of the tools of the teaching profession as ethics educators craft experiences that mediate what constitutes the spirit of an ethical professional and inspires the spirit of their students to evidence ethical competence and continue doing the same in their in-service professional practice.

Reframing pedagogy in this way upends common notions associated with pedagogical expertise. Mastery of the contents of the curriculum, the skilled application of the technologies associated with communicating those contents, and doing so in a way that is both inspirational and motivational at the same time, important as these are, support pedagogy yet are secondary to the process. When *Bildung* is the desiderium, the spirit of the ethics educator—a continuously self-perfecting and self-possessed professional—is what reveals expertise. To this end, ethics educators reveal the spirit of an ethical pedagogue who exemplifies ethics and enact ethical competence in the practice of their chosen profession. This represents the "value-added" proposition that applied ethics education offers the pre-service training curriculum.

CONCLUSION

When *Bildung* provides *terminus ad quem* for applied ethics education, those teaching pre-service professionals might be better characterized as "educational connoisseurs" (Eisner, 1985)—artists expressing their distinctive spirit in a studio—than as "educational experts"—scientists implementing a uniform method in a laboratory.

Connoisseurship complicates pedagogical decision making because the spirit animating each ethics educator and student differs, making it near to impossible to identify "one best way" to teach applied ethics. Furthermore, although the curriculum and pedagogical methods implemented tend to be fairly standard—the content of ethics, case studies, codes of ethics, lectures, discussions, and assessment activities—decision making about what constitutes how best to teach the subject is fraught with numerous complicating factors, making these decisions more a matter of interpretation and artistry than skill and its rote implementation (Burlingame & Sergiovanni, 1993).

This continuous professional self-formation provides the substantive purpose identifying *why* pre-service professionals need to be educated *in* ethics—"to redeem humanity one by one"—as well as its critically important role in pre-service professional training. This purpose also provides a rationale supporting why a required course in applied ethics is necessary, that is, if pre-service professionals are to liberate the spirit Nature has endowed them with from any extrinsic factor that otherwise might impinge upon if not constrain it from being perfected.

The eight preceding chapters in this volume have eloquently addressed the ethics of teaching applied ethics directing attention to the pedagogical struggle applied ethics educators seek to resolve as they make *Bildung* central to their teaching in an academic culture that prizes science above philosophy, techniques above aesthetics, demonstrable facts above normative principles, efficiency above effectiveness, and characteristics above character. For pre-service professionals, these efforts have assisted in clarifying the general contours of this chapter's reframing of applied ethics education—*Bildung*—including its subject, curriculum, and pedagogy, the foundation of which is an education *in* ethics. However, the process of and assessing this continuous self-formation across the trajectory of a professional's career through in-service professional development is a matter requiring further study (Siewert & Udani, 2016; Wittmer, 2000; Wyatt-Nichol & Franks, 2009).

Once that matter is synthesized and as the early German romantics hoped, this continuous self-formation will perfect in-service professionals to "redeem" both themselves and their professions continuously *in* ethics. Then, utilizing a variety of empirical and quasi-empirical methods the efficacy of applied ethics education can be assessed. While the contours of what constitutes in-service applied ethics training are apparent, professional associations will have to decide the content of the curriculum in collaboration with academics and accrediting agencies. In this way, in-service ethics training as *Bildung* will promote the continuous development of ethical character so that in-service professionals will express their spirit and bring glory, first, to themselves and, second, to the profession from which they sprang.

REFERENCES

Adams, G. B., & Balfour, D. L. (2014). *Unmasking administrative evil* (3rd ed.). Routledge.

Anand, P. (1993). *Foundations of rational choice under risk*. Oxford University Press.

Aristotle. (1958). The Nicomachean ethics (W. D. Ross, Trans.). In J. D. Kaplan (Ed.), *The pocket Aristotle* (pp. 158–274). Simon & Schuster.

Augustine. (1949). *The greatness of the soul & the teacher* (J. M. Colleran, Trans.). Newman Press.

Augustine. (1997). *The confessions* (M. Boulding, Trans.). New City Press.

Beiser, F. C. (2003). Romanticism. In R. Curren (Ed.), *A companion to the philosophy of education* (pp. 130–142). Blackwell Publishing. https://www.jstor.org/stable/j.ctt1c99bkt

Burlingame, M., & Sergiovanni, T. J. (1993). Some questions about school leadership and communication theory. *Journal of Management Systems, 5*(2), 51–61.

Candy, P. C. (1991). *Self-direction for lifelong learning*. Jossey-Bass.

Carr, D. (1991). *Educating the virtues: Essay on the philosophical psychology of moral development and education*. Routledge.

Cooper, T. L. (2012). *The responsible administrator: An approach to ethics for the administrative role* (6th ed.). Jossey-Bass Publishers.

Cooper, T. L., & Menzel, D. C. (2013). *Achieving ethical competence for public service leadership*. Routledge.

De Graff, G., & Van Exel, J. (2008). Using Q methodology in administrative ethics. *Public Integrity 11*(1), 63–78.

Dewey, J. (2013). *Democracy and education. An introduction to the philosophy of education*. CreateSpace.

Eisner, E. W. (1985). *The educational imagination*. MacMillan Publishing Co.

Federal Bureau of Investigation. (n.d.). *Training* [webpage]. https://www.fbi.gov/services/training-academy

Federal Bureau of Investigation. (2011). *The FBI integrity and compliance program* [webpage]. https://www.fbi.gov/audio-repository/news-podcasts-thisweek-the-fbi-integrity-and-compliance-program.mp3/view

Federal Bureau of Investigation. (2017a). *Becoming an agent: An inside look at what it takes: Part 2—Inside the classroom* [webpage]. https://www.fbi.gov/news/stories/becoming-an-agent-part-2

Federal Bureau of Investigation. (2017b). *Becoming an agent: An inside look at what it takes: Part 1—The first week* [webpage]. https://www.fbi.gov/news/stories/becoming-an-agent-part-1

Jacobs, R. M. (2019). Teaching public administration ethics: A 20-year public integrity retrospective. *Public Integrity, 21*(Sup 1).

Kaptein, M., Huberts, L., Avelino, S., & Lasthuizen, K. (2005). Demonstrating ethical leadership by measuring ethics: A survey of U.S. public servants. *Public Integrity, 7*(4), 299–311.

Kelling, G. L., & Moore, M. H. (1988, November). The evolving strategy of policing. *Perspective in Policing, 4.* National Institute of Justice.

Kohlberg, L. (1981). *Essays in moral development.* Harper and Row.

Lawton, A. (2008). The language of ethics: Understanding public service ethics through discourse. *Public Integrity, 11*(1), 45–62.

Levine, I. N. (1978). *Physical chemistry.* Mc-Graw-Hill.

MacCrimmon, K. R. (1968). Descriptive and normative implications of the decision-theory postulates. In K. Borch & J. Mossin (Eds.), *Risk and uncertainty* (pp. 3–32) [International Economic Association Conference Volumes, Numbers 1–50]. Palgrave Macmillan.

Mann, H. (1957). *The republic and the school: Horace Mann on the education of free men* (Classics in Education, No. 1, L.A. Cremin, Ed.). Teachers College Press.

Maritain, J. (1943). *Education at the crossroads.* Yale University Press.

Maslow, A. (1954). *Motivation and personality.* Harper.

Menzel, D.C. (2010). *Ethics moments in government: Cases and controversies.* CRC Press.

Merezhkovsky, D. (1908). *The romance of Leonardo da Vinci: The forerunner.* G. P. Putnam's Sons.

National Law Enforcement Officers Memorial Fund. (n.d.). *Important dates in law enforcement history* [webpage]. https://nleomf.org/facts-figures/important-dates-in-law-enforcement-history

Newman, J. H. (1981). *The idea of a university* (Notre Dame Series in the Great Books). University of Notre Dame Press.

Nieuwenburg, P. (2003). Can administrative virtue be taught?: Educating the virtuous administrator. *Public Integrity, 5*(1), 25–38.

Peterson, A., & Arthur, J. (2021). *Ethics and the good teacher: Character in the professional domain.* Routledge/Taylor & Francis Group.

Peterson, M. (2009). *An introduction to decision theory.* Cambridge University Press.

Plato. (1981). Phaedo. In G. M. A. Grube (Ed.), *Plato: Five dialogues* (pp. 89–155). Hackett Publishing Co.

Rachels, J., & Rachels, S. (2015). *The elements of moral philosophy* (8th ed.). McGraw Hill.

Ricoeur, P. (1973a). The task of hermeneutics. *Philosophy Today, 17*(2), 112–128.

Ricoeur, P. (1973b). The hermeneutical function of distanciation. *Philosophy Today, 17*(2), 129–141.

Rohr, J. A. (1978). *Ethics for bureaucrats: An essay on law and values.* Marcel Dekker.

Sarason, S. B. (1999). *Teaching is a performing art.* Teachers College Press.

Sergiovanni, T. J. (1986). Understanding reflective practice. *Journal of Curriculum and Supervision, 1*(4), 353–359.

Sergiovanni, T. J. (1995). *The principalship: A reflective-practice perspective* (3rd ed.). Allyn and Bacon.

Siewert, W., & Udani, A. (2016). Missouri municipal ethics survey: Do ethics measures work at the municipal level? *Public Integrity, 18*(3), 269–289.

Simon, Y. R. (1993). *Philosophy of democratic government*. The University of Notre Dame Press.

Simpson, D. J., & Sacken, D. M. (2021). *Ethical dilemmas in schools: Collaborative inquiry, decision-making, and action.* Cambridge University Press.

Stephens, J. P. (2021). How the show goes on: Using the aesthetic experience of collective performance to adapt while coordinating. *Administrative Science Quarterly, 61*(1), 1–41.

Svara, J. (2015). *The ethics primer for public administrators in government and nonprofit organization* (2nd ed.). Jones & Bartlett Learning.

Swisher, L. L., Rizzo, A-M., & Marley, M. A. (2001). Moral reasoning among public administrators: Does one size fit all? *Public Integrity, 3*(1), 53–68.

Tyack, D., & Hansot, E. (1982). *Managers of virtue: Public school leadership in America, 1820–1980.* Basic Books.

Von Maravić, P. (2008). Studying methods, not ethics: Exploring the methodological character of administrative ethics research. *Public Integrity, 11*(1), 9–34.

Vygotsky, L. S. (1978). *Mind in society: The development of higher psychological processes.* Harvard University Press.

Walton, C. (2000). Where the code meets the road: Professional ethics and the need for sanctions. *Public Integrity, 2*(4), 329–346.

West, J. P., & Berman, E. M. (2004). Ethics training in U.S. cities: Content, pedagogy, and impact. *Public Integrity, 6*(3), 189–206.

Wheeland, C. M. (2013). Gregory G. Smith: A township manager effectively managing ethical dilemmas. *Public Integrity, 15*(3), 265–282.

Wilson, W. (1887). The study of administration. *Political Science Quarterly, II*(2), 197–222. http://www.commentary.com/admin_thoughts_1887.pdf

Wittmer, D. (2000). Individual moral development: An empirical exploration of public- and private-sector differences. *Public Integrity, 2*(3), 181–194.

Wood, A. W. (2003). Hegel on education. In A.O. Rorty (Ed.), *Philosophers on education: New historical perspectives* (pp. 300–317). Routledge.

Wyatt-Nichol, H., & Franks, G. (2009). Ethics training in law enforcement agencies. *Public Integrity, 12*(1), 39–50.

Zinner, S. E. (2011). The stories public administrators tell. *Public Integrity, 13*(4), 385–396.

CHAPTER 10

THE CORE VALUES OF THE SERVICE PROFESSIONS AND AN EFFECTIVE CURRICULUM TO HELP STUDENTS INTERNALIZE THEM

Neil Hamilton
University of St. Thomas School of Law

This chapter analyzes both the core values that educators in each of the eight professions included in this volume are asking their students to understand and internalize and the core values emphasized in the earlier Carnegie Foundation for the Advancement of Teaching's studies of higher education for five professions. The chapter does a similar analysis of the most effective curricular principles the eight authors and the earlier Carnegie studies have recommended to foster student development to internalize these core values. The chapter recommends creating a learning community of educators across the professions to build stage development models on the most foundational core values that educators in all the professions are emphasizing.

Keywords: Applied Ethics Education; Ethics Curriculum; Effective Ethics Teaching

Educating in Ethics Across the Professions: A Compendium of Research, Theory, Practice, and an Agenda for the Future, pages 213–230.
Copyright © 2023 by Information Age Publishing
www.infoagepub.com

INTRODUCTION

All eight of the service professions in this volume have the same challenge: To help each new entrant understand and internalize the core values of that profession. A major question for this volume is whether educators of applied ethics in the different professions can learn from each other across the service professions how most effectively to foster each new entrant's developmental growth toward the core values of the profession. This chapter answers this question strongly in the affirmative.

Following this introduction, this chapter is divided into four major sections. The section titled "Core Values of the Eight Professions" analyzes the core values that each of the eight professions are asking new entrants to understand and internalize. A synthesis of the core values of the eight professions included in this volume and the core values of five professions included in an earlier major study of higher education for the professions follows. The section titled "Effective Curriculum for Applied Ethics Learning Outcomes on the Core Values of the Eight Professions" summarizes all eight chapters' analyses of effective curriculum concerning the core values. The section titled "Recommendations on Next Steps to Move toward a More Effective Applied Ethics Curriculum across the Professions" puts forward a significant step that educators in all eight professions could take to foster each student's growth toward later stages of ownership over the student's continuous professional development.

This volume's chapters concerning education in applied ethics across eight professions build upon the earlier Carnegie Foundation for the Advancement of Teaching's five studies of higher education for the professions. In 2001, the Carnegie Foundation for the Advancement of Teaching initiated a series of studies of higher education for the professions in the United States (including site visits to a number of schools in each profession) focusing upon clergy (2006), lawyers (2007), engineers (2009), nurses (2010), and physicians (2010). Each study included analysis of acculturation into that profession's ethics. The Carnegie Foundation sought "to discover what is common among the many forms of professional education, while also exploring the distinctive approaches to teaching and learning that mark specific professional domains" (Foster et al., 2006, p. 2). In *Educating Clergy*, the first study to be published, then-Carnegie Foundation President Lee Shulman explained that all professions have some similar characteristics and obligations; as a result, pedagogies for one profession "will reappear in our future studies of other professions, often under different names, but predictably with similar functions" (pp. ix, xii). The Carnegie Foundation did not ultimately analyze the common approaches to acculturating new entrants into the core values of the profession across all five professions because of a change in the leadership of the foundation.

In 2012, I analyzed the five Carnegie studies to pull out "lessons learned" across the professions' educational programs regarding how to foster each student's growth to internalize the ethics of the profession (Hamilton, 2012). The Carnegie Foundation defined the challenge of these programs regarding each profession's ethics in the context of the three general apprenticeships that the new entrant to each profession endeavors to master: the cognitive apprenticeship, the practical apprenticeship, and the apprenticeship of professional formation (Foster et al., 2006).

The cognitive apprenticeship "focuses the student on the knowledge and way of thinking of the profession" (Sullivan et al., 2007, p. 28). In other words, the cognitive apprenticeship concentrates upon the analytical skills unique to each profession applied to the doctrinal knowledge of that profession. This apprenticeship is the focus of classroom education in each profession.

The second apprenticeship is "a practical apprenticeship to learn skilled know-how and clinical reasoning" (Benner et al., 2010, p. 25). These are the practical (not analytical) skills necessary for effective practice and include, for example, all the relationship skills necessary to engage with clients and colleagues. This apprenticeship usually involves practice-based learning and is the major focus of experiential education in each profession such as clinics, externships, and simulation courses.

The third apprenticeship is the apprenticeship of professional formation, which "introduces students to the purposes and attitudes that are guided by the values for which the professional community is responsible." The essential goal of this apprenticeship "is to teach the skills and inclinations, along with the ethical standards, social roles, and responsibilities that mark the professional" (Sullivan et al., 2007, p. 28). Ethics educators in the five professions had different descriptors for this third apprenticeship. For example, the Carnegie Foundation studies use the terms "professional formation," "formation of professional identity," "ethical comportment," "professionalism," and "professionalism and ethics" to describe the educational objective. In many respects, these are synonyms. This apprenticeship is the most foundational since it defines the purpose of the first two apprenticeships and should drive the entire learning process.

William Sullivan (2009), the Co-Director of all five Carnegie Foundation for the Advancement of Teaching studies of higher education for the professions, concluded that the "chief formative challenge" for higher education in the professions is to help each student entering a profession to change from thinking like a student where he or she learns and applies routine techniques to solve well-structured problems toward the acceptance and internalization of responsibility to others (particularly the person served) and for the student's own pro-active development toward excellence as a practitioner at all of the competencies of the profession. Each person served (e.g., a client or patient) needs to trust that the professional serving the person is dedicated above all else to care for the person with all of the professional's ability. This is essentially a fiduciary disposition, using "fiduciary" in the general meaning of founded on trustworthiness. Each student must internalize a fiduciary disposition to others, particularly the persons served by the profession (Sullivan, 2013).

Similarly, the authors of the Carnegie Foundation's fifth and final study—on medical education—*Educating Physicians*—conclude that "The physician we envision has, first and foremost, a deep sense of commitment and responsibility to patients, colleagues, institutions, society, and self, and an unfailing aspiration to perform better and serve with excellence. Such commitment and responsibility involve habitual searching for improvement in all domains...." (Cooke et al., 2010, p. 41).

My analysis points toward "professional formation" as the best descriptive term that captures the multi-faceted developmental growth toward the core values that applied ethics educators in the professions want to foster. As *Educating Physicians* notes, the term "professional formation" indicates that the third apprenticeship is "an ongoing self-reflective process involving habits of thinking, feeling, and acting" (Cooke et al., 2010, p. 41). It is a lifelong commitment to continued progress toward excellence and the aspirational core value of deep responsibility and care for the persons served by the profession.

THE CORE VALUES OF THE EIGHT PROFESSIONS

To what degree do educators in the eight professions included in this volume identify core values similar to those identified in the earlier Carnegie studies? This section analyzes the eight chapters to identify the core values identified for each profession.

Legal Education

Professor Judith McMorrow observes that the dominant theme in applied ethics in legal education is to emphasize the law of lawyering and precise legal analysis, not the core values of the profession. The presence of a large body of law governing lawyers overwhelms nuanced discussion of professional and personal core values. Based upon over 30 years of teaching the required professional responsibility course in law schools, my experience is similar to that of McMorrow. There are professional core values embedded in the law of lawyering like competence, confidentiality, loyalty, and independent professional judgment. But, the required professional responsibility course is generally taught as a type of compliance course emphasizing knowledge of and legal analysis applied to the law of lawyering, with little time spent on the core values of the profession and how the core values inform all of the discretionary decisions a lawyer makes every day.

Many of the legal profession's core values are stated in the Preamble to the ABA Model Rules of Professional Conduct. For example, "A lawyer is also guided by personal conscience and the approbation of professional peers. A lawyer should strive to attain the highest level of skill, to improve the law and the legal profession, and to exemplify the profession's ideals of public service" (American Bar Association, 2020). The major ABA and Conference of Chief Justices reports on professionalism emphasize that each lawyer agrees to act as a fiduciary where his or her self-interest is overbalanced by devotion to the serving the client and the public good in the profession's area of responsibility, namely, justice (Hamilton, 2008).

There is good reason to believe that law schools will be giving more attention to fostering each student's growth toward these core values. In 2022, the ABA adopted revisions to accreditation Standard 303(b) which now state:

> A law school shall provide substantial opportunities to students for: (1) law clinics or field placement(s); (2) student participation in pro bono legal services, including law-related public service activities; and (3) **the development of a professional identity** (emphasis added).

> Interpretation 303-5: Professional identity focuses on what it means to be a lawyer and the special obligations lawyers have to their clients and society. The development of professional identity should involve an intentional exploration of the values, guiding principles, and well-being practices considered foundational to successful legal practice. Because developing a professional identity requires reflection and growth over time, students should have frequent opportunities for such development during each year of law school and in a variety of courses and co-curricular and professional development activities. (American Bar Association, 2022)

Medical Education

Professor Greg Moorlock notes that undergraduate medical education in the United Kingdom is guided by the U.K.'s regulator of the medical profession, the General Medical Council (GMC) and its Outcomes for Graduates, and similarly in the United States by the accreditor for M.D. programs, the Liaison Committee on Medical Education (LCME), and its accreditation standards. Both accrediting bodies articulate core values for the medical profession.

The GMC lists 20 learning outcomes relating to ethical and professional principles, but they can be grouped into three general categories (General Medical Council, 2018):

- Five learning outcomes that focus specifically on internalizing responsibility to the patient: to make sure the fundamental needs of the patient are addressed with compassion; to maintain patient confidentiality; to protect patients from any risk posed by the caregiver's own health; to demonstrate person-centered care; and, to seek patient consent and provide options to the patient;
- Seven learning outcomes that focus on professional development and lifelong learning: take personal and professional responsibility for the

student's actions; recognize professional limits and seek help when necessary; be open and honest with colleagues and employers when things go wrong; demonstrate the importance of professional development and lifelong learning; access and analyze reliable sources of current clinical evidence; demonstrate the importance of engagement with revalidation including maintaining a professional development portfolio; and, learn from experience and feedback and respond constructively to assessments; and,

- Five learning outcomes that focus on general relational competencies: act with integrity and be polite, considerate, and trustworthy; recognize personal biases; act with an inclusive approach; raise concerns through informal communication with colleagues; and, work as a mentor for the interprofessional team.

One learning outcome requires each graduate to be able to summarize the current ethical dilemmas in healthcare practice and everyday clinical decision-making and to apply ethical reasoning to situations that may be encountered in the first years after graduation.

The LCME learning outcomes include self-directed and lifelong learning and a general outcome "to require medical students to behave ethically in caring for patients and in relating to patients' families and others involved in patient care" (Liaison Committee on Medical Education, 2021). The LCME outcomes also include recognition of bias, communication skills with patients and other stakeholders, and collaboration skills.

The Accreditation Council for Graduate Medical Education (ACGME) is the accrediting body for the residency programs in the United States. The ACGME specifically includes a learning outcome that residents must demonstrate competence to "continually improve patient care based on constant self-evaluation and lifelong learning" plus a learning outcome that residents must demonstrate "responsiveness to patient needs that supersedes self-interest," and "compassion, integrity, and respect for others" (Accreditation Council for Graduate Medical Education, 2020).

Nursing Education

Professor Pamela Grace emphasizes that "Ethical practice in nursing at its most basic is the intention to provide the best possible care to patients, in a way that is sensitive to the particular patient's needs, the possibilities of environmental and/or contextual impediments, and the need to anticipate and minimize potential harms. A critical element for new nurses or nurses working in unfamiliar environments is to grasp the limits of their knowledge and seek appropriate assistance."

The American Association of Colleges of Nursing (AACN) 2021 publication, *The Essentials: Core Competencies for Professional Nursing Education* also emphasizes that

Person-centered care is the core purpose of nursing as a discipline… Foundational to person-centered care is respect for diversity, differences, preferences, values, needs, resources, and the determinants of health unique to the individual. The person is a full partner and the source of control in team-based care. Person-centered care requires the intentional presence of the nurse seeking to know the totality of the individual's lived experiences and connections to others (family, important others, community). As a scientific and practice discipline, nurses employ a relational lens that fosters mutuality, active participation, and individual empowerment. This focus is foundational to educational preparation from entry to advanced levels irrespective of practice areas. (American Association of Colleges of Nursing, 2021)

The AACN *Essentials* also include learning outcomes on the formation and cultivation of a sustainable professional identity, including accountability, perspective, collaborative disposition, and comportment, that reflects nursing's characteristics and values. *The Essentials* also includes learning outcomes on professional development requiring participation in activities and self-reflection that contribute to life-long learning.

Engineering Education

Professor José-Félix Lozano identifies essential features of engineering stating "It is science-based, systematic, synthetic and creative, goal-oriented, dynamic and people-oriented. The first five are essentially positivist materialist and naturalistic in their approach and focused upon calculative strategic rationality. The sixth, people-oriented, has an idealistic and social component…."

Professor Lozano also notes that the Accreditation Board for Engineering and Technology adopted accreditation standards that require learning outcomes including "an ability to apply engineering design to produce solutions that meet specified needs with consideration of public health, safety, and welfare, as well as global, cultural, social, environmental, and economic factors." The learning outcomes must also include "an ability to recognize ethical and professional responsibilities in engineering situations and make informed judgments, which must consider the impact of engineering solutions on global, economic, environmental, and societal contexts" and "the ability to acquire and apply new knowledge as needed, using appropriate learning strategies." (Accreditation Board for Engineering and Technology, 2021, p. 5). The professional organizations for engineers also emphasize that an engineer should meet the specified needs of a client or employer as a faithful agent keeping paramount the safety, health, and welfare of the public while also continuing one's professional development (National Society of Professional Engineers, 2019).

Urban Planning Education

Professor Jeffrey Chan notes that for urban planners in the United States, the American Institute of Certified Planners (AICP) has some influence regarding the core values of the profession. The AICP's first principle is that planners shall continuously pursue and faithfully serve the public interest. The second principle is to do so with integrity. The third principle is to work to achieve economic, social, and racial equity. The fourth principle is to safeguard the public trust. The fifth principle is to improve knowledge and techniques and increase public understanding (American Institute of Certified Planners, 2021). The American Planning Association Statement of Ethical Principles in Planning emphasizes similar core values (American Planning Association, 2021).

Business Education

Professor Ronald Sims observes there is disagreement among educators about the goals and core values in business education. With no major organization of business professionals having articulated core values and a code of ethics like the other service professions included in this volume, Sims points out that a major accreditor, the American Association of Collegiate Schools of Business (AACSB), has been influential in requiring ethics as a part of a business degree. The AACSB's accreditation standards require that a school's curriculum promote and foster "a lifelong learning mindset" and the ability to have a "positive societal impact" in each student (American Association of Collegiate Schools of Business, 2020). Survey research indicates business employers greatly value relationship skills like teamwork, oral, and written communication, leadership, and customer orientation that flow from an internalized responsibility to and care for others. (Hamilton, 2018, Appendix C).

Public Administration Education

Professor Jonathan West finds that ethics education in public administration is controversial because there is little agreement about what to teach. However, West notes the importance of both the American Society for Public Administration (ASPA) formed in 1939 to advance excellence in public service and the Network of Schools of Public Administration (NASPAA) formed in 1970 and recognized as the accreditor of Master's Degree programs in the field.

ASPA has adopted a code of ethics with a first core value of "Promote the interests of the public and put service to the public above service to oneself." Other core values are to uphold the Constitution and the law, promote democratic participation, strengthen social equity, fully inform and advise government officials, demonstrate personal integrity, strengthen personal capacities to act competently and ethically, and encourage the professional development of others (American Society for Public Administration, 2013).

The NASPAA accreditation standards for Master's Degree Programs require the curriculum to demonstrably emphasize public service values which include pursuing the public interest with accountability and transparency, acting ethically to uphold the public trust, and promoting participation and inclusiveness (Network of Schools of Public Administration, 2019).

Military Education

Professor Andrew Corbett writes that the core values of the military go beyond the laws of armed conflict to foster judgment about what "should" be done in the use of lethal force based on a set of core moral values. The specific core values for the British Air Force are respect, integrity, service, and excellence. The United States Air Force core values are integrity first, service before self, and excellence in all we do. The British Navy and Army core values are commitment, courage, discipline, respect for others, integrity, and loyalty. The United States Navy core values are honor, courage, and commitment. The United States Army core values are loyalty, duty, respect, selfless service, honor, integrity, and personal courage (Department of Defense, 2020).

SYNTHESIS: THE CORE VALUES

Educators in the eight professions are asking each new entrant to grow from being a passive student, doing what the faculty asks, toward a core value of an internalized pro-active ownership over continuous professional development. Educators in the eight professions are also asking each new entrant to grow from a self-interest orientation toward a core value of an internalized ethic of responsibility to and care for others served by the profession.

Synthesizing the core values emphasized in this volume's eight chapters with the core values identified in the Carnegie studies discussed earlier, I suggest there are two foundational learning outcomes for applied ethics education regarding core values across the professions.

Each student should demonstrate an understanding and integration of:

- pro-active continuous professional development toward excellence at all the competencies needed to serve others in the profession's work well; and,
- an internalized deep responsibility to others whom the student serves as a professional in widening circles as the student matures.

These two foundational core values across the professions represent an opportunity for educators from the different professions to help each other understand what is the most effective curriculum that will foster student development toward these core values. It is also clear both of these core values across the professions build on each new entrant's earlier development of these values before entering education for a particular profession. Some new entrants, particularly those with significant life and work experience, may be at a significantly later stage of development on either or both of these core values. Some new entrants may be at a very early stage of development. An effective curriculum will need to take this into account.

AN EFFECTIVE CURRICULUM FOR DESIRED
APPLIED ETHICS LEARNING OUTCOMES

This section first analyzes the eight chapters plus Jacobs' chapter to identify what the chapter authors recommend in terms of an effective curriculum that fosters each student's growth to later stages of development regarding these two core values.

Table 10.1 summarizes the frequency with which the different authors recommend specific curricular approaches.

Table 10.1 identifies each chapter author's analysis of the most effective curriculum to foster student development in applied ethics education. These analyses are based not only on any empirical study of the applied ethics curriculum in each of the professions, but rather each chapter is an experienced educator's observation of the field. This is an important data point but it would be highly beneficial to have more empirical research identifying how different schools have designed and assessed effective curriculum. Table 10.2 provides other important data points based on the Carnegie Foundation's site visits to a number of schools in each profession.

A synthesis of Tables 10.1 and 10.2 indicates that the most effective curriculum to foster each new entrant's developmental growth toward the core values of each profession will integrate:

1.   an understanding of the core values (responsibilities) of the profession, knowledge of theories of applied ethics, and critical analysis/ethical reasoning
2.   case studies/common real-world and current dilemmas and experiential education (authentic professional experiences)
3.   repeated opportunities for each student's guided reflection to foster growth from the student's current developmental stage on a core value to the next developmental stage.

Several recent articles provide an in-depth analysis of guided reflection, coaching, and the importance of major transitions for the student in their development toward later stages of the two foundational values (Hamilton, 2021b, 2022a,b).

TABLE 10.1.   The Most Effective Curriculum Identified to Foster Student Development in Applied Ethics Education

Curriculum Principles	Law	Medicine	Nursing	Engineering	Urban Planning	Business	Public Admin.	Military	Jacobs' synthesis
Case studies/common real-world dilemmas/current dilemmas	X	X	X	X	X	X	X	X	X
Understanding core values of the profession		X	X	X	X		X	X	X
Knowledge of theories of applied ethics		X	X	X	X	X	X		X
Critical analysis using ethical theories/ethical reasoning	X	X	X	X	X	X	X		X
Importance of guided reflection[1]		X	X			X	X		X
Importance of experiential education including simulations (authentic professional experiences)		X	X			X	X		X
Applied ethics engagements throughout the curriculum	X	X	X			X	X	X	X
Open dialogue with others on applied ethics in safe environment		X	X		X			X	X
Usefulness of the Four Component Model framework (which recognizes stages of development on each component)[2]		X	X	X				X	X
Role Modeling		X	X					X	X
Coaching/ Mentoring		X	X					X	X

TABLE 10.2.   The Most Effective Curriculum to Foster Student Professional Formation From the Carnegie Foundation Studies of Higher Education for Five Professions
(Hamilton, 2012)

Curriculum Principles	MEDICINE	NURSING	CLERGY	ENGINEERING	LAW
Reflection on the responsibilities of the profession	X	X	X	X	X
Inteqratinq the three apprenticeships	X	X	X	X	X
Actively seek feedback, dialoque, reflection, and self-assessment	X	X	X	X	X
Clinical education and practical experiences	X	X	X (learninq by doing)	X (practical experience)	X
Modeling	X	X	X	X	X
Coaching	X	X	X	X	X
Teacher-quided discussion of ethics	X	X		X	X
Broad curricular attention to professional formation	X	X		X	X

RECOMMENDATIONS: NEXT STEPS TO MOVE TOWARD A MORE EFFECTIVE APPLIED ETHICS CURRICULUM ACROSS THE PROFESSIONS

This final section offers recommendations regarding next steps to move toward more effective applied ethics curriculum across the professions which emphasizes the same two foundational core values—a pro-active continuous professional development toward excellence at the competencies needed to serve others well in the profession's work and an internalized deep responsibility to others whom the student serves as a professional in widening circles as the student matures. Applied ethics curriculum across the professions also emphasizes repeated opportunities for each student's guided reflection to foster growth from the student's current developmental stage on a core value to the next developmental stage. It would be very useful if applied ethics educators across the professions could work toward a clear framework of developmental stages through which students must progress on either of these foundational core values.

Medical education for residency certification has tried to create developmental stage models of this type. The Accreditation Council for Graduate Medical Education uses the term "milestones" to describe narrative models regarding how student development of a core competency moves through stages toward a level of competency necessary for a licensed physician to serve clients adequately (Holmboe & Englander, 2018). The milestones on a specific competency provide a "shared mental model" of professional development starting as a student and progressing to competent practitioner and, beyond, to mastery. A milestone model defines a logical learning trajectory of professional development. It also highlights and makes transparent significant points in student development using a narrative that describes demonstrated student behavior at each stage. Milestones can be used for formative and summative assessment as well as program assessment.

When faculty adopt a milestone model for a particular competency, they also are building consensus concerning what competent performance looks like which will foster interrater reliability of the assessments. Because milestones describe what a trajectory should look like, learners can track their progress toward becoming competent at a particular competency and programs can recognize students who are advancing well or in need of extra help. Overall, each milestone reflects the Dreyfus model of development from novice to expert at any competency. Level 1 describes what would be expected of a novice in the field and Level 4 is a graduation target (Eno et al., 2020).

Inherent in a milestone model is the idea that learners ultimately take ownership over their continuous professional development to later stages on each competency required (Holmboe & Englander, 2018). This matches up squarely with the first core value—ownership of continuous professional development toward excellence at the major competencies needed by the profession.

Table 10.3 identifies the substantial benefits of a milestone model on the major competencies required for a law student. These benefits should be the same for all the professions in this volume if there were milestone models for the two foundational core values.

A good milestone model draws the particular core value at issue and its stages of development into view, enabling more purposeful and effective work at every step by everyone involved. A principal challenge for law faculty who teach professional responsibility with respect to the two foundational core values is that, unlike a traditional learning outcome like knowledge of the law of lawyering and critical analysis, the faculty do not have a clear shared understanding of the two foundational core values to define the level of competence a student must achieve by graduation and the stages of development to get there. This may also be a challenge for applied ethics educators in other professions.

A first step in formulating a milestone model is to embrace the idea that a student may have begun the development of a professional competencies before matriculating in higher education, and then progresses in stages of development

TABLE 10.3. The Purpose and Function of Milestones for the Two Foundational Core Values (adapted from Eno et al., 2020)

Constituency or Stakeholder	Purpose/Function
Law Students	• Provide a descriptive roadmap to foster development toward later stages (new entrant students don't know what they don't know and need to be shown later stages). • Increased transparency of performance requirements • Encourage informed self-assessment and self-directed learning • Facilitate better feedback to the student • Guide personal action plans for improvement
Law Schools, Faculty, and Staff	• Provide a meaningful framework/shared mental model of student development • Guide curriculum and assessment tool development • Provide more explicit expectations of students • Support better systems of assessment • Enhance opportunity for early identification of under-performers so as to support early intervention
ABA Accreditation and the Public	• Accreditation – enable continuous monitoring of programs and lengthening of site visit cycles • Public Accountability – report at an aggregated national level on competency outcomes • Community of practice for evaluation and research, with a focus on continuous improvement

on these same competencies during higher education and well into professional life after graduation. The Holloran Center has developed the competency alignment model. In this model, a "competent learner" is ready to take the bar examination and begin the professional practice after passing the exam (Hamilton, 2021a) (Figure 10.1).

This same type of alignment model for the two foundational core values can be aligned well with the models that employers use to assess their professionals on the same core value or competency. In this way, the school's learning outcomes and curriculum thus will meet employer needs and students will be able to communicate their value to potential employers using the employers' language.

What might a milestone model for one of the two core values look like? Since 2017, the Holloran Center has organized working groups to create milestone models for the most common learning outcomes the law schools are adopting. The consensus of these expert panels creates some content validity for the models. The current Holloran Center Milestone Model of continuous professional development toward excellence at all the competencies needed to serve others as a lawyer (Table 10.4). Applied ethics educators in other professions could adapt this milestone model for their students.

Students can self-assess their developmental stage for an internalized continuous professional development (as well as listing the specific evidence demonstrating the student's stage of development). Faculty observers can assess the student's stage of development. With faculty providing guided reflection, students can create written professional development plans to grow to the next level (with appropriate supporting evidence). Students with significant work and life experience may already have achieved the competent learner or later stages.

During Law School

| Novice Learner | Intermediate Learner | Competent Learner | Exceptional Learner |

| Beginning Practicing Lawyer | Early Practicing Lawyer | Skilled Practicing Lawyer | Mastery Level Practicing Lawyer |

After Law School

FIGURE 10.1.   The Holloran Competency Alignment Model

TABLE 10.4.   Holloran Center Milestone Model on Assessment of Student's Ownership of Continuous Professional Development (Self-Directedness)

Sub-Competencies of Ownership/ Self-Directedness	Novice Learner (Level 1)	Intermediate Learner (Level 2)	Competent Learner (Level 3)	Exceptional Learner (Level 4)
1. **Self-Assesses and Identifies Strengths and Areas for Growth** *Understands full range of lawyering competencies and diagnoses learning needs*	RARELY demonstrates understanding of full range of lawyering competencies and diagnoses learning needs	SOMETIMES demonstrates understanding of full range of lawyering competencies and diagnoses learning needs	OFTEN demonstrates understanding of full range of lawyering competencies and diagnoses learning needs	CONSISTENTLY demonstrates understanding of full range of lawyering competencies and diagnoses learning needs
2. **Articulates Goals and Follows a Plan** *Implements a written professional development plan reflecting goals that are specific, measurable, achievable, relevant, and time-bound[1]*	RARELY creates and implements a written professional development plan reflecting goals that are specific, measurable, achievable, relevant, and time-bound	SOMETIMES creates and implements a written professional development plan reflecting goals that are specific, measurable, achievable, relevant, and time-bound	OFTEN creates and implements a written professional development plan reflecting goals that are specific, measurable, achievable, relevant, and time-bound	CONSISTENTLY creates and implements a written professional development plan reflecting goals that are specific, measurable, achievable, relevant, and time-bound
3. **Acquires and Learns from Experience** *Seeks experiences to develop competencies and meet articulated goals, and seeks and incorporates feedback received during the experiences*	RARELY seeks experiences or seeks and incorporates feedback received during the experiences	SOMETIMES seeks experiences and seeks and incorporates feedback received during the experiences	OFTEN seeks experiences and seeks and incorporates feedback received during the experiences	CONSISTENTLY seeks experiences and seeks and incorporates feedback received during the experiences
4. **Reflects and Applies Lessons Learned** *Uses reflective practice[2] to reflect on performance, contemplate lessons learned, identify how to apply lessons learned to improve in the future, and applies those lessons*	RARELY uses reflective practice to reflect on performance, contemplate lessons learned, identify how to apply lessons learned to improve in the future, and applies those lessons	SOMETIMES uses reflective practice to reflect on performance, contemplate lessons learned, identify how to apply lessons learned to improve in the future, and applies those lessons	OFTEN uses reflective practice to reflect on performance, contemplate lessons learned, identify how to apply lessons learned to improve in the future, and applies those lessons	CONSISTENTLY uses reflective practice to reflect on performance, contemplate lessons learned, identify how to apply lessons learned to improve in the future, and applies those lessons

[1] Goals that exhibit these factors are referred to as SMART Goals: Specific—clear goals including what, why, and how; Measurable—including a clear method for evaluation of progress; Achievable—including obstacles and realistic solutions; Relevant—including connection to core values; and Time-bound—including a clear timeline of steps.

[2] Reflective practice requires learners to: focus on their own performance (what?); consider multiple perspectives, including their own, and contemplate lessons learned (so what?); and identify how to apply lessons learned to improve in the future (now what?).

CONCLUSION

Educators in all the professions want students to internalize a core value of ownership of continuous professional development. As Jacobs recommended earlier in this volume, there would be significant benefit to create a learning community including educators in the different professions to discuss the most effective curriculum including assessment to foster each student's growth toward later stages of development on this core value. If this learning community were successful, educators in applied ethics across the professions could build upon this success to consider effective curriculum and assessment for other core values.

REFERENCES

Accreditation Board for Engineering and Technology. (2021). *ABET accreditation policy and procedure manual.* https://www.abet.org/accreditation/accreditation-criteria/accreditation-policy-and-procedure-manual-appm-2021-2022/

Accreditation Council for Graduate Medical Education. (2020). *Common program requirements* (residency). https://lcme.org/wp-content/uploads/filebase/standards/2022-23_Functions-and-Structure_2021-10-28.docx

American Association of Colleges of Nursing. (2021). *The essentials: Core competencies for professional nursing education* [pamphlet]. https://www.aacnnursing.org/Portals/42/AcademicNursing/pdf/Essentials-2021.pdf

American Association of Collegiate Schools of Business. (2020). *AACSB 2020 guiding principles and standards for business accreditation.* https://www.aacsb.edu/-/media/documents/accreditation/2020-aacsb-business-accreditation-standards-july-2021.pdf?rev=80b0db4090ad4d6db60a34e975a73b1b&hash=D210346C64043CC2297E8658F676AF94

American Bar Association. (2020). *Model rules of professional conduct.* American Bar Association.

American Bar Association. (2022). *American Bar Association adopted by the House of Delegates 2022 Midyear Meeting February 14, 2022.* American Bar Association. https://www.americanbar.org/content/dam/aba/directories/policy/midyear-2022/300-midyear-2022.pdf

American Institute of Certified Planners. (2021). *AICP code of ethics and professional conduct* [webpage]. https://www.planning.org/ethics/ethicscode/

American Planning Association. (1992). *APA ethical principles in planning.* https://www.planning.org/ethics/ethicalprinciples/

American Society for Public Administration. (2013). *ASPA code of ethics.* https://www.aspanet.org/ASPA/Code-of-Ethics/Code-of-Ethics.aspx

Benner, P., Sutphen, M., Leonard, V., & Day, L. (2010). *Educating nurses: A call for radical transformation.* Jossey-Bass.

Cooke, M., Irby, D. M., & O'Brien, B. C. (2010). *Educating physicians: A call for reform of medical school and residency.* Jossey-Bass.

Department of Defense. (2020). *Department of defense core values.* https://diversity.defense.gov/Portals/51/Documents/Resources/Commission/docs/Issue%20Papers/Paper%2006%20-%20DOD%20Core%20Values.pdf

Eno, C., Correa, R., Stewart, N. H., Lim, J., Westerman, M. E., Holmboe, E. S., & Edgar, L. (2020). *Milestones guidebook for residents and fellows*. Accreditation Council for Graduate Medical Education.

Foster, C. R., Dahill, L. E., Golemon, L. A., & Tolentino, B. W. (2006). *Educating clergy: Teaching practices and pastoral imagination*. Jossey-Bass.

General Medical Council. (2018). *Outcomes for graduates*. https://www.gmc-uk.org/-/media/documents/outcomes-for-graduates-2020_pdf-84622587.pdf?la=en&hash=35E569DEB208E71D666BA91CE58E5337CD569945

Hamilton, N. (2012). Fostering professional formation/professionalism: Lessons from the Carnegie Foundation's five studies on educating professionals. *Creighton Law Review, 45*(3), 763–797.

Hamilton, N. (2018). *Roadmap: The law student's guide to meaningful employment*. ABA Press.

Hamilton, N. (2021a). The gap between the foundational competencies clients and legal employers need and the learning outcomes law schools are adopting. *UMKC Law Review, 89*(3), 559–82.

Hamilton, N. (2021b). The major transitions in professional formation and development from being a student to being a lawyer present opportunities to benefit the students and the school. *Baylor Law Review, 73*(1), 139–69.

Hamilton, N. (in press, a). The foundational skill of reflection in the formation of a professional identity. *St. Mary's Journal on Legal Malpractice and Ethics, 12*(2).

Hamilton, N. (in press, b). Mentor/coach: The most effective curriculum to foster each student's professional identity. *University of St. Thomas Law Journal, 17*(2).

Holloran Center for Ethical Leadership in the Professions. (2019). *Self-directedness milestone*. https://www.stthomas.edu/media/hollorancenter/pdf/Revisedself-directednessrubricDecember2019.pdf

Holmboe, E., & Englander, R. (2018). What can the legal profession learn from the medical profession about next steps? *University of St. Thomas Law Journal, 14*(2), 345–56.

Liaison Committee on Medical Education. (2021). Functions and structure of a medical school. https://lcme.org/wp-content/uploads/filebase/standards/2022-23_Functions-and-Structure_2021-10-28.docx

National Society of Professional Engineers. (2019). *Code of ethics for engineers*. https://www.nspe.org/sites/default/files/resources/pdfs/Ethics/CodeofEthics/NSPECodeofEthicsforEngineers.pdf

Network of Schools of Public Policy, Affairs, and Administration. (2019). *NASPAA accreditation standards for master's degree programs*. https://www.naspaa.org/sites/default/files/docs/2019-11/NASPAA%20Accreditation%20Standards%20-%202019%20FINAL%20with%20rationale.pdf

Sullivan, W. M. (2009). Foreword. *Teaching medical professionalism* (2d ed.). Cambridge Univ. Press.

Sullivan, W. M. (2013). Align preparation and assessment with practice. *New York State Bar Association Journal, 85*(7), 41–43.

Sullivan, W. M., Colby, A., Wegner, J. W., Bond, L., & Shulman, L. S. (2007). *Educating lawyers: Preparation for the profession of law*. Jossey-Bass.

EPILOGUE

EDUCATING IN ETHICS

Today's Desired Reality and Agenda for the Future

Richard M. Jacobs

Villanova University

An ethics center can provide an invaluable service to promote this agenda and ensure its success by uniting applied ethics educators across the professions who, for the most part, practice their craft oftentimes in isolation from one another on the peripheries. Developing this center appears to be essential if the fundamental reconception of teaching applied ethics detailed here is to succeed. If it does, applied ethics educators *across* the professions will strengthen ethics education within the *professions* by educating the spirit of pre-service and in-service professionals *in* ethics as they foster their formation as professionals which is today's desired present reality.

—*Richard M. Jacobs*

This volume's Prologue proposed three goals that identify a *terminus ad quo*—a portrait of what Oettingen (2012) called the "present reality"—concerning the

Educating in Ethics Across the Professions: A Compendium of Research, Theory, Practice, and an Agenda for the Future, pages 231–252.
Copyright © 2023 by Information Age Publishing
www.infoagepub.com
All rights of reproduction in any form reserved.

history, challenges, and future vision for those who teach and will be teaching applied ethics across the professions.

The contributors to the eight chapters comprising this volume's first three sections provided the content depicting a present reality evidencing four challenges:

- *Being bounded within independent disciplinary silos with little if any discourse among and between those who teach applied ethics across the professions.* This lack of collaboration has limited the positive impact applied ethics education has had and could potentially have upon those independent disciplines.
- *Looking to other scholarly disciplines for clues about how to improve the teaching of ethics.* While this aspect of the field's history has illuminated some of the pedagogical challenges within the professions and demonstrates the potential for interdisciplinary research to improve the teaching of professional ethics, it has also limited identifying the particular purpose, nature, and significance of this field for training professionals across the professions.
- *Using different terminology to describe similar ideas and concepts.* Across the professions, there is no lexicon of commonly accepted definitions. Important terms—ethics, applied ethics, and ethical practice—and concepts—ethical professional, ethical professional practice, ethical competence—denote different things to different people both within and across the professions, making it difficult for applied ethics educators to communicate effectively both within and across the professions.
- *Expecting much of the same, including further marginalization to the peripheries.* Accrediting associations have contributed in part to this disconcerting finding, many of which—presumably out of respect for academic freedom—don't mandate ethics courses and allow the content to be infused into courses across the curriculum, all the while steadily moving away from promoting normative, universal ethical principles and in the direction of promoting utilitarian global values.

Compounding these challenges in the present reality are four questions that colleagues who teach discipline specific courses periodically raise and which applied ethics educators have had to contend with, perhaps from the day when the idea was first advanced that professionals need some form of ethics education. Those questions include:

1. Can ethics be taught?
2. How should applied ethics be taught?
3. Who should teach applied ethics?
4. Should applied ethics be taught in a standalone course, be integrated into courses across the curriculum, both, or be relegated to the professional associations?

Assuming this *terminus ad quo* accurately depicts the present reality, those who teach and will be teaching applied ethics must consider how they might substantively change the present reality.

This Epilogue offers a solution: That applied ethics educators across the professions join forces to collaborate in envisioning a *terminus ad quem*—today's "desired present reality"—toward which those who currently teach and will be teaching applied ethics can direct their efforts to change the present reality substantively.

To stimulate discourse that can frame an agenda for the future of teaching applied ethics across the professions, this Epilogue suggests a "desired reality." Reflecting upon the contents of this volume's fourth section—educating the spirit of pre- and in- service professionals as well as forming ethical professionals—those who teach applied ethics can identify objectives and goals that respond to those four questions and chart a way forward to arrive at today's "desired reality" in the most efficient and effective way possible, given what's currently known.

FOUR THEMES EMERGING FROM THIS VOLUME'S CONTENTS

This desired reality is framed by four themes emerging from this volume's contents: 1) insufficient academic preparation to teach applied ethics; 2) forming ethical professionals who demonstrate ethical competence; 3) a framework for forming ethical professionals; and, 4) a lack of systematic assessment.

These themes represent the "meta-challenges" contributors to this volume's first three sections voiced and, moving forward, the problems ethics educators across the professions must resolve if they are break down the artificial walls of the disciplinary silos insulating them from one another and to form what DiBella and Nevis (1998) call a "community of practice." In turn, success in changing the present reality substantively will evidence itself as applied ethics educators seek not only to strengthen the practice of their craft but also to solidify their important role and place in the curriculum of their training program. Success in making progress toward today's desired reality will evidence itself as the practice of the ethical professionals demonstrates increasing levels of ethical competence tomorrow and into the foreseeable future.

Theme #1: Insufficient Academic Preparation to Teach Applied Ethics

The gulf demarcating ethical theorists from applied ethics educators concerns the latter's lack of adequate academic preparation in the former's area of academic expertise. In light of this lacuna, the former rightly ask: "How can someone teach what one doesn't know?"

Having been trained in professional disciplines, theoretical ethics represents a foreign terrain for many who teach applied ethics across the professions and an assignment to teach it may require considerable self-education. Noble as efforts in this regard may be, this approach may not suffice not only because the contents of theoretical ethics are not only difficult to master but also because mastery doesn't provide the self-assurance that's needed to communicate a principled rationale when reasonable challenges are raised concerning proposed solutions to dilemmas. In addition, ethical decisions require time for deliberating, proficiency in exercising higher-order thinking skills, clarity about one's roles and responsibilities, and the possession of a sufficient power of will to select and then enact the best possible decision, given the situation and circumstances. Lastly, explaining the decision's rationale requires facility not just with the language of ethics but also a certain *savoir faire* to make the decision understandable to ethicists and non-ethicists as well as to proponents and opponents alike (Cooper, 2014).

Unlike the contents of the professional fields of academic inquiry, the contents of applied ethics aren't so neatly categorized. With the goal being to cultivate each student's ability to synthesize a principled rationale while accounting for the strengths and weakness of multiple ethical theories, those who are new to teaching this body of content oftentimes don't appreciate the challenges they will confront. Then too, cultivating sufficient conversancy with the contents takes time—perhaps several semesters. For the first few iterations, neophytes may find themselves struggling just to "stay one chapter ahead of the students." Lastly, other professional responsibilities—research, teaching, and service, among others deplete the scarce resource of time. If ethics education is to be accorded its rightful place in the curriculum, the historical record implicit in the present reality depicted by the contributors to the first three sections of this volume indicates the current approach to prepare applied ethical educators across the professions for this assignment doesn't serve anyone's best interest.

An agenda to change the present reality substantively must include preparing those who teach applied ethics to develop sufficient conversancy with theoretical ethics so they can speak authoritatively regarding the application of theoretical ethics to the dilemmas of professional practice as well as to utilize its terminology with sufficient dexterity. While this preparation doesn't require earning the equivalent of a Bachelor's or Master's degree in ethics, it does require learning the content of ethics, grasping its subtle nuances, and demonstrating sufficient conversancy with those contents to communicate them competently and confidently if applied ethics educators are to assist students learn to apply those contents appropriately to the dilemmas of professional practice and demonstrate basic ethical competence as well.

Beyond the classroom, developing sufficient conversancy with theoretical ethics and its language system will also assist those teaching applied ethics to advocate more concretely and convincingly the value applied ethics adds to the professional training curriculum. Advocating articulately the "why" and "what" pre-service professionals need so they can learn to demonstrate ethical competence in their chosen profession will assist, at a minimum, to ameliorate the source of some of the underlying challenges those four questions raise concerning the value that ethics education adds to the curriculum.

Conversely, the gulf demarcating ethical theorists from applied ethics educators also evidences the former's lack of sufficient knowledge of each profession's practice and, in particular, inadequate conversancy with the realities and subtle nuances that make practice *professional*. Quite rightly, the latter ask: "How can someone speak authoritatively about a profession's practice in which one has little or no experience?" While it is also true, pedagogically speaking, the goal of applied ethics is to assist pre- and in- service professionals to learn to make those applications with increasing alacrity and precision, that goal begs the question—especially when it comes to pre-service professionals—concerning the lack of a sufficient base of experience to know how to make those applications. Even informed guesses are guesses, not professional judgments.

The question this first theme raises isn't so much the "what" theoretical ethicists need to know. Given their depth of knowledge and understanding, the question is: "How might theoretical ethicists cultivate in applied ethics educators across the professions what theoretical ethicists know and understand as professional ethicists?

The COVID-19 pandemic offers what may be an opportunity in this regard.

When the pandemic forced most universities and colleges to cancel in-person classes and send students home, educators had to devise alternatives to traditional pedagogy. With "in person," classroom education all but impossible, exigencies beyond the control of educators forced them to experiment with new technologies. What this experiment taught educators—forged in reaction to an emergency as they applied technology's promise for improving teaching—applied ethics educators can perfect by conceiving of a "center and periphery" (Shils, 1975) with the center—for example, an applied ethics clearinghouse—offering a way to conceive of how training applied ethics educators across the professions might unfold. This center would provide an array of services—training programs, networks, downloadable resources, among others—to applied ethics educators across the professions irrespective of their current stage of conversancy with theoretical ethics or experience teaching it (Figure 1).

The center would function akin to a wheel's axle around which applied ethics educators on the peripheries would use technology (e.g., Internet conferencing platforms like Zoom, Adobe Connect, Blackboard, Skype)—the wheel's spokes—to connect to the center and network with their collaborators on the peripheries across the professions. Providing the education those on the peripheries need to develop conversancy with ethical theory, to "talk through" its challenges, strengths, weaknesses, and nuances, and to strengthen their fluency in using its conceptual and language system, the center would facilitate the formation of a "community of practice" (DiBella & Nevis, 1998).

Completing this basic training would assist participants to improve teaching applied ethics in their respective professions, modeling for them and preparing

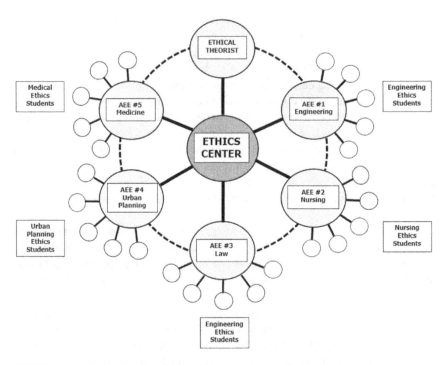

FIGURE 1.   Training Applied Ethics Educators *Across* the Professions

them, in turn, to form similar communities of practice with their students, whether those students are taking an ethics course in pre-service classrooms or taking ethics training as in-service professionals practicing their craft in different locales.

This approach to training applied ethics educators across the professions would demonstrate two substantive changes: Providing education in ethics irrespective of the participants' physical location and at a low cost.

Theme #2: Forming Ethical Professionals Who Demonstrate Ethical Competence

Providing training in ethical theory as well as its conceptual and language systems doesn't address what arguably may be the most crucial aspect of ethics education across the professions: Forming ethical professionals who demonstrate ethical competence.

Commensurate with Strong (1997), the contributors to this volume's first three sections offer images of classrooms that applied ethics educators can adapt or refashion to align better with their idiosyncratic needs (e.g., urban planning suggests the architecture of a design studio; medical, nursing, and law suggest a model of clinic; military ethics suggests the arduous and challenging process of an after-action report). These images can stimulate the development of new training experiences that would encourage students to form themselves in ethics as well as to form learning communities whose members collaborate to consider how they might resolve the typical dilemmas of practice emerging within their respective professions and which neophytes should be capable of solving competently.

As the contributors to this volume's fourth section remind readers, the foundation of these experiences demarcates instruction *about* ethics from education *in* ethics (Carr, 1991). Although some of the former is required for pre-service professionals to develop facility with ethical theory, if the latter is to flourish, ethics educators need to provide experiences that challenge students intrinsically to perfect their spirit—the inner desire to flourish as ethical professionals in their chosen profession do—so as to develop facility with and apply ethical theory, to deliberate about it for the concrete problems of practice, and to render and implement decisions demonstrating ethical competence.

Reconceiving classrooms as well as ensuring the appropriate balance of theory and practice also requires those who teach ethics across the professions to reconceive the best use of time for the purposes of instruction *about* ethics and education *in* ethics across the years of a career (Al-Zahrani, 2015; Kong, 2014; Munir et al., 2018; Simpson & Sacken, 2021).

Once again, the "center and periphery" model can assist applied ethics educators to reconceive these matters substantively. By connecting applied ethics educators on the peripheries within a profession, the center would provide the important and valuable service of networking ethics educators teaching in different locales to form a "community of practice" (DiBella & Nevis, 1998). For example, the center can connect an experienced engineering ethics professor with other engineering ethics professors—who may be new to teaching in the field, are interested in perfecting their pedagogy, or currently are experimenting with new methods. The experienced professor would facilitate experiences developing the type of learning participants have requested (see Figure 2).

The model would facilitate learning about, exchanging best practices, and reflecting upon practice as well as researching and sharing literature from other disciplines and professions, all in a collaborative effort to develop new experiences that can be field tested in their classrooms within their respective professions. The primary primarily benefit of this model is the training of educators within a profession to improve teaching applied ethics irrespective of the participant's physical location. Connected to but not physically present at the center, this approach also saves time and money if similar training and collaborative learning were to be offered, for example, at a profession's annual national conference.

Theme #3: A Framework for Forming Ethical Professionals

With many occupations that developed into professions during the 20th century, lists identifying the constitutive elements of the professions have proliferated (e.g., Flexner, 1910; Schein, 1972). One common element is a set of principles or

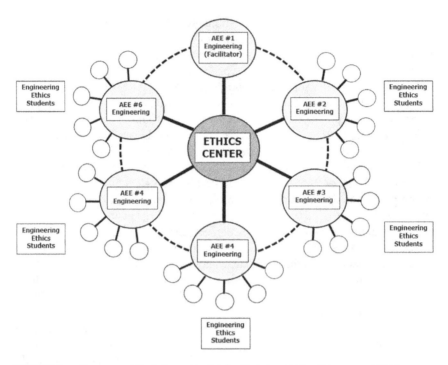

FIGURE 2. Center and Periphery Model for Training Ethics Educators *Within* a Profession

values specifying a profession's ethical practice and a mechanism to enforce its principles and values (Bullock, & Trombley, 1999).

Yet, to this day, the formation of ethical professionals who will demonstrate those principles and values—the "how to"—remains a much-contested concept.

Historically and as the present reality affirms, that formation has emphasized instructing pre-service professionals about ethics in traditional classrooms. Assuming that ethics can be taught and commensurate with Gallie's (1968) theory of contested concepts, the rationale for this approach reveals two conflicting perspectives. While some have argued this formation begins with an ethics course introducing students to ethical theory and its practice with a profession, others have argued it involves infusing ethical theory as well as its concepts and language system across the curriculum. While the culmination of both approaches has featured the awarding of an academic degree from an accredited professional training institution, the influence each perspective has exercised over the decades exhibits itself historically in the variability of accreditation standards and ethics requirements both within and across the professions.

Then too, naysayers have argued that ethics cannot be taught and therefore should not be included in the curriculum. From this perspective, the formation of ethical professionals has little if anything to do with ethics instruction but is the purview of professional associations whose code of ethics and practices specify what's required of members. This approach has resurfaced in recent decades through training programs offered at annual professional conferences including panels, symposia, workshops, lectures, and demonstrations, to name but a few. Ironically, much of this approach to training has resembled a traditional classroom where experts provide training based upon the profession's code of conduct as well as updates to best practice. To keep one's membership current, some associations award participants continuing education units (CEUs).

The two authors of this volume's fourth section offer an alternative. Applying the Carnegie Foundation for the Advancement of Teaching's most recent call for a fundamental reconception of professional education (Carnegie Foundation for the Advancement of Teaching, n.d.)[1], the authors think through how professionals across the professions might be formed. Both press beyond the Foundation's objective of "forming the mind for practice" with the objective being to "form the character of an ethical professional" which includes educating the mind, hand, and heart *in* ethics.

This reconception—today's desired reality—treats *applied ethics education* as an umbrella term spanning the course of a career, beginning with pre-service *ethics instruction* and continuing across the years and decades through in-service *ethics training*. Throughout, the focus is intentional: Forming the character of professionals *in* ethics through a series of continuous, progressive, and developmental learning experiences designed to assist both pre-service and in-service professionals inculcate into their character the virtues specified by their chosen profession's code of ethics and practices. The objective is for ethics instruction to provide the experiences professionals will need across their career to form their character and conduct themselves as virtuous members of their profession as they demonstrate increasing levels of ethical competence (Jacobs, 2021) (see Figure 3).

Pre-Service Ethics Instruction. For the past century, pre-service ethics instruction has transpired for the most part in classrooms, with the curriculum conveying, primarily, a profession's declarative knowledge and emphasizing theory and skills, and secondarily, their integration in practice.

Retrospectively, the focus could have been more intentionally formative—"theory-for-practice"—because the focus of pre-service ethics instruction is to assist students in forming their minds to begin thinking as ethical practitioners think (Argyris & Schön, 1974). The suggested reconception of pre-service ethics

---

[1] Between 1997 and 2009, the Carnegie Foundation for the Advancement of Teaching (Sullivan & Rosin, 2008) investigated student acculturation into five professions—clergy (Foster, Dahill, Golemon, & Tolentino, 2005), lawyers (Sullivan, Colby, Wegner, Bond, Shulman, 2007), engineers (Sheppard, Macatangay, Colby, & Sullivan, 2008), nurses (Benner, Sutphen, Leonard, & Day, 2009), and physicians (Cooke, Irby, & O'Brien, 2010). The reports invoked metaphor of "apprenticeship" to describe the process and content of a curriculum to form ethical professionals.

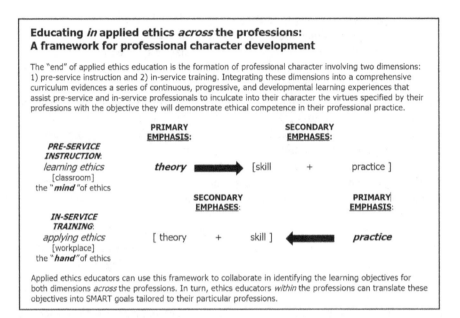

Educating *in* applied ethics *across* the professions:
A framework for professional character development

The "end" of applied ethics education is the formation of professional character involving two dimensions:
1) pre-service instruction and 2) in-service training. Integrating these dimensions into a comprehensive
curriculum evidences a series of continuous, progressive, and developmental learning experiences that
assist pre-service and in-service professionals to inculcate into their character the virtues specified by their
professions with the objective they will demonstrate ethical competence in their professional practice.

	PRIMARY EMPHASIS:		SECONDARY EMPHASES:
PRE-SERVICE INSTRUCTION: *learning ethics* [classroom] the "*mind*"of ethics	***theory*** ➡	[skill +	practice]

	SECONDARY EMPHASES:		PRIMARY EMPHASIS:
IN-SERVICE TRAINING: *applying ethics* [workplace] the "*hand*"of ethics	[theory +	skill] ⬅	***practice***

Applied ethics educators can use this framework to collaborate in identifying the learning objectives for
both dimensions *across* the professions. In turn, ethics educators *within* the professions can translate these
objectives into SMART goals tailored to their particular professions.

FIGURE 3. A Framework for Teaching Applied Ethics

instruction implements the Carnegie report's first two apprenticeships, emphasizing primarily the cognitive apprenticeship to introduce pre-service professionals to the knowledge, theory, skills, and reasoning processes associated with effective practice in specific professions. While the cognitive apprenticeship figures more prominently in pre-service ethics instruction than does the practical apprenticeship where "on the job" experience will assist them to envision how in-service professionals hone their integration of both apprenticeships (Callahan & Bok, 1980; Englehardt & Pritchard, 2018), the practical apprenticeship is introduced to pre-service professionals to assist them to begin integrating the content of ethics with practice (e.g., case studies, formulating scenarios and projecting probable consequences, as well as critiquing the code of ethics of their chosen profession). The goal is for pre-service professionals to develop their profession's "perspectival lens" of its purpose and practice objectives (Grace, 2001).

Aiming to form "the mind of ethics," successful completion of this dimension of the curriculum—what Haug observed as fueling the move toward "credentialism" in the 20th century (1973, p. 203)—will evidence itself in pre-service professionals who demonstrate ethical competence by making basic ethical decisions and communicate both the "what" and "why" of those decisions to others with sufficient refinement.

In-Service Ethics Training. With the present reality indicating that in-service ethics training has not been pervasive across the professions, those which have required it—the healthcare and legal professions, in particular—anecdotal evidence as well as some authors in the first three sections of this volume suggest this approach has had little if any demonstrable impact upon practice. As these contributors maintain, in-service ethics training needs to be more systematic, focusing upon workplace dilemmas and featuring professionals who work in collaborative groups to integrate their pre-service ethics instruction and professional experience with the dictates of their profession's virtues. The Carnegie report's second apprentice is ideally suited for this task, providing a potential model curriculum each profession can adapt.

Many professional associations underappreciate the significance of the Carnegie report's third apprenticeship—continuous in-service formation as ethical professionals—which builds upon and extends the formation initiated in the first and second apprenticeships, namely, cultivating the "mind" of ethics. These experiences extend the challenges presented in the second apprenticeship, in particular, the objective being that in-service professionals will demonstrate increasingly sophisticated levels of ethical competence in their practice. The challenge this third apprenticeship presents ethics educators is to identify the experiences which constitute and differentiate the achievement of a basic, advanced, and accomplished level of ethical competence in professional practice.

Prospectively, this purpose of this third apprenticeship must be intentional—"theory-in-practice" (Argyris & Schön, 1974)—focusing in-service ethics training upon ethical practice. The experiences would introduce in-service professionals to and engage them in cultivating the disciplined habit of reflective practice (Sergiovanni, 1986) by exploring the level of ethical competence they currently exhibit in the dilemmas of practice they have resolved. Cultivating this habit would assist in-service professionals to perfect their character by extending the foundation of their pre-service ethics instruction as they strengthen their powers of mind to do right things by holding themselves accountable for conducting themselves more ethically—exhibiting the "hand" of an ethical professional in professional practice.

As these experiences develop greater sensitivity and increase responsiveness to the contextual variables implicit in dilemmas and assist participants in this formative program to overcome "ethical blindspots" (Cooper & Menzel, 2013, p. 17), this aspect of professional formation also challenges in-service professionals to develop "ethical imagination" (Cooper, 2012, p. 31).

First introduced during their pre-service instruction, in-service professionals would be immersed in four experiences:

1. The descriptive task (identifying the dilemma's conflict of values and contextual variables as well as one's professional roles and responsibilities);
2. The prescriptive task (complicating one's their understanding of the dilemma by formulating principled and conflicting scenarios and rehears-

ing a defense for each and, then, selecting the best scenario and subjecting it to a rigorous "*New York Times*" or "*60 Minutes*" investigative
reporter's interrogation);

3. The decision-making task (determining what one will do and why one
    will do it aware of the decision's strengths and weaknesses as well as any
    opportunities and interesting possibilities that may result from it); and,

4. Communicating the decision in a way that demonstrates ethical compe-
    tence (conducting oneself in a way that's commensurate with the profes-
    sion's code of ethics and practices, exhibiting ethical character and pro-
    moting ethical practice, and inspiring others in the profession to conduct
    themselves similarly).

Heeding the Carnegie Foundation's recommendations, this substantive reconception of ethics education aims to cultivate the mind, hand, and heart of professionals across the professions by focusing upon their chosen profession's purpose. The process consists of three apprenticeships: a cognitive apprenticeship;
a practical apprenticeship; and, a professional formation apprenticeship. The first
two require pre-service professionals to demonstrate mastery of a particular body
of declaratory knowledge and process of thought that's unique to each profession (doctrinal knowledge and analytical skills), develop the "know how" and
clinical reasoning required for effective practice (practice-based learning). The
educational outcome of these apprenticeships would be professionals who are
well-prepared to exemplify the profession's purpose in their practice (i.e., the
integration of its values, skills, inclinations, ethical standards, social roles, and
responsibilities) and who—through the experiences of the third apprenticeship—
develop into exemplars of their profession's practice (Sullivan & Rosin, 2008).

This comprehensive approach to educating professionals *in* ethics assists them
to appreciate *why* they do *what* they do. Viewing *applied ethics education* across
the professions as spanning the course of an entire career, its two dimensions—
pre-service *ethics instruction* and in-service *ethics training*—then enables those
teaching applied ethics across the professions to identify *how* they will do what
they do.

The work of identifying the "*how*"—the teaching objectives and learning goals
for educating professionals *in* ethics *across* the curriculum—is contextualized by
considering this volume's fourth theme which evidences itself in present reality:
The lack continuous and comprehensive of assessment in ethics education across
the professions in its two dimensions.

Theme #4: Lack of Systematic Assessment

With the present reality drawing attention to four problems—being bounded
within independent disciplinary silos, looking to other scholarly disciplines for
clues concerning how to improve the teaching of ethics within those independent
disciplinary silos, using different terminology to describe similar ideas, and ex-

pecting much of the same to transpire, including further marginalization to the peripheries, while autonomy represents one aspect of a profession—accountability ensures that professionals will demonstrate fidelity to their profession's purpose (Haug, 1973, pp. 205–208). For this reason, the pervasive lack of systematic assessment represents a major source, if not the source of these problems.

Holding applied ethics educators accountable is no small undertaking. The methodological challenges involved in assessing the development of ethical competence across the span of a career are daunting: observability of conduct, clarity of goals and techniques, and a rationale for linking techniques to goals; developing longitudinal research studies; designing valid and reliable instruments; gathering data; and, conducting systematic assessments. In diffuse and indeterminate areas like teaching applied ethics, objectives are particularly difficult to identify, goals are difficult to operationalize, skills oftentimes are amorphous, and the connection between theory, skill, and wise judgment is hazy. All of this has raised widespread debate concerning the appropriate means to the desired ends (Daniels, 1972, as cited in Haug, 1973, p. 207).

As daunting as this undertaking would be, the reconception of teaching applied ethics across the professions described above offers a meta-perspective to consider how applied ethics educators, with the assistance of educational researchers, might surmount the many impediments. More importantly, success would to a long way in ameliorating the problems generating the present reality, yield evidence that can be used to improve teaching applied ethics, and provide a sound rationale concerning the value applied ethics education adds to training programs across the professions.

What follows is a process for assessment that's intended to stimulate thought concerning how applied ethics education across the professions might be assessed. Adapting Hamilton's model to form a template, the process unfolds first by identifying benchmarks and then assessing the level of ethical competence evidenced when pre-service professionals first undertake and then complete their pre-service instruction. The process continues, second, through periodic assessments during in-service training that use the same benchmarks. Comparing the latter data to the former would identify the degree of competence being developed across a professional career.

This process consists of four steps that aim to form the spirit of an ethical professional:

1. Applied ethics educators across the professions define the object of assessment (i.e., ethical competence).
2. Knowing the object, ethics educators develop a metaview of applied ethics education (e.g., the center and periphery model).
3. With the foundation constructed, ethics educators formulate teaching objectives to guide applied ethics education toward its object (i.e., professionals who develop ethical competence).

4. Applied ethics educators then specify subsidiary learning goals and levels of proficiency attained as well as levels of proficiency attained (e.g., not proficient, proficient, and mastery) for its two dimensions to guide ethics education towards its subject (i.e., professionals who continuously educate themselves in ethics across the trajectory of their career).

In this regard, the ethics center can provide two invaluable services: 1) networking applied ethics educators from *across* the professions to define the object of assessment and a metaview of applied ethics education across (the first and second steps) and 2) networking applied ethics educators *within* the professions to make this process more concrete to formulate those teaching objectives and learning goals (the third and fourth steps).

First: Defining "Ethical Competence." If researchers are to formulate general teaching objectives, what they aim to form—ethical professionals who continuously educate themselves in ethics and exhibit ethical competence at increasing levels of proficiency—must first be defined.

To commence this process, Cooper and Menzel (2013) have defined ethical competence as "the quest for knowledge and action that defines right and wrong behavior." Professionals exhibit ethical competence, they maintain, in a positive dynamic and synthetic relationship involving the knowledge of ethics codes and laws, the ability to engage in ethical reasoning, the identification of a profession's ethics and values, the commitment to high ethical standards, and advocating ethical practices and conduct in professional practice.

Helpful as this definition is to understand better what ethical competence is and what developing ethical competence involves and requires, ethical competence is evidenced not by arriving at the best possible destination in the most efficient and effective way possible but by its demonstration. In addition, with the gamut of ethical professionals spanning from neophytes to veterans, there are many ethical competencies which professionals need to hone if they are to demonstrate ethical competence (De Schrijver & Maesschalck, 2013). For his part, Sennett (2008) observes that a pre-service craftsman cannot be expected to make the kind of sophisticated decisions an experienced in-service professional tacitly and routinely makes. Developing ethical competence requires patience, practice, and persistence that's cultivated not in mastering ethical theory and decision making but in the crucible of practicing one's profession through which one strengthens its various competencies.

Moreover, professionals cultivate ethical competence not by taking what appears to be the best, most straightforward path to resolve a dilemma but by combining what a broad base of education, common sense, and experience suggest is the best path. Assessments of progress along the path toward the object provide direction concerning where the path is currently headed and any course correction that may be necessary. However, with situations and circumstances oftentimes more dynamic than static, cultivating ethical competence unfolds at various speeds at different points in time.

Additionally, ethical competence is career-long, progressive and developmental endeavor. It's cultivated by reflecting upon missed opportunities, detours, and dead-ends as well as by identifying ethical blind spots. Of this jumble, Menzel observes: "All too often, however, one only knows when he has failed to achieve ethical competence by an unforgiving ethical moment when reality makes abundantly clear that ethical competence remains a cherished but elusive destination" (2016, p. 3).

If applied ethics educators across the professions are to assess the outcomes resulting from the practice of their craft, they need to formulate a shared definition they can translate into competencies that, in turn, they can translate into teaching objectives and learning goals so the object—ethical competence—can be assessed validly and reliably.

Second: Generating a Metaview of the Trajectory. Heeding Aristotle's observation that ethical competence is demonstrated in "do[ing] this to the right person, to the right extent, at the right time, with the right motive, and in the right way... (1958: II.9: 195), its achievement suggests a standard for assessing the degree of ethical competence exhibited at a particular moment in time, when confronting a particular dilemma, and at a particular place in a professional's experience. This standard facilitates the development of metrics to differentiate between the levels of ethical competence professionals can be expected to achieve at various points across the trajectory of a career (e.g., not proficient, proficient, mastery).

With the overarching purpose of ethics education across the professions being to form the spirit of professionals *in* ethics so they will exhibit ethical competence in professional practice, I have advocated elsewhere utilizing Lonergan's "method of insight." This method offers a "metaview"—a pathway—of the trajectory applied ethics education takes that can assist in framing appropriate teaching objectives and learning goals as well as to develop subsidiary metrics for both (Jacobs, 2016).

Applying Lonergan's paradigm to the task at hand, the challenge confronting professionals at all levels of experience involves generating an insight into what the *best* resolution to a dilemma is at this time and given the dilemma's idiosyncratic situation and circumstances. As Lonergan observed, that kind of resolution doesn't emerge *ex nihilo* but is the result of well-developed intellectual discipline (Figure 4).

Questioning begins by perceiving a dilemma and asking, "What is this?" The answer requires gathering relevant factual evidence to grasp the dilemma's context—its situation and circumstances—as well as to describe it as accurately as possible. Cooper calls the refined ability to question and describe a dilemma accurately the "expressive" level of ethical inquiry (2012, p. 31).

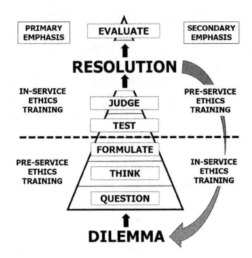

FIGURE 4.   A Metaview of Applied Ethics Education

Thinking builds upon questioning as professionals recall ethical theory as well as their various roles and responsibilities. Applying this information to the facts generated by questioning, professionals ask "What is this?" once again, seeking to ensure they are perceiving the dilemma accurately. While questioning precedes thinking and each represents a discrete mental operation, the act of synthesizing both operations is the culmination of thinking. These mental operations identify what Cooper calls the "descriptive task" which clarifies the issue—the conflict of values—generating the dilemma.

The third mental operation, formulating, requires applying the results of what has preceded by generating multiple scenarios—resolutions to the dilemma—and projecting the probable consequences of each to identify what appears to be the best scenario. The process isn't linear but "dynamic" and requires revisiting one's roles and responsibilities, rehearsing potential defenses, revisiting relevant ethical principles to support the defense, and an anticipatory self-appraisal ("Will I be able to live with myself having made this decision?"). Importantly, the adjective "best" denotes "optimal" because the final decision will necessarily involve making a tradeoff between efficiency (not wasting time) and effectiveness (promoting virtue). The most efficacious decision will not always be what the most optimal scenario presents but the one that maximizes efficiency and effectiveness. For this reason, Cooper notes the best decision—the "state of resolution"—exhibits ethical imagination, autonomy, and integrity—evidencing the degree of "ethical character"—achieved and will be expressed when implementing the final decision.

Commensurate with Kohlberg's (1981) three-level, six-stage developmental model of moral reasoning that many who teach applied ethics have implemented into their syllabi over the past four decades, questioning, thinking, and formulating comprise the "pre-ethical" level of ethical decision making. However, what's crucial is that the final decision represents "ethical" level of ethical decision making (i.e., it fulfills the requirements of Cooper and Menzel's definition of ethical competence). In addition, this intellectual formation provides the primary focus of pre-service ethics instruction: demonstrating basic ethical competence—the refined competencies of perceiving, identifying, and describing a dilemma by mastering the dynamic relationship between projecting probable consequences and assessing those in light of one's role and responsibilities, potential defenses, ethical principles, and anticipatory self-appraisal. The achievement of basic ethical competence can then be assessed in a variety of ways, many of which already appear in course syllabi across the professions.

Moving higher up Kohlberg's model of moral reasoning, the fourth mental operation of Lonergan's paradigm—testing—is the implementation of the preferred scenario and the gathering of data concerning the scenario's efficacy—its "state of resolution" (Cooper, 2012, p. 31). Oftentimes, a dilemma's situation and circumstances will change, and the incomplete data set generated to this point in time will indicate a mid-course adjustment may be necessary to arrive at the desired state of resolution. Awareness of the scenario's unfolding—for better or for worse—and making necessary course adjustments is where professionals honing cultivating ethical competence, moving from the "ethical level" to the "post-ethical level," commensurate with Kohlberg's movement from the "conventional" to the "post-conventional" levels.

The fifth mental operation—judgment—involves analyzing and assessing the data to determine their efficacy for professional practice. Engaging in reflective practice (Sergiovanni, 1986, 1995), data sets which indicate success *and* failure afford professionals the opportunity to further cultivate ethical competence as the data reaffirm success or indicate missed opportunities, having taken detours, turned down dead-ends, or realizing one's ethical blind spots.

Evaluating—the sixth mental operation which builds upon the reflective practice perfected by judging—is perhaps the most critical of the six. Evaluating is the act of drawing out of the experience not just the lessons learned or reaffirmed but also identifying the level of ethical competence achieved or yet to be achieved in the attempt to resolve the dilemma, successful or not. This achievement, a qualitative variable, represents a professional's informed, subjective determination of relative position along the pathway to being ethically competent. It is assessed by comparing different current performance against the level of ethical competence demonstrated in one's pre-service ethics instruction and any further development in one's in-service education in ethics along the way.

While testing, judging, and evaluating provide the focus for in-service training, these advanced mental operations of Lonergan's method are first introduced in pre-service instruction to orient pre-service professionals to the method's scope and sequence through which ethical professionals discipline themselves to develop ethical competence continuously as they integrate into their character the rational and affective dimensions of ethical decision making. In this sense, judging and evaluating constitute Kohlberg's "post-ethical" level of ethical decision making in that decisions reveal the social contract and universal ethical principles being factored into the best decision, given the dilemma's situation and circumstances. They also represent the level of ethical competence—ethical imagination, autonomy, and integrity—currently achieved.

These six mental operations clarify the teaching objectives through which those who teach applied ethics will assist professionals to develop basic ethical competence as they master the Lonergan's method and gain insight into the conflict of values characterizing ethical dilemmas.

To facilitate building upon this foundation, the ethics center—by networking expert applied ethics educators *across* the professions to define ethical competence and generate a metaview of the process of educating professionals in ethics—provides yet another invaluable service.

Fourth: Formulating Teaching Objectives and Learning Goals to Inculcate Ethical Competence. The challenge confronting ethics educators *within* each profession involves translating the broad purpose and trajectory of applied ethics education into competencies to identify each profession's idiosyncratic teaching objectives and learning goals.

To facilitate completing this task, the center once again can provide an invaluable service to the periphery by networking expert applied ethics educators *within* the professions in formulating learning goals for each, using as a starting point the six teaching objectives currently found in most syllabi across the professions (e.g., Svara & Baizhanov, 2019; West, 2017) as well as to specify learning goals for each objective, assigning appropriate emphasis to the those objectives and goals which figure prominently in pre-service ethics instruction and in-service training. Those objectives include: the profession's ethics codes and laws, its ethical principles and practices, ethical theory, ethical decision making, demonstrating a commitment to high ethical standards, and advocating ethical practice and conduct in professional practice (see Figure 5).

The intersection of each objective across the professions and each goal within each profession identifies the competencies—the specific knowledge, skills, abilities, and attitudes—associated with exhibiting ethical competence in each profession. The completed chart will identify what pre-service and in-service professional will learn, each goal stating, "The participant will (know or exhibit [the learning])...."

With several taxonomies already identifying cognitive, affective, and kinesthetic learning goals (Anderson & Krathwohl, 2000; Bloom & Krathwohl, 1956; Fink, 2013; Krathwohl, 2002; Simpson, 1972; Wiggins & McTighe, 2005) and with many professions already having well-articulated learning goals, the center can then network experts within each profession with educational researchers to formulate strong, operationalized goals. These learning goals will enable those teaching applied ethics in each profession to identify assessment activities

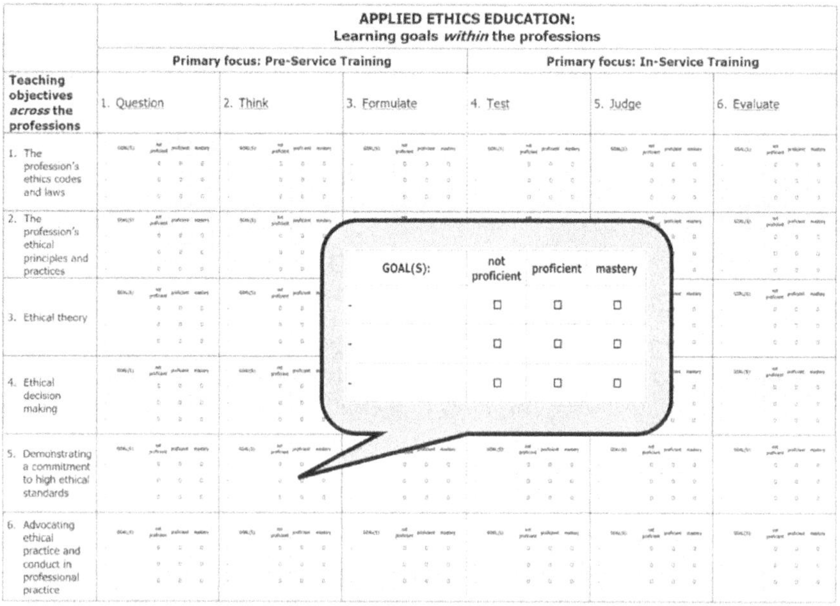

FIGURE 5.   Formulating a Model Applied Ethics Curriculum *Within* a Profession

through which mastery of each goal will be demonstrated at one of three levels, "not proficient," "proficient, or "expert."

Mastery of those goals does not demonstrate the achievement of ethical competence, rather its constitutive competencies. Cultivating and honing these through ongoing professional practice demonstrates "ethical craftsmanship" at three levels: an apprentice (the cognitive apprenticeship to develop basic proficiency), a journeyman (the practice practical apprenticeship to develop professional proficiency), and a master (the professional formation apprenticeship to develop expert proficiency) (Foster et al., 2005).

To sum up: These four steps identify the foundational elements for longitudinal assessment which would proceed as experts in educational research design an instrument that would validly and reliably identify the degree to which pre-service instruction (the hand of ethics) and in-service training (the hand in professional practice of ethics) have been integrated in professional practice, evidencing the increasing development of ethical competence (the heart of ethics) across the trajectory of a career.

Again, the ethics center would provide the invaluable service of networking applied ethics educators *within* a profession who are located on the peripheries with educational researchers for the purpose of gathering data for assessment and evaluation. Ideally, pre-service professionals will demonstrate basic proficiency for all goals emphasized in their pre-service instruction and perhaps professional proficiency at some of the goals emphasized at the in-service level. These professionals will demonstrate professional proficiency at all goals for in-service training and perhaps exhibiting expert proficiency of some goals. Longitudinally, the data would indicate progressive increase in mastery—the development of ethical competence—from pre-service instruction to in-service training, with "master ethical professionals" demonstrating mastery of all learning goals, that is, ethical competence.

A FINAL WORD

The contents of this Epilogue offer an agenda to conceive of a future for teaching applied ethics across the professions— a terminus *ad quo*—where its teaching is improved within the professions. Dealing effectively with the issue of the pervasive lack of assessment across the professions will enable applied ethics educators to solve those four problems evidencing themselves in the present reality.

An ethics center would provide an invaluable service to promote this agenda and ensure its success by uniting applied ethics educators across the professions who, for the most part, practice their craft oftentimes in isolation from one another on the peripheries. Developing this center appears to be essential if the substantive reconception of teaching applied ethics envisioned and detailed herein is to succeed. If it does, applied ethics educators *across* the professions will strengthen ethics education within the *professions* by educating the spirit of pre-service and in-service professionals *in* ethics as they foster their self-formation as professionals which is today's desired reality.

REFERENCES

Al-Zahrani, A. M. (2015). From passive to active: The impact of the flipped classroom through social learning platforms on higher education students' creative thinking. *British Journal of Educational Technology, 46*, 1133–1148. Available online: https://doi.org/10.1111/bjet.12353

Anderson, L. W., & Krathwohl, D. R. (Eds.). (2000). *Taxonomy for learning, teaching, and assessing: A revision of Bloom's taxonomy of educational objectives.* Pearson.

Argyris, C., & Schön, D. A. (1974). *Theory in practice: Increasing professional effectiveness.* Jossey-Bass.

Aristotle. (1958). Nicomachean ethics (W. D. Ross, Trans). In *The pocket Aristotle* (pp. 158–274). Washington Square Press.

Benner, P., Sutphen, M., Leonard, V., & Day, L. (2009). *Educating nurses: A call for radical transformation.* Jossey-Bass.

Bloom, B. S., & Krathwohl, D. R. (1956).*Taxonomy of educational objectives: The classification of educational goals, Handbook I: Cognitive domain.* Longmans, Green.

Bullock, A., & Trombley, S. (1999). *The new Fontana dictionary of modern thought.* Harper Collins.

Callahan, D., & Bok, S. (Eds.). (1980). *Ethics teaching in higher education* (The Hastings Center series in ethics). Springer. Available online: https://doi.org/10.1007/978-1-4613-3138-4_12

Carnegie Foundation for the Advancement of Teaching. (n.d.). *About us: Past work and related resources* [webpage]. https://www.carnegiefoundation.org/about-us/past-work-and-related-resources/

Carr, D. (1991). *Educating the virtues: Essay on the philosophical psychology of moral development and education.* Routledge.

Cooke, M., Irby, D. M., & O'Brien, B. C. (2010). *Educating physicians: A call for reform of medical school and residency.* Jossey-Bass.

Cooper, T. L. (2012). *The responsible administrator: An approach to ethics for the administrative role* (6th ed.). Jossey-Bass Publishers.

Cooper, T. L., & Menzel, D. C. (Eds.). (2013). *Achieving ethical competence for public service leadership.* M. E. Sharpe.

De Schrijver, A., & Maesschalck, J. (2013). A new definition and conceptualization of ethical competence. In T. L. Cooper & D. C. Menzel (Eds.), *Achieving ethical competence for public service leadership* (pp. 29–50). M.E. Sharpe.

DiBella, A., & Nevis, E. C. (1998). *How organizations learn: An integrated strategy for building learning capability.* Jossey-Bass.

Englehardt, E. E., & Pritchard, M. S. (2018). *Teaching practical ethics* (pp. 117–130). Springer Nature. Available online: https://doi.org/10.1007/978-3-319-78939-2_2

Fink, L. D. (2013). *Creating significant learning communities.* Jossey Bass.

Flexner, A. (1910). *Medical education in the United States and Canada: A report to the Carnegie Foundation for the Advancement of Teaching (Bulletin No. 4). The Carnegie Foundation for the Advancement of Teaching.* http://archive.carnegiefoundation.org/publications/pdfs/elibrary/Carnegie_Flexner_Report.pdf

Foster, C. R., Dahill, L., Golemon, L., & Tolentino, B. W. (2005). *Educating clergy: Teaching practices and pastoral imagination.* Jossey Bass.

Gallie, W. B. (1968). Essentially contested concepts. In *Philosophy and the historical understanding* (pp. 157–191). Schocken Books.

Grace, P. J. (2001). Professional advocacy: Widening the scope of accountability. *Nursing Philosophy, 2*(1), 151–162.

Haug, M. R. (1973). Deprofessionalization: An alternative hypothesis for the future. *Sociological Review Monographs, 20,* 195–211.

Jacobs, R. M. (2016). Developing insight in aspiring researchers: Challenges confronting public administration teachers and scholars. *Teaching Public Administration, 34*(2), 178–205.

Jacobs R. M. (2021). Ethics education in the professions: Those who have taught and what they have taught. In D. C. Poff & A. C . Michalos (Eds.), *Encyclopedia of business and professional ethics.* Springer, Cham. https://doi.org/10.1007/978-3-319-23514-1_1187-2

Kohlberg, L. (1981). *Essays in moral development.* Harper and Row.

Kong, S. C. (2014). Developing information literacy and critical thinking skills through domain knowledge learning in digital classrooms: An experience of practicing flipped classroom strategy. *Computer Education, 78,* 160–173. https://doi.org/10.1016/j.compedu.2014.05.009

Krathwohl, D. R. (2002). A revision of Bloom's taxonomy: An overview. *Theory Into Practice, 41*(4), 212–264.

Menzel, D. C. (2016). Ethical competence. In A. Farazmand (Ed.), *Global encyclopedia of public administration, public policy, and governance.* https://link.springer.com/refe renceworkentry/10.1007%2F978-3-319-31816-5_2458-1

Munir, M. T., Baroutian, S., Young, B. R., & Carter, S. (2018, April). Flipped classroom with cooperative learning as a cornerstone. *Education for Chemical Engineers, 23,* 25–33. https://doi.org/10.1016/j.ece.2018.05.001

Oettingen, G. (2012). Future thought and behaviour change. *European Review of Social Psychology, 23*(1), 1–63. https://doi.org/10.1080/10463283.2011.643698

Schein, E. H. (1972). *Professional education: Some new directions.* McGraw-Hill.

Sennett, R. (2008). *The craftsman.* Yale University Press.

Sergiovanni, T. J. (1986). Understanding reflective practice. *Journal of Curriculum and Supervision, 1*(4), 353–359.

Sergiovanni, T. J. (1995). *The principalship: A reflective-practice perspective* (3rd ed.). Allyn and Bacon.

Sheppard, S. D., Macatangay, K., Colby, A., & Sullivan, W. M. (2008). *Educating engineers: Designing for the future of the field.* Jossey Bass.

Shils, E. A. (1975). Center and periphery. In *Center and periphery: Essays in macrosociology* (pp. 3–16). University of Chicago Press.

Simpson, D. J., & Sacken, D. M. (2021). *Ethical dilemmas in schools: Collaborative inquiry, decision-making, and action.* Cambridge University Press.

Simpson, E. J. (1972). *The classification of educational objectives in the psychomotor domain.* Gryphon House.

Strong, M. (1997). *The habit of thought: From Socratic seminars to Socratic practice.* New View Publications.

Sullivan, W. M., Colby, A., Wegner, J. W., Bond, L., & Shulman, L. S. (2007). *Educating lawyers: Preparation for the profession of law.* Jossey Bass.

Sullivan, W. M., & Rosin, M. S. (2008). *A new agenda for higher education: Shaping a life of the mind for practice.* Jossey-Bass.

Svara, J. H., & Baizhanov, S. (2019). Public service values in NASPAA programs: Identification, integration, and activation. *Journal of Public Affairs Education, 25*(1), 73–92. 10.1080/15236803.2018.1454761

West, J. P. (2017). *What is actually taught and how it is taught in public administration ethics courses.* A paper presented at the NASPAA 2017 Annual Conference, Washington, DC.

Wiggins, G., & McTighe, J. (2005). *Understanding by design – Facets of understanding* (2nd ed.). ASCD.

BIOGRAPHIES

ABOUT THE EDITOR

Richard M. Jacobs is Professor of Public Administration at Villanova University where he has been teaching organization theory and leadership ethics to MPA students for 30 years. His research interests include: organization theory, leadership ethics, and ethical competence as well as teaching and learning in public administration. Jacobs earned his Ph.D. in educational leadership from the University of Tulsa. During his tenure at Villanova, Jacobs has authored six books and monographs as well as numerous book chapters and articles spanning a variety of topics, in particular, those relating applied philosophy in administration, teaching, and learning. He has served as the Acquisitions Editor and member of the Editorial Board of *Public Integrity* and a contributing quarterly ethics columnist for the *PA Times*. Jacobs has served as Chair of the American Society for Public Administration's Section on Ethics and Integrity in Governance (2017–2021). In 2016, The Matthew J. Ryan Center for the Study of Free Institutions and the Public Good named Jacobs one of its Faculty Associates.

Educating in Ethics Across the Professions: A Compendium of Research, Theory, Practice, and an Agenda for the Future, pages 253–257.
Copyright © 2023 by Information Age Publishing
www.infoagepub.com

ABOUT THE CONTRIBUTORS

Jeffrey K. H. Chan is an assistant professor in the Humanities, Arts and the Social Sciences (HASS) cluster at the Singapore University of Technology and Design (SUTD). Chan's research focuses on design ethics, and he has taught a planning ethics module to young planners at the Urban Redevelopment Authority (URA), Singapore. Chan is the author of *Urban Ethics in the Anthropocene* (Palgrave, 2019).

Andrew Corbett is a teaching fellow at King's College London's Defence Studies Department. His first career in the Royal Navy submarine service spanned the end of the Cold War and included Command of 2 Trident submarines, capability management in the MOD, and development of 21st century NATO deterrence and defence strategy. Corbett's research interests concern the use of nuclear deterrence as a strategic tool in the 21st century. His current research project is focused upon the ethics of nuclear deterrence.

Pamela Grace is an experienced critical care nurse, primary care advanced practice nurse, and educator. She is a research associate professor in the William F. Connell School of Nursing at Boston College and an external nurse scientist at the Munn Center for Nursing Research at Massachusetts General Hospital where she collaborates with colleagues on nursing ethics research endeavors. Grace collaborated on a 3-year HRSA grant—The Clinical Ethics Residency for Nurses—aimed at developing nurses' ethical expertise in two metropolitan hospitals. A past fellow in medical ethics at Harvard University's School of Social Medicine and Fulbright Senior Scholarship, Dr. Grace's scholarship includes: professional ethics, nursing ethics, moral decision making, justice in healthcare, and advocacy. She is an active member of the newly reinstated American Academy of Nursing's Bioethics Expert panel. Her book *Nursing Ethics and Professional Responsibility in Advanced Practice* is used internationally and is in its 3rd edition.

 **Neil W. Hamilton** is Holloran Professor of Law and Founding Director of the Holloran Center for Ethical Leadership in the Professions at the University of St. Thomas School of Law. He served as Interim Dean in 2012 and Associate Dean for Academic Affairs twice at St. Thomas. From 1980–2001, he served as Trustees Professor of Regulatory Policy at William Mitchell College of Law. He has taught Professional Responsibility and an ethics seminar to law students and professionals for over 30 years. Author of five books, over 100 law journal articles, and over 150 shorter articles, he will publish his newest book in 2022 with Cambridge University Press, *Law Student Professional Development and Formation: Bridging Law School, Student, and Employer Goals.* In 2004, the Minnesota State Bar Association bestowed upon Hamilton its highest honor, the Professional Excellence Award.

 **Jose Félix Lozano** is a Tenured Lecturer for Business Ethics, Engineering Ethics, and Responsible Research Innovation, at the *Universidad Politécnica de Valencia* (Spain). An associated researcher at the *Intituto Ingenio* (CSIC-UPV), his research interests include: Business Ethics, business ethics education, Engineering Ethics, and RRI. Formerly a Fellow of the *DAAD* (German academic exchange program) and the *Studienstiftung des deutschen Volkes* (Foundation of German Students), Lozano has published articles in the *Journal of Business Ethics*, *Science and Engineering Ethics*, *Journal of Philosophy of education*, and *Journal of Academic Ethics*, among others. He is author of two books (*Códigos éticos para el mundo empresarial*, and *¿Qué es la ética de la empresa?*) and co-editor of the handbook, *Responsabilidad Social Corporativa* (Pearson). He has worked as a consultant for public and private organizations in Spain and Latin America and currently is a member of the Research Ethics Committee at the *Universitat Politécnica de Valencia.*

 **Judith A. McMorrow** Professor Judith A. McMorrow serves as the Associate Dean of Experiential Learning and Global Engagement at Boston College Law School, where she teaches Torts, Professional Responsibility, Semester-in-Practice and related courses. Her scholarship is primarily in the area of professional responsibility and legal ethics. She has co-authored two books, *Lawyers and Fundamental Moral Responsibility* (with Daniel R. Coquillette & R. Michael Cassidy) and *The Federal Law of Attorney Conduct* (with Daniel R. Coquillette) (Moore's Federal Practice), authored a free Torts textbook, and published over 25 articles and book chapters. McMorrow is active in pro bono and service activities, including over 20 years on the board of Com-

munity Legal Services and Counseling Center, 10 years on the Massachusetts SJC Committee on Judicial Ethics, work with the ABA Center for Professional Responsibility, and earlier work in representing women in Massachusetts seeking commutation based on Battered Woman Syndrome.

Greg Moorlock is an Associate Professor at the Wawrick Medical School (UK), specializing in bioethics. His current project explores ethical issues that arise from transplant patients using the Internet to find willing living donors.

Ronald R. Sims is the Floyd Dewey Gottwald Senior Professor in the Raymond A. Mason School of Business at William & Mary where he teaches leadership, change management, human resources management (HRM), and business ethics. His research focuses on a variety of topics to include leadership, change management, human resource management (HRM), business ethics, employee training, and management and leadership development (i.e., Human Resource Development), and cyber-security resilience. Sims is the author or co-author of 40 books, 84 chapters and more than 90 articles that have appeared in a wide variety of scholarly and practitioner journals.

Jonathan P. West was Professor of Political Science and Director of Graduate Studies at the University of Miami. His research interests included human resource management, productivity, local government, and public service ethics. He was co-author of *Public Service Ethics: Individual and Institutional Responsibilities* (Routledge, 2022, 3rd edition) and *Human Resource Management in Public Service: Paradoxes, Processes, and Problems* (Sage/CQ Press, 2022, 7th edition). For 16 years, he served as Managing Editor of *Public Integrity*. Professor West's chapter in this volume is his final work, as he passed away in January 2022 before its publication."

 **David Whetham** is Professor of Ethics and the Military Profession in the Defence Studies Department of King's College London. He is the Director of the King's Centre for Military Ethics and delivers or coordinates the military ethics component of courses for between two and three thousand British and international military officers a year at the UK's Joint Services Command and Staff College. Whetham supports military ethics education in many different countries and has held Visiting Fellowships at the Stockdale Center for Ethical Leadership, US Naval Academy Annapolis, the Centre for Defence Leadership and Ethics at the Australian Defence College in Canberra. He was a Mid Career Fellow at the British Academy in 2017–18 and is currently a Visiting Professorial Fellow at the University of New South Wales. Whetham is the Vice President of the European Chapter of the International Society for Military Ethics (Euro ISME).

CPSIA information can be obtained
at www.ICGtesting.com
Printed in the USA
JSHW050429130723
44662JS00001B/30